THE GROWTH AND DEVELOPMENT

OF

THE PENNSYLVANIA RAILROAD COMPANY

A REVIEW OF THE CHARTER AND ANNUAL REPORTS
OF THE PENNSYLVANIA RAILROAD COMPANY
1846 TO 1926, INCLUSIVE

BY

H. W. SCHOTTER
Assistant Treasurer

DECEMBER, 1927

PRESS OF
ALLEN, LANE & SCOTT,
PHILADELPHIA, PA.

DIVIDENDS PAID IN EVERY YEAR SINCE 1848

The Pennsylvania Railroad Company

General Office, Broad Street Station,

A. J. County,
Vice President-Treasury, Accounting and Corporate Work.

Philadelphia, December 15, 1927.

I heartily commend this practical and concise Review of Important Events in the Life of The Pennsylvania Railroad Company, and congratulate Mr. Schotter, Assistant Treasurer, in compiling this volume and placing it at the disposal of the Company. It should prove invaluable to officers and employes who wish to increase their knowledge of the underlying policies of the Company, and will interest those who know its traditions and have helped to shape its policies and progress. It also gives a clear understanding of the growth of the System, and will increase our appreciation of the foresight, devotion and ability of our predecessors. Through these qualities, and by sound policies of administration, the Company has been gradually developed into one of the great transportation systems of the World.

A. J. County,

Vice-President.

THIS review of the growth and development of The Pennsylvania Railroad Company was begun some years ago, and represents the use, to a large extent, of leisure hours. Its preparation was inspired by a desire to know more about how the Company grew to its present powerful position in the field of transportation. As this information was not available in condensed form or chronological order, it was necessary to go back to the origin of the Company, over 80 years ago, and resort very largely to its Annual Reports to secure the data.

No references are made to many minor events, which are inseparable from the growth of every large corporation, the purpose being to simply record the more important facts. To have done otherwise would have considerably enlarged the work without correspondingly adding to its value to those interested in obtaining a brief account of the inception and growth of a really great transportation system.

I gratefully acknowledge the helpful suggestions received from the various Departments.

H. W. S.

THE CHARTER

THIS review of the growth and development of The Pennsylvania Railroad Company into the largest transportation system in the Country may appropriately begin with a brief recital of the struggle to obtain a charter by the public spirited citizens who promoted and believed in the enterprise. They proceeded in the face of strong opposition from those who could see nothing but a repetition of the unprofitable experience of the State of Pennsylvania in the operation of its line of Public Works, and the results far exceeded their most optimistic expectations. The completion of the Pennsylvania Railroad from Harrisburg to Pittsburgh gave new life to the business and industries of the State, and it soon became, and has since continued to be, the greatest single factor in the material prosperity of Pennsylvania. The fact that this State leads all others in the Union, so far as industrial and railroad developments are concerned, is to a great extent due to the courage and foresight of those men who early planned and constructed the Pennsylvania Railroad from Harrisburg to Pittsburgh, which, with the State-owned Philadelphia & Columbia Railroad and the privately owned Harrisburg, Portsmouth, Mt. Joy & Lancaster Railroad, constituted the first all-rail avenue of transportation across the State of Pennsylvania.

PHILADELPHIA LOSES PRESTIGE

Until the completion of the Erie Canal in 1825, Philadelphia had been the commercial and financial centre of the United States, as well as its largest city in population, but the opening of that canal and the subsequent failure of a number of its large financial institutions and industrial concerns, caused it unwillingly to surrender its prestige to New York as the commercial metropolis of the Country. The City of Philadelphia, therefore, had to stand aside in its weakened condition and see the profitable trade of the West seeking tidewater at New York through the newly constructed canal, or going to Baltimore over the Baltimore & Ohio Railroad, which had been constructed as far as Cumberland, Md., in 1842, and stood at the border line of Pennsylvania waiting for legislative authority to extend its road to Pittsburgh, a distance of 150 miles.

PENNSYLVANIA'S FIRST RAILROAD

True, the State of Pennsylvania had embarked on the construction of its Main Line of Public Works across the State; in fact as early as March 31st, 1823, or more than a Century ago, a charter was granted to private interests led by John Stevens for a railroad known as "the Pennsylvania Railroad" (a forerunner of the present The Pennsylvania Railroad Company), which was the oldest charter under which any railroad promotion was ever undertaken and finally carried out on the American Continent. It was to be constructed between Philadelphia and the Susquehanna River at Columbia, Pa., a distance of about 81 miles. The intention of the incorporators was to ultimately extend the railroad westward to Pittsburgh; thence through Ohio and up to the Great Lakes and eastwardly to New York City, a territory later served by the present Pennsylvania Railroad. For the next three years a great deal of work was done and money spent in organizing the project, making preliminary surveys, and appealing for subscriptions to the Capital Stock, but no construction work was undertaken.

During this period there had been some criticism of certain provisions in the Act of 1823, and to eliminate the objectionable features a new Act was passed on April 7th, 1826, authorizing private interests to construct a railroad on the same route to be known as "the Columbia, Lancaster and Philadelphia Railway," which thus preserved and continued the project begun in 1823. A further effort was made to induce private capital to build the road, but as it could not be secured in sufficient amount, an appeal was finally made for State aid, which resulted in the passage of a new Act on March 24th, 1828. Under this law, the State of Pennsylvania was to furnish the funds and construct "the

Pennsylvania Railroad" between Philadelphia and Columbia, which meant the consummation of the original plan evolved by John Stevens and his associates in 1823. Its construction was actively undertaken by the State and it was opened for operation on April 16th, 1834, as part of the State-owned Public Works. The Philadelphia & Columbia Railroad, as it was then popularly known, was purchased by the Pennsylvania Railroad Company in 1857, together with the other portions of the Main Line of Public Works owned by the State, so that it has in its System today a railroad which was built as originally conceived and planned more than a century ago.

In the period 1832-1838, the rail route was extended from a point just west of Lancaster (where connection was made with the Philadelphia & Columbia Railroad) to Harrisburg by a privately owned Company known as the "Harrisburg, Portsmouth, Mt. Joy & Lancaster Railroad Company," whose first President was James Buchanan, and who later became President of the United States. A branch of this latter railroad from a point near Middletown (now Royalton), to a connection with the Philadelphia & Columbia Railroad at Columbia was completed on August 14th, 1850.

THE STATE WORKS OF PENNSYLVANIA

The Main Line of Public Works owned by the State extended from Philadelphia to Pittsburgh, and consisted of a double track railroad from Philadelphia to Columbia, 81 miles in length; the Eastern and Juniata Divisions of the Pennsylvania Canal from Columbia to Hollidaysburg, a distance of 173 miles; the double track Allegheny Portage Railroad, with five inclined planes on each side of the mountain, from Hollidaysburg to Johnstown, 36 miles in length; and the Western Division of the Pennsylvania Canal from Johnstown to Pittsburgh, a distance of 105 miles, making the total length from Philadelphia to Pittsburgh 395 miles.

The State also owned a system of branch canals, the most important of which were the Susquehanna Division extending from Duncan's Island (north of Harrisburg) to

Northumberland, 39 miles; West Branch Division, Northumberland to Farrandsville, 72 miles; North Branch Division, Northumberland to Lackawanna Creek (near Wilkes-Barre), 72 miles; Delaware Division, Bristol to Easton, 60 miles, and the Erie Extension extending from near New Castle to Erie, 106 miles. None of these branches was included in the sale of the Public Works to the Pennsylvania Railroad Company, to which reference is later made. They were subsequently sold by the State to the Philadelphia & Erie Railroad Company for $3,500,000., and later the Susquehanna, West Branch and North Branch Divisions were acquired by the Pennsylvania Canal Company, which was controlled by the Pennsylvania Railroad Company.

STATE WORKS WERE A FAILURE

The State Works had proven a failure not only from the standpoint of the financial losses sustained by the State in constructing and operating them, but by reason of their inability to attract the competitive traffic between the West and the Atlantic Seaboard. The principal reasons for the unsatisfactory results in operating these Works were the delays and inconvenience caused by the use of inclined planes in crossing the mountains; the fact that the canals were closed by ice for three or four months of the year, and the Spring operations were hampered by floods and freshets. It, therefore, became apparent that if Philadelphia and the State of Pennsylvania were to be restored to their former preeminence, it was necessary to provide a more modern system of transportation, especially since the Baltimore & Ohio Railroad Company was ready to proceed, upon securing legislative authority, with the extension of its road westward to the Ohio River.

TWO APPLICATIONS BEFORE LEGISLATURE

Therefore, the year 1846 found two large influential bodies of men at the Seventieth Session of the Pennsylvania Legislature contesting for State authority to proceed with their respective projects. One represented those who were determined to secure a charter in the name of The Pennsylvania Railroad Company, and to construct an all-rail line across the State from Harrisburg to Pittsburgh and the Ohio River. The other group were supporters of the Baltimore & Ohio Railroad Company, which was seeking the right to extend its line from Cumberland, Md., to Pittsburgh, the delegation from the southern city being reinforced by representatives from the southwestern counties of Pennsylvania, who claimed that they were badly treated in the matter of railroad improvements, and attributed it to Philadelphia interests.

The Pennsylvania Legislature had previously granted the Baltimore & Ohio Railroad Company the right to construct this extension, but having failed to do so within the specified time, that Company was seeking a re-enactment of the grant. The struggle between the two interests became intense, both in and out of the Legislature, but the climax finally being reached two Bills were passed, one incorporating The Pennsylvania Railroad Company, and the other granting the Baltimore & Ohio Railroad Company the right to construct the desired extension from Cumberland, Md., to Pittsburgh. The Act creating The Pennsylvania Railroad Company was signed by Governor Francis Rawn Shunk on April 13th, 1846, and his signature was affixed to the Baltimore & Ohio Railroad Company Bill on April 21st, 1846.

CONDITIONAL RIGHTS GRANTED P. R. R. AND B. & O. R. R.

The Act granting the Baltimore & Ohio Railroad Company the right to construct its extension to Pittsburgh was not to become effective until July 30th, 1847. There was a further condition attached to it that if the Legislature during the Session of 1846 should pass an Act giving the right to a Company to build a railroad from Harrisburg to Pittsburgh within the limits of Pennsylvania, and if certain conditions were complied with, the construction rights granted to the Baltimore & Ohio Railroad Company were to be null and void. These conditions were that $3,000,000. would have to be subscribed to the Stock of such Company, with 10%

thereof actually paid in, and Letters Patent issued by the Governor, within one year from the passage of such an Act; also that thirty miles or more of its railroad would have to be placed under contract on or before July 30th, 1847. It was furthermore provided that the Act creating The Pennsylvania Railroad Company would not take effect unless the stockholders of that Company should pay into its Treasury, before July 30th, 1847, the sum of $1,000,000., representing subscriptions to Capital Stock, and fifteen miles of road were placed under contract at the Pittsburgh end of the road.

P. R. R. CHARTER MADE EFFECTIVE—B. & O. RIGHTS VOID

A strong appeal was made to the civic pride and commercial interests of Philadelphia, and after a door to door canvass for even single share subscriptions, and the decision of Philadelphia City Council to take 30,000 shares, in addition to a conditional subscription of 20,000 shares, together with the fact that some subscribers paid up their Stock in full, the required amount of cash representing paid-in subscriptions was received. The necessary steps were also taken to place 30 miles of the road under contract, and, therefore, the Governor, on February 25th, 1847, issued Letters Patent to The Pennsylvania Railroad Company. This, of course, put an end to whatever hopes the Baltimore & Ohio Railroad Company had of extending its line to Pittsburgh at that time, and on August 2nd, 1847, the Governor issued a proclamation declaring the right of that Company in this respect null and void.

IMPORTANT PROVISIONS OF CHARTER

The Act incorporating the Company gave the President and Board of Directors, which latter was to consist of thirteen members, all to be residents of Pennsylvania and owners of at least twenty shares of the Capital Stock of the Company (subsequently changed to fifty shares), the power to determine the most advantageous route for its railroad, track, bridges, branches and facilities, beginning at a connection with the Harrisburg, Portsmouth, Mt. Joy & Lancaster

Railroad at Harrisburg westward to the City of Pittsburgh. It also gave authority to construct a branch to the Great Lakes at Erie, and such other branches into Counties through which its Main Line passed as in the judgment of the Board of Directors might be advantageous. The State was given the power to purchase the road at the end of any twenty-year period, which latter privilege was cancelled when the State-owned Public Works were bought by the Pennsylvania Railroad Company. The Company was authorized to issue $7,500,000. of Capital Stock represented by 150,000 shares of a par value of $50. each, and with the right to increase this to $10,000,000., or 200,000 shares, without securing additional Legislative authority.

FREIGHT AND PASSENGER RATES PRESCRIBED

When completed the railroad was to be used for the conveyance of passengers and the transportation of freight, and the Company was authorized to charge for its own passengers a sum not exceeding 3 cents per mile for through passengers and 3½ cents for local passengers. The charter gave to any person owning the necessary vehicle the privilege of having it conveyed over the railroad of the Company upon the payment of a charge for motive power, which was the same method of operation practiced on the State-owned Philadelphia & Columbia Railroad. The charge for this service could not exceed 2½ cents per mile for each passenger, 3 cents per mile for each ton of freight, 3 cents per mile for each passenger or baggage car, and 2 cents per mile for each freight car, every 4 wheels being computed a car.

TONNAGE TAX

The Company was required, under its Charter, to pay to the State 5 mills per mile for each ton of freight carried more than 20 miles over the road between March and December of each year, but not for the Winter months, because the canal could not then be operated and the Pennsylvania Railroad would not then be competing with the Public Works of the State. This tax was levied to protect the investment of the State in these Public Works, especially the canal, as this new railroad project was looked upon as a competitor. A supplement to the original Act provided for the reduction of the tonnage tax to 3 mills per ton per mile *during the entire year,* instead of 5 mills between the months of *March and December,* and if after completion of the road this reduction should not yield as much revenue to the State as the 5-mill rate, the latter was to be restored at the option of the Legislature.

LIMIT ON DEBTS AND LIABILITIES

The Charter also provided that the "whole amount of debts or other liabilities including loans, shall not at any time exceed one-half of the amount of capital actually paid in." This provision was, of course, later amended to give the Company greater latitude in increasing its bonded debt.

INTEREST TO BE PAID ON CAPITAL STOCK SUBSCRIPTIONS

Another provision was that after contracts had been made for the immediate construction of fifteen miles of the road at each end of the line, a sum equal to 5% per annum (increased to 6% by Act approved March 27th, 1848, hereinafter referred to) on the paid-in capital of the Company was to be estimated and credited to the holders of the Capital Stock, the amount of such interest to be charged to the cost of construction. This provision was to remain in force until 100 miles of the railroad, that is 50 miles thereof at both the eastern and western termini, were completed and in use, when, if a sufficient profit were earned, it could be disbursed to the stockholders in the form of a dividend in the months of May and November of each year.

THE PRESIDENTS

IN a review of this kind, covering an eighty-year period, it was felt that interest would be added to the work if it were divided into the Administrations of the ten Presidents, who have so ably served the Company since its incorporation. An opportunity is thus presented to show at the close of each Administration how the physical growth during such period was reflected in greater earnings and financial returns, and also adds a personal touch to a work which must necessarily deal so little with the personalities of the Directors, officers and employes, past and present, who have made it one of the greatest transportation systems in the Country.

In passing, it may be interesting to point out that during the past eighty years, the Company has been fortunate in having as its responsible head men who were peculiarly fitted to solve the many intricate problems confronting the Management during their respective Administrations. This is the result of a policy adopted very early in the history of the Company of selecting as its Chief Executives those officers, who from long experience were familiar with the Company's operations, traffic conditions and finances, who knew its traditions and policies, and through well-merited promotion had previously served in important official capacities.

FIRST AND SECOND

Samuel Vaughan Merrick and William Chamberlain Patterson, the First and Second Presidents, respectively, were prominently identified with the industrial and financial interests of Philadelphia. They were the type of men required to give the project the necessary impetus, and encourage subscriptions to the Capital Stock of the Company.

THIRD

Then followed John Edgar Thomson, the Third President, who, as Chief Engineer, located and began construction of the road from Harrisburg to Pittsburgh, and later, as President, laid the foundation of the present Pennsylvania Railroad System in its greatest period of expansion from 1852 to 1874. At the close of his Administration the System embraced a territory extending westward from the Atlantic Seaboard to the Mississippi River, and from the Ohio and Potomac Rivers on the south to the Great Lakes on the north. With few exceptions this is practically the same territory it serves at the present time, the growth and development of the System since 1874 having been largely internal.

FOURTH, FIFTH AND SIXTH

To the successors of John Edgar Thomson was left the important task of strengthening and compacting the System he had laid out. Therefore, the succeeding Administrations of Thomas Alexander Scott, George Brooke Roberts and Frank Thomson, the Fourth, Fifth and Sixth Presidents, respectively, were characterized by large expenditures for internal improvements, such as the construction of branch lines, additional running tracks, enlarged yards, terminals, etc.; the financing, consolidation and acquisition of a number of subsidiary companies, and the solution of many perplexing problems incident to the rapid growth of the System.

SEVENTH

They were followed by the Administration of Alexander Johnston Cassatt, the Seventh President, who, with remarkable vision and foresight, saw that the Country would soon emerge from the financial and business depression of the 90's. The Company, therefore, began a program of huge expenditures for improvement work on the Main Line between New York and Pittsburgh, including the New York Tunnel Extension and Station, which was unparalleled in its history up to that time. As a result, it was prepared to handle the enormous growth in traffic which came with the general prosperity from 1901 to 1906.

EIGHTH AND NINTH

The Administrations of James McCrea and Samuel Rea, the Eighth and Ninth Presidents, respectively, were marked by further compacting and rounding out of the System, but their efforts in other directions were greatly handicapped by business depressions, hostile railroad regulation, and the effects of the World War and Federal Control of the Railroads.

Notwithstanding the future of the railroads was so uncertain, the Pennsylvania Railroad Company joined with other railroads of the Country in a huge program of capital expenditures for the improvement of the transportation service in the reconstruction period following the termination of Federal Control in 1920, which to some extent is responsible for the fact that they are now operating with greater efficiency than ever before. Another significant fact, as indicating public confidence in the Pennsylvania Railroad Company and its Management, is that notwithstanding the earning power of the Company was impaired by reason of conditions over which it had no control, the number of stockholders nearly doubled during President Rea's Administration. There were 75,155 stockholders at the beginning of 1913 and during the year 1925, before he retired, there were 147,185, which is the greatest number on record up to the present time.

TENTH

William Wallace Atterbury, the Tenth President, began his Administration on October 1st, 1925, and this review, therefore, covers only one full year (1926) of his term as President. In that year the recovery from the War and Federal Control conditions, which began in 1923, became more pronounced. Further substantial improvement was made in the earning power of the Company, and in restoring the railroad, the efficiency of the Organization, and the service to their former standards. There is, however, no indication that the problems of railroad construction, operation, or management will be less difficult than those which faced his predecessors, but it is safe to say that they will be solved, as they have been in the past, in the best interest of the public, the owners and the employes.

SUMMARY

The following is a list of the Presidents from the time the Organization of the Company was effected in 1847 up to the present date, and in subsequent pages the important events which have characterized its growth during this long and eventful period are reviewed in chronological order:—

Samuel Vaughan Merrick........March 31, 1847 to September 1, 1849;
William Chamberlain Patterson..September 1, 1849 to February 2, 1852;
John Edgar Thomson...........February 3, 1852 to May 27, 1874;
Thomas Alexander Scott.........June 3, 1874 to June 1, 1880;
George Brooke Roberts..........June 1, 1880 to January 30, 1897;
Frank Thomson................February 3, 1897 to June 5, 1899;
Alexander Johnston Cassatt......June 9, 1899 to December 28, 1906;
James McCrea.................January 2, 1907 to January 1, 1913;
Samuel Rea...................January 1, 1913 to October 1, 1925;
William Wallace Atterbury......October 1, 1925 to date.

SAMUEL VAUGHAN MERRICK
First President—March 31st, 1847, to September 1st, 1849.

SAMUEL VAUGHAN MERRICK

FIRST PRESIDENT, 1847-1849

ORGANIZATION

ON March 30th, 1847, the stockholders of the newly incorporated Pennsylvania Railroad Company held a meeting for the election of Directors, and on March 31st, 1847, the Directors so chosen elected Samuel Vaughan Merrick as President. He was born at Hallowell, Maine, on May 4th, 1801, and early devoted his energies along mechanical lines. Prior to his election, Mr. Merrick, as the head of the Franklin Institute, had charge of the erection of the Philadelphia Gas Works, and was an active partner in a large manufacturing establishment in that city. While not possessing the technical training of an engineer, he had a great deal of practical knowledge of that profession, and was regarded as well fitted to manage and inspire confidence in the enterprise.

On April 9th, 1847, the engineering organization was perfected, John Edgar Thomson (later President) being appointed Chief Engineer, and W. B. Foster, Jr., and Edward Miller, Associate Engineers.

On April 21st, 1847, the President announced that he had appointed Committees on Road, Finance and Accounts. The Company secured offices on the second floor of what was then the American Fire Insurance Company Building, Nos. 308 and 310 Walnut Street, Philadelphia, for a term of five years.

Of course, the most important work in President Merrick's administration, with the possible exception of raising the necessary capital to go forward with the project, was to locate and begin the construction of the road. The greatest obstacle in the way of this was the crossing, without the use of inclined planes, of the natural barrier between the East and West, namely, the Allegheny Mountains, and to select the most advantageous point at which to do so.

ADOPTED ROUTE—HARRISBURG TO ALTOONA

Many routes had previously been proposed across the State, and after the Chief Engineer had made an inspection of each on the ground, and the rugged character of the country through which they would pass, he wisely selected the valley of the Juniata River as the most feasible, whether considered from the standpoint of grade or general directness.

The route adopted by the Board of Directors commenced at the Harrisburg depot of the Harrisburg, Portsmouth, Mt. Joy & Lancaster Railroad; thence passing through Harrisburg, it followed the sloping ground between the Pennsylvania Canal and the Capitol Ridge for about 4 miles, where it crossed the Canal and, touching the point of Blue Mountain, crossed the Susquehanna River by bridge and passed to the west side. It then followed the Susquehanna River through the village of Duncannon to the Juniata River, along the southern side of which it continued through Newport and Perrysville to a point a short distance above Lewistown. Here the line crossed to the north side and within a short distance re-crossed the Juniata to save about a mile of road and 180 degrees of curvature. From this point westward the river was crossed several times to a point called "Jack's Narrows," and finally the route passed to the north side of the river through Huntingdon to the Little Juniata above Petersburg (Huntingdon County), and thence after crossing the river twelve times and tunneling Tussey's Mountain, near Spruce Creek, Logan's Narrows was reached at the eastern base of the Allegheny Mountains.

CROSSING THE ALLEGHENIES

The line had then reached a point where it was necessary to determine the best location to cross the mountainous barrier between the East and the West. A great deal of time and study were given to this most important section of the road, as well as a careful examination on the ground of every feasible route, and the number and power of locomotives required to make the ascent. It was finally decided that the best location was to pursue a course from Logan's Narrows nearly in a direct line to Sugar Run Gap, which would pass through a beautiful valley over comparatively favorable ground, with gradual elevation until it reached Robinson's Summit (now Altoona), which was the base of the mountain proper. The route, as described, began to ascend at Harrisburg, where it was 310 feet above tide, and followed the Susquehanna and Juniata Rivers to Robinson's Summit which was 1,174 feet above tide, at which point started the actual ascent of the mountain. At Lewistown it had risen to 488 feet above tide; at Huntingdon, 610 feet; at Tyrone, 886 feet; and at Robinson's Summit the line was at an elevation of 1,174 feet above tidewater, leaving but 984 feet to reach the height found most suitable for crossing the mountains, which was 2,158 feet above tide. The crossing was to be made on a maximum grade of 84½ feet per mile upon straight lines and 75 feet on curves for 12¼ miles, with a tunnel 3,570 feet long through the crest of the mountain. This grade was not unusual at that time, as the Baltimore & Ohio Railroad, in overcoming the Alleghenies, had a grade of 116 feet per mile for 11½ miles.

WESTWARD TO PITTSBURGH

Careful thought and study were then given to the most feasible of the several routes surveyed from the crossing of the mountain to Pittsburgh, and it was finally determined that the route should descend along the valley of the Conemaugh River to Johnstown, the chief obstacle to overcome being the building of a tunnel 600 feet in length through Pringle's Point, a short distance below Jefferson, but as the route crossed the Allegheny Portage Railroad (part of the State Works of Pennsylvania) five times by bridges and once upon a level, it possessed the advantage of being able to connect with it, thus bringing each portion of the line into profitable use as fast as it was completed. From Johnstown the route crossed the Conemaugh River and thence extended westward by way of Blairsville, Loyalhanna and Greensburg to the head of Brush Creek, which was followed to its confluence with Turtle Creek, and thence via the latter stream to the banks of the Monongahela River; then following a northwesterly direction to Wilkinsburg and East Liberty, it reached its terminus at Pittsburgh. The line made a gradual descent from the top of the mountain, to Johnstown, where it was 1,184 feet above tide; thence along the Conemaugh Valley and Packsaddle Gap, and across the country to Greensburg, where its elevation was 1,091 feet. At Pittsburgh the elevation was 748 feet, being 438 feet higher at the western terminus than at Harrisburg. The total distance from Harrisburg to Pittsburgh on the route described was 249 miles. A more northerly route by the west branch of the Susquehanna River would have encountered less elevation at the principal summits, but it would have been a much longer line than through the valley of the Juniata.

OTHER ROUTES EXAMINED

An examination was made of a proposed southern route, which followed the Cumberland Valley Railroad to near Shippensburg, passing through the Blue Mountains and thence westward. Another route left the Cumberland Valley Railroad at Chambersburg, and, turning the end of Blue Mountain, would have gone toward the low depression at Cowan's Gap in Tuscarora Mountain, but this would have been too circuitous compared with the line from Shippensburg. The principal objections, however, to both of these routes were the high gradients and the rugged character of the country which they proposed to accommodate. Aside from the disadvantages of the Shippensburg route, it was found that this section of the State could be provided with equally as good transportation facilities, with less expenditure of capital, by constructing the Main Line in the valley of the Juniata and building branches through the level valleys lying between the parallel mountains on the adopted Juniata route. In this connection it may be well to point out that Chief Engineer Thomson early adopted a policy, which, if it had been adhered to by other railroad managements in the earlier days of railroad construction, would have saved much additional and unprofitable mileage, that is, not to turn from a direct course to accommodate local developments to the detriment of the principal object to be accomplished, when the same interest could be served equally as well with a branch line.

CONNECTION WITH ALLEGHENY PORTAGE RAILROAD

Pending the completion of the Western Division of the Pennsylvania Railroad, arrangements were made to connect the Eastern Division with the State-owned Allegheny Portage Railroad by the construction of a branch from Altoona to Hollidaysburg at the "Y" switches, a distance of a little more than 6 miles. There would then be available within a few years an all-rail line from Philadelphia to Johnstown, a distance of 279 miles, through the use of the Philadelphia & Columbia Railroad from Philadelphia to a connection with the Harrisburg, Portsmouth, Mt. Joy & Lancaster Railroad just west of Lancaster; the latter road from said point of connection to Harrisburg; the Pennsylvania Railroad from Harrisburg to Hollidaysburg "Y" switches, and the Allegheny Portage Railroad from there to Johnstown.

DESCRIPTION OF ALLEGHENY PORTAGE RAILROAD

As the Allegheny Portage Railroad was to temporarily become an important connecting link in the through line to the West, the following description of it is interesting, it having been published by the Passenger Department of the Pennsylvania Railroad Company in 1875 from information furnished by Solomon W. Roberts, who was one of the Principal Assistant Engineers in its construction:—

> "The Portage Road, over the Allegheny Mountains, was during all the time it remained in operation one of the wonders of America. It consisted of eleven levels or grade lines and ten inclined planes. The ascent from Johnstown to the summit was 1,171½ feet in a distance of 26½ miles, and the descent from the summit to Hollidaysburg was 1,399 feet in a distance of ten miles (a total length of 36 miles). The planes were numbered east-

wardly, the one nearest Johnstown being number one and that nearest Hollidaysburg number ten. The length and rise of the planes were as follows:

	Length	*Rise*
No. 1	1,607 ft.	150 ft.
No. 2	1,760 ft.	132 ft.
No. 3	1,480 ft.	130 ft.
No. 4	2,195 ft.	187 ft.
No. 5	2,628 ft.	201 ft.
Summit Level		*Fall*
No. 6	2,713 ft.	266 ft.
No. 7	2,655 ft.	260 ft.
No. 8	3,116 ft.	307 ft.
No. 9	2,720 ft.	189 ft.
No. 10	2,295 ft.	180 ft.

The cars were passed over these planes by means of wire ropes attached to stationary engines, and it is a notable fact that during the twenty years the road was used no serious accidents ever occurred upon it. Boats used on the Canal for carrying through freight were built in sections, which sections were placed upon trucks and carried over the railroad."

ESTIMATES TO COMPLETE AND EQUIP THE ROAD

The Chief Engineer had prepared two estimates of the cost of constructing and equipping the road. The first was based on building the entire 249 miles of railroad, graded for double track, but laid with a single track, and it also included the purchase of locomotives and cars. On this basis the estimated cost was approximately $11,100,000. The other estimate was based on making the road available for traffic between Harrisburg and Pittsburgh at the earliest possible date by using the Allegheny Portage Railroad between Hollidaysburg and Johnstown, a distance of 36 miles. It was estimated that the cost, including equipment, under a plan of this kind, could be reduced to $7,860,000., and the Management proceeded on this basis pending the completion of the Mountain Division.

CAMPAIGN FOR SUBSCRIPTIONS TO CAPITAL STOCK

By strong and persistent efforts the Company up to 1849 had secured subscriptions to its Capital Stock amounting to over $5,500,000., payable in ten installments of $5.00

each, leaving $2,360,000. to be subscribed to complete the work on a reduced scale. The City of Philadelphia had originally taken 30,000 shares, and subsequently subscribed to 20,000 shares additional, making a total investment of $2,500,000. With this substantial interest in the enterprise, and other large and small subscriptions throughout the City, the citizens of Philadelphia set a creditable example for other sections of the State, which were to share in the general prosperity incident to the expansion of the trade and traffic of Pennsylvania, through the medium of the transportation facilities to be provided by the Pennsylvania Railroad Company. The citizens throughout the State were urged to invest their capital, with the most implicit confidence in the future of the project, and with the assurance of a fair return on their investment until the road was opened to Pittsburgh, when it was felt regular dividends of 8% would be paid. A report of the progress of construction was widely published and the people of the State were advised of the strenuous efforts being made by neighboring railroads and communities to secure the prize in the trade of the West, when the Pennsylvania Railroad had the shortest and most natural route to reach it. Attention was called to the estimate of earnings prepared by the Management showing the profit that should accrue to the Company, which was based on the results of operations of other roads in the East, and did not take into consideration the advantages the Pennsylvania Railroad had in its shorter route, easier grades and lower cost of operation because of its accessibility to very cheap fuel for motive power purposes.

MANAGEMENT'S POLICY QUESTIONED

In the midst of the efforts to secure additional subscriptions, some question was raised by the leading firms engaged in transportation upon the State Works, with respect to the manner in which the Management intended to conduct the business of the Company, especially with regard to the matter of cars. This had been a very profitable source of income to those who owned equipment on the State Works, and who hired it out at remunerative rates, they receiving a much larger profit, in proportion to the capital employed, than that derived from the operations of the road and motive power. They were informed that it was the intention of the Company to conduct operations with its own cars and engines as much as possible consistent with the rights reserved to individuals in the Charter. This decision led to attempts to mislead prospective stockholders, and to raise questions as to the propriety of using the capital of the Company in furnishing equipment instead of devoting it to building the road. Of course, the question of profit was an important element in the decision of the Management to provide its own equipment, but it also had in mind the reduction of the cost of transportation to a minimum price, thus accomplishing the main object in promoting the enterprise, which was to benefit the trade and commercial relations of the whole State of Pennsylvania. In accordance with this policy, contracts were entered into for the first equipment of the Company, viz: 75 freight cars and 3 freight locomotives to be delivered on May 1st, 1849, when the road was expected to be completed as far west as Lewistown.

INCREASED INTEREST PAYMENTS

The clause in the Charter requiring the payment of 5% interest per annum on the actual paid-in capital of the Company, after contracts had been made for the construction of 15 miles at each end of the road, was given serious consideration because that rate of interest was not deemed sufficient to attract subscriptions to Capital Stock. Therefore, the Legislature was asked to amend the Charter to increase the rate to 6%, and a supplemental Act was passed on March 27th, 1848, authorizing the Company to pay that rate of interest semi-annually in the months of May and November until the road was completed. Interest payments, therefore, began in the month of May, 1848, and covered the period from the date the first installment ($5.00 per share) was paid in April, 1847. It may not seem to have been a wise policy for the Company to pay interest on its paid-in capital when nothing was being earned, yet the factor of interest, and probably at usurious rates, would have been an element in any event if other methods had been used to raise the capital to construct the road. The Directors felt that it was not fair to ask subscribers to forego their income while the work was in progress when, by the payment of a reasonable return on their investment, additional capital could probably be induced to participate in the enterprise.

LOOKING WESTWARD

The Management early gave its attention to the bright prospect of securing the large and profitable traffic from the West, in addition to the revenue to be derived from local traffic in the rich and populous section served by its railroad in the State of Pennsylvania. The adopted line of the Pennsylvania Railroad was directly in the path of a route that would be most advantageous for the location of a railroad from the Mississippi River through the centre of the great agricultural, mining and manufacturing districts to the Atlantic Seaboard. The Management, therefore, looked with favor upon the efforts of the citizens and merchants of Ohio and western Pennsylvania to construct a line from the western terminus of the Pennsylvania Railroad across the State of Ohio. They had secured a Charter in 1848 under the name of the Ohio & Pennsylvania Railroad Company (now part of Pittsburgh, Ft. Wayne & Chicago Railway), and as sufficient Stock had been subscribed along its proposed route to enable them to organize, it was not hard to understand the willingness of many citizens in the western part of Pennsylvania to change their former unfriendly feelings toward the Pennsylvania Railroad Company. As a result the County of Allegheny in 1848 authorized a subscription to 20,000 shares ($1,000,000.) of its Capital Stock upon the fulfillment of certain conditions as to the prompt commencement of construction work upon the western end of the line, the location of the terminus in Pittsburgh, and the payment of interest upon their subscription, all of which, it is needless to say, were readily met.

OPERATION OF HARRISBURG, PORTSMOUTH, MT. JOY & LANCASTER R. R.

Realizing the importance and necessity of extending the operations of the Pennsylvania Railroad over as long a route as possible, and of placing all motive power and cars under one Management, even before its own railroad was completed and in operation, arrangements were made on November 1st, 1848, with the Harrisburg, Portsmouth, Mt. Joy & Lancaster Railroad (with which the Pennsylvania Railroad proposed to connect at Harrisburg), by which the latter Company was to conduct the operations of the smaller road. The important features in this contract, which was to be effective for 20 years from September 1st, 1849, were that the Pennsylvania Railroad Company was to purchase all the equipment of the Harrisburg, Portsmouth, Mt. Joy & Lancaster Railroad Company, which, with that owned by the Pennsylvania Railroad, was to be used exclusively on both railroads. The charges for the local business, or that which did not pass over the Pennsylvania Railroad, were to be regulated by the Harrisburg, Portsmouth, Mt. Joy & Lancaster Railroad Company, but the charges upon all freight and passenger traffic passing over any portion of the Pennsylvania Railroad were to be governed by its rates. This agreement with the Harrisburg, Portsmouth, Mt. Joy & Lancaster Railroad Company later took the form of a lease for 999 years, but as it was consummated in another Administration, it will be dealt with in a subsequent chapter.

RESIGNATION OF PRESIDENT MERRICK

With the construction of the road progressing satisfactorily, and the prospect that sufficient capital would be raised for its completion, President Merrick tendered his resignation on August 29th, 1849, and relinquished the responsibilities of the office of President, effective September 1st, 1849, but retained his membership in the Board of Directors.

BRIGHT PROSPECTS

Prospects were bright at the close of President Merrick's administration for the successful completion of the entire line at a not distant date. With the acknowledged superiority of the route to the West, both as to grades and distance, and the well known advantage of all-rail transportation over the then existing rail, canal and stage coach, there seemed to be substantial basis for the belief that the Company would have a profitable career, notwithstanding the impression that if the State Works did not yield a profit, it was hardly possible for this new road to have sufficient earnings to pay anything like a fair return on the capital invested. The answer was readily given that if the capital obligations of the State Works represented an amount equal to the reproductive cost of the property, instead of being so greatly in excess of it, there was hardly a question but what it would pay with judicious and economical management.

CONSTRUCTION ACCOUNT

The following statement shows the Construction Account for the first three years of the Company's existence (fiscal year ending October 31st), and as the road was then in course of construction, there are no operating results to present:

	1847	*1848*	*1849*
Amount received from stockholders in payment of subscriptions..............	$1,017,725.00	$1,623,710.00	$3,622,035.00
Of which there was expended	64,421.14	1,108,269.31	3,123,364.71
Leaving a balance of.......	$953,303.86	$515,440.69	$498,670.29
Stock subscriptions to be collected..............................		1,520,000.00	1,900,000.00
Amount available for construction work...........	$953,303.86	$2,035,440.69	$2,398,670.29

DIRECTORS

It may be of interest to give the names and terms of service of the Directors of the Pennsylvania Railroad Company since its incorporation, and this information will be found at the close of each Administration for the Directors who served during such period. A supplement to the original Charter was approved on March 27th, 1848, which authorized Municipalities subscribing to the Capital Stock of the Company to elect one Director for each 10,000 shares subscribed, but limiting the number so elected to three for each Municipality. Under this authority, Allegheny County had two representatives on the Board up to 1859 when it sold its holdings, and the City of Philadelphia had three members up to 1879 when the Pennsylvania Railroad Company purchased its ownership of Capital Stock.

As a result of subscriptions to the required amount of Capital Stock, two Municipal Districts of Philadelphia, namely, Spring Garden and Northern Liberties, also had one member each on the Board of Directors for several years prior to 1855. When these Municipal Districts were consolidated with the City of Philadelphia under an Act approved March 11th, 1854, they ceased to have representation on the Board as the City of Philadelphia then had the full quota permitted under the Charter of the Company.

The following is a list of the Directors who served during President Merrick's Administration, together with the dates of their election and the end of their service:—

Name of Director	*Elected*	*End of Service*
Samuel Vaughan Merrick....	March 30, 1847,	February 2, 1852;
Thomas P. Cope...........	"	April 26, 1848;
Robert Toland.............	"	July 19, 1848;
David S. Brown............	"	February 4, 1852;
James Magee...............	"	December 4, 1848;
Richard D. Wood..........	"	"
Stephen Colwell............	"	December 18, 1850;
George W. Carpenter........	"	January 6, 1858;
Christian E. Spangler.......	"	September 19, 1857;
Thomas T. Lea.............	"	February 4, 1852;
William C. Patterson	"	February 2, 1852;
Henry C. Corbit...........	"	May 17, 1847;
John A. Wright.............	"	December 4, 1848;
Jesse Godley...............	May 17, 1847,	December 4, 1848;
Robert F. Stockton.........	December 4, 1848,	December 3, 1849;
John Wiegand..............	"	December 21, 1848;
Morris L. Hallowell.........	"	December 3, 1849;
George Howell..............	"	March 2, 1857;
John H. Shoenberger.......	"	December 26, 1851;
William Wilkins............	"	February 7, 1853;
John Yarrow...............	January 17, 1849,	December 2, 1850;
"	December 18, 1850,	December 18, 1855.

WILLIAM CHAMBERLAIN PATTERSON

Second President—September 1st, 1849, to February 2nd, 1852.

WILLIAM CHAMBERLAIN PATTERSON

SECOND PRESIDENT, 1849–1852

WILLIAM CHAMBERLAIN PATTERSON was elected President on August 29th, 1849, effective September 1st, 1849. He was born in Claiborne County, Tenn., on February 1st, 1813, and came prominently before the public through his efforts in managing the Bill for the consolidation of the City and County of Philadelphia, and as the result of his work in settling the tangled affairs of the defunct Pennsylvania Bank. He possessed unusual financial and practical ability, which qualified him to act as the administrative head of the Pennsylvania Railroad Company.

OPENING OF SECTIONS OF THE ROAD

On the first day of his Administration as President, namely, September 1st, 1849, the Pennsylvania Railroad was completed between Harrisburg and Lewistown, a distance of 61 miles, that being the first section opened for operation. The time table issued by the Company at that time showed one passenger train over the road each way daily. The westward train left Dillerville on the Harrisburg, Portsmouth, Mt. Joy & Lancaster Railroad at 12.00 o'clock, noon, arriving at Lewistown, a distance of 97 miles, at 5.30 in the afternoon. The eastward train left Lewistown at 10.00 o'clock in the morning, and arrived at Dillerville at 3.10 in the afternoon. The freight trains at that time ran only twice a week between these points.

On December 24th, 1849, the road was completed to McVeytown, a distance of 72 miles from Harrisburg; to Shaeffer's Aqueduct, near Mount Union, 85 miles, on April 1st, 1850; to Huntingdon, 97 miles, on June 10th, 1850, and to the State-owned Allegheny Portage Railroad, near Hollidaysburg, 137 miles, on September 17th, 1850. The actual connection was not made until October 1st, 1850, and then only for the purpose of testing the facilities, as operations were not commenced over the Allegheny Portage Railroad, so far as Pennsylvania Railroad traffic was concerned, until the following Spring. When this large section of the road was in active operation, it was expected the earnings would afford the stockholders sufficient evidence of the safety and productiveness of the capital which they had invested in the Pennsylvania Railroad Company. The road was laid with iron rails, contracted for at the rate of $61.50 per ton, which was about $10. less than the market price at that time. Experiments were made with the use of coal, wood and coke for fuel purposes, which resulted in the use of coal and wood combined, the experience with coke proving very unsatisfactory.

MOUNTAIN DIVISION

While the Pennsylvania Railroad had been completed to a connection with the Allegheny Portage Railroad, and arrangements made to temporarily use that avenue of transportation over the mountains, the Management felt that this means of conveyance, although temporarily answering the purpose, should be discontinued as promptly as capital could be raised. The use of inclined planes not only prevented the carriage of live stock from points west of the mountains to the eastern markets, thus cutting off a material source of revenue, but the time consumed on this section of the road made it anything but an inviting route for travelers and shippers. Added to this was the fact that it was mismanaged, owing to the numerous changes in State and local politics. Therefore, that portion of the road crossing the Allegheny Mountains from Altoona to the Stone Viaduct over the Conemaugh River, just east of Conemaugh, a distance of 31½ miles, known as the "Mountain Division," had been considered by the Chief Engineer as a separate section of the road in his estimates, and no effort had been made to proceed with its immediate construction, as sufficient capital could not be had to justify this action. However, with the Eastern Division of the line finished and partly in operation, and rapid progress being made on the Western

Division from Pittsburgh to the Stone Viaduct, a distance of 85 miles, the Chief Engineer was naturally anxious to begin construction work on the connecting link across the mountains, which it was estimated would cost close to $2,000,000.

B. & O. R. R. AGAIN IN THE FIELD

He was especially desirous of completing this section of the road because the Baltimore & Ohio Railroad Company had secured the right to build an extension from Cumberland, Md., to the Ohio River, upon which rapid progress was being made. It was felt that if the Pennsylvania Railroad were to continue the use of the Allegheny Portage Railroad over the mountains and be subject to its frequent delays and interruptions, it could not hope to be a strong competitor of the Baltimore & Ohio Railroad when the latter road reached the Ohio River, to which point it was expected to be completed by 1852. It was recognized that it was a difficult task at that time to raise $2,000,000. to build the Pennsylvania Railroad over the mountains, and the additional amount to complete the Western Division and provide the necessary equipment, but the advantages to be gained were considered to be worth the effort.

EARNINGS SHOULD EQUAL THOSE OF B. & O.—COMPETITION FOR WESTERN TRAFFIC

In further substantiation of the claim that the Pennsylvania Railroad would prove a profitable investment for capital, reference was made to the Baltimore & Ohio Railroad, which was earning 8½% upon its Stock, and it was argued if that Company could operate so successfully, it was unquestionable, with the smaller capital investment of the Pennsylvania Railroad Company, its greater length of road and more favorable grades and curvature, that it should do at least as well, or even better than the southern company. Further, the Baltimore & Ohio Railroad Company, instead of disbursing the 8½% earned on its Capital Stock, was using it in the vigorous prosecution of its extension westward in an endeavor to secure the trade of the West, as it was expected that before the Pennsylvania Railroad was built to Pittsburgh, a continuous all-rail line would be constructed from the latter point to Cleveland and Cincinnati, and probably into Indiana, and both companies were extremely anxious to provide the outlet to the Atlantic Coast for this traffic.

TONNAGE TAX

It was in the year 1850 that the Management of the Pennsylvania Railroad Company first called attention to the tonnage tax imposed under the Charter granted to the Company, and the great injustice it would do if allowed to remain, the tax having been levied for the alleged purpose of protecting the investment of the State in its line of Public Works. The injurious effects of this measure on the prospects of the new enterprise were continually kept before the State authorities, and efforts were made to show that instead of the Pennsylvania Railroad being a competitor of the State Works, it was really the only means of retaining the important trade of the West within the limits of Pennsylvania. It was pointed out that as the result of the delays and inconveniences incident to the movement of traffic on the State Works, it would sooner or later find an outlet over the Baltimore & Ohio Railroad on the south, or the New York & Erie Railroad and Erie Canal on the north, which companies were the real competitors of the State in the operation of its transportation facilities, and thus the through business from the West would almost cease to flow through the State of Pennsylvania. Therefore, all attempts to secure it to the State Works by a tonnage tax or other penalties on traffic passing over the Pennsylvania Railroad were not only unreasonable, but unjust, and the tax imposed was just that much of an advantage to its competitors on the north and south.

FINANCING WITH CAPITAL STOCK

When subscriptions to the Capital Stock had reached close to the $10,000,000. authorized in the Charter, a controversy arose over the method to be pursued in raising the balance of $2,500,000. required to complete the road, as subscriptions to the Stock were not being received in very large amounts. The advisability of making a loan was considered, but it was claimed by the opponents of this plan that it would be a departure from the declared policy of the Company to complete the line unencumbered by debt. On the other hand it was recognized that a resort to loans was inevitable unless substantial subscriptions were received from the citizens and large institutions. Serious discussion was had on the question, and as a result the Board of Directors concluded to continue the efforts to raise new capital through the medium of Capital Stock.

REDUCTION IN PASSENGER RATES

The Charter of the Company having fixed the maximum charge for local passengers at 3½ cents per mile, and through passengers at 3 cents per mile, the Management deemed it advisable to charge those rates, but as it did not seem fair to discriminate against local travel, which it was urged should be encouraged, it was decided that the abolition of the distinction between local and through passengers would ultimately yield a larger net revenue. Accordingly passenger rates were fixed at the uniform rate of 3 cents per mile on and after January 1st, 1850, except for emigrant traffic, which could be carried at slow speed and consequently at very low rates.

CONSTRUCTION PROGRESS—EARNINGS—OPERATING ORGANIZATION

While the Pennsylvania Railroad had been constructed to a connection with the Allegheny Portage Railroad, a distance of 137 miles from Harrisburg, the average length of road in use during the year 1850 was only 90 miles, and, therefore, it was felt it would not be fair to place the net earnings against the total cost of road and equipment in figuring the percentage earned on the money invested. A further reason was that an Operating Organization had just been perfected, consisting of four Departments, viz: Conducting Transportation, Maintenance of Way, Motive Power, and Maintenance of Cars, and the minor positions, though not unimportant, were necessarily filled with inexperienced men, as the operation of railroads was then something of a new undertaking.

The early part of the year 1851 found the Pennsylvania Railroad in operation as far west as Altoona, the terminus of the Eastern Division, with a connection to the Allegheny Portage Railroad. During that year portions of the Western Division, which embraced that section of the road from the Stone Viaduct over the Conemaugh River to Pittsburgh, were brought into operation, and the movement of traffic between Philadelphia and Pittsburgh was then conducted over five or six separate links forming a broken chain of transportation facilities between the two cities. However, despite these unsatisfactory conditions, the gross earnings of the Company during the year 1851 were much greater than those for the previous year, but, of course, the increase in the length of road operated was responsible for a large portion of this very creditable showing. The net earnings indicated a return equivalent to 6¾% upon the cost of the road and equipment then in use, including interest during construction.

ORIGIN OF NAME "ALTOONA"

As the City of Altoona occupies such an important place in the growth and development of the Company, it would perhaps be interesting at this point to give the origin of its name. There are several versions, but after careful research and examination of the records it was found that when the Company had purchased property there, which consisted largely of farm land, the town was tentatively named "Allatoona," presumably after the picturesque "Allatoona Pass" in Georgia, in which State John Edgar Thomson had been engaged in engineering work before his connection with the Pennsylvania Railroad Company. This first name is confirmed by reference to the note books of the late James R. McClure, Assistant Engineer in charge of building the railroad and the Logan House at that point in the latter part of 1850. Later when the town was laid out and lots placed on the market for sale, a final name had to be given to it and "Altoona" was selected as being shorter and perhaps more euphonious.

OHIO & PENNSYLVANIA RAILROAD COMPANY

Great pressure was brought upon the Management in 1851 to subscribe to $250,000. of Stock of the Ohio & Pennsylvania Railroad Company, the line of which commenced at Pittsburgh and was to be constructed to Crestline, O. It was suggested that this subscription could be paid for by the issue of Bonds of the Pennsylvania Railroad Company, provided an amount equivalent to the interest on such Bonds was paid by the Ohio & Pennsylvania Railroad Company. The matter was carefully considered by a Committee of Stockholders, and while their report set out how vastly important it was, not only to the Pennsylvania Railroad Company, but to the whole State of Pennsylvania, to aid in the completion of this western connection, the Committee did not deem it advisable at that time to participate in the project, as its own railroad was in an unfinished condition, and it was only after much persuasion that additional capital could be induced to support that project. The Management, however, did not long maintain this attitude toward the Ohio & Pennsylvania Railroad Company, as subsequent chapters indicate.

RESIGNATION OF PRESIDENT PATTERSON

A difference of opinion in the Management as to the course to be pursued in financing the needs of the Company and its general business policies led to the resignation of President Patterson, effective February 2nd, 1852, and the election to the Presidency on February 3rd, 1852, of John Edgar Thomson, who had been Chief Engineer of the Company.

EARNINGS—CONSTRUCTION ACCOUNT

The following statements give the results of operation during President Patterson's administration, and the financial condition of the Company during that period. The road had been opened to Lewistown on September 1st, 1849, and as the fiscal year of the Company then ended on October 31st, the results of operation during September and October, 1849, are omitted. They are included in the operations for the year ending December 31st, 1850, as the fiscal year of the Company was changed to the last day of the year by an Act of the Legislature dated April 26th, 1850:—

EARNINGS

	1850	*1851*
Gross Earnings	$339,452.51	$1,039,565.49
Operating Expenses	172,244.28	706,640.19
Net Earnings	$167,208.23	$332,925.30

CONSTRUCTION ACCOUNT

	1850	*1851*
Amount received from stockholders in payment of subscriptions	$5,822,210.00	$8,103,465.00
Of which there was expended	5,095,546.12	7,978,089.82
Leaving a balance of	$726,663.88	$125,375.18
Stock subscriptions to be collected	1,013,640.00	1,472,585.00
Amount available for construction work	$1,740,303.88	$1,597,960.18

DIRECTORS

The following is a list of the Directors who served during President Patterson's Administration, together with the dates of their election and the end of their service:—

Name of Director	*Elected*	*End of Service*
Samuel Vaughan Merrick	March 30, 1847,	February 2, 1852;
Stephen Colwell	"	December 18, 1850;
George W. Carpenter	"	January 6, 1858;
Christian E. Spangler	"	September 19, 1857;
Thomas T. Lea	"	February 4, 1852;
William C. Patterson	"	February 2, 1852;
David S. Brown	"	February 4, 1852;
Robert F. Stockton	December 4, 1848,	December 3, 1849;
George Howell	"	March 2, 1857;
Morris L. Hallowell	"	December 3, 1849;
John H. Shoenberger	"	December 26, 1851;
William Wilkins	"	February 7, 1853;
Washington Butcher	December 3, 1849,	May 28, 1861;
"	December 27, 1865,	January 8, 1873;
Edward M. Davis	December 3, 1849,	February 12, 1852;
John Yarrow	January 17, 1849,	December 2, 1850;
"	December 18, 1850,	December 18, 1855;
Alexander J. Derbyshire	December 2, 1850,	February 5, 1855;
"	February 26, 1873,	March 26, 1878;
William Robinson, Jr	December 26, 1851,	March 3, 1856.

JOHN EDGAR THOMSON
Third President—February 3rd, 1852, to May 27th, 1874.

JOHN EDGAR THOMSON

THIRD PRESIDENT, 1852–1874

JOHN EDGAR THOMSON was born in Morton, Delaware County, Pa., on February 10th, 1808, and was educated principally by his father. He began his eventful railroad career at the age of 19 on one of the engineering corps engaged in surveying the Philadelphia & Columbia Railroad, which was later constructed by the State of Pennsylvania. The knowledge and experience gained in this work and in supervising the construction of other railroads was later used to the great advantage of the Pennsylvania Railroad Company. After leaving the service of the State, he secured employment with the Camden & Amboy Railroad, and subsequently became Chief Engineer of the Georgia Railroad, with which road he remained until his appointment as Chief Engineer of the Pennsylvania Railroad Company early in 1847. In June, 1849, the Board of Directors also committed to Mr. Thomson the duties of General Superintendent, which position he retained until January, 1851, and on February 3rd, 1852, he was elected President. He was one of the foremost civil engineers of his time, and the location and building of the Pennsylvania Railroad is a tribute to his engineering skill.

During his term as President, extending over a period of 22 years, he laid the foundation of the Pennsylvania Railroad System, which at the close of his Administration embraced a territory extending as far west as the Mississippi River, and from the Ohio and Potomac Rivers on the south to the Great Lakes on the north. Furthermore, he was responsible for the first organization adopted by the Company for conducting its business, which, while enlarged to meet changing conditions and the needs of the Company, has stood the test of time and experience. He lived to see its operations grow to extremely large proportions, which left no doubt as to the profitableness of the enterprise and its vast importance not only to the State in the development of its industries and natural resources, but to the whole economic welfare of the Country.

FURTHER REDUCTION IN PASSENGER RATES

So great was the desire to secure the trade of the West that the Management of the Company proposed to make the passenger rates almost without regard to profit, and so low as to preclude the successful interference of any rival route. With this policy in mind the first class passenger fares were reduced on and after March 1st, 1852, to a uniform rate of 2½ cents per mile.

INCREASED CAPITAL STOCK

A supplemental Act was passed by the Legislature on April 23rd, 1852, authorizing the issuance of 60,000 additional shares of Capital Stock, having a par value of $3,000,000., to complete the Mountain Division. Shortly afterward, on May 6th, 1852, legislation was secured to further increase the Capital Stock 20,000 shares, par value $1,000,000., making a total authorized issue of 280,000 shares with a par value of $14,000,000. Although strong efforts were made to dispose of this Stock the response was not encouraging, and this means of raising capital was temporarily abandoned; but as the Company would have been seriously embarrassed if it had not been able to complete the Mountain Division and furnish equipment and other facilities at the earliest practicable date, in order to become an important competitor with other routes for the trade of the West, it was necessary to employ other means of raising the funds.

FIRST BOND ISSUE

Therefore, with the approval of the stockholders of the Company, a First Mortgage for $5,000,000. was executed, dated October 14th, 1852, providing for the issuance of 5,000 $1,000. Bonds, or 5,000 Bonds of 200 Pounds Sterling each; the Dollar Bonds to bear 6% interest and the Sterling Bonds 5% interest. These Bonds were to mature on December 31st, 1880, with the privilege to the holders to convert them into Capital Stock at par up to December 1st, 1860. They were all issued as Dollar Bonds bearing 6% interest, and $3,000,000. of them were disposed of on favorable terms in the year 1852 and the balance in 1853, the selling price being slightly above par. The proceeds were to be used for the purpose of completing a single track road from Harrisburg to Pittsburgh, including equipment and other facilities, thus avoiding the use of the objectionable inclined planes on the Allegheny Portage Railroad. However, the demands of increased business had made it very apparent that an additional track was necessary, estimated to cost $3,600,000., throughout the entire length of the road, and the Chief Engineer was accordingly instructed to proceed with this work as soon as the financial resources of the Company would permit.

CONTINUOUS RAILROAD OPENED

It was with great pleasure that the Management reported to the stockholders that a continuous single track railroad had been opened to trade and travel on December 10th, 1852, between Philadelphia and Pittsburgh, including a branch to Blairsville nearly 3 miles in length. It was the first all-rail line to be built from the Atlantic Seaboard to Pittsburgh. However, the State-owned Allegheny Portage Railroad with its inclined planes and the Philadelphia & Columbia Railroad continued to form a part of the route.

BRANCHES

While the Management realized the importance of early completing its road to Pittsburgh, they were not unmindful of the possibilities of developing the territory adjacent to the Main Line by the construction of branches. In accordance with this policy a location had been made for a branch 16½ miles in length from Blairsville to Indiana, Pa., to be paid for partly by Stock subscriptions of residents along the route, and surveys were being made for a branch to Uniontown, Pa. It was felt that with the completion of the Main Line of the Company, the foregoing branches, and the western railroads then being constructed through Ohio, Indiana and Illinois, an enormous amount of traffic would be thrown on the Pennsylvania Railroad; in fact so much that a two-track line would soon be overcrowded, thus necessitating a third track in congested sections, giving the road greatly increased capacity and a consequent ability to reduce transportation charges to compete with the low rates charged on western shipments via the Erie Canal route. With this prospect, it was argued that the tide of the western trade would soon be turned toward Philadelphia, from which City it had been diverted by the opening of that route.

PHILADELPHIA TERMINAL

By an Act of the Legislature of March 3rd, 1853, the Pennsylvania Railroad Company was given the right to operate its cars over the Philadelphia & Columbia Railroad, and as this arrangement necessitated the construction of a station in Philadelphia for the accommodation of its passenger trains, property was secured at Eleventh and Market Streets for that purpose. A station was subsequently built on this site and opened for use on May 20th, 1854. The Company was also the owner of property at Thirteenth and Market Streets, now occupied by the Wanamaker Store, on which a large freight station was erected. It was placed in operation in 1855, and was said to be the largest of its kind in the United States at that time.

AIDING WESTERN CONNECTIONS

President Thomson realized early in his Administration that to judiciously invest capital in the several railroads projected in Ohio and Indiana was almost as important for the concentration of traffic from these States and the great central region of the West upon the Pennsylvania Railroad, as it was to provide funds for the completion of the latter road itself. Therefore, a number of subscriptions were made to the Capital Stock of various western railroad companies, and financial aid was otherwise extended to them. As it was necessary to secure legislative authority therefor, a supplement to the Act incorporating the Pennsylvania Railroad Company was passed on March 23rd, 1853. This Act authorized and empowered it to subscribe to the Capital Stock or guarantee the Bonds of such railroad companies in other States as the Board of Directors deemed wise to promote the trade of the State of Pennsylvania and the interest of the Pennsylvania Railroad Company, but not in excess of 15% of the actual subscribed Capital Stock of the latter Company.

OHIO & PENNSYLVANIA RAILROAD COMPANY

Of the several lines that were being built in Ohio, through which the Pennsylvania Railroad expected to receive its share of the western trade, the Ohio & Pennsylvania Railroad Company (afterward merged into the Pittsburgh, Ft. Wayne & Chicago Railroad Company) made the greatest progress. This road under its Charter had the right to build a line from the eastern to the western boundary lines of Ohio and into Pittsburgh, and as the means for completing the Pennsylvania Railroad's Main Line had been furnished by the sale of $5,000,000. of its First Mortgage Bonds, the Management felt that it could safely invest $300,000. in the Capital Stock of the Ohio & Pennsylvania Railroad Company, a portion of which was to be used to construct a bridge across the Allegheny River so as to reach the depot of the Pennsylvania Railroad in Pittsburgh. It was finally determined not to build this road further west than Crestline, O., from which point it was opened for traffic to Pittsburgh on April 11th, 1853.

OHIO & INDIANA RAILROAD COMPANY

The Pennsylvania Railroad also agreed to help finance the Ohio & Indiana Railroad Company (also later merged into the Pittsburgh, Ft. Wayne & Chicago Railroad Company), which was chartered to build a line from Crestline, O., to Fort Wayne, Ind., it being really an extension of the Ohio & Pennsylvania Railroad from Crestline to Ft. Wayne. This railroad had been partly constructed, and as it was estimated that it would cost about $300,000. to complete it, the Pennsylvania Railroad agreed to subscribe to that amount of the Capital Stock of the Company. As a result it was completed between those cities and opened for traffic in November, 1854. An extension of this route was projected from Ft. Wayne to Chicago, for the construction of which the Fort Wayne & Chicago Railroad Company (this being another of the Companies afterward merged into the Pittsburgh, Ft. Wayne & Chicago Railroad Company) was organized.

PITTSBURGH, FT. WAYNE & CHICAGO RAILROAD COMPANY FORMED

On May 6th, 1856, the Ohio & Pennsylvania Railroad Company, the Ohio & Indiana Railroad Company, and the Fort Wayne & Chicago Railroad Company were merged into the Pittsburgh, Ft. Wayne & Chicago Railroad Company. The whole length of the road when completed was to be 468 miles, forming a continuous railroad from Pittsburgh to Chicago. As a result of this consolidation, the Pennsylvania Railroad Company received $769,850. of Stock in the new Company for its investment of $600,000. in two of the three consolidated companies.

MARIETTA & CINCINNATI RAILROAD COMPANY

The Pennsylvania Railroad Company also aided the Marietta & Cincinnati Railroad Company, which was engaged in the completion of a line from Wheeling, W. Va., to Marietta, O., a distance of 76 miles. This road was designed as a connecting link between a line originating at Cincinnati (then in course of construction from that point eastwardly to Marietta), and a road from Pittsburgh to Wheeling, W. Va., which was being built as rapidly as the character of the country traversed would permit. To construct this connecting link, the Pennsylvania Railroad was asked to subscribe to $750,000. of the Capital Stock of the Marietta & Cincinnati Railroad Company, and after the route had been examined by the Chief Engineer of the Pennsylvania Railroad Company, and an estimate had been prepared of the probable amount of traffic it would divert to its road at Pittsburgh for eastern markets, as well as the advantages to be secured in having a through line from Pittsburgh to Cincinnati, he strongly recommended the project. The Company thereupon subscribed $750,000. to the Capital Stock of the Marietta & Cincinnati Railroad Company, the subscription to be paid for either in Capital Stock of the Pennsylvania Railroad Company, or cash, with the proviso that the Marietta Company should agree to pay 6% on the Stock issued by it and not sell the Pennsylvania Railroad Company Stock at less than par without the consent of the latter Company. Subsequently, $100,000. of the investment in the Marietta & Cincinnati Railroad Company was exchanged for a like amount of Stock in the Maysville & Big Sandy Railroad Company, which road, through the Scioto Valley Railroad, connected with the Marietta & Cincinnati Railroad, and by means of which Philadelphia was to be placed in direct connection with the heart of Kentucky at Lexington.

SPRINGFIELD, MT. VERNON & PITTSBURGH RAILROAD COMPANY

In addition to the foregoing, the Springfield, Mt. Vernon & Pittsburgh Railroad Company received financial aid from the Pennsylvania Railroad Company in the form of a subscription to $100,000. of its Capital Stock, which was done largely to secure an early connection with Cincinnati by a route, which, while longer than the line via Wheeling and Marietta, had lighter gradients and easy curvature. Subsequently the Pennsylvania Railroad Company exchanged its interest in this Company for a like amount of stock of the Steubenville & Indiana Railroad Company, to which reference is hereinafter made. In 1861 the completed portion of the Springfield, Mt. Vernon & Pittsburgh Railroad between Springfield and Delaware, O., was sold to what is now the Cleveland, Cincinnati, Chicago & St. Louis Railway Company (part of the New York Central System). The uncompleted section later formed part of the road constructed from Millersburg to Columbus, O., by a predecessor of the Pennsylvania, Ohio & Detroit Railroad Company, all of the Capital Stock of which is owned in the interest of the Pennsylvania Railroad Company.

STEUBENVILLE & INDIANA RAILROAD COMPANY

While these roads extending in a northwesterly and southwesterly direction from the Pennsylvania Railroad terminus at Pittsburgh were aggressively pushing their respective lines to completion, the Management realized the importance and value of securing a more direct railroad communication with the rich agricultural and commercial section of the West lying about parallel with Philadelphia. The Steubenville & Indiana Railroad Company (now part of the Pittsburgh, Cincinnati, Chicago & St. Louis Railroad Company), which was chartered to build a line from Steubenville, O., to the Indiana State line, occupied this territory and had been diligently proceeding with the construction of its line without heretofore asking aid of the Pennsylvania Railroad Company. The gauge of the two roads was the same, affording a material advantage in the interchange of cars for through traffic, which unfortunately had not been the case in the exchange of business with the Ohio & Pennsylvania Railroad. The advantage in the form of a direct connection with the Steubenville & Indiana Railroad was offered to the Pennsylvania Railroad if it would guarantee the Bonds of the former company to the extent of $500,000., the proceeds from the sale of which were to be used in the completion of its line between Steubenville and Columbus. This the Pennsylvania Railroad agreed to do, and with this guarantee the Company had reached the limit to which it could extend aid to roads in other States under the supplement to its Charter. The connection with the Steubenville & Indiana Railroad was to be made through the Pittsburgh & Steubenville Railroad, which was to be built from a connection with the Pennsylvania Railroad in Pittsburgh to Steubenville, and the completion of these roads, it was stated, would furnish the shortest route to Cincinnati and the middle West from Philadelphia and New York.

To summarize, the Pennsylvania Railroad Company had up to the end of 1854, in addition to this guarantee, the sum of $1,450,000. invested in the Capital Stocks of the following Western railroads:—

Ohio & Pennsylvania R. R. Co.	$300,000.
Ohio & Indiana R. R. Co.	300,000.
Marietta & Cincinnati R. R. Co.	650,000.
Maysville & Big Sandy R. R. Co.	100,000.
Springfield, Mt. Vernon & Pittsburgh R. R. Co.	100,000.
	$1,450,000.

MOUNTAIN DIVISION COMPLETED

The Mountain Division of the Pennsylvania Railroad, which was the most difficult section of the whole road to construct, was completed on February 15th, 1854, thus bringing the entire line of the Pennsylvania Railroad into use from Harrisburg to Pittsburgh. There were three through westward trains daily from Philadelphia to Pittsburgh and the same number eastward, the time consumed in making the journey being 13, 15, and 17 hours, respectively. That portion of the line crossing the mountain was laid with two tracks, but the double tracking on other sections of the route was temporarily discontinued in 1854 owing to the difficulty in raising capital.

SECOND MORTGAGE BONDS

The Company under date of April 18th, 1854, secured an amendment to its Charter, which authorized debts and loans up to the full amount of its paid-in capital, and having by this time sold all the Bonds issued under its First Mortgage, it created a Second Mortgage, dated June 1st, 1854, in the authorized sum of $5,000,000. with the provision that these Bonds could be issued either as Dollar or Sterling Bonds, to bear 6% interest, and have the privilege of conversion into Capital Stock at par. The Annual Report for 1854 states that owing to the embarrassed financial conditions in this Country in that year, they were not pressed on the market. The Company, however, beginning in the year 1855 sold over $2,000,000. of these Bonds abroad, bearing

6% interest, and payable in Sterling. The balance of the $5,000,000. issue was subsequently sold in this Country, bearing 6% interest, and payable in Dollars, the entire amount issued under the Second Mortgage maturing March 31st, 1875.

DOUBLE TRACKING

The double tracking work was partially resumed in 1855, and it may be interesting to note the following statement of the completed and uncompleted portions of the *second* track at the close of that year:—

Harrisburg to Lewistown	37	miles finished,	24	miles unfinished
Lewistown to Huntingdon	6	" "	30	" "
Huntingdon to Altoona	8	" "	26	" "
Altoona to Johnstown	38½	" "	0	" "
Johnstown to Blairsville Intersection	0	" "	25	" "
Blairsville Intersection to Pittsburgh	43¼	" "	10¾	" "
Totals	132¾	" "	115¾	" "

FIRST DIVIDEND

The Pennsylvania Railroad Company had been paying interest at the rate of 6% per annum beginning in 1848 on all paid-in subscriptions to its Capital Stock from the date when the first installment was paid in April, 1847. In May, 1856, it paid what is described in the Annual Report for that year as Dividend No. 1 at the rate of 4% on its Capital Stock. The Company accordingly ceased to pay interest on fully paid subscriptions to Capital Stock in November, 1855.

INTEREST PAID STOCKHOLDERS TAKEN OUT OF CONSTRUCTION ACCOUNT

Under its Charter the Company was authorized to charge interest paid to the stockholders, prior to the inauguration of dividend payments, to its Construction Account, and this was done while the road was under construction. However, as soon as a substantial part of it was opened for operation and the net earnings permitted, the Management pursued the conservative policy of taking the item of stockholders' interest out of the Construction Account and charging it to net earnings. The total amount of interest paid to the stockholders up to November 1st, 1855, when interest payments ceased, was over $2,800,000., which sum had by that time been entirely eliminated from the Construction Account of the Company.

INDIANA BRANCH

The Indiana Branch from Blairsville to Indiana, Pa., was opened for use on June 9th, 1856. It was 16¼ miles long, making the entire distance from the connection with the Main Line at Blairsville Intersection to Indiana about 19 miles.

PURCHASE OF THE MAIN LINE OF PUBLIC WORKS

AGITATING SALE

When the Pennsylvania Railroad was finished and in operation, it soon became evident that the Pennsylvania State Works could not profitably compete with that improved avenue of transportation, or indeed with those to the north and south of it, and the people of Pennsylvania began to agitate the sale of their railroad and canal improvements to some suitable purchaser. These properties had been constructed to preserve the trade and commercial relations of the State with other communities, and while that purpose had to a limited extent been accomplished, it was done at great expense to the State Treasury. Now that a private corporation had provided a medium of transportation, with which it was most unwise and unprofitable to compete, the citizens were anxious to rid themselves of the burden of meeting yearly deficits in the operation of the Public Works.

LEGISLATIVE AUTHORITY

Therefore, in 1854 legislation was enacted by the State providing for the sale of the Main Line of Public Works, but the terms and conditions were such that neither the Pennsylvania Railroad Company, nor other interests, would make a bid. A somewhat similar Act was passed in 1855, but it too proved ineffective in securing a purchaser, although the Company submitted a proposition offering to purchase the said Works for $7,500,000. It also agreed to purchase the Philadelphia & Columbia Railroad at its cost of construction to be determined by a Commission of three civil engineers upon which sum so ascertained the Pennsylvania Railroad Company would forever pay to the State semi-annually an amount equivalent to the dividend paid to its stockholders upon an equal amount of its Capital Stock. This offer, however, was not accepted, but it practically formed the basis, except for the latter feature, of a subsequent Act passed by the Legislature, under which the Pennsylvania Railroad Company purchased the entire State Works.

TONNAGE TAX

Meanwhile the Company had continued to voice its protest against the burdensome tonnage tax imposed by the State, and as a result the Legislature, by the passage of an Act on May 7th, 1855, partially yielded to this pressure by repealing the tax on coal and lumber, provided the rates charged by the Pennsylvania Railroad Company would be correspondingly reduced. It was at once apparent that the traffic in these commodities was greatly stimulated by this concession, and shippers of other commodities insisted upon similar treatment. In the midst of this agitation the Commonwealth again offered to sell its Main Line of Public Works, a third Act to accomplish this purpose being passed on May 16th, 1857.

DETAILS OF ACT

The most important feature of this Act was that it fixed the minimum price for the sale of the Main Line at $7,500,000., and provided that if the Pennsylvania Railroad Company should become the purchaser, it should, in addition to the sum of $7,500,000., pay $1,500,000. in its 5% bonds, and thereupon the Pennsylvania Railroad Company and the Harrisburg, Portsmouth, Mt. Joy & Lancaster Railroad Company would in consideration thereof be discharged by the Commonwealth forever from the payment of all taxes upon tonnage or freight carried over said railroads, and the Pennsylvania Railroad Company would be released from the payment of all other taxes or duties on its Capital Stock, Bonds, dividends or property.

PURCHASED BY PENNSYLVANIA RAILROAD

The property was, therefore, offered for sale in accordance with the terms in the Act on June 25th, 1857, at the Merchants Exchange in the City of Philadelphia and the Pennsylvania Railroad Company, being the highest and best bidder, purchased it for $7,500,000. The Secretary of State made the conveyance on July 31st, 1857, and on August 1st, 1857, the Pennsylvania Railroad Company entered into possession of what had been the Main Line of Public Works of Pennsylvania.

TERMS OF PURCHASE

Under the terms of the purchase 5% Bonds of the Pennsylvania Railroad Company were to be delivered to the State in the sum of $7,500,000., of which $100,000. were to become due on July 31st, 1858, and $100,000. on July 31st annually thereafter until July 31st, 1890, when $1,000,000. of said Bonds were to be paid; $1,000,000. annually thereafter on July 31st until 1893, inclusive, and the balance of $300,000. on July 31st, 1894; interest was to be paid on the 31st day of January and July in each year. The State also surrendered its right to purchase the Pennsylvania Railroad as provided in the Charter of the Company.

PROPERTY PURCHASED

The purchase included 105 miles of canal on the west and 173 miles on the east side of the Allegheny Mountains; 36 miles of railroad, part double and a portion single track over these mountains between Johnstown and Hollidaysburg, and 81 miles of double track road between Philadelphia and Columbia, Pa., together with all the real estate, locomotives, cars and all other property connected therewith. The Allegheny Portage Railroad with its inclined planes, which had been in operation since 1834, had been abandoned and its place taken by a standard railroad built by the State and opened for traffic on July 1st, 1855. It was known as the "New Portage Railroad." However, when the Pennsylvania Railroad Company came into possession of the property, this section was operated only to the end of October, 1857, as operations over its own road crossing the mountains could be conducted much more economically. Therefore, the work of dismantling the New Portage Railroad was begun in 1858, and some of the rails taken up were used in extending the Pittsburgh, Ft. Wayne & Chicago Railroad from Plymouth, Ind., to Chicago, Ill.

All of the facilities, as well as the equipment, were in a more or less dilapidated condition owing to the lack of repairs and renewals, and the expenditure to put them in good working order was necessarily heavy. The Company was not only burdened with this outlay, but in addition no material had been purchased by the Commonwealth between June 25th, 1857, when the property was sold, and the date of delivery on August 1st, 1857, except that absolutely necessary to keep the Works in operation. The material included in the Bill of Sale was used to repair and maintain the property for the thirty-six days intervening, while the State appropriated the receipts.

REPEAL OF TONNAGE TAX UNCONSTITUTIONAL

The Supreme Court of the State, however, declared unconstitutional that portion of the Act repealing the tonnage tax, and releasing the Company from the payment of all other taxes on its Stock, Bonds, dividends and property. Therefore, it found itself in the position of being the owner of the Main Line of the State Works, and at the same time burdened with a tonnage tax originally assessed to compensate the State for any diminution in the receipts from the operation of said Public Works by reason of the competition resulting from the construction of the Pennsylvania Railroad. The Company, under advice of counsel, decided to withhold the payment of the tonnage tax, and threatened to test its constitutionality in the Courts. The Management clearly set forth that the construction of the Pennsylvania Railroad had not only failed to impair the net revenues of the Main Line of Public Works, but had made profitable the Philadelphia & Columbia Railroad, which was the only portion of the whole property having any value as an investment; that the motive for the tax had been removed by the sale of the Public Works at a cost far in excess of their value to the State, or indeed to any independent purchaser, and, therefore, a continuance of its exaction would be a most oppressive and arbitrary use of the power of the Commonwealth.

SETTLEMENT FINALLY REACHED

A bitter controversy arose over the question. Many merchants favored the removal of the tax rather than to suffer the loss of business resulting from the tax discrimination, while State bondholders, who feared that a repeal would seriously reduce the revenues of the State, allied themselves with the opposition. The final outcome was the passage of an Act on March 7th, 1861, commuting the tonnage tax imposed upon the Pennsylvania Railroad Company and the Harrisburg, Portsmouth, Mt. Joy & Lancaster Railroad Company, provided the former Company would agree to pay the State of Pennsylvania the sum of $460,000. annually until July 31st, 1890, part of which sum was to represent installments of principal and interest on account of the purchase of the State Works, and the balance as a tribute to the State for the commutation of the tonnage tax. The final cost to the Company, including interest, as indicated in subsequent pages, was $15,565,654.94.

ASSISTING OTHER ROADS

Meanwhile the tonnage tax, which the Company had refused to pay from 1857 to 1861, had amounted to $850,000., and under the terms of the Act of 1861, the Pennsylvania Railroad Company was obligated to use this sum in purchasing the First Mortgage Bonds of the following companies, whose roads were in various stages of completion, and were in need of additional capital. All of these roads are today embraced in the Pennsylvania Railroad System, viz:—

Bald Eagle Valley Railroad Company..............	$200,000.
Tyrone & Clearfield Railroad Company..............	75,000.
Ebensburg & Cresson Railroad Company............	66,500.
Bedford Railroad Company.........................	100,000.
Western Pennsylvania Railroad Company............	250,000.
Pittsburgh & Steubenville Railroad Company........	158,500.
Total....................................	$850,000.

A PANIC YEAR

The panic year of 1857 seriously affected the operations of the Pennsylvania Railroad Company, though it suffered to no greater extent than any other transportation or industrial corporation. While a 4% cash dividend was paid in May of that year, and the earnings were sufficient to justify the payment of a reasonable cash dividend in November, the financial outlook was far from promising, and the Management deemed it advisable not to pay the usual semi-annual dividend in November. In addition the salaries of the employes were reduced 10%, 15% and 25% depending upon the amount of compensation received, this action becoming effective on November 1st, 1857.

AID FOR TYRONE & CLEARFIELD RAILROAD

An appeal for aid was made in 1858 to complete the Tyrone & Clearfield Railroad, 23 miles in length, and after giving the subject careful consideration, the Pennsylvania Railroad Company agreed to accept in payment of passenger fares and amounts due on freight traffic interchanged with that road, 60% in cash and 40% in First Mortgage Bonds, provided the amount of the First Mortgage, which was not to exceed $200,000., should complete the line from Tyrone to Philipsburg, Pa. The road was located in a region rich in mine and forest products, and it was felt that when finally completed it would prove a valuable tributary to the Pennsylvania Railroad and develop a section of the State theretofore without adequate transportation facilities. This was one of the roads which later secured additional aid from the Pennsylvania Railroad Company under the State Act repealing the tonnage tax.

MARIETTA & CINCINNATI INVESTMENT CHARGED TO PROFIT AND LOSS

The Marietta & Cincinnati Railroad Company, which the Pennsylvania Railroad Company had aided by a subscription to $750,000. of its Capital Stock, became so hopelessly involved that the money advanced for its construction between Marietta and Wheeling was used without the consent of the Pennsylvania Railroad Company to meet debts incurred on the line west of Marietta. In consequence of this misapplication of the means furnished by the Pennsylvania Railroad Company, and the very large sum that would have been required to complete the line, it was not deemed prudent to attempt to save the original investment, which was accordingly charged to Profit and Loss in 1858.

DELAWARE EXTENSION AUTHORIZED

While Legislative authority had been secured on April 18th, 1856, to extend what was then the Philadelphia & Columbia Railroad from the west bank of the Schuylkill River to the Delaware (later known as the "Delaware Extension"), the Management deemed it advisable, during the period in which the Country was passing through the financial crisis of 1857, to defer all expenditures not absolutely necessary for the maintenance of the property. However, in the early part of 1859 the financial and industrial situation began to improve, and the subject again became active. A report made by President Thomson on January 26th, 1859, indicated the great advantages to be derived from such an extension, one of which was that it would avoid the hauling of cars through the City by horse power, and the conclusion of the Management was to authorize the selection of a convenient location on the Delaware River front for a terminal depot to be reached by locomotive steam power. After considerable study, it was decided to locate the terminus at the foot of Washington Avenue, just above the Navy Yard. The extension was completed and placed in operation in January, 1862.

SINKING FUND INVESTMENT IN CUMBERLAND VALLEY RAILROAD

The gratifying results in operating the Pennsylvania Railroad in 1859 led the Management to create a Sinking Fund for the redemption of its $3,948,680. Second Mortgage Bonds due in 1875. The funds furnished to the Trustees for this purpose were invested in $157,520., par value, of Preferred and $322,500. of Common Stock of the Cumberland Valley Railroad Company, which represented a controlling interest in that Company. This road extended from Harrisburg to Hagerstown, Md., a distance of 74 miles. It was a very important feeder to the Pennsylvania Railroad, and was located in a valley rich in agricultural products and bounded on both sides by mountain ranges containing valuable deposits of iron ore.

REORGANIZATION OF PITTSBURGH, FT. WAYNE & CHICAGO RAILROAD COMPANY

It was deemed advisable by the Management to give additional assistance to the Pittsburgh, Ft. Wayne & Chicago Railroad Company in building its line from Plymouth, Ind., to Chicago, which was opened for traffic on December 25th, 1858. This aid consisted principally of iron rails taken from the New Portage Railroad in 1858, which was no longer of use to the Pennsylvania Railroad by reason of having its own route across the Allegheny Mountains. The cost of removing this material, together with the value of the rails, was secured by a pledge of $650,000. of First Mortgage Bonds of the Pittsburgh, Ft. Wayne & Chicago Railroad Company. However, as the three lines forming the consolidated company, to which reference has been made, were not soundly financed, due to the large floating debt they had accumulated, and which was carried into the new Company, the First Mortgage Bondholders, for self-protection, applied to the United States District Court and secured the appointment of a Receiver on December 7th, 1859, but under a subsequent arrangement a new Receiver was appointed on January 17th, 1860. The plan of reorganization adopted by the Bondholders on October 20th, 1860, provided for the sale of the road to a Purchasing Committee of five persons, appointed by the Bondholders, and the road was sold to this Committee on October 24th, 1861, and then reorganized. Under this reorganization a new corporation was created, and the holders of the First Mortgage Bonds of the several original companies forming the consolidated company received $5,250,000. new First Mortgage 7% Bonds, which sum was equal to the par value and unpaid coupons of the First Mortgage Bonds of the three original companies. The Second Mortgage Bonds of the three original companies and the Construction Bonds of the Pittsburgh, Ft. Wayne & Chicago Railroad Company, including unpaid coupons to October 1st, 1859, were funded by a new issue of $5,160,000. Second Mortgage 7% Bonds. The coupons accruing after that date and to April 1st, 1862, and the floating debt were covered by the issuance of $2,000,000. Third Mortgage Income Bonds, bearing a contingent interest (equivalent to a Preferred Stock) not exceeding 7% per annum. The original shareholders were to retain their full interest in the new Company. The Purchasing Committee continued to operate the road until March 2nd, 1862, when it was transferred to a new corporation called the Pittsburgh, Ft. Wayne & Chicago *Railway* Company. The plan of reorganization limited the amount of Capital Stock of the new Company to $6,500,000.; of this amount $6,250,000. was exchanged for Stock of the Pittsburgh, Ft. Wayne & Chicago *Railroad* Company, and the balance sold and applied to construction purposes.

CONSTRUCTION OF JUNCTION RAILROAD

Under a Charter secured from the Pennsylvania Legislature in 1860, the Pennsylvania Railroad Company, jointly with the Philadelphia, Wilmington & Baltimore Railroad Company and the Philadelphia & Reading Railroad Company, organized the Junction Railroad Company, the object of which was to connect these three railroads by a line along the west bank of the Schuylkill River in Philadelphia. The new road was to extend from a connection with the Philadelphia & Reading Railroad near Peter's Island to the junction with the Philadelphia, Wilmington & Baltimore Railroad at Gray's Ferry, and intersect the Pennsylvania Railroad near the bridge over the Schuylkill River in Fairmount Park. By this means an interchange of traffic between the three roads could be effected without passing through the congested sections of the City. The Pennsylvania Railroad Company subscribed to its proportionate share of the Capital Stock of the Junction Railroad Company and agreed to guarantee, with the other owning companies, the principal and interest of that Company's Bonds issued for construction purposes. The northern section from Peter's Island (Belmont) to 35th Street was completed and placed in operation on November 23rd, 1863, and the southern portion from the Market Street Tunnel to Gray's Ferry was opened for traffic on July 1st, 1866. The total length of the road was about three miles. Subsequently the Stock owned by the other railroads was purchased by the Pennsylvania Railroad Company and the Junction Railroad was absorbed and operated as part of its lines.

LEASE OF HARRISBURG, PORTSMOUTH, MT. JOY & LANCASTER RAILROAD

On January 1st, 1861, the Pennsylvania Railroad Company leased the Harrisburg, Portsmouth, Mt. Joy & Lancaster Railroad for a term of 999 years, agreeing to guarantee the payment of 7% dividends on $1,182,550. of Capital Stock representing 23,651 shares, par value $50. each; the principal of, and 6% interest on, $700,000. First Mortgage

Bonds; and organization expenses amounting to $2,000. per annum. This road extended from Harrisburg to Dillerville, a distance of about 36 miles, with a branch from Royalton to Columbia, about 18 miles in length, or a total of approximately 54 miles. The lease superceded the previous contract entered into between these companies, which proved to be an unprofitable arrangement for the Pennsylvania Railroad Company, and which still had eight years to run. The terms of the lease gave the stockholders of the Harrisburg, Portsmouth, Mt. Joy & Lancaster Railroad Company the right to exchange their Stock prior to 1871 at par for shares of the Pennsylvania Railroad Company. As it was estimated the new lease would result in a saving of from $30,000. to $60,000. per annum, the Management proposed to set aside in a Sinking Fund such sums as were saved for the remaining eight years of the unexpired contract to purchase the shares of the leased company not converted into Stock of the Pennsylvania Railroad Company. The lease of this road placed the entire line of transportation facilities from Philadelphia to Pittsburgh under the control and management of the Pennsylvania Railroad Company.

PENNSYLVANIA RAILROAD IN THE CIVIL WAR

While the historical events of the Civil War were not given any special prominence in the Annual Reports, yet as the Pennsylvania Railroad Company and its officers and employes took such a prominent part in the movement of troops and munitions of war, it might be interesting to refer to the important work performed by Thomas A. Scott, who was at that time a Vice-President (later President) of the Pennsylvania Railroad Company. Colonel Scott had been aiding Governor Curtin of Pennsylvania in the transportation of troops and supplies to the South, and as there had been attempts to interrupt their passage through Baltimore by partisans of the South, the Secretary of War sent the following communication to him, under date of April 22nd. 1861:—

> "This department needs, at the moment, a man of great energy and decision, with experience as a railroad officer, to keep open and work the Northern Central Road from Harrisburg to Baltimore, for the purpose of bringing men and munitions to this point.
>
> You are, to my mind, the proper man for this occasion and this duty. Will you report to me to-morrow morning?"

Colonel Scott replied that as he was then serving on the staff of Governor Curtin, he could not leave Harrisburg without the permission of the Governor. However, the destruction of a vital part of the Northern Central Railway by Southern sympathizers made it absolutely necessary that another avenue of transportation should be opened to Washington, and after numerous calls for his services, Colonel Scott was relieved of duty at Harrisburg and reported to the Secretary of War. He was instructed by that Officer to open a road by way of Annapolis to Philadelphia and the East and North. The following order was issued by the Government, dated April 27th, 1861:—

> "To Whom it May Concern:
>
> Thomas A. Scott has been appointed to take charge of the railways and telegraphs between Washington City and Annapolis. Parties in charge thereof will place Mr. Scott in possession, and in future conform to his instructions in all matters pertaining to their management.
>
> Simon Cameron,
> *Secretary of War.*"

Calling to his assistance a few efficient railroad men, one of whom was Frank Thomson, who later became President of the Company, he opened a line by way of Perryville and Annapolis to Washington. Shortly afterward on May 3rd, 1861, he was appointed Colonel of the District of Columbia Volunteers, and on August 1st, 1861, Assistant Secretary of War, being the first person to fill that position.

In the following letter to the President and Board of Directors of the Pennsylvania Railroad Company, dated

August 21st, 1861, Colonel Scott explained his connection with the Government service:—

"In consequence of my protracted absence from Philadelphia, I deem it my duty to make a frank statement for your information and such action under the circumstances as to you may seem advisable.

In April last at the time our National Capitol was supposed to be in imminent danger, I was summoned to Washington City by the Secretary of War. I responded to the call and found on arrival that my services were desired by the Government to take charge of Railways and Telegraphs in order to get troops there for the defense of the Capitol. Believing that my services there were of value to the country at large and of material consequence to the interests of our own Company I remained by consent of the President from time to time. A few weeks since it was determined by Congress to create the position of Assistant Secretary of War which I was solicited by the Secretary of War and other heads of Departments to take charge of, at least for a short period. After full consultation again with our President I accepted the position with the distinct understanding that I could retire about the First of October if desired by myself or the Pennsylvania Rail Road Company—my connection with which I had no idea of severing.

The brief statement will explain to the Board the exact position in which I am placed. I have endeavored by my labors at Washington to aid our struggling country and at all times when possible have been careful to protect the interests of our Company.

I should be glad to have an expression from the Board in regard to the course I have pursued."

The Board of Directors of the Company on August 21st, 1861, took the following action:—

"*Resolved*, That the communication of Thomas A. Scott, Esq., Vice-President explaining his relations as Assistant Secretary of War to be temporary, be received and entered on the Minutes, and that the Board expresses its approval of his prompt response to the demand of Government and its gratification that it does not contemplate any severance of his connection with this Company."

Andrew Carnegie was Superintendent of the Pittsburgh Division at this time, and assisted Colonel Scott while the latter was Assistant Secretary of War.

On June 1st, 1862, Colonel Scott resigned his position as Assistant Secretary of War, and resumed his duties as Vice-President of the Pennsylvania Railroad Company. On his retirement from Government services he received the following letter from the Secretary of War:—

"June 1st, 1862.

Dear Sir:

In taking leave of you, in consequence of your resignation of the office of Assistant Secretary of War, it is proper for me to express my entire satisfaction with the manner in which you have discharged your duties during the whole period of our official relations. Those duties have been confidential and responsible, requiring energy, prudence and discretion; and it gives me pleasure to say that to me you have proved to be, in every particular, an able and faithful assistant.

Yours truly,

Edwin M. Stanton,

Secretary of War."

Colonel Scott again went into the service of the Government in 1863 to aid in the dispatch of troops, and at the termination of this work, he returned to his active official duties with the Pennsylvania Railroad Company.

STOCKHOLDERS' RESOLUTIONS

As there had been signs of discontent among a few of the stockholders of the Company as to its general policy, a Special Committee was appointed at the annual meeting in February, 1861, "to make a full examination into the general policy of the Company." This Committee after a careful examination expressed its views in the following resolutions, which were presented at the Stockholders' meeting in February, 1862, and referred to the incoming Board of Directors:—

"*Resolved*, That from the inquiries and examination of the Committee into the condition and management of the Company, they are satisfied that it is in a prosperous condition, and that the present system and regulations for the freight and forwarding business are calculated to promote the interests of the stockholders and the accommodation of the public.

Resolved, That this Committee is convinced of the integrity, ability and fidelity of the management of the Company.

Resolved, That this Committee, exercising the discretion invested in them by the resolution of the stockholders, do not deem it expedient to submit a report, and that the above resolutions be presented to the next annual meeting of the stockholders."

The foregoing resolutions were agreed to by six of the seven members of the Committee, the exception being James Page, who submitted a minority report, in which he questioned the integrity of the majority of the Committee, and criticized the Management and its methods in general. His minority report closed with the following recommendations:—

"*First:*—That the real estate, equipment and construction accounts should be closed.

Second:—That the dividends should be suspended until the track and outfit were restored to undoubted efficiency, and that the Board should be instructed not to make any dividends in future unless earned.

Third:—That the Board be directed hereafter to consider Philadelphia and Pittsburgh the termini of the road, and that they should not cripple the local trade of the road.

Fourth:—That a Committee of investigation should be appointed to examine into the affairs of the Company in the manner adopted by the Committee of the New York Central Company, by passing over the whole track on a hand car, examine the condition of the locomotives, cars and all property."

The Management replied to these criticisms in a special report, in which the recommendations of the minority report were answered in the following manner:—

"The first proposition supposes that the road has reached its full capacity, and nothing is required but to finish its double track to render it complete.

In this limited view of the future operations of the line the Board do not concur, and to provide for the enlargement of the business of the road, have made, and are making, large additions to their accommodations at Pittsburgh as well as at Philadelphia. It will be observed, however, by a careful examination of the accounts of the Company for several years past, that these expenditures have been met from the profits of the road after paying dividends, without materially augmenting the debts of the Company.

The second simply assumes that the track and machinery of the Company have greatly deteriorated, when the facts are that as a whole this property is much more valuable than when it was first brought into use.

The third recommends that policy which has always been pursued by your Board.

The fourth provides for a Perambulating Committee, such as the New York Central once created, which Committee, candidly reported that their investigations were of no practical value, as they did not understand the anatomy of the subject examined.

Your Board in this connection will state that it is believed that by the termination of next year, under the operation of the sinking fund created for the extinguishment of the obligations of the Company, the second mortgage bonds will be provided for when they fall due in 1875. The debts of the Harrisburg and Lancaster Railroad will be purchased when it matures without further appropriations to the object than the savings effected by the new lease, and that the payment annually of $460,000., the debt due to the State, will be extinguished in 1890, leaving no incumbrance upon the road unprovided for but a first mortgage of $5,000,000., which can readily be continued upon the credit of the Company at a reduced rate of interest.

These gratifying facts, so widely different from those presented by the Minority Report, will excuse the Board from pursuing the subject further."

PHILADELPHIA & ERIE RAILROAD

On January 6th, 1862, the Pennsylvania Railroad Company entered into a contract to complete the Philadelphia & Erie Railroad, and on the same date it also agreed to lease that railroad for 999 years. This road had originally been chartered on April 3rd, 1837, as the Sunbury & Erie Railroad Company, and was authorized to construct its line from Sunbury to Erie, a distance of 288 miles. While the promoters of the new road were enthusiastic over its prospects, there was no great promise of traffic through the region it traversed, as Williamsport was then of little importance; Lock Haven practically a new town and other sections of the line nothing more than wilderness. Erie, however, was a thriving city, aided to a large extent by the United States Government, which had spent large sums of money in harbor improvements, and by an unprecedented increase in real estate values. While the Company had been incorporated in 1837, the first section of the line from Milton to Williamsport, a distance of 28½ miles, was not finished until December 18th, 1854. The work on the remaining sections proceeded so slowly, owing to the unsettled conditions prior to the financial crisis of 1857, that at the close of the year 1859 there were but 158 miles constructed, and in 1860 the work was practically suspended, because of the inability of the Company to dispose of its Bonds.

This was the situation when the Pennsylvania Railroad Company became interested in the project. The Management felt that if it did not step in, the road would be entirely completed and placed in operation by some other Company, probably one that would be adverse to the Pennsylvania Railroad, and as the charter of the latter Company authorized the building of a branch to Erie on the Great Lakes, the Philadelphia & Erie Railroad could be utilized for that purpose. The road was then in use between Erie and Warren on the west and from Sunbury to Lock Haven on the east, and by a re-arrangement of its finances the Company had placed a Mortgage of $1,000,000. at 7% on the completed portion of its line between Sunbury and Williamsport. It had also issued $1,200,000. of a $5,000,000. Mortgage at 6% on the remaining section. Therefore, under contract dated January 6th, 1862, the Pennsylvania Railroad Company agreed to advance the money to the

Philadelphia & Erie Railroad Company to complete its line, and take the remaining $3,800,000. of unissued 6% Bonds at the rate of one $1,000. Bond for every $850. advanced for construction purposes; also to guarantee the principal of, and interest on, $1,200,000. of 6% Bonds already issued and the $3,800,000. to be delivered to it in payment for construction advances.

Simultaneously with the making of this construction contract, the Pennsylvania Railroad Company leased that portion of the Philadelphia & Erie Railroad which had been completed, and the section to be constructed, for a term of 999 years, agreeing to appropriate 30% of the gross earnings of the road to pay taxes and assessments levied against the latter road; organization expenses; interest on all Mortgage Bonds, and the Sinking Fund payments required by one of its Mortgages. The balance of the gross earnings was to be applied by the Pennsylvania Railroad Company to the payment of motive power charges and operating expenses. The Company entered into the possession of the road on February 1st, 1862, and while construction work was promptly started on the uncompleted sections of the line, slow progress was made on account of the scarcity of labor during the Civil War period, and the road was not finished until October 17th, 1864.

BRANCH ROADS COMPLETED

The amounts allotted to the small roads under the Act discharging the Company from the payment of the State tonnage tax were insufficient to render them of service to the public, or make them profitable. Therefore, further advances were made to several of the Companies, which finally resulted in the completion and placing in operation in July, 1862, of the Ebensburg & Cresson Railroad, extending from Cresson to Ebensburg, a distance of 11 miles, and the Tyrone & Clearfield Railroad at the same time from Tyrone to Philipsburg, a distance of 16 miles. The Bald Eagle Valley Railroad had been completed in January, 1863, from its connection with the Tyrone & Clearfield Railroad, about 3 miles north of Tyrone, to Milesburg, a distance of 27 miles, and the remaining portion of the line to a connection with the Philadelphia & Erie Railroad at Lock Haven was completed on May 1st, 1865, making a total length of 51 miles. The Bedford Railroad was completed between Hopewell and Bloody Run, a distance of 12½ miles, in July, 1863.

FIRST STOCK DIVIDEND

As the accumulated surplus profits of the Company had amounted to over $5,500,000. at the close of 1863, which, it was stated, were represented by good securities in its Treasury, the Management felt justified in declaring an extra dividend of 30% payable in stock on May 2nd, 1864, to shareholders as registered on the books of the Company on February 15th, 1864. This prosperous condition of the Treasury was all the more creditable, as the Country was then in the midst of a Rebellion, and its operations were necessarily conducted with serious difficulty and at greatly increased cost of labor and supplies. It meant that a continually increasing traffic had to be handled by a decreasing number of experienced men, as the Government had drafted a great many of the Company's employes to operate its military railways.

CONSTRUCTION OF CONNECTING RAILWAY

Work was started in 1864 on the Connecting Railway, which was chartered on April 14th, 1863, to construct a line connecting the Pennsylvania Railroad in West Philadelphia with the Philadelphia & Trenton Railroad at Frankford Junction, a distance of 6¾ miles. The Pennsylvania Railroad Company agreed to guarantee the principal of, and interest on, $1,000,000., of Bonds of the Connecting Railway Company, it being the owner of nearly all of that Company's Capital Stock.

SALE OF FORT WAYNE SECURITIES

The Management in its annual report for 1864 stated that the investments made by the Pennsylvania Railroad

Company in the Stock and Bonds of the Pittsburgh, Ft. Wayne & Chicago Railway Company, to insure its completion, had all been sold except 1,200 shares of its Stock and $200,000. of Third Mortgage Bonds at a considerable advance over their cost. The Management felt that its arrangements for the interchange of through traffic with this road were secure, but, as hereinafter explained, it was only a few years later that the Pennsylvania Railroad Company found it necessary to lease the Ft. Wayne Road in order to be assured of the traffic from this important Western connection.

STEUBENVILLE & INDIANA RAILROAD REORGANIZED

The Steubenville & Indiana Railroad, one of the western roads to receive aid from the Pennsylvania Railroad Company by having its bonds guaranteed to the extent of $500,000., became involved in financial difficulties by reason of the failure of the Pittsburgh & Steubenville Railroad to complete its line between Pittsburgh and Steubenville. The road, however, was successfully reorganized and its line extended from Newark to Columbus, O., a distance of 33 miles by the purchase in 1864 of a one-half interest in this section of the Central Ohio Railroad Company, whose road was constructed between those cities.

THREE ROUTES TO THE WEST

In looking back over the history of the Western Lines, it will be seen that the Management selected three avenues of transportation to the West, which it was hoped would cause to be delivered to the Pennsylvania Railroad at its western terminus, Pittsburgh, a sufficient traffic to compensate it for advances made to these western lines—one to Cincinnati by way of Wheeling and Marietta, which had proven a failure; the second to Chicago over the lines which had been consolidated and subsequently reorganized as the Pittsburgh, Ft. Wayne & Chicago Railway Company, and the third—the Columbus road via the Steubenville & Indiana Railroad and the Pittsburgh & Steubenville Railroad. The latter became financially embarrassed several times before its completion, and the work was finally taken up by the Western Transportation Company, in which the Pennsylvania Railroad Company was the principal stockholder, and prosecuted with vigor until its completion in 1865, thus making a through line operated under one control from Pittsburgh to Columbus, a distance of 196 miles.

The connecting link between the Steubenville & Indiana Railroad and the Pittsburgh & Steubenville Railroad was built by the Holliday's Cove Railroad Company, which consisted of a bridge over the Ohio River and an extension from the west end of the bridge to the depot of the Steubenville & Indiana Railroad in Steubenville. The bridge and extension were completed in 1865.

CONSTRUCTION OF WESTERN PENNSYLVANIA RAILROAD

On August 1st, 1865, the Western Pennsylvania Railroad, which was one of the roads to receive financial aid under the Act commuting the tonnage tax, was completed and placed in operation for a distance of 36 miles from Blairsville to Freeport, Pa. On December 1st, 1866, the Pittsburgh Branch of this road was completed from Freeport to Allegheny City, a distance of 28 miles, it having been built on the west side of the Allegheny River on the route of the old Pennsylvania Canal abandoned in the previous year. Subsequently the road was extended on the west from Butler Junction to Butler, Pa., and on the east from Blairsville to Bolivar, Pa.

Under date of August 1st, 1865, the Pennsylvania Company leased the Western Pennsylvania Railroad, and agreed to guarantee the principal of, and interest on, the 6% Bonds of the latter Company in the sum of $1,158,600.

FAST FREIGHT LINES

After many years of unsuccessful effort to induce the New York trunk lines to abandon their policy of giving a portion of their fast freight traffic to private companies, the Management of the Pennsylvania Railroad Company pointed out in the annual report for 1865 that it had agreed to the introduction of a similar service on its line, so as to counteract the diversion of traffic from its route, and also to provide equally as good facilities for the transportation of this class of traffic for the merchants of Philadelphia. The chief element of profit to these fast freight lines was the margin paid to them above the ordinary railroad freight rates by shippers, who preferred to patronize a medium of transportation where the responsibility was direct from the point of shipment to destination, which services, for obvious reasons, could not at that time be accorded to merchants by any single railroad company.

CONSERVATIVE FINANCIAL POLICY

President Thomson, whose sound judgment and experience had saved the Company from many financial difficulties in the early days of its existence, was largely responsible for the policy of charging all the interest paid on subscriptions during the construction of the road, together with discounts on Bonds sold and all doubtful investments, against net earnings in order to prevent the over-capitalization of the Company, which was the unfortunate experience of a great many corporations in the early days of railroad construction. Therefore, there was nothing in the accounts of the Company of fictitious value, but on the other hand, the property was worth more than it was represented on the books, due mainly to the foregoing reasons, and also that the Main Line and branches were constructed under contracts for cash when the price of labor was just about one-half of that paid during the Civil War period. As a consequence of this conservative policy, the stockholders of the Pennsylvania Railroad Company had received from the date of the payment of each installment on their subscription an average of 6% interest upon their investment until May, 1862, since which date and up to the end of 1865, the regular and extra cash and Stock dividends had averaged over 18% per annum.

NEW FINANCIAL PROGRAM

An Act was passed by the Pennsylvania Legislature on March 21st, 1866, which authorized an increase of 200,000 shares in the Capital Stock of the Company, and the creation of a Mortgage, not exceeding the paid-in Capital Stock of the Company, the Bonds to be issued thereunder to bear interest at the rate of 6% per annum. This additional capital was necessary to provide enlarged facilities to keep pace with the rapid growth of the territory served by the Company's lines, and also to make additional advances to those roads which had already received financial assistance. In this latter situation the Management saw no other alternative than to meet the difficulty by the adoption of a liberal policy, and thus bring all of these lines into productive use as quickly as possible, or suffer the loss of the amounts theretofore advanced. Three methods of disposing of the additional Stock were suggested—First, by a sale of the Stock; second, by Stock subscription in which each shareholder would have the right to participate in proportion to his holdings; and third, by a Stock dividend. The first plan was deemed inexpedient, the second, which seemed to be the most desirable, was objected to by the City of Philadelphia, as a stockholder, owing to alleged lack of legal authority to take part in such a plan; the third suggestion, that of Stock dividends was, therefore, deemed to be the most desirable to carry out, and the following resolution embodying that plan was presented to the stockholders at the annual meeting held on February 19th, 1867:—

> "*Resolved*, That for the purpose of consolidating the Bonded and other indebtedness of the Pennsylvania Railroad Company and to raise funds to meet the annual demands upon the Treasury of the Company for new tracks, additional equipment, enlargement of depots, extensions of sidings, and to meet the legitimate demands of the traffic of the Country drained by the road of said Company and its branches, for increased railroad accommodations, and also to preserve the proper relation between the share capital and debts of the Company, the following financial programme be and the same is hereby adopted:

First:—That the Bonds of the Pennsylvania Railroad Company secured by the First and Second Mortgages, and those due the Commonwealth issued for the purchase of the Main Line of Public Works, and other indebtedness be paid out of the proceeds of, or be retired by, Bonds to be secured by a Consolidated Mortgage upon the whole or such portion of the line from Philadelphia to Pittsburgh, with its equipment, and for such amounts as the President and Board of Directors may determine, and the issue of the Bonds secured thereby shall at no time exceed the Capital Stock as the same may from time to time be increased.

Second:—Dividends to be made semi-annually of not exceeding four per cent. from the net profits of the Company payable in cash, free of United States and State taxes, and that a Stock dividend of five per cent. based upon profits already earned be declared at the regular dividend term in May next, and thereafter, in addition to the semi-annual cash dividend, a Stock dividend of five per cent. per annum be declared, annually, if the net earnings of the Company will warrant the same."

This resolution was considered and adopted at the adjourned annual meeting of the stockholders on April 30th, 1867.

While Stock dividends did not bring additional capital into the Treasury, their payment to the stockholders was equivalent to having the latter subscribe to the Capital Stock at par, because the earnings of the Company warranted the payment of larger cash dividends than were actually paid. By the adoption of this policy, the Company was able to utilize its surplus earnings for improvements, and in addition it was able to increase its margin for raising capital through the sale of Bonds by reason of the increase in the outstanding Capital Stock.

STOCKHOLDERS' INVESTIGATION

At the annual meeting of the stockholders of the Pennsylvania Railroad Company held on February 19th, 1867, the usual resolution was offered to accept the annual report, when Col. James Page, a discontented stockholder, offered a substitute as follows:—

"*Resolved*, That the report be referred to a special Committee of seven Stockholders for examination, and that the said Committee be further specially authorized and directed to examine into and report upon the expediency of issuing additional stock and borrowing more money, and further to examine into and report upon the operation and working of the systems of discrimination, of free passes, and of private freight expresses, and to what extent the officers and employes are interested in the last, and the effect these have had and still have upon the earnings of the Road and the rights and interests of the Stockholders with power to send for persons and papers, and report the result of their investigations to an adjourned meeting of the Stockholders, to be held on the last Tuesday in April next, at such hour and place as notice may be given by public advertisement—the Board of Directors in the meanwhile to cause the Annual Report to be printed for the information of the Stockholders."

This resolution was adopted and a Committee of seven Stockholders appointed by the Chairman of the Annual Meeting, who were to report at an adjourned meeting to be held on April 30th, 1867. This Committee accordingly proceeded with its work with much diligence and on the date named their report was submitted. Colonel Page, however, did not concur in the views of the Committee and declined to sign the report, but as the other six members were unanimous in their conclusions, they submitted it in the following form:—

"The undersigned, a Special Committee appointed in accordance with a resolution passed at the last Annual Meeting of the Stockholders of the Pennsylvania Railroad Company for the purpose set forth in said resolution, have attended to the duties assigned them, and do now submit the following report of their proceedings and conclusions:

Upon the organization of the Committee the President of the Company was notified of the fact, and he appointed the following day for the commencement of our investigations, at which time we met the President and a Committee of the Directors.

These officers expressed a willingness and desire to grant us every facility for the performance of our duties, and they, and the subordinate officers of the Company, have in all ways and at all times throughout the examination aided and furthered the Committee in its work.

The Committee, finding it convenient and proper so to do, will treat the subjects referred to them in the following order: 'System of Discrimination,' 'Free Passes,' 'Private Freight Expresses,' 'Report of the Board of Directors, and the expediency of issuing more stock and of borrowing more money.'"

"*First:*—Of the 'System of Discrimination.'

We learn, on inquiry, that this Company has no such system nor have we found any authenticated case of discrimination between parties shipping freight under the same circumstances. At one of the sessions of our Committee we were informed that certain parties made accusations against this Company on this matter, and we at once invited them to come before the Committee and prove their charges; but they declined or did not appear for that or any other purpose and the charges of the said parties are therefore unworthy of further notice.

Charges of discrimination are, in many cases, based as we believe on mere suspicions; and in other cases they spring from misapprehension of circumstances which the parties making the charges do not understand. All experienced managers of transportation companies know that fair and equal rates are, in the long run, most productive to themselves and most satisfactory to the public; and in the absence of all testimony to sustain charges of discrimination against this Railroad Company, we cannot believe that its very able officers are guilty of a practice at variance with the well-established principles of the business over which they preside."

"*Second:*—In regard to 'Free Passes': Passes of this kind are issued to some extent by all the Railroad Companies of this Country, and the issue within strict and narrow limits is justifiable; but the practice when carried beyond such limits is improper and unjust. The granting of free passes to all the members of our State Legislature, and to members of our City Councils is of pernicious tendency, and ought to be abolished. That the issue of such passes has been heretofore too much extended by this Railroad Company, is shown by the fact that the Directors themselves became aware of the evil, and on the 9th of January last, at a meeting of the Board, passed a resolution 'to decline to issue free passes except for purely charitable purposes, and such others as in the opinion of the President may be absolutely required by the interests of the Company,' and we hope that the President will carry out this resolution in its letter and spirit."

"*Third:*—Of 'Private Freight Expresses': There are no expresses of this kind, or with this title, on the roads of this Company; but there are 'Fast Freight Lines,' one on the Pennsylvania Railroad known as the 'Union Line,' and another on the Philadelphia and Erie, called the 'Empire Line'; both of them owned by incorporated companies, and running to and from Western States.

These lines own the cars used by them—more than 2,000 in number; their average haul of each ton of freight during the year 1866, without trans-shipment, or breaking of bulk, was nearly 1,000 miles; and their cars are run not only over the Pennsylvania, but over about (4,500) four thousand five hundred miles of other roads, whose own equipment is hardly sufficient for their ordinary business; and, therefore, the additional equipment furnished by these 'Fast Lines' brings over the said roads to the Pennsylvania Railroad much freight which it could not get without such additional freight cars.

The statements of the President and other officers of this Company in regard to the said lines, given in answer to interrogatories put by us, have been fully confirmed by a mass of testimony taken by Committees of the Pennsylvania State Legislature. The said statements and testimony show conclusively that these 'fast lines' are at this time, and have been since their establishment, a direct and positive benefit to the Pennsylvania Railroad Company; because this Company, has, by means of them, regained freight which had been lost by the prior establishment of similar 'fast lines' on other competing roads."

"This Committee was also instructed to examine 'to what extent the officers and employes of this Company are interested in these lines,' and we have accordingly made inquiry, and have learned that neither the President, Vice-Presidents, nor any of the Directors have any pecuniary interest therein. These officers have the control of this matter as they have of all other matters relating to this Company, and they can exclude these lines at short notice from their road; as appears by the original contract between said lines and the Pennsylvania Railroad Company, which has been read by this Committee. One of its conditions is, that the Pennsylvania Railroad Company, by giving six months notice of its intention so to do, may, at any time, terminate the contract.

Some of the subordinate officers of this Company own, in the aggregate, a small percentage of the stock of said lines; but your Committee cannot believe that these officers control the Company they serve; nor can the Committee perceive how 'the rights and interests of the stockholders can be affected by such ownership in said lines'."

"*Fourth:*—Of the 'Report of the Board of Directors and of the expediency of issuing additional stock, and borrowing more money.'

The financial part of our inquiry being of great importance, a Sub-Committee composed of three members of this Committee, gave special attention to it, and made a thorough examination of it. This Sub-Committee (Messrs. Johnson, Davis and Wheeler) verified the cash account of the Treasurer; the cash in bank (as appeared by the bank books), and on hand December 31st, 1866, being equal 'to the balance in the hands of the Treasurer,' as stated in the last annual report of the Directors. The same Sub-Committee entered the fire-proof vaults and carefully examined and counted all the bonds, stocks and other securities of the Company; and on inquiry we learned from well informed parties that the value of the same is, at this time, greater than is set forth in said annual report. These securities pay in the aggregate an annual income of about ten per cent. on their cost; and for this, as well as other good reasons, we think it important that the Company should continue to hold them. Another Sub-Committee of three took in hand the original leases of all the railroads held by this Company, and read them, or the essential parts of them; and made inquiry about other matters in regard to which it was thought information might be of importance. But the undersigned, omitting details of these and of other unimportant matters which could lead to no useful results, will make the general statement that this investigation has disclosed nothing in any way at variance with the last annual report of the Directors, except only as regards the valuation of assets, of which an instance has been given above.

The undersigned have been over the lands of the Company on the Delaware River at Greenwich Point; where a large outlay of capital is required for wharves, storehouses and other accommodations for business, to make this valuable property useful and productive.

In order to make our investigation of the affairs and property of the Company complete, we have passed over its main line from West Philadelphia to Pittsburgh, stopping at the principal stations and examining the real estate, depots, machine shops, rolling stock, machinery, and other equipment, as well as the permanent way itself, and we found the whole in excellent order and condition.

The value of the rolling stock (which we could most readily estimate) is much greater than the amount which stands to the 'debit of equipment of road' in the account on page 6 of the last annual report; and we now say that in our investigations, we have nowhere discovered a case of an over-estimate of property, but have found many items which, in the judgment of the Committee, are under-estimated and we have no doubt that the actual value of the aggregate assets of this Company is much above the sum of them as stated on page 6 of the report.

The books and accounts at the office of the Company in Philadelphia, and at the other principal stations, were opened and laid before us for inspection and scrutiny. The system on which these accounts are kept is a very perfect one, and it is carried out with great accuracy in details and results, so far as we had time for examination, great care being taken in every department by checks and otherwise to correct errors and prevent frauds.

At these offices and on the road we have had intercourse with many of the officers and employes of the Company, and we bear willing testimony to the efficiency with which they perform their respective duties, and to the courtesy and intelligence which characterize all of them.

At the conclusion of this report of our proceedings we will say that our journey over the Main Line of this Company, and over the Western Pennsylvania and

Bald Eagle Valley Railroads, and over portions of the Philadelphia and Erie and Northern Central Railroads, has given us a knowledge of the Main Line, its large equipment and extensive connections, which we could have acquired in no other way so well; and has enabled us to understand and appreciate the policy of the President and Directors better than we otherwise could have done. This policy has for its object the increase of the commerce of our City, and the development of the great resources of our State, as well as the promotion of the direct interests of the Shareholders of the Company; but unless ample pecuniary means are provided, this policy cannot be continued and carried out to successful results to meet the continually growing wants of our country. Believing that such means, if provided, will be so used as to conduce to the public good of our City and State, we do now recommend to the Shareholders of this Company the acceptance of the Report of the Directors and the adoption of the resolution appended thereto.

The undersigned having finished the work committed to them, submit this report of it to the Stockholders, and ask to be discharged."

Israel H. Johnson,
Henry Winsor,
John C. Davis,
Alan Wood,
Wm. P. Cresson,
Charles Wheeler.

This report was adopted by the stockholders and the Committee discharged with a vote of thanks for the efficient, conscientious and satisfactory manner in which the responsible duties entrusted to them were performed.

AUTHORITY FOR INCREASED STOCK AND DEBT—SALE OF GENERAL MORTGAGE BONDS

On March 22nd, 1867, an Act was passed by the Legislature authorizing the Pennsylvania Railroad Company to issue not exceeding 300,000 shares of Capital Stock for the purpose of retiring the indebtedness of the Company, whether by Bond or otherwise, and provide for the enlargement of the facilities made necessary by the increased business. The

Act of March 21st, 1866, which gave authority to issue 200,000 shares was repealed. The 1867 Act also authorized the issuance of Bonds bearing interest not to exceed 6% per annum in an amount not in excess of the Capital Stock outstanding at the time such Bonds were issued. The stockholders by resolution directed the issuance of the said Capital Stock to the authorized amount at such time and in such manner as the Board of Directors deemed advisable, and the creation of one Mortgage for $35,000,000. The purpose of this mortgage was to consolidate the bonded and other indebtedness of the Company, and to raise funds to meet the annual demands upon the Treasury of the Company for new tracks, additional equipment, etc., and also to preserve the proper relation between the Capital Stock and the bonded indebtedness of the Company. It was known as the General Mortgage, was dated July 1st, 1867, and approximately $20,000,000. of bonds were issued under it, the Consolidated Mortgage of 1873, to which reference will later be made, taking its place as the next medium for the raising of capital through Bond issues. Of approximately $20,000,000. issued, bearing 6% interest, nearly $13,500,000. were sold abroad and were payable in Sterling. They matured on July 1st, 1910.

SALE OF PENNSYLVANIA CANALS

In accordance with authority received from the stockholders at the annual meeting in 1866, the Pennsylvania Railroad Company disposed of its interest in the Pennsylvania Canals to the Pennsylvania Canal Company, which had been incorporated by an Act of the Pennsylvania Legislature in 1866. The property was sold for the sum of $2,750,000., which figure was arrived at by estimating the value when purchased from the State at $1,000,000. and the balance representing interest and the cost of renewals and enlargement. The transfer to the Canal Company was made on April 15th, 1868, the Pennsylvania Railroad Company agreeing to take 55,000 shares of full paid Capital Stock of the Pennsylvania Canal Company, with a par value of $50. per share, for the purchase price. The Pennsylvania

Canals had been owned and operated by the Pennsylvania Railroad Company since August 1st, 1857. In December, 1865, the Western Division, extending from Johnstown to Pittsburgh, 105 miles in length, was finally abandoned for the purposes of navigation, leaving the Juniata and Eastern Divisions, 173 miles, to be kept and operated as required by law.

PENNSYLVANIA CANAL TRAFFIC—ADDITIONAL CANALS ACQUIRED

The Canals when they came into the possession of the Company were in a very dilapidated condition throughout, so filled up and out of repair that they were unfit for use at many places. The through trade had been wholly diverted from them to the Pennsylvania Railroad, and the only remaining tonnage which paid expenses was coal and lumber coming in at the mouth of the Juniata. About one-half of this trade stopped at different points on the Eastern Division, and the balance passed on to Tidewater. The average distance the tonnage was carried, and for which tolls were received, did not exceed 30 miles, while the whole line had to be maintained and operated. The Pennsylvania Canal Company subsequently purchased, with its First Mortgage Bonds, a majority of the shares of the West Branch Canal Company, extending from the Juniata River up the Susquehanna and its West Branch to Farrandsville, near Lock Haven, 123 miles, and consolidated its shares with those of the Wyoming Valley Canal Company, which occupied the North Branch of the Susquehanna from Northumberland to Wilkes-Barre, a distance of 64 miles, making in all 360 miles of canal. The two latter canals were acquired so as to bring under one control what was then known as the Susquehanna System of canals, as under separate ownership it was impossible for them to successfully compete with the railroads operating in that territory. The Pennsylvania Railroad Company agreed to pay the interest on these Bonds of the Canal Company if the earnings of the latter Company were inadequate for that purpose.

CONNECTING RAILWAY COMPLETED

In June, 1867, the Connecting Railway was completed, this road extending from a connection with the Pennsylvania Railroad at Mantua (1½ miles west of the West Philadelphia Passenger Station), to a junction with the Philadelphia & Trenton Railroad at Frankford Junction, a distance of about 6¾ miles. It was opened for freight traffic in July, 1867, and for passenger service in October of that year. Under date of January 1st, 1868, the road was leased, with the concurrence of the Pennsylvania Railroad Company, to the Philadelphia & Trenton Railroad Company, the rental being 6% per annum, clear of all taxes, on the cost of construction. This rental was twice the amount of the annual interest charges on the Bonds issued to build the road. This lease was assigned to the Pennsylvania Railroad Company effective December 1st, 1871.

Through the construction of this connecting link, a new through route was provided for traffic between the East and the West, the Pennsylvania Railroad having previously used the co-called "Allentown Route" between New York and Harrisburg via the Central Railroad of New Jersey from New York to Allentown and the Philadelphia & Reading Railroad from the latter point to Harrisburg. Both routes were used for some years afterward, the one via Allentown being 12 miles shorter. However, the Pennsylvania Railroad Company having leased the lines of the United New Jersey Railroad & Canal Company and Philadelphia & Trenton Railroad Company between New York and Philadelphia in 1871, and as its own route passed through Philadelphia, there was apparently no necessity for operating both of them, and the use of the "Allentown Route" was discontinued in the Spring of 1872.

CASH AND STOCK DIVIDENDS

Under the financial plan approved at the adjourned annual meeting of the Pennsylvania Railroad Company in April, 1867, cash dividends of 3% each were paid in May and November of that year, which, together with a 5% dividend paid in stock, made the total dividends disbursements 11% for the year 1867. Similar cash and Stock dividends were paid in 1868.

ADVANCES TO PHILADELPHIA & ERIE RAILROAD

The poor results from operating the Philadelphia & Erie Railroad was a matter of considerable concern to the Management, and as a continuance of heavy losses could only be prevented by large expenditures for renewals and replacements, the Pennsylvania Railroad Company was forced to provide the funds for this purpose. This it did to the extent of nearly $4,000,000., in addition to the advances previously made, in return for which it received 31,636 shares of Common and 48,000 shares of Preferred Stock of the Philadelphia & Erie Railroad Company, a sufficient amount to control the future policy of that Company.

EARNINGS USED FOR IMPROVEMENTS 1854-1867

It may be of interest to point out that in 1867 the cost of constructing the Pennsylvania Railroad from Harrisburg to Pittsburgh stood upon the books of the Company at about the same figure ($13,540,950.) as it did in 1854, when it was opened as a continuous single track railroad between those cities. This gratifying situation was the direct result of paying for a second track throughout the entire length of the road, except for about 3 miles, and other improvements, costing nearly $7,000,000., out of the net earnings, instead of incurring additional Mortgage debt or selling more Stock.

PITTSBURGH & STEUBENVILLE RAILROAD REORGANIZED

While the Pittsburgh & Steubenville Railroad had been constructed between Pittsburgh and the east bank of the Ohio River opposite Steubenville, yet, in consequence of the great cost and long delay in completing the road, it became involved in further financial difficulties, to free it from which it was sold under a Court decree. After the sale of the road it was reorganized on January 14th, 1868, under the name of the Pan Handle Railway Company, in which the Pennsylvania Railroad Company was the majority stockholder.

FORMATION OF PITTSBURGH, CINCINNATI & ST. LOUIS RAILWAY COMPANY

On April 20th, 1868, the Pan Handle Railway Company, the Holliday's Cove Railroad (Steubenville Bridge) and the Steubenville & Indiana Railroad Company were consolidated into the Pittsburgh, Cincinnati & St. Louis Railway Company, the railroad of the new Company extending from Pittsburgh to Columbus, O., a distance of 196 miles. The interest held by the Pennsylvania Railroad Company in the Capital Stock and Bonds of the consolidated company was sufficient to control its policy and stood upon its books at a cost of $5,633,450.09. It was an indispensable connection for the Pennsylvania Railroad with the West and Southwest, and it was the belief that the road would eventually pay a fair rate of dividend to its stockholders.

BRANCH LINE EXTENSIONS IN WESTERN PENNSYLVANIA

The Mifflin & Centre County Railroad, which was operated under lease to the Pennsylvania Railroad Company from near Lewistown to Reedsville, Pa., completed an extension of its road to Milroy, Pa., a distance of about six miles, on January 6th, 1868.

On February 1st, 1869, the extension of the Tyrone & Clearfield Railway from Philipsburg to Clearfield, a distance of 17 miles, was completed and placed in operation.

STATE CHANGES A RAILROAD INVESTMENT

In 1869 the State of Pennsylvania disposed of its lien of $3,500,000. upon the Philadelphia & Erie Railroad to the Allegheny Valley Railroad, accepting therefor a second lien upon the line the latter Company was building from the Philadelphia & Erie Railroad at Driftwood to the Allegheny Valley Railroad at Red Bank, Pa., known as the "Low Grade Line"; the Bonds given to the State in exchange being guaranteed by the Pennsylvania Railroad, Philadelphia & Erie Railroad and Northern Central Railway Companies, over whose lines the traffic of the new road was to pass to Philadelphia and Pittsburgh. This insured to the

State the ultimate payment of its original claim of $3,500,000. on the Philadelphia & Erie Railroad Company for the canals purchased by the latter Company, which were not included in the Public Works sold to the Pennsylvania Railroad Company.

FORT WAYNE ROUTE IN DANGER

While the original policy of the Pennsylvania Railroad Company was to reach the traffic of the Northwest and Southwest by assisting in the construction of connecting lines leading to the markets of these sections, and not to lease or control their operations, the rapid growth of the western country and the help received from the Pennsylvania Railroad Company placed a number of the roads traversing that territory in strong financial condition, particularly the Pittsburgh, Ft. Wayne & Chicago Railway Company, which extended from Pittsburgh to Chicago, a distance of 468 miles, and which had pledged its business flowing toward the Atlantic seaboard to the Pennsylvania Railroad. After the Fort Wayne Company had reached this favorable position, its Board of Directors decided that it would be preferable to have an independent line to the East, notwithstanding its obligations to the Pennsylvania Railroad Company, and extensive surveys of the country east of Pittsburgh were made to find a suitable route over which it could send its traffic, which was later followed by large advances to a railway company, whose road it was proposed to use as a part of this rival line. During the progress of these negotiations an effort was made by the Erie Railroad Company to absorb not only the Pittsburgh, Ft. Wayne & Chicago Railway Company, but nearly all of the Western connections of the Pennsylvania Railroad, which failed of its purpose only from a misapprehension of the law under which they proposed to carry out their plan.

LEASE OF PITTSBURGH, FT. WAYNE & CHICAGO RAILWAY

In view of this extraordinary situation, it became evident to the Management of the Pennsylvania Railroad Company that it should have closer relations with its Western connections, and after extended negotiations with the Pittsburgh, Ft. Wayne & Chicago Railway Company, a lease for a term of 999 years was agreed upon and signed on June 7th, 1869, and the Pennsylvania Railroad Company entered into possession of that road on July 1st, 1869. While the terms were considered very onerous at the time, the Management felt justified, in view of the foregoing circumstances, in making the lease.

The provisions of the lease required the Pennsylvania Railroad Company to pay an annual rental of $1,380,000., which was equal to 12% upon the $11,500,000. of Capital Stock then outstanding. The Fort Wayne Company thereupon, in accordance with the understanding reached in the lease negotiations, increased (by over 71%) the outstanding Stock to $19,714,285.71, which made the annual guaranteed rental of $1,380,000. equivalent to 7% upon the increased amount of Stock.

The Pennsylvania Railroad Company also assumed all the obligations of the latter Company, including the payment of the principal of, and interest on, its First, Second and Third Mortgage Bonds and Equipment Bonds. The leases of the New Castle & Beaver Valley Railroad, the Lawrence Railroad, and the Massillon & Cleveland Railroad to the Ft. Wayne Company; the contracts of December 15th, 1862, and February 16th, 1866, with the Cleveland & Pittsburgh Railroad Company for joint operation and division of earnings; the one-half Stock ownership of the Fort Wayne Company in the Indianapolis & St. Louis Railway Company, which had a lease of the St. Louis, Alton & Terre Haute Railroad, were all assigned to the Pennsylvania Railroad Company.

Another provision in the lease was that the Pennsylvania Railroad Company should assume the obligations of the Fort Wayne Company under a contract with the Grand Rapids & Indiana Railroad Company, under which it endorsed $4,000,000. of 7% First Mortgage Bonds of the latter Company. This was done to aid in the construction of the

Grand Rapids & Indiana Railroad from Fort Wayne, Ind., to Little Traverse Bay, Mich., a distance of about 320 miles, from which the Fort Wayne road was to receive all the interchange traffic.

FT. WAYNE LEASES AND CONTRACTS TRANSFERRED TO PENNSYLVANIA COMPANY

All of these leases and contracts were subsequently transferred to the Pennsylvania Company (to which reference is later made) upon its formation in 1870, except the lease of the Massillon & Cleveland Railroad Company, which was assigned to the Cleveland, Mt. Vernon & Delaware Railroad Company (a predecessor of the Pennsylvania, Ohio & Detroit Railroad Company) on January 22nd, 1870, that Company taking possession on May 1st, 1870, but in October, 1880, the lease of the road was transferred to the Pennsylvania Company.

SALE OF CLEVELAND, ZANESVILLE & CINCINNATI RAILROAD

On November 4th, 1869, the Pittsburgh, Ft. Wayne & Chicago Railway Company and the Pennsylvania Railroad Company sold to the Pittsburgh, Mt. Vernon, Columbus & London Railroad Company (which later became the Cleveland, Mt. Vernon & Delaware Railroad Company), the Cleveland, Zanesville & Cincinnati Railroad, which was formerly the Akron Branch of the Cleveland & Pittsburgh Railroad. It was constructed from Hudson to Millersburg, O., 61 miles, and had been purchased by the Pittsburgh, Ft. Wayne & Chicago Railway Company on July 1st, 1865, and transferred under the lease to the Pennsylvania Railroad Company.

LEASE OF ANOTHER ROUTE TO CHICAGO

The same reasons which induced the Pennsylvania Railroad Company to become the lessee of the Pittsburgh, Ft. Wayne & Chicago Railway Company, prompted the Pittsburgh, Cincinnati & St. Louis Railway Company to lease the Columbus, Chicago & Indiana Central Railway, which extended from Columbus, O., to Chicago, Ill., Indianapolis, Ind., and State Line, Ill., a total distance of about 581 miles. The lease was for 99 years, renewable for like periods at the option of the lessee, taking effect as of February 1st, 1869. Under its terms the lessor company was to receive 30% of the gross earnings, which the lessee guaranteed would amount to 7% interest on $22,000,000. Mortgage Bonds, but under an amendment to the lease dated February 1st, 1870, the liability of the Pittsburgh, Cincinnati & St. Louis Railway Company was reduced to the interest on $15,821,000. of Funded Debt.

LEASE OF LITTLE MIAMI RAILROAD

Under date of February 23rd, 1870, effective December 1st, 1869, the Pittsburgh, Cincinnati & St. Louis Railway Company leased the Little Miami Railroad, through which line the Pennsylvania Railroad connection with Cincinnati was established, thus enabling it to share in the growth and prosperity of that City. The lease was for 99 years, renewable forever, the Pennsylvania Railroad Company guaranteeing the performance of the covenants on the part of the Pittsburgh, Cincinnati & St. Louis Railway Company. The lease included the Columbus & Xenia Railroad, Dayton & Western Railroad and the portion of the Richmond & Miami Railway leased by it, which roads were already controlled by lease to the Little Miami Railroad Company; also the Cincinnati Street Connection Railway and the Dayton, Xenia & Belpre Railroad. The rental was the sum of $480,000. per annum, equivalent to a dividend of 8% per annum upon the aggregate Capital Stock of the Little Miami Railroad Company and the Columbus & Xenia Railroad Company, amounting to $6,000,000., to which sum their combined Capital Stock was by the terms of the lease increased.

The railroads included in the foregoing lease extended from Columbus to Cincinnati via Xenia, and from Xenia northward to Springfield and westward to the Ohio-Indiana State Line at New Paris, a total distance of about 195 miles.

TWO CONNECTIONS WITH ST. LOUIS

Under the lease of the Pittsburgh, Ft. Wayne & Chicago Railway Company, the Pennsylvania Railroad Company became possessed of one-half the shares of the Indianapolis & St. Louis Railroad Company, extending from Indianapolis to Terre Haute, which had a lease of the old line between Terre Haute, Alton and St. Louis, and which was known as the St. Louis, Alton & Terre Haute Railroad Company. The Pennsylvania Railroad Company had previously acquired a majority of the shares of the new and shorter line between Terre Haute and St. Louis, via Vandalia, and known as the St. Louis, Vandalia & Terre Haute Railroad Company, thus completing two connections with St. Louis. The latter route was retained, but the former was subsequently sold to what is now the Cleveland, Cincinnati, Chicago & St. Louis Railway Company (part of the New York Central System), to which reference is later made.

LEASE OF ERIE & PITTSBURGH RAILROAD

Under date of March 24th, 1870, taking effect March 1st, 1870, the Pennsylvania Railroad Company leased the entire railroad and property of the Erie & Pittsburgh Railroad Company for 999 years, which lease was subsequently assigned to the Pennsylvania Company. This road was constructed from New Castle to Girard Junction, Pa., a distance of about 80 miles, with a branch about three miles long in Erie, Pa. Under the lease the Erie & Pittsburgh Railroad Company received annually as a dividend fund for its stockholders $140,000., which was equal to 7% upon $2,000,000. Capital Stock, and $2,500. annually to provide for the expense of maintaining its corporate organization. The lessee also guaranteed the payment of the principal of, and interest on, the Bonded Debt of the lessor company.

The Erie & Pittsburgh Railroad was not built beyond Girard Junction, except for the three mile branch extending westwardly from Erie, for the reason that it had secured trackage rights over the New York Central Lines between Girard Junction and Erie. This agreement was made in 1863 for a 25-year period, and upon its expiration in 1888 was renewed for 20 years, except that the freight trains of the Pennsylvania Company, which was then operating the Erie & Pittsburgh Railroad, were confined to the use of the tracks of the New York Central Lines between Girard Junction and Dock Junction, to which latter point the Erie & Pittsburgh Railroad had built its branch from Erie. The agreement was again renewed in 1908, and now runs until terminated by either party on 18 months notice.

PURCHASE OF ERIE CANAL COMPANY

In order to protect the interests of the Erie & Pittsburgh Railroad Company, the Pennsylvania Railroad Company in 1870 secured control of the privately owned Erie Canal Company by the purchase of the Stock and Bonds of that Company and judgments against it amounting to $1,200,000., paying therefor $350,000. in Equipment Bonds of the Erie & Pittsburgh Railroad Company. The canal was operated for about one year under an arrangement with the Erie & Pittsburgh Railroad Company, when executions were issued on the judgments against the Canal Company, and the canal from Erie to the mouth of Beaver River was sold by the sheriffs of the Counties through which it ran, and purchased by W. L. Scott in the interest of the lessee and the Erie & Pittsburgh Railroad Company. The canal property was subsequently sold to parties living along the line of the canal, and the proceeds were used in retiring part of the Equipment Bonds which were given for its purchase, the Canal Company being dissolved.

POLICY IN MAKING WESTERN LEASES

As bearing on the various leases and consolidations of the Lines West of Pittsburgh, it may be interesting to quote from the General Remarks of the annual report of the Pennsylvania Railroad Company for the year 1870, the following paragraphs:—

"In consequence of the failure of the mixed system of canals and railroads of the Commonwealth of Pennsylvania, and their connecting lines beyond Pittsburgh to attract a reasonable share of the traffic between the East and West, or successfully compete with the avenues built by New York, all the lines of railway that were first built in the West to reach the Atlantic market were directed towards Buffalo as the then best and cheapest route to the East, leaving to this Company, if it entered the list of competitors for this distant traffic, to endeavor without delay to secure in its interest railway connections with the commercial centres of the West as feeders to your Main Line. Sensible of the prejudice against large corporations since the failure of the United States Bank, the policy of this Company was first directed to the procuring of these connections by securing the organization of independent railway companies, and their construction by such pecuniary assistance as was required to effect this necessary object under contracts for the mutual interchange of business. This course it was confidently expected would meet the objects desired without involving this Company in the direct management of distant enterprises.

It, however, soon became evident, after securing such feeders, that their success in diverting the traffic of the West from the channels it had become accustomed to follow, stimulated the older rival interests to endeavor to overcome it by obtaining the control of such feeders with a view to embarrass our business and augment their own. The efforts proved nearly successful and were only prevented by promptly meeting the exigency by securing the absolute control of these lines for this Company. The Board think that they would have been derelict in their duty if they had yielded to timid counsels and permitted this opportunity to secure their object to pass unimproved. It is not proposed nor is it desired to manage these lines in a manner to divert traffic from its natural markets or channels, but solely with a view to secure to this Company its fair share of the business of the West, which it was found impossible to otherwise obtain."

PURCHASE OF CONTROLLING INTEREST IN NORTHERN CENTRAL RAILWAY COMPANY

The annual report for 1870 refers to the circumstances under which the Pennsylvania Railroad Company acquired a controlling interest in the Northern Central Railway Company, which at that time was constructed from Baltimore, Md., to Sunbury, Pa., a distance of 138 miles, and through contracts and leases, as well as traffic connections, practically extended to Buffalo, N. Y. This road for a time was under the control of the Baltimore & Ohio and Philadelphia & Reading Railroad Companies, whose interests were inimical to the Pennsylvania Railroad Company, and, therefore, the task of securing the much desired connection with Washington and the South was rendered that much more difficult. However, during the monetary panic in Baltimore immediately following the election of President Lincoln (1861), the holdings of the Baltimore & Ohio Railroad Company and many others, were thrown upon the market, and 43,614 shares with a par value of $2,180,700. were purchased by the Pennsylvania Railroad Company and placed in its Sinking Fund. The remaining shares necessary to secure a majority ownership were purchased in London. It was at first thought that the acquisition of an interest in the Northern Central Railway would prove a burden, but after placing the road in better operating condition and providing it with additional equipment, it was able to pay quarterly dividends at the rate of 8% per annum, with a fair surplus remaining.

EARLY RAILROAD CHARTERS FOR CONSTRUCTION—BALTIMORE, MD., TO YORK, PA.

It is a matter of interesting railroad history that one of the predecessors of the Northern Central Railway Company—the Baltimore & Susquehanna Railroad Company—had one of the earliest charters granted to steam railroads in this Country. It was incorporated in the State of Maryland on February 13th, 1828; construction was commenced in August, 1829, and the road was completed from Baltimore to the Pennsylvania-Maryland State Line, a distance of nearly 36 miles, in September, 1832. Other predecessors of the Northern Central Railway Company built from that point northward, one of which, the York & Maryland Line Railroad Company (incorporated in Pennsylvania in 1832), completing its road from a connection with the northern end of the Baltimore & Susquehanna Railroad to York, Pa., in August, 1838.

FROM BALTIMORE TO THE SOUTH

The acquisition of the Northern Central Railway proved satisfactory so far as securing a line to Baltimore was concerned, but to reach the Capital of the Nation the Baltimore & Ohio Railroad had to be used. Naturally the latter Company was not favorably disposed toward a competitive line, and it refused to allow the sale of through tickets, the right to check through passenger baggage, or to run through trains. Rather than remain in such a position steps were taken in co-operation with the Northern Central Railway Company to build an independent line from Baltimore to Washington. The construction of this road was begun in 1868 by the Baltimore & Potomac Railroad Company. Owing to the difficulty in securing a charter to build from Baltimore to Washington, and to overcome the objections of those who were opposed to it, the Company was given the right by the State of Maryland to build a Main Line of railroad from Baltimore to Popes Creek, Md., a distance of about 73 miles, with power to construct branches not exceeding 20 miles in length. The road was, therefore, being built to Popes Creek and a "branch" 19 miles long was being constructed from Bowie, Md., to Washington. From this it will be seen that what is now part of the Main Line of the Philadelphia, Baltimore & Washington Railroad between Bowie and Washington was originally built as a "branch" of the Baltimore & Potomac Railroad.

It was necessary to secure authority of Congress to construct this "branch" into the District of Columbia, and by an Act approved February 5th, 1867, the Company was authorized to extend its railroad to the Potomac River. This was supplemented by an Act, approved June 21st, 1870, giving the right to continue it over the Long Bridge to a connection with any railroads constructed, or to be constructed, in the State of Virginia. By an Act of Congress, approved March 3rd, 1871, the Baltimore & Potomac Railroad Company was also authorized to build a passenger station in Washington, which, according to the terms of the Act, was to be "of the same style of architecture as the depot of the Pennsylvania Railroad Company at the city of Lancaster, in the State of Pennsylvania." Through a supplemental Act, approved May 21st, 1872, which repealed the previous Act, the location of the station, which was to be on a site known as "The Mall," was slightly changed, and the peculiar feature designating the style of architecture was omitted.

When the Baltimore & Potomac Railroad had reached Washington, it was the purpose to continue the routh South to Richmond, Va., via the Alexandria & Washington Railway and the Alexandria & Fredericksburg Railway (later consolidated to form the Washington Southern Railway) and the Richmond, Fredericksburg & Potomac Railroad. This would connect it with the whole system of southern railroads controlled by the Southern Railway Security Company, in which the Pennsylvania Railroad Company had become a shareholder to secure the traffic from the roads south of Richmond, Va.

PULLMAN SERVICE

On January 27th, 1870, a contract was made with the Pullman Palace Car Company for the use of its equipment on the lines of the Pennsylvania Railroad Company. The latter had previously used the equipment of the Central Transportation Company in furnishing this class of service, and prior to that time had a contract, dated September 15th, 1858, with T. T. Woodruff & Company for the operation of its sleeping cars, which contained patented seats and couches, on the Pennsylvania Railroad and its affiliated lines. The Pullman Company had acquired the entire equipment of the Central Transportation Company, and the contract which had been made with the former Company would, it was stated, result in the introduction of a great many parlor and sleeping cars of improved type on the Pennsylvania Railroad System.

BRANCH OF WESTERN PENNSYLVANIA R. R.

On March 1st, 1871, the Butler Branch of the Western Pennsylvania Railroad was completed from Butler Junction to Butler, Pa., a distance of 21 miles.

CREATION OF PENNSYLVANIA COMPANY

In order to secure greater efficiency, economy and harmony in the management of the numerous Western connections of the Pennsylvania Railroad Company, extending westwardly and northwardly from Pittsburgh, and more effectively promote the welfare of the public and the companies themselves, a Charter was secured from the State of Pennsylvania for a corporation known as the Pennsylvania Company on April 7th, 1870.

Under the Act of Incorporation, it was authorized to issue $100,000. of Capital Stock in shares of $50. each, with authority to increase it to any required amount. At a meeting of the stockholders on January 20th, 1871, the authorized Capital Stock was increased to $12,000,000., consisting of $8,000,000., par value, of Preferred and $4,000,000. of Common Stock. The Pennsylvania Railroad Company received $8,000,000. of this Preferred Stock as a consideration for selling and transferring to the Pennsylvania Company, as of April 1st, 1871, the securities, leases, etc., of the corporations hereinafter named on the following terms:—

19,376 shares common stock Pittsburgh, Cincinnati and St. Louis Railway Company, at $12. per share	$232,512.
56,200 shares preferred stock Pittsburgh, Cincinnati and St. Louis Railway Company, at $50. per share	2,810,000.
Claim against the Pittsburgh, Cincinnati and St. Louis Railway Company for 48,000 shares Cincinnati and Muskingum Valley Railroad Company, to be received by the former company, at $8.75 per share	420,184.
29,000 shares Indianapolis and Vincennes Railroad Company, at $8.75 per share	253,866.
6,000 shares Indianapolis and St. Louis Railroad Company, at $50. per share	300,000.

13,500 shares St. Louis, Vandalia and Terre Haute Railroad Company, at $70. per share	$945,000.
6,000 shares Holliday's Cove Railroad Company	100.
Mortgage on property in Steubenville, purchased for Pittsburgh, Cincinnati and St. Louis Railway Company, and accrued interest	72,038.
A lease of the railway, depots and property as then occupied or used by the Pittsburgh, Cincinnati and St. Louis Railway Company, between Union Depot, Pittsburgh, and the Washington turnpike (Steubenville Extension)—the Pennsylvania Railroad Company (the owner) to complete the bridge and double track between those points	1,250,000.
A lease of the Pittsburgh, Fort Wayne and Chicago Railway	200.
A lease of the Erie and Pittsburgh Railroad	100.
For rolling stock on said railroads, belonging to the Pennsylvania Railroad Company	759,650.
50 Logansport city bonds (Indiana), 80 per cent	40,000.
3 Junction Railroad bonds (Indiana)	2,000.
300 Bonds, Indianapolis, Cincinnati and Lafayette Railroad Company, 75 per cent	225,000.
811 general mortgage bonds, Pittsburgh, Cincinnati and St. Louis Railway Company, 85 per cent	689,350.
Total	$8,000,000.

The following securities having a value of $1,154,550. were received by the Pittsburgh, Cincinnati & St. Louis Railway Company with the lease of the Little Miami Railroad, and they were to be transferred without charge to the Pennsylvania Company and could be used in purchasing new equipment, in erecting depots, in building new works, or be cancelled at the discretion of the Directors:—

Columbus and Xenia Railroad Company Stock	$519,550.
General Mortgage Bonds, Pittsburgh, Cincinnati & St. Louis Railway Company	189,000.
Cincinnati Street Connection Bonds issued by Little Miami-Cincinnati and Indiana Railroad Companies	335,000.
Columbus and Xenia Railroad Company First Mortgage Bonds	54,000.
Little Miami Railroad Company First Mortgage Bonds	33,000.
Dayton and Western Railroad Company Bonds	24,000.
Total	$1,154,550.

The Pennsylvania Company, effective November 1st, 1876, made a sublease for 25 years of the bridge across the Monongahela River and adjoining tracks, known as the Steubenville Extension of the Pennsylvania Railroad, to the Pittsburgh, Cincinnati & St. Louis Railway Company.

Thomas A. Scott was elected President of the Pennsylvania Company, William Thaw, Vice-President, and the general management of the properties, aggregating 3,200 miles, was assigned to J. N. McCullough, who had a long and successful experience in the operation of the Pittsburgh, Ft. Wayne & Chicago and Cleveland & Pittsburgh Railroads.

HOLDINGS OF ADDITIONAL SECURITIES OF WESTERN CONNECTIONS

In addition to the interests of the Pennsylvania Railroad Company in the West to be transferred to the Pennsylvania Company, it still held 22,000 shares (a large majority) of the stock of the Cleveland, Mt. Vernon & Delaware Railroad Company. This road, as heretofore stated, was a predecessor of the Pennsylvania, Ohio & Detroit Railroad Company, and by September 1st, 1873, was completed from Hudson to Columbus, O., a distance of 144 miles. This interest was received with the lease of the Pittsburgh, Ft. Wayne & Chicago Railway Company and promised to become a profitable investment. The Pennsylvania Railroad Company also held $1,049,000. of Bonds of the Newport & Cincinnati Bridge Company, which was then erecting a bridge over the Ohio River to connect the Little Miami Railroad with the Kentucky system of railroads; $4,446,000. of General Mortgage Bonds of the Pittsburgh, Cincinnati & St. Louis Railway Company; $1,766,000. of Second Mortgage Bonds of the St. Louis, Vandalia & Terre Haute Railroad Company; and $807,000. of First Mortgage Bonds of the Cincinnati & Muskingum Valley Railroad Company, the line of which was built from Zanesville to Morrow, 132 miles, and was then being extended from Zanesville to Dresden, O., 16 miles, on the Pittsburgh, Cincinnati & St. Louis Railway.

LEASE OF CLEVELAND & PITTSBURGH RAILROAD

Under date of October 25th, 1871, taking effect December 1st, 1871, the Cleveland & Pittsburgh Railroad was leased to the Pennsylvania Railroad Company for 999 years.

This road extended from Rochester, Pa., on the Pittsburgh, Ft. Wayne & Chicago Railway, by way of Wellsville, O., to Bridgeport and Cleveland, which, with branches, gave it a length of about 202 miles. The lessee guaranteed the payment of 7% upon the Capital Stock as increased at the time of the lease; the payment of principal of, and interest on, the Funded Debt; and also the necessary Sinking Fund payments. The lease was assigned to the Pennsylvania Company under date of April 14th, 1873, taking effect as of December 1st, 1871.

ACQUISITION OF WRIGHTSVILLE, YORK & GETTYSBURG RAILROAD

On June 21st, 1870, the Wrightsville, York & Gettysburg Railroad, extending from York to Wrightsville, Pa., opposite Columbia, Pa., a distance of about 13 miles, came into possession of the Pennsylvania Railroad, thus establishing a connection with the Northern Central Railway at York, Pa., and permitting through service between Philadelphia and York. The bridges on this road were all destroyed by the Confederate forces during their raids into Pennsylvania just prior to the Battle of Gettysburg. The Capital Stock and Bonds of this Company, which were entirely owned by the Pennsylvania Railroad Company, were cancelled in 1874, and 6,000 shares of the Stock of the latter Company, amounting at par to $300,000., were issued in lieu thereof, and held in its Treasury.

COLUMBIA BRIDGE

The Pennsylvania Railroad Company had previously purchased the bridge across the Susquehanna River between Wrightsville and Columbia. This bridge had been owned by a Company known as "The Columbia Bank and Bridge Company," under which it conducted a banking as well as a bridge business. However, the risks were too great in operating the bridge property and it was, therefore, determined to separate the banking from the bridge business. Accordingly in 1852, "The Columbia Bank" was formed and efforts were made to dispose of the bridge property, but it was not until 1864 that it was finally sold to interests affiliated with the Pennsylvania Railroad, which had formed the "Columbia Bridge Company." On July 1st, 1871, the entire property and franchises of the latter Company were conveyed to the Pennsylvania Railroad Company. The bridge was first opened for traffic in 1814; was badly damaged by a freshet in 1832; was rebuilt (with two railroad tracks) in 1834; was destroyed by fire by the Northern Armies during the Civil War (1863) as a matter of protection against invasion by the armies of the South; was rebuilt and opened for traffic in 1869; was again destroyed by a violent wind storm in 1896, and rebuilt as a steel structure and placed in operation in 1897.

ALLEGHENY VALLEY RAILROAD COMPLETED TO PITTSBURGH

The Allegheny Valley Railroad having completed its line to Pittsburgh and connected its tracks with those of the Pennsylvania Railroad at that point, a contract was entered into between the two Companies for the use of the Union Passenger Depot, and that Company commenced operating its trains into the Station on October 20th, 1870.

AMERICAN STEAMSHIP COMPANY

For a number of years prior to 1871 the Pennsylvania Railroad had been urged to take some interest, with the citizens and municipal authorities of Philadelphia, in a line of steamships which was to furnish a service between Philadelphia and Liverpool. The project was not looked upon with much favor until 1871, when the Pennsylvania Railroad Company agreed to guarantee the Bonds of the American Steamship Company, which was incorporated for this purpose, to the extent of $1,500,000., and also subscribe to $400,000. of an issue of $704,700. of Capital Stock to thus control the policy of the Company. Four steamers were to constitute the fleet and they were all contracted for through William Cramp & Sons at a total cost of $2,080,000. The steamers were to be of the same general type, the length of each to be 355 feet, and the breadth of beam 43 feet, with sufficient capacity to carry 76 first class and 854 steerage passengers. The four vessels were to be named after the States through which the lines of the Pennsylvania Railroad passed, namely, "Pennsylvania," "Ohio," "Indiana" and "Illinois." The Company also entered into a contract with the International Navigation Company, which proposed to establish a line of steamships between Philadelphia and Antwerp, Belgium, stopping at Southampton, England, and which it was believed would develop the foreign trade of Philadelphia to and from points in Europe not reached by the steamers of the American Steamship Company, and consequently result in an increase of traffic to and from the lines of the Pennsylvania Railroad. The Annual Report for 1872 states that the "Pennsylvania" had been launched and was expected to be ready for service in May, 1873.

LOW GRADE LINE—ALLEGHENY VALLEY RAILROAD

Rapid progress was made on the construction of the Low Grade Line of the Allegheny Valley Railroad which was being built especially for freight traffic and designed for cheap transportation at low rates of speed. This new line intersected the Philadelphia & Erie Railroad at Driftwood and proposed to use about 120 miles of the eastern end of the latter road for traffic destined to eastern points, which it was felt would not only materially add to the revenues of the Philadelphia & Erie Railroad, but would likewise prove profitable to the Allegheny Valley Railroad.

MORRISON'S COVE EXTENSION

On May 1st, 1871, the Morrison's Cove Extension of the Hollidaysburg Branch was completed to McKee's, and on December 25th of that year, the line was completed to Henrietta, a distance of nearly 20 miles from Hollidaysburg. This extension was constructed in order to reach the valuable hematite iron ore deposits at Morrison's Cove, and it was believed that the traffic from this field would more than compensate the Company for the outlay.

BRANCH FROM GREENSBURG TO CONNELLSVILLE, PA.

On March 16th, 1871, a Charter was secured in the name of the South West Pennsylvania Railway Company to construct a branch line from Greensburg on the Main Line to Connellsville, a distance of about 25 miles, which latter point was the centre of valuable coke producing fields, the products from which found their way to Pittsburgh and other markets in the East and West. This branch was completed on April 1st, 1873.

LEASE OF UNITED CANAL AND RAILROAD COMPANIES OF NEW JERSEY

It was early in 1870 that the Management of the Pennsylvania Railroad Company began to consider the propriety of leasing the railways and canals of the United Canal & Railroad Companies of New Jersey (now known as United New Jersey Railroad & Canal Company), with which it had interchange traffic agreements, whereby Pennsylvania Railroad traffic was sent via that route to and from New York. The principal objects of the lease were to secure ample facilities for the accommodation of the heavy traffic it could send to the City of New York, the metropolis of the Country; the great desirability of having a continuous line of railroad between this important eastern gateway and the West under one Management, so as to insure through train service, and the use of unrivaled terminal facilities in New York, Jersey City and South Amboy, N. J.

Onerous terms were demanded for the lease of these lines, but the Management of the Pennsylvania Railroad Company felt that their acceptance was justified by the very great importance of having under its control a line reaching the Hudson River and the establishment of an eastern gateway for its traffic. Therefore, the Pennsylvania Railroad Company agreed to take over these railroads and the canal, and a lease providing therefore was signed on June 30th, 1871, taking effect on July 1st, 1871. The terms of the lease provided for the payment annually of a 10% dividend on the $19,485,000. of Capital Stock of the United

Companies; also the payment of the principal of, and interest on, their outstanding Bonded Debt, amounting in the aggregate to $16,942,419.50; and in addition $10,000. per annum to enable them to maintain their corporate organization. The lease was to run for 999 years, and included the delivery by the United Companies of all their stocks, bonds, cash, real estate, equipment, rents, assets or other property of every kind whatsoever, belonging to the said Companies. The Stocks and Bonds delivered under the lease amounted in the aggregate at par to $5,714,444., valued at the time the lease was signed at $4,065,225., and yielding a revenue in 1872 of $171,629.92. These securities were largely those of companies owning the railroads, canals and ferries hereinafter mentioned, and they also included Stocks and Bonds of Bridge, Telegraph, Plank Road and Horse Car Railroad Companies.

PHYSICAL PROPERTY

The following Railroad and Canal Companies were parties to the agreement, viz:—

	Miles
Camden & Amboy Railroad and Transportation Company, owning a railroad with branches, extending from the Delaware River at Camden to the Raritan Bay at South Amboy, N. J.	63.28
New Jersey Railroad & Transportation Company, owning a railroad with branches extending from Jersey City to a point 3½ miles west of New Brunswick, N. J.	38.44
The Joint Companies (C. & A. R. R. & T. Co., N. J. R. R. & T. Co., and D. & R. C. Co.), owning a railroad from a point 3½ miles west of New Brunswick, N. J., to Trenton, N. J., together with various branches	43.02
Total railroads owned	144.74
Delaware & Raritan Canal Company, owning a canal and feeder extending almost across the State of New Jersey, connecting the Delaware and Raritan Rivers	66.00

The Philadelphia & Trenton Railroad Company, in which the United Canal & Railroad Companies owned a majority interest, was also a party to the lease, its road extending from Trenton to Frankford Junction, a distance of about 24 miles. The Connecting Railway, the lease of which was assigned by the Philadelphia & Trenton Railroad

Company to the Pennsylvania Railroad Company, effective December 1st, 1871, completed the connecting link, it extending from Frankford Junction to a connection with the Pennsylvania Railroad at a point 1½ miles west of the West Philadelphia Passenger Station.

The following railroads, which had previously been leased by either the United Companies or the Philadelphia & Trenton Railroad Company, or in which these Companies had a large Stock and Bond interest, came with the lease of the parent companies:—

	Miles
Camden & Burlington County R. R.:	
Camden to Pemberton, N. J	22.46
Mt. Holly to Burlington, N. J	7.15
Pemberton & Hightstown R. R.:	
Pemberton to Hightstown, N. J	24.47
Vincentown Branch of Burlington County R. R.:	
Ewansville to Vincentown, N. J	2.84
Rocky Hill R. R. & Transportation Co.:	
Kingston to Rocky Hill, N. J	2.38
Mt. Holly, Lumberton & Medford R. R.:	
Mt. Holly to Medford, N. J	6.19
Perth Amboy & Woodbridge R. R.:	
Rahway to Perth Amboy, N. J	6.40
Millstone & New Brunswick R. R.:	
East Millstone to New Brunswick, N. J	6.65
Connecting Railway:	
Frankford Junction to Mantua Junction (Philadelphia)	6.75
Frankford & Holmesburg R. R.:	
Holmesburg Junction to Bustleton, Pa	4.16
Trenton Delaware Bridge:	
Morrisville to Trenton, N. J.,	0.19
Total	89.64

In addition to the foregoing, the United Companies held a large, and in some cases controlling, interest in a number of other transportation companies which were included in the lease, the most important of which were as follows:—

	Miles
Associates of the Jersey Company:	
Ferry from Jersey City to New York	2.13
Belvidere Delaware R. R.:	
Trenton, N. J., to Manunka Chunk, Pa	67.49
Branch from Lambertville to Flemington, N. J	11.67

	Miles
Camden & Philadelphia Steamboat Ferry Co.:	
Ferry from Philadelphia to Camden, N. J.	.53
Freehold & Jamesburg Agricultural R. R.:	
Jamesburg to Sea Girt, N. J.	27.54
West Jersey R. R.:	
Camden to Cape May, N. J.	81.47
Branches: Glassboro to Bridgeton, N. J.	19.60
Elmer to Salem, N. J.	17.12
Total	227.55

The terms of the lease required the delivery of the railways and canals on July 1st, 1871, but an injunction was secured by some dissatisfied shareholders of the United Canal & Railroad Companies of New Jersey, which delayed the transfer until December 1st, 1871.

The State of New Jersey, as a large stockholder in the Camden & Amboy Railroad & Transportation Company and the Delaware & Raritan Canal Company, validated the lease by Act approved March 27th, 1873.

On April 26th, 1872, the Delaware & Raritan Canal Company, the Camden & Amboy Railroad & Transportation Company, and the New Jersey Railroad & Transportation Company were consolidated to form the United New Jersey Railroad & Canal Company. The consolidation was carried out under an Act of the Legislature of New Jersey approved March 14th, 1872, and was effective May 18th, 1872.

TRENTON DELAWARE BRIDGE COMPANY

There came with the lease of the Philadelphia & Trenton Railroad Company, its ownership of a majority of the Capital Stock of the Trenton Delaware Bridge Company. This Stock interest was acquired prior to 1835, at which time the cars of the Philadelphia & Trenton Railroad were moved over the bridge by animal power, but in 1839 the bridge was so altered as to permit locomotives to haul the cars. The Trenton Delaware Bridge Company had a very old charter, it being incorporated in New Jersey on March 3rd, 1798, and in Pennsylvania on April 4th, 1798. An interesting feature of the charter was that no other bridge or bridges could be erected over the Delaware River at any place within 3 miles of the bridge built by this Bridge Company without its consent. During the year 1875, it was replaced by a new and improved double track iron bridge. The arrangement for the use of the bridge tracks took the form of a trackage agreement, dated June 20th, 1877, and running for over 993 years, between the Philadelphia & Trenton Railroad Company and the Trenton Delaware Bridge Company, which was assigned on the same date to the Pennsylvania Railroad Company.

A new four-track stone arch bridge having been completed in August, 1903, over the Delaware River south of the one owned by the Trenton Delaware Bridge Company, the steel superstructure of the latter, which was in good serviceable condition, was sold to the Philadelphia, Baltimore & Washington Railroad Company and used in connection with the rebuilding of its bridge over the Potomac River at Washington. This left only the highway section of the Trenton Delaware Bridge, and in 1918 it was sold to the States of Pennsylvania and New Jersey and made free of tolls.

LEASE OF SUNBURY & LEWISTOWN RAILROAD

The Sunbury & Lewistown Railroad, extending between Lewistown on the Pennsylvania Railroad and Selinsgrove on the Northern Central Railway, a distance of 44 miles, was leased under a contract dated October 2nd, 1871, by the Pennsylvania Railroad and opened for traffic on December 1st, 1871. This road was to be operated at cost, and any surplus turned over to the Sunbury & Lewistown Railroad Company.

EXTENSION OF LEWISBURG, CENTRE & SPRUCE CREEK RAILROAD

The extension of the Lewisburg, Centre & Spruce Creek Railroad from Lewisburg to Mifflinsburg, a distance of 10 miles, was completed on November 1st, 1871.

PITTSBURGH, VIRGINIA & CHARLESTON RAILWAY

The difficulties in operating freight trains from the south branch of the Monongahela River through the tunnel under

Grants Hill in Pittsburgh, and the yards of the Pennsylvania Railroad adjacent thereto, became so serious that it was deemed advisable to build a line through Birmingham (opposite Pittsburgh) under the Charter of the Pittsburgh, Virginia & Charleston Railway, and to construct a branch across the Monongahela River at Port Perry to the Pennsylvania Railroad near Turtle Creek Station. This could be done on a route of better gradients and shorter distance than via the Main Line. The Pittsburgh, Virginia & Charleston Railway was to be continued by way of the valley of the Monongahela through a populous region containing very large fields of high grade bituminous coal, the traffic from which assured the profitableness of the extension. The Monongahela Valley Railroad Company had been incorporated for this purpose on April 8th, 1867, but the corporate title of this Company was changed to the Pittsburgh, Virginia & Charleston Railway Company on February 4th, 1870.

LEASE OF CHARTIERS RAILWAY

The Chartiers Railway, a branch line completed in 1871 by the Pennsylvania Railroad Company, aided by the citizens along its route, from Mansfield (now Carnegie, Pa.) on the Pittsburgh, Cincinnati & St. Louis Railway, to Washington, Pa., a distance of 22 miles, was leased to the latter road on December 8th, 1871, effective January 1st, 1872. It was to be operated at cost and the profits turned over to the owners of the Stocks and Bonds of the Chartiers Railway Company. The Pennsylvania Railroad Company owned a majority of the Capital Stock of this Company.

ADDITIONAL ROUTE TO CINCINNATI

The Cincinnati & Muskingum Valley Railway, which was constructed through a rich agricultural section of Ohio, intersecting the Little Miami Railroad at Morrow, O., was connected in 1871 with the Pittsburgh, Cincinnati & St. Louis Railway by the construction of a line from near Dresden to Zanesville, O., a distance of 16 miles. This road formed an additional through route to Cincinnati and was controlled by the Pennsylvania Company through the ownership of a large majority of its shares.

CONSTRUCTION FROM TOLEDO JUNCTION (NEAR MANSFIELD) TO TOLEDO, O.

The construction of the Mansfield, Cold Water & Lake Michigan Railroad was commenced in 1871 under a construction contract with the Pennsylvania Company. This road was to extend from Mansfield, O. (Toledo Junction), to Allegan, Mich., a distance of about 216 miles, with a branch from Tiffin to Toledo, O. The Pennsylvania Company agreed to fully equip the line when the roadbed had been constructed, for which it received the First Mortgage Bonds of the Mansfield, Cold Water & Lake Michigan Railroad Company and a controlling interest in its Stock. Under this contract about 80 miles of track were laid, and that portion from Toledo Junction (on the Pittsburgh, Ft. Wayne & Chicago Railway west of Mansfield) to Tiffin, O., a distance of about 37 miles, was placed in operation on May 1st, 1873, as part of the through route to Toledo, O., opened at that time. The road north of Tiffin to Toledo was built by two companies. One was the Toledo, Tiffin & Eastern Railroad, extending from Tiffin to Woodville, O., nearly 25 miles, which was controlled in the interest of the Pennsylvania Railroad Company, and the other was the Toledo & Woodville Railroad, which extended from Woodville to Toledo, a distance of about 18 miles. This latter road was owned by the City of Toledo at that time and was leased to the Toledo, Tiffin & Eastern Railroad Company.

CONTROL OF INDIANAPOLIS & VINCENNES RAILROAD

The Pennsylvania Railroad Company on July 2nd, 1870, secured control of the Indianapolis & Vincennes Railroad Company, the line of which extended from Indianapolis to Vincennes, Ind., a distance of 117 miles, through its ownership of the Pittsburgh, Cincinnati & St. Louis Railway Company, which latter Company, with others, entered into a contract with the Indianapolis & Vincennes Railroad Company on August 1st, 1868, for construction and lease of its road. This agreement was cancelled in 1870, the Pennsylvania Railroad Company becoming the guarantor of the First Mortgage 7% Bonds amounting to $1,700,000., and also $1,402,000. Second Mortgage 6% Bonds of the Indianapolis & Vincennes Railroad Company. These latter Bonds were issued in exchange for $1,402,000. of Capital Stock, which was surrendered to the Pennsylvania Railroad Company in accordance with an agreement dated July 2nd, 1870. On April 24th, 1872, the Pennsylvania Railroad Company transferred the entire Capital Stock of the Indianapolis & Vincennes Railroad Company to the Pennsylvania Company. Effective January 1st, 1879, the latter Company leased this road for 99 years, and agreed to pay the net earnings to the Indianapolis & Vincennes Railroad Company to be used in the payment of interest on its Bonds and other obligations.

CONTROL OF ROUTE TO CAIRO, ILL.

In addition to the foregoing the Pennsylvania Company entered into satisfactory arrangement for the control of the Cairo & Vincennes Railroad after it was completed, thus extending its control of railroads to Cairo, Ill., from which latter point the Cairo & Fulton Railroad proposed to connect with the International Railway then being built southwestwardly into Texas.

LEASE OF SOUTHWESTERN LINES

Under date of December 26th, 1871, the Pittsburgh, Cincinnati & St. Louis Railway Company, in order to secure greater traffic from the Southwest, leased the Jeffersonville, Madison & Indianapolis Railroad Company, which extended from Indianapolis to Louisville, a distance of 110 miles; Madison to Columbus, Ind., 45 miles; and Columbus to Cambridge City, Ind., 65 miles, or a total of 220 miles. The road was leased for 999 years from August 1st, 1871, the rental to be equivalent to the interest on the Funded Debt; Sinking Fund payments; and a dividend of 7% per annum on the $2,000,000. of Capital Stock. The terms of the lease on the part of the Pittsburgh, Cincinnati & St. Louis Railway Company were guaranteed by the Pennsylvania Railroad Company.

LEASE OF DANVILLE, HAZLETON & WILKES-BARRE RAILROAD COMPANY

Under date of February 21st, 1872, the Pennsylvania Railroad Company leased the Danville, Hazleton & Wilkes-Barre Railroad for a term of 33 years and agreed to operate it at cost. Any surplus earnings were to be applied to the payment of the coupons on $1,400,000. of 7% Bonds issued by the leased Company, and if they were not sufficient for that purpose, the Pennsylvania Railroad Company agreed to purchase the coupons at their face value. This road was constructed in the anthracite coal regions of Pennsylvania and extended from Sunbury to Tomhicken, Pa., a distance of about 44 miles.

FIRST DIVIDEND ON PENNSYLVANIA COMPANY STOCK

The first dividend of 6% was paid on $8,000,000. of Preferred Stock of the Pennsylvania Company on October 1st, 1872. The Preferred Stock was also to participate equally with the Common Stock in any dividends above 6% per annum.

PURCHASE OF UNION FAST FREIGHT LINE

When the Union Railroad & Transportation Company, known as the "Union Line," was organized for the rapid carriage of freight traffic between the East and the West, the Management of the Pennsylvania Railroad Company, as has been heretofore stated, was loathe to enter into a contract with that Company, feeling that the service performed by its own lines was efficient and adequate, but as the several railroad companies competing with it for the extensive traffic of the West had contracted for this fast freight service, it was compelled in self-defense to also provide that character of transportation on its own lines. The Pennsylvania Railroad Company accordingly entered into an agreement in 1872 with the Union Railroad & Transportation Company, whose cars traversed thousands of miles of railways in the West, and which could gather up the traffic from the markets in that territory, and bring it to the East over the lines of the Pennsylvania Railroad Company if the goods were destined to points reached by it. However, since the Company had by acquisitions and leases extended its System to the Mississippi River, it was found that with this additional mileage and increased facilities, it could provide a similar service to that furnished by the Union Railroad & Transportation Company, and accordingly negotiations were entered into and arrangements made for the purchase of the property, equipment, franchise rights, etc., of that Company for the sum of $3,000,000., payment being made by the issuance of that amount of Common Stock of the Pennsylvania Company at par.

COMPLETION OF BALTIMORE & POTOMAC RAILROAD

On July 2nd, 1872, the Baltimore & Potomac Railroad was, with the exception of the tunnel in Baltimore, completed and placed in service between the latter City and Washington. The tunnel in Baltimore was not completed and opened for traffic until June 29th, 1873, at which time the road from Bowie to Popes Creek, a distance of about 48 miles, was also completed and placed in operation.

LEASE OF BEDFORD & BRIDGEPORT RAILROAD

Effective September 23rd, 1872, the Bedford & Bridgeport Railroad, extending from Mt. Dallas, Pa., which was the terminus of the Huntingdon & Broad Top Mountain Railroad, to the Pennsylvania State Line, a distance of about 38 miles, was leased to the Pennsylvania Railroad Company, to be operated at cost, the surplus, if any, to be turned over to the stockholders of the Bedford & Bridgeport Railroad Company.

PHILADELPHIA & ERIE RAILROAD EARNINGS DISAPPOINTING

The net earnings of the Philadelphia & Erie Railroad were a continued source of disappointment to its owners which was not due to the amount of traffic handled, but the rates it received for transporting the same, the year 1872 ending with a net loss of nearly $38,000. The failure of this road to become profitable was due, first, to the fact that its projectors started with insufficient capital; second, instead of crossing the valuable coal deposits of the Allegheny Mountains via Driftwood, Brookville, Franklin and thence northwardly to Erie, it was constructed north of this rich coal region in order to secure the alleged benefit of two local subscriptions to its stock at Ridgway and Warren; and, third, starting construction work at both ends of the line, when the Company did not have enough capital to execute any great portion of the road at either end. In passing it might be interesting to point out that the lease of this road was only offered to the Pennsylvania Railroad after the Philadelphia & Reading Railroad had declined to take an interest in the property, and when all other plans for raising the capital to complete the line, without a great sacrifice of its Stock, had failed. With all of these adverse influences it was felt that the Philadelphia & Erie Railroad could be made profitable only by the gradual development of its local business, as its through traffic had necessarily to be carried at rates which could not be remunerative, and indeed might be forced lower by the competition of rival lines.

PROPOSED LEASE OF NORTHERN CENTRAL RAILWAY

The Northern Central Railway, in which the Pennsylvania Railroad held a controlling interest, did not earn its dividend in 1872, as the result of the low rates received for the service it rendered, the deficit incurred in paying the dividend being taken from previous surplus profits. To enable that Company to earn a greater return on its Stock, it was necessary to raise large sums of money for the purchase of equipment, and to provide additional facilities to handle the traffic in the most economical manner. It was, therefore, suggested that the capital could best be obtained by a lease of the road to the Pennsylvania Railroad, but this plan was not looked upon with favor by the Management of the latter Company at that time, except as a means of promoting its interest in the Northern Central Railway as the majority stockholder.

LEASE OF CINCINNATI & MUSKINGUM VALLEY RAILWAY

On January 1st, 1873, the Cincinnati & Muskingum Valley Railway Company leased its road to the Pittsburgh, Cincinnati & St. Louis Railway Company for 99 years, the net earnings to be paid to the Cincinnati & Muskingum Valley Railway Company. It was provided that in case the net earnings were not sufficient to meet the interest on the First Mortgage Bonds, the lessee was to advance the amount needed, which was to be returned out of subsequent net earnings. The lease was executed on March 25th, 1873, and the Pittsburgh, Cincinnati & St. Louis Railway Company commenced operating the road on May 1st, 1873.

PURCHASE OF ANTHRACITE COAL LANDS

In the early 70's it was realized that if the Pennsylvania Railroad Company did not follow the example of other roads in the State of Pennsylvania, which were acquiring large tracts of anthracite coal lands, this source of revenue to the Pennsylvania Railroad would be taken away, and the traffic handled by competing roads. The latter were quietly but rapidly securing the best anthracite coal properties, and thus tying the traffic from these mines to their roads. Therefore, in accordance with the laws which had been enacted by the State of Pennsylvania to encourage the development of its natural resources, and to retain some of this coal traffic for its own lines, the Pennsylvania Railroad Company secured control of about 28,000 acres of anthracite coal lands in the vicinity of its lines, as shown by the following statement:—

	Number of Acres
In Wilkes-Barre Coal Region	5,823
In Hazleton Coal Region	2,119
In Shamokin Coal Region	7,808
In Lykens' Valley Coal Region	12,300
Total	28,050

All of these anthracite coal fields had outlets to tide-water over the railroads and canals controlled by the Pennsylvania Railroad Company, and it was contemplated to operate them to an extent that would insure a profit upon the investment in the coal lands and supply a heavy tonnage to these railroads and canals.

AUTHORITY FOR INCREASED STOCK AND DEBT

In order to meet the annual requirements for capital to improve and enlarge the railroads owned and controlled by the Pennsylvania Railroad Company, an Act of Legislature was secured on February 18th, 1873, which authorized an increase of 100% in the Capital Stock of the Company, with the privilege of raising additional funds by the issue of Bonds to an amount equal to the Capital Stock when so increased, which were to be secured by a mortgage of the Company's property. With this authority the Pennsylvania Railroad Company could issue its Capital Stock to the extent of $151,700,000.

CREATION AND SALE OF CONSOLIDATED MORTGAGE BONDS

On July 1st, 1873, when the par value of its Capital Stock outstanding was $65,047,850., the Consolidated Mortgage of the Pennsylvania Railroad Company was created, providing for the issue of $100,000,000. of Bonds thereunder. The principal object of the Management was to create a mortgage that would be comprehensive enough to provide for the issue of successive series of Bonds limited to a fixed total sum, without requiring the creation of a new mortgage as each issue of Bonds thereunder matured. It was made a first lien on the railroad property and rolling stock of the Company, as well as certain after-acquired property, subject, however, to about $35,000,000. of prior lien mortgages. The series of Bonds to be issued could vary in amount; in the rate of interest, which, however, was not to exceed 7%, and at the time of maturity and when one issue became due and was paid, or for any other reason cancelled, the Company could authorize the issue of an equal amount of Bonds to become due at some other fixed time, the only restraint being as to the rate of interest and that the amount of bonds outstanding at any one time could not exceed $100,000,000., nor be in excess of the Capital Stock then outstanding. There were pledged under this mortgage as additional security various Bonds and Stocks owned by the Company having an approximate value of $50,000,000., which, under certain conditions, were subject to substitution or release.

The first and second issues of Consolidated Mortgage Bonds were sold abroad. The first was for £2,000,000, bearing 6% interest, and dated July 1st, 1873. The second was for £3,000,000, bearing the same rate of interest, and dated July 1st, 1874. Both issues matured July 1st, 1905. With Sterling at $4.85 per pound, the principal of these Bonds amounted to $24,250,000. They were sold at a discount which was charged to Profit & Loss. The proceeds from the sale of these Bonds were used largely to acquire securities of affiliated companies, meet the maturity of the General Mortgage Bonds in 1875, and provide funds for capital expenditures consisting principally of equipment purchased in 1873.

These Bonds were sold abroad because of the great financial strain in this Country incident to the panic of 1873 and its aftermath. It was a policy which the Company had adopted as early as 1855 when it began the sale of its Second Mortgage Bonds in England, the principal and interest of which were payable in Sterling. The same course was followed in later years when the American markets were such that its requirements could not be financed on reasonable terms in this Country.

PENNSYLVANIA & DELAWARE RAILROAD COMPLETED

On July 1st, 1873, the Pennsylvania & Delaware Railroad, extending from Pomeroy, on the Main Line of the Pennsylvania Railroad, to Delaware City, Del., a distance of 38 miles, was completed and operated as a branch of the Philadelphia Division.

COMPLETION OF GRAND RAPIDS & INDIANA RAILROAD

On November 25th, 1873, the Grand Rapids & Indiana Railroad was completed and opened for operation from a connection with the Pittsburgh, Fort Wayne & Chicago Railway at Fort Wayne, Ind., to Petoskey, Mich., a distance of about 333 miles. The extension from the latter point to Mackinaw City, Mich., on the Straits of Mackinac, a distance of 34 miles, was completed and placed in operation in July, 1882.

The Grand Rapids & Indiana Railroad Company had completed only 20 miles of its road up to December, 1867, and as it did not have the financial means to proceed further, it made a contract, under date of May 1st, 1869, with the Continental Improvement Company, under which the road was completed as heretofore stated. The Continental Improvement Company was reimbursed through the issuance to it of $8,000,000. First Mortgage 7% Bonds of the Grand Rapids & Indiana Railroad Company and, in addition, $100,000. of its Capital Stock for every 20 miles of road constructed. The latter Company also assigned to the Continental Improvement Company a land grant of over 850,000 acres located north of Grand Rapids, Mich., which had been conferred upon it to assist in constructing its railroad.

Under a contract dated September 30th, 1869, the Pittsburgh, Fort Wayne & Chicago Railway Company guaranteed the principal of, and interest on, $4,000,000. of these First Mortgage Bonds. As a consideration therefor, the Grand Rapids & Indiana Railroad Company agreed to transfer to Trustees named by the Pennsylvania Railroad Company (which had assumed the obligation of the Fort Wayne Company), such amounts of Capital Stock of the Grand Rapids & Indiana Railroad Company as would at all times give these Trustees control of a majority thereof.

WAGES REDUCED

While the financial and industrial depression of 1873 did not affect the earnings of the Pennsylvania Railroad Company as severely as many other railroad and industrial companies, it was found necessary to reduce expenses wherever possible, in consequence of which the wages of every officer and employe of the Company were reduced 10%.

SEMI-ANNUAL DIVIDEND PAID IN SCRIP

The usual cash dividend of 5% was paid by the Pennsylvania Railroad Company in May, 1873, but as the prevailing rates of money during the panic in the latter part of that year were so high—and indeed exorbitant—the Management decided that rather than pass the usual semi-annual dividend in November, as was done in the panic of 1857, it would issue scrip equivalent to a 5% dividend, redeemable in cash in 15 months, with interest at 6%, which met with general approval on the part of the stockholders.

CANAL OPERATIONS

The net profits from the operation of the canal system controlled by the Pennsylvania Railroad in 1873, were $147,580., all of which was invested in canal boats and other equipment, in order to keep the outstanding obligations of these works at as low a figure as possible. The canal system then consisted of the main stem from Columbia to Wilkes-Barre, 151 miles, with a branch from Northumberland to Lock Haven, on the west branch of the Susquehanna River, 71 miles in length, and a branch from the mouth of the Juniata River to Williamsburg, 113 miles (the section from Williamsburg to the terminus at Hollidaysburg having been abandoned), making in all 347 miles of canal, including the Wisconisco feeder, 12 miles in length, purchased from the Wisconisco Canal Company. The controlling interest held by the Pennsylvania Railroad Company in the Pennsylvania Canal Company was represented by 70,231 shares out of a total capitalization of 89,143 shares, 55,000 of which ownership represented the price paid by the Canal Company to the Pennsylvania Railroad Company for the canals which the latter Company purchased from the State of Pennsylvania in 1857.

INVESTMENT IN SOUTHERN RAILWAY SECURITY COMPANY CHARGED OFF

As the investment made by the Pennsylvania Railroad Company beginning in 1871 in the Southern Railway Security Company proved itself of doubtful value, the whole sum was charged to Profit & Loss in 1873, although it was believed that the outlay would in time yield a favorable return and bring traffic of some value to the roads controlled by the Pennsylvania Railroad, for the benefit of which the investment was originally made.

This interest in the Southern Railway Security Company consisted of a one-sixth ownership of its Capital Stock, which had cost $783,000., and an advance of $1,825,000. This money was used to assist in the construction of the Atlanta & Richmond Air Line Railroad from Charlotte, N. C., to Atlanta, Ga., this road having been completed in 1873. The Security Company was an important factor at that time in promoting the construction of railroads in the South, and, with the exception of a few intervening links, with which it had alliances, it controlled three independent routes converging from Richmond, Va., viz:—

First:—Atlantic Coast Route, via Weldon and Wilmington to Charleston, S. C., branching from Florence to Columbia, S. C., and Augusta, Ga., connecting there with the Georgia system of railroads;

Second:—Middle Route via Danville, Greensboro, Charlotte, Atlanta, Montgomery and Mobile, Ala.;

Third:—Interior Route, via Bristol, Knoxville and Chattanooga to Memphis, Tenn., on the Mississippi River.

The Pennsylvania Railroad was able to reach these lines at Richmond, Va., by reason of its control of the Alexandria & Washington and Alexandria & Fredericksburg Railways running from Washington to Quantico, Va., and through traffic arrangements with the Richmond, Fredericksburg & Potomac Railroad extending from the latter point to Richmond, Va.

The Security Company became financially embarrassed in the panic of 1873, and had to dispose of all its interests except in the Atlantic Coast Route. The securities of roads in the Middle Route, consisting principally of the Stock, Bonds and Notes of the Richmond & Danville Railroad Company and the Atlanta & Richmond Air Line Railroad Company, were conveyed to the Pennsylvania Railroad Company in settlement of its claim for $1,825,000. The Security Company again became involved in financial difficulties several years later, and the roads it then controlled finally found their way, to a large extent, into the present Southern Trunk Lines. A controlling interest in the Stock of the Richmond & Danville Railroad Company was of more value than any of the other securities which the Pennsylvania Railroad Company received for its advances. This was retained until 1880 when it was sold for $1,200,000., and it later became a part of the Southern Railway System.

DEATH OF PRESIDENT THOMSON

On May 27th, 1874, John Edgar Thomson, after 47 years of service in the railroad profession, 27 of which were with the Pennsylvania Railroad Company, passed away, and his death brought sorrow and regret not only to his associates in the railroad field, but to all whose privilege it had been to know him.

No one can read the history of his 27 years of service with the Pennsylvania Railroad Company without being profoundly impressed with the remarkable energy, experience and skill of this great central figure in its growth and prosperity, which naturally sustained the greatest loss in his death. Fortunately, however, the period of railroad expansion had temporarily passed, and with the Pennsylvania Railroad and its affiliated lines firmly entrenched in the important industrial centres East of the Mississippi, there was left to his successors the task of operating the property in a manner that would prove satisfactory to the public and profitable to the stockholders.

The following resolutions were adopted by the Board of Directors of the Company on May 29, 1874, in recording the death of President Thomson:—

"*Resolved,* That it be entered upon the minutes of this Corporation—1st, That John Edgar Thomson, its President, died at his residence in Philadelphia, at twenty minutes before twelve o'clock, of the evening of Wednesday, May 27, 1874.

2d, That the association, thus severed by death, began in 1847, within one year after the incorporation of the Company, with his election to the office of Chief Engineer, and the location and construction of its main line of railway, in which his marvelous engineering skill, and the ability with which he discharged important duties, attested his title to rank with the great Civil Engineers of the age.

3d, That it was continued by his election in 1852 to the office of President, which he continued to hold by successive annual re-election until his death, developing the business relations of the Company from feeble beginnings to their present importance, with the breadth of view, an excellence of judgment, a financial sagacity, a profound comprehension of the laws of trade and, above all, a pure, lofty and spotless integrity and dignity of character, which, while they won for him the absolute confidence of the whole country, have entitled him to a place among the foremost of the men whose wisdom, character and public services have so largely contributed to our National growth and prosperity.

Resolved, That in the death of Mr. Thomson, not only this Corporation, but our city, our state and the whole country have lost an eminent public servant and benefactor, whose memory should be always cherished and honored.

Resolved, That we will attend the funeral of our late President, wearing the usual badge of mourning; and that the proper officer of the Company direct every usual and proper mark of respect to be shown Mr. Thomson's memory, in the several departments of the Company's service.

Resolved, That we tender to the family of Mr. Thomson, an expression of our great respect and sincere sympathy, praying that in addition to the comfort derived from the recollection of his public life and services, they may have abundantly those higher consolations which are not of earth.

Resolved, That the Secretary of the Company prepare and furnish to the family of Mr. Thomson, a duly certified copy of these resolutions, and have the same published in the daily journals of this city."

STATISTICAL DATA

It will be interesting to note on the following pages the operating, traffic, and financial statistics of the Pennsylvania Railroad Company during President Thomson's Administration, which will give some idea of its wonderful progress in this period. These figures, however, do not reflect the full extent of the growth, because they cover only the operations of the Pennsylvania Railroad Company and its leased lines East of Pittsburgh and Erie, which embraced 1,574 miles of railroads and canals at the end of 1873. The Company controlled at that time nearly 6,000 miles of railroads and canals, some of which had separate organizations, while others West of Pittsburgh were operated by the Pennsylvania Company. Their operating results were not included with those of the Pennsylvania Railroad Company until they were acquired or leased, or their operation directly assumed by it, which was largely in the period 1900 to 1922, inclusive.

REVENUE, EXPENSES, OPERATING INCOME, AND RENTALS, 1852 TO 1873, INCLUSIVE

All Lines East of Pittsburgh and Erie Directly Operated

Year	Miles	Gross Revenue	Operating Expenses	Operating Income	Rentals Paid	Net Operating Income to Penna. R. R. Co.
1852......	No Record	$1,943,827.81	$1,326,801.94	$617,025.87	....	$617,025.87
1853......	"	2,774,889.37	1,673,681.29	1,101,208.08	....	1,101,208.08
1854......	"	3,512,295.13	2,049,918.53	1,462,376.60	....	1,462,376.60
1855......	"	4,270,015.56	2,440,738.02	1,829,277.54	....	1,829,277.54
1856......	"	4,720,193.71	2,814,567.98	1,905,625.73	....	1,905,625.73
1857......	"	4,855,669.76	3,000,742.90	1,854,926.86	....	1,854,926.86
1858......	"	5,185,330.68	3,021,885.04	2,163,445.64	....	2,163,445.64
1859......	367.	5,362,355.21	3,130,738.15	2,231,617.06	....	2,231,617.06
1860......	367.	5,932,701.48	3,636,299.08	2,296,402.40	....	2,296,402.40
1861......	438.	7,300,000.95	3,653,062.76	3,646,938.19	$128,847.96	3,518,090.23
1862......	645.	10,729,978.57	5,652,412.47	5,077,566.10	260,163.37	4,817,402.73
1863......	716.	12,628,071.31	7,087,651.46	5,540,419.85	380,723.30	5,159,696.55
1864......	797.	15,890,205.64	11,461,741.49	4,428,464.15	540,881.35	3,887,582.80
1865......	856.	19,533,310.28	14,913,969.41	4,619,340.87	848,778.46	3,770,562.41
1866......	887.	19,124,934.63	14,726,484.53	4,398,450.10	1,019,412.25	3,379,037.85
1867......	890.	18,673,916.30	13,941,538.39	4,732,377.91	962,147.80	3,770,230.11
1868......	896.	20,037,747.67	13,697,035.73	6,340,711.94	1,186,647.34	5,154,064.60
1869......	915.	20,513,517.02	14,321,479.55	6,192,037.47	1,341,280.48	4,850,756.99
1870......	927.	20,675,751.53	13,591,878.62	7,083,872.91	947,073.13	6,136,799.78
1871......	1,028.	22,262,100.58	14,296,696.68	7,965,403.90	1,202,040.33	6,763,363.57
1872......	1,530.	36,448,503.36	24,112,901.01	12,335,602.35	4,746,166.08	7,589,436.27
1873......	1,574.	39,983,138.91	26,237,850.05	13,745,288.86	5,117,926.18	8,627,362.68

The statistics in the following statements are available only for the last ten years of President Thomson's Administration, but they indicate a tremendous growth in the traffic of the Pennsylvania Railroad Company during that period:—

TONNAGE, MILEAGE, REVENUE, EXPENSES, AND AVERAGES ON FREIGHT BUSINESS, 1864 TO 1873, INCLUSIVE

All Lines East of Pittsburgh and Erie Operated Directly

Year	Tons	Tons One Mile	Revenue	Average Revenue per Ton per Mile	Expenses	Average Expenses per Ton per Mile	Average Net Revenue per Ton per Mile
				Cents		Cents	Cents
1864*.....	3,189,259	436,591,940	$10,907,036.77	2.498	$8,336,168.69	1.909	0.589
1865......	3,090,681	452,183,478	12,277,490.68	2.715	10,610,867.32	2.347	0.368
1866......	4,001,455	579,839,073	13,453,592.72	2.320	10,625,075.12	1.832	0.488
1867......	4,501,232	646,231,881	13,464,201.69	2.083	9,974,596.36	1.544	0.539
1868......	5,518,729	806,376,652	14,983,779.28	1.858	9,712,567.62	1.204	0.654
1869......	6,294,066	927,714,156	15,439,739.81	1.664	10,602,820.27	1.143	0.521
1870......	7,041,688	1,014,652,970	15,252,314.99	1.503	9,971,625.98	0.983	0.520
1871......	8,404,334	1,244,328,216	16,852,662.82	1.354	10,777,144.98	0.866	0.488
1872......	13,246,456	1,629,613,645	23,797,237.02	1.460	16,181,517.88	0.993	0.467
1873......	15,647,509	1,870,537,537	26,987,820.76	1.443	18,286,725.39	0.978	0.465

* Information not available for prior years.

PASSENGERS, MILEAGE, REVENUE, EXPENSES, AND AVERAGES ON PASSENGER BUSINESS, 1864 TO 1873, INCLUSIVE

All Lines East of Pittsburgh and Erie Operated Directly

Year	Passengers	Passengers One Mile	Revenue	Average Revenue per Passenger per Mile	Expenses	Average Expenses per Passenger per Mile	Average Net Revenue per Passenger per Mile
				Cents		Cents	Cents
1864*.....	2,952,696	163,094,736	$4,357,880.64	2.672	$3,125,572.80	1.916	0.756
1865......	3,611,086	232,019,815	6,376,079.14	2.748	4,303,071.37	1.855	0.893
1866......	3,368,983	162,395,880	4,681,191.66	2.883	4,101,409.41	2.526	0.357
1867......	3,983,028	147,540,084	4,256,343.52	2.885	3,966,942.03	2.689	0.196
1868......	4,376,498	156,632,079	4,241,585.82	2.708	3,984,468.11	2.544	0.164
1869......	4,880,401	169,772,834	4,304,101.45	2.535	3,718,659.28	2.190	0.345
1870......	5,014,924	169,972,984	4,364,481.43	2.568	3,611,554.05	2.125	0.443
1871......	5,384,869	172,678,024	4,483,535.42	2.596	3,504,276.14	2.029	0.567
1872......	13,967,690	361,676,659	9,637,166.69	2.665	6,915,345.64	1.912	0.753
1873......	15,057,153	372,048,475	9,887,634.75	2.658	7,613,540.51	2.046	0.612

* Information not available for prior years.

DIVIDENDS AND ALLOTMENTS ON CAPITAL STOCK—THE PENNSYLVANIA RAILROAD COMPANY

DATE	Capital Stock on which Dividend or Allotment was Declared	DIVIDEND				ALLOTMENTS OF STOCK ON SUBSCRIPTION	
		CASH		SCRIP OR STOCK			
		Per Cent.	Amount	Per Cent.	Amount	Per Cent.	Amount
*May, 1856.	$10,886,004 25	4	$435,440 17				
November, "	10,994,840	4	439,793 60				
May, 1857.	11,372,700	4	454,908				
May, 1858.	11,883,650	3	356,509 50				
November, "	11,962,450	3	358,873 50				
May, 1859.	11,988,867	3	359,666				
November, "	11,997,350	3	359,920 50				
May, 1860.	12,020,650	3	360,619 50				
November, "	12,021,400	3	360,642				
May, 1861.	12,060,800	3	361,824				
November, "	12,057,300	3	361,719				
May, 1862.	13,274,100	4	530,964				
November, "	13,274,100	4	530,964				
May, 1863.	13,363,700	4	534,548				
November, "	13,430,250	5	671,512 50				
May, 1864.	13,848,650	5	692,432 50	30	$4,130,750 00 stock.		
November, "	18,016,600	5	900,830	......	....	10	(At par $1,843,500 00
May, 1865.	19,957,500	5	997,875				
November, "	19,987,800	5	999,390				
May, 1866.	20,000,000	5	1,000,000				
November, "	20,000,000	4	800,000				
May, 1867.	20,000,000	3	600,000	5	1,000,000 00 stock.		
November, "	21,045,750	3	631,372 50				
May, 1868.	21,045,750	3	631,372 50	5	1,051,937 50 stock. October, 1869, $37.50 was redeemed in cash.	25	(At par) 5,102,700 00
November, "	26,578,037 50	5	1,328,901 87				
February, 1869.	26,869,287 50	......	....	......	....	25	(At par) 6,301,000 00
May, "	26,874,687 50	5	1,343,734 37				
November, "	32,725,450	5	1,636,272 50				
May, 1870.	33,500,000	5	1,675,000				
November, "	33,500,000	5	1,675,000				
April, 1871.	34,200,000	......	....	......	....	16⅔	(At par) 5,642,400 00
May, "	34,200,000	5	1,710,000				
November, "	39,541,200	5	1,977,060				
February, 1872.	39,836,550	......	....	......	....	30	(At par) 11,303,050 00
May, "	40,008,650	5	2,000,432 50				
November, "	50,285,750	5	2,514,287 50				
March, 1873.	53,350,550	......	....	......	....	33⅓	(At par) 14,113,350 00
May, "	53,585,000	5	2,679,250				
November, "	66,014,050	......	....	5	3,269,750 00	......	Scrip redeemable in cash in 15 months, with interest at 6 per cent.

*The first payments to the stockholders designated as "dividends" are shown in the Annual Report for 1856 as "Dividends Nos. 1 and 2." The Charter of the Company provided that interest at the rate of 5% per annum was to be estimated and credited on paid-in subscriptions to the Capital Stock of the Company until 100 miles of road had been completed and placed in operation. However, before any interest payments were made, it was realized that a 5% interest rate would not attract subscriptions, and, under date of March 27th, 1848, a supplement to the Charter was secured authorizing the payment of 6% interest on all paid installments until the road was completed. Therefore, beginning with May, 1848, interest at this rate was paid from the date of the payment of the first installment, which was in April, 1847, until November 1st, 1855, the dividend payments in 1856 covering the 14 months from November 1st, 1855, to December 31st, 1856.

DIRECTORS

The following is a list of the Directors who served during President Thomson's Administration, together with the dates of their election and the end of their service:—

Name of Director	*Elected*	*End of Service*
David S. Brown	March 30, 1847,	February 4, 1852;
Geo. W. Carpenter	"	January 6, 1858;
Christian E. Spangler	"	September 19, 1857;
Thomas T. Lea	"	February 4, 1852;
George Howell	December 4, 1848,	March 2, 1857;
William Wilkins	"	February 7, 1853;
Washington Butcher	December 3, 1849,	May 28, 1861;
"	December 27, 1865,	January 8, 1873;
Edward M. Davis	December 3, 1849,	February 12, 1852;
John Yarrow	January 17, 1849,	December 2, 1850;
"	December 18, 1850,	December 18, 1855;
Alexander J. Derbyshire	December 2, 1850,	February 5, 1855;
"	February 26, 1873,	March 26, 1878;
John Edgar Thomson	February 2, 1852,	May 27, 1874;
William Ayres	"	February 6, 1854;
Samuel Jeanes	March 3, 1852,	June 14, 1854;
Edward T. Mott	"	February 5, 1855;
William Robinson, Jr	December 26, 1851,	March 3, 1856;
John Farnum	February 7, 1853,	October 28, 1857;
William R. Thompson	March 1, 1852,	April 3, 1861;
William B. Foster, Jr	May 20, 1853,	March 4, 1860;
William Neal	February 6, 1854,	March 3, 1856;
Thomas Scott	December 27, 1854,	February 5, 1855;
"	February 7, 1855,	March 1, 1858;
Herman Haupt	March 3, 1856,	December 24, 1856;
John H. Bringhurst	"	March 2, 1857;
Josiah Bacon	"	February 3, 1881;
Thomas Mellon	"	March 7, 1864;
William M. Lyon	"	March 1, 1858;
John Robbins, Jr	December 24, 1856,	March 7, 1859;
Samuel Megargee	March 2, 1857,	March 5, 1860;
John G. Brenner	"	March 7, 1859;
John Hulme	October 24, 1857,	March 4, 1867;
Geo. D. Rosengarten	November 25, 1857,	March 21, 1866;
Wistar Morris	January 29, 1858,	March 23, 1891;
Geo. W. Cass	January 5, 1859,	December 27, 1865;
Benjamin T. Curtis	March 7, 1859,	December 4, 1859;
Horatio C. Wood	"	March 5, 1860;
Joseph M. Thomas	"	March 9, 1859;
John M. Kennedy	February 8, 1860,	March 2, 1863;
"	April 6, 1864,	March 5, 1866;
"	April 4, 1866,	February 25, 1880;
William H. Smith	March 5, 1860,	March 6, 1865;
Thomas A. Scott	March 21, 1860,	June 1, 1880;
William Martin	April 4, 1860,	March 4, 1861;
"	March 3, 1862,	October 18, 1862;
J. Craig Miller	"	July 3, 1862;
Edward C. Knight	March 4, 1861,	March 2, 1863;
"	March 7, 1864,	February 25, 1874;

Name of Director	Elected	End of Service
Samuel T. Bodine	February 8, 1860,	March 24, 1874;
Joseph B. Myers	July 3, 1862,	February 26, 1873;
David Salomon	March 2, 1863,	February 3, 1864;
Hugh Craig	"	March 6, 1865;
Sylvester J. Megargee	"	"
Herman Lombaert	May 27, 1863,	January, 1872;
John Rice	March 6, 1865,	March 24, 1874;
John Derbyshire	"	August 23, 1865;
Alexander Nimick	"	April 1, 1868;
Lewis Elkin	December 13, 1865,	March 1, 1869;
"	March 7, 1870,	March 6, 1871;
William Anspach	March 4, 1867,	March 25, 1879;
G. Morrison Coates	"	March 26, 1878;
George Black	April 1, 1868,	August 5, 1872;
Morton McMichael	March 1, 1869,	March 7, 1870;
George B. Roberts	May 3, 1869,	January 30, 1897;
Edmund Smith	"	March 1, 1873;
"	June 29, 1874,	June 30, 1888;
Alexander M. Fox	March 6, 1871,	October 6, 1907;
John Scott	November 2, 1872,	March 26, 1878;
Samuel M. Felton	February 26, 1873,	September 12, 1883;
Alexander Biddle	March 24, 1874,	May 2, 1899;
Henry M. Phillips	"	August 28, 1884;
N. Parker Shortridge	"	January 3, 1915.

THOMAS ALEXANDER SCOTT

FOURTH PRESIDENT, 1874–1880

THOMAS ALEXANDER SCOTT was born on December 28th, 1824, in Franklin County, Pa., and being thrown on his own resources early in life through the death of his father, he secured employment with the State of Pennsylvania as a Clerk on its Public Works at Columbia in 1841, before he was 17 years of age. In 1850 he entered the service of the Pennsylvania Railroad Company as Station Agent at Duncansville, Pa. His ability soon attracted attention and resulted in his promotion in 1852 to the Third Assistant Superintendent in charge of the Western Division of the road at Pittsburgh. The intelligent manner in which he conducted the affairs of this office lessened to a great degree the feeling of animosity toward the Pennsylvania Railroad Company in Pittsburgh, which had arisen because the granting of its charter had for some years prevented the extension of the Baltimore & Ohio Railroad to that City, and this, it was alleged, had delayed the development of the industries and natural resources in the Pittsburgh District. On January 1st, 1858, he was made General Superintendent at Altoona, Pa., which was followed on March 21st, 1860, by his election as a Vice-President, and on June 3rd, 1874, he attained the Presidency. His valuable services to the Government at the time of the Rebellion, when the military rank of Colonel was conferred upon him, and he was appointed Assistant Secretary of War, virtually having entire charge of the transportation of the troops and munitions of war for the Northern Armies, have already been recounted. His unusual executive ability and wide knowledge and experience gained from close association with the late President John Edgar Thomson, admirably fitted him to become the directing head of the vast interests of the Pennsylvania Railroad Company.

THOMAS ALEXANDER SCOTT

Fourth President—June 3rd, 1874, to June 1st, 1880.

FINANCIAL DIFFICULTIES OF ALLEGHENY VALLEY RAILROAD

The Allegheny Valley Railroad Company was again confronted with financial difficulties of a serious nature in 1874, due to the fact that it had no adequate means of providing for its floating indebtedness. The creditors of that Company held a number of meetings and an arrangement was finally perfected by which it created a new mortgage to secure $10,000,000. of 7% Income Bonds, out of which the creditors were to receive at par the amount of indebtedness due them, with interest to October 1st, 1874. To effect this arrangement with the creditors, other than the Pennsylvania Railroad and Philadelphia & Erie Railroad Companies, it became necessary for these two companies and the Northern Central Railway Company to set apart 10% of the revenue derived from the freight traffic to and from the Allegheny Valley Railroad and apply the same to the payment of interest upon the Income Bonds taken by such creditors. The practical effect of this plan was to give to the three foregoing roads 90% of the revenues on all freight traffic to and from the Allegheny Valley Railroad in cash, which yielded a fair profit, and the remaining 10% in Income Bonds of the Allegheny Valley Railroad Company. There was a further condition that if any portion of this 10% was not required to pay said interest, it was to be invested in these Income Bonds at the lowest current market values, each Company receiving the Bonds so purchased in proportion to its traffic contribution.

COMPLETION OF LOW GRADE LINE

The Low Grade Line of the Allegheny Valley Railroad, to which reference has heretofore been made, extending from Red Bank to Driftwood, a distance of 110 miles, and connecting at the latter point with the Philadelphia & Erie Railroad, was completed and opened for traffic on June 1st, 1874.

PENNSYLVANIA COMPANY MINORITY STOCK ACQUIRED

Arrangements were made in 1874 to acquire the $3,000,000. of Common Stock of the Pennsylvania Company, which was issued at par to pay for the property of the Union Railroad & Transportation Company, to which reference has been made, and a plan was adopted providing that the owners of this Stock should receive Bonds of the Pittsburgh, Cincinnati & St. Louis Railway Company in exchange par for par. Nearly all of the stockholders accepted the offer, which when finally consummated would place the entire Capital Stock of the Pennsylvania Company in the Treasury of the Pennsylvania Railroad Company.

IMPARTIAL RATE COMMISSION INEFFECTIVE

In 1874 a meeting of the Officers of the New York Central, Erie and Pennsylvania Railroad Companies was held for the purpose of devising some plan, in the interest of economy, for abolishing commissions, agencies and outside expenses in connection with the solicitation and movement of freight traffic; also with the further object of creating a Commission of three persons familiar with railway traffic, but disinterested and in no way connected with either of the three roads, to have power to make such moderate rates from time to time as would be reasonable and just to the public and give equal and uniform rates to every shipper. This Commission was appointed and for a short time performed its duties promptly and satisfactorily, and with strict impartiality as between the companies interested. While the Baltimore & Ohio Railroad Company did not join in this arrangement, it agreed to abolish all commissions and agencies of every kind, and to adhere to the freight rates made from time to time by its officers.

This plan, however, did not prove effective in stabilizing the rate structure. Early in 1875 the competition for through traffic at unremunerative rates was renewed with vigor, which continued until 1877, when, as the result of co-operative efforts, an arrangement was entered into between the four Trunk Lines whereby the westbound business was divided among them on the basis of the actual volume of traffic which they had handled under open competition. This placed all westbound business on an equal basis, and as the rates then in effect were below the average for the previous five years, the shippers were assured that no attempt would be made by these railroads to exact unreasonable charges as a result of the co-operative plan. The new arrangement was placed under the supervision of Mr. Albert Fink, who was appointed Commissioner for the Trunk Lines, and who had long been connected with important railroads of the Country.

A very interesting description of the struggle which had taken place is contained in the book of Arthur T. Hadley (1885), former President of Yale University, and for many years a student of railroad economics, entitled "Railroad Transportation," from which the following is quoted:—

> "They (the railroads) not only stopped fighting, but they made arrangements to prevent such fighting in future by pools. Trunk-line pools had not been quite unknown; but they had generally been managed by outside parties (eveners), in such a way as to intensify the abuses to which the system was liable. Now the roads took the matter in hand themselves. The division of west-bound traffic was arranged in 1877. The east-bound pooling arrangements were more complicated, owing to the number of initial points of shipment; and it was two years before they could arrange any division at all. Meantime, an association, something like that of the southern roads, had been formed by the trunk lines and their connections, under the title of the Joint Executive Committee. Albert Fink was at its head. It never attained the thoroughness of organization which there has been in the South. There was no clearing-house system, and no means of forming pooling contracts by any central authority—only by the voluntary action of the roads in each individual case."

While the new arrangement brought some measure of stability to the railroad situation, it was not lasting and several years later the struggle began anew with other railroads also entering into it. Meanwhile, public indignation was growing against the granting of privileges and preferences to favored shippers, such as special rates, rebates and other forms of discrimination. The feeling of hostility toward the railroads was also aroused by the alleged over-capitalization and manipulation of railroad securities, all of which finally crystalized itself in the enactment of the Interstate Commerce Act of 1887, to which reference is later made.

EXTENDING PENNSYLVANIA RAILROAD ORGANIZATION OVER SUBSIDIARIES

On December 8th, 1874, James Donald Cameron, after having served as President of the Northern Central Railway Company for many years, tendered his resignation, and as the Pennsylvania Railroad Company owned a controlling interest in the Stock of that Company, it was deemed advisable to have its President act in a similar capacity for the Northern Central Railway Company, and accordingly a reorganization of the official staff was effected on the same date. It also became necessary to revise the organization of the Baltimore & Potomac Railroad Company, in which the Pennsylvania Railroad Company had a majority Stock ownership, and as both lines were important subsidiaries of that Company, it was determined to extend its general working organization over these lines, and thus secure the greatest economy in the operation of the two roads and furnish the best possible service to the public.

JERSEY CITY PASSENGER STATION COMPLETED—HARSIMUS COVE DEVELOPMENTS

The new passenger station of the Company in Jersey City was completed in 1874. At Harsimus Cove in the same city the facilities for receiving and forwarding freight were greatly extended, and the new railroad to connect with the Harsimus Cove property was also opened for use in the same year through a portion of Bergen Hill from its connection with the Main Line of the New York Division.

NO FURTHER EXPANSION—INTERNAL DEVELOPMENT TO BE FUTURE POLICY

In 1874 the Management of the Pennsylvania Railroad Company decided that as it had secured lines and extensive terminal facilities at Philadelphia and New York and, through roads controlled by it, at Baltimore and Washington, in the east; the control of roads to Erie, Ashtabula, Cleveland and Toledo on Lake Erie, with connecting roads working in harmony to Buffalo; the control of lines through the lumber regions of Michigan, and those in the west having termini at Chicago, St. Louis, Louisville, Cincinnati, Wheeling and other important commercial centres, with connections beyond those points; having also perfected communications with the entire oil region of Pennsylvania, the Connellsville coke region, the city of Cumberland and the Cumberland coal region; and with Frederick and Hagerstown in Maryland and Martinsburg in West Virginia, it should adopt a general policy that no further extensions of its lines should be made, or obligations assumed, either by lease or otherwise, excepting to complete such small branches and extensions as were then in progress, and that thereafter the energies of the Management should be devoted to the internal development of the Pennsylvania Railroad System as then constituted.

STOCKHOLDERS' INVESTIGATION COMMITTEE

At the annual meeting of the stockholders of the Pennsylvania Railroad Company on March 10th, 1874, a resolution was passed requesting the Chairman of that meeting, who was Hon. William S. Stokley, then Mayor of Philadelphia, to appoint a Committee of seven stockholders entirely disconnected from the management and operations of the Company, to make an appraisement of the value of the roads, shops, machinery, real estate, depots, bonds, stock, and all other assets of the Company; also, to examine the liabilities and obligations of the Company, including all its guarantees for other lines, with the sources of revenue to meet the same; also its contracts and relations with other Companies and parties of every kind, and to make report to the stockholders of the results of this examination when completed. In accordance with this action the Mayor named as such Stockholders' Committee the following gentlemen, who were all prominently identified with large financial, commercial and manufacturing interests in Philadelphia, and whose knowledge and experience would be of great value in making the investigation contemplated by the resolution. They were:—

William A. Stokes, *Chairman,*
Wm. H. Kemble,
A. Loudon Snowden, *Secretary,*
David E. Small,
John S. Irick,
Wm. C. Longstreth,
John A. Wright.

THE REPORT

This Committee made a most thorough examination of every branch of the Company's service, including all of its financial operations, the obligations it had assumed through leases, contracts, etc., and indeed no Department was overlooked. Their report, which was unanimous, was presented by Colonel Snowden at a special meeting of the stockholders held on October 3rd, 1874, at which meeting it was voted to dispense with reading the report of the Committee on account of its great bulk (240 pages), and the further fact that a copy had been sent to each stockholder. It was suggested, however, that the resolutions attached to the report be taken up and discussed, but before this was done President Scott stated that there had been some delay in the receipt of copies of the report by European stockholders, who had cabled him asking that its consideration be delayed until the next annual meeting of the Company in March, 1875, which was agreed to by the meeting and a resolution passed to make this action effective. A resolution, however, was passed accepting the report of the Committee, and tendering the thanks of the stockholders to them for the ability, care and fidelity which they had exercised in preparing their full and comprehensive report. It took the Committee seven months to make their investigation and report, and the Management stated that it was considered by experts, both in this Country and Europe, to be one of the most exhaustive and valuable documents ever prepared in connection with any railroad company.

A part of the Investigating Committee's Report consists of tables of earnings and expenses and other financial statements, some of which can readily be omitted. However, there are portions of it so interesting that they have been condensed into as few pages as possible, consistent with giving an intelligent idea of the scope of the work undertaken by the Committee, and as fully describing the Pennsylvania Railroad and its interests at that time.

SECURITIES OWNED

The Committee suggested some alterations and reductions in the book value of securities owned by the Company, and there was incorporated in its report the following list of Stocks and Bonds owned on December 31st, 1873, showing their par value and the Committee's estimate of their cash value per share and per bond, with the totals:—

LIST OF STOCKS OWNED BY THE PENNSYLVANIA RAILROAD ON DECEMBER 31st, 1873

Number of Shares	Name of Security	Par Value Per Share	Cash Value Per Share	Total Cash Value
41,500	Allegheny Valley R. R. Co	$50.	$10.00	$415,000.
4,000	American Steamship Co	100.	20.00	80,000.
3,682	Bald Eagle Valley R. R. Co	50.	50.00	184,100.
36,572	Baltimore & Potomac R. R. Co	50.	1.00	36,572.
6,179	Bedford & Bridgeport R. R. Co	50.	1.00	6,179.
6,500	Chartiers Railway Co	50.	10.00	65,000.
22,000	Cleveland, Mt. Vernon & Delaware R. R. Co., common	50.	1.00	22,000.
5,802	Cleveland, Mt. Vernon & Delaware R. R. Co., preferred	50.	40.00	232,080.
25,547	Connecting Railway Co., 6% guaranteed	50.	50.00	1,277,350.
5,286	Cresson Springs Co	25.	....	50,000.
4,744	Cumberland Valley R. R. Co., preferred	50.	60.00	284,640.
19,516	Cumberland Valley R. R. Co., common	50.	60.00	1,170,960.
15,251	Harrisburg & Lancaster R. R	50.	50.00	762,550.
1,130	Junction R. R. Co	50.	50.00	56,500.
19,217	Jeffersonville, Madison & Indianapolis R. R Co	100.	85.50	1,643,054.
5,624	Little Miami R. R. Co	50.	50.00	281,200.
374	Lewistown & Tuscarora Bridge Co	20.	2.00	748.
3,759	Louisville Bridge Co	100.	100.00	375,900.
6,040	Lykens Valley Coal Co	50.	....	395,765.
7,200	Newport & Cincinnati Bridge Co	100.	7.50	54,000.
250	New Jersey Stock-Yard & Market Co	100.	80.00	20,000.
48,420	Northern Central Railway Co	50.	40.00	1,936,800.
70,231	Pennsylvania Canal Co	50.	15.00	1,053,465.
160,000	Pennsylvania Company, preferred	50.	50.00	8,000,000.
40,984	Pennsylvania R. R. Co	50.	50.00	2,049,200.
6,798	Pennsylvania Steel Co	100.	75.00	509,850.
31,636	Philadelphia & Erie R. R., common	50.	....	....

LIST OF STOCKS OWNED BY THE PENNSYLVANIA RAILROAD ON DECEMBER 31st, 1873
—Continued

Number of Shares	*Name of Security*	*Par Value Per Share*	*Cash Value Per Share*	*Total Cash Value*
48,000	Philadelphia & Erie R. R., preferred	$50.	$10.00	$480,000.
250	Philadelphia & Merion R. R., one installment only paid		5.00	1,250.
80	Philadelphia & Southern Mail Steamship Co	125.	37.50	3,000.
60,000	Pittsburgh, Cincinnati & St. Louis Railway Co., preferred	50.	....	....
12,800	Pittsburgh, Ft. Wayne & Chicago Ry. Co., special 7% guaranteed	100.	90.00	1,152,000.
51	Pittsburgh, Ft. Wayne & Chicago Ry. Co., common	100.	85.00	4,335.
8,100	Pittsbg., Virginia & Charleston Ry. Co	50.	40.00	324,000.
1,233	Pullman Palace Car Co	100.	100.00	123,300.
39,263	Shamokin Coal Company	25.	10.00	392,630.
5,500	South West Pennsylvania R. R. Co	50.	37.50	206,250.
25,048	Summit Branch R. R. Co	50.	45.00	1,127,160.
10,000	Susquehanna Coal Co	100.	100.00	1,000,000.
10,176	Tyrone & Clearfield R. R. Co	50.	50.00	508,800.
2,498	West Chester & Philadelphia R. R. Co., preferred	50.	50.00	124,900.
19,453	Western Pennsylvania R. R. Co	50.	50.00	972,650.
1,551	West Jersey R. R. Co., second and third installments	50.	50.00	54,285.
6,341	Wrightsville, York & Gettysburg R. R. Co	50.	....	170,541.
	Total			$27,608,014.

LIST OF BONDS OWNED BY THE PENNSYLVANIA RAILROAD COMPANY ON DECEMBER 31st, 1873

Par	*Name of Security*	*Value (Per Cent.)*	*Total Cash Value*
$8,500.	Allegheny County—" Penna. R. R. Loan " 6%	100	$8,500.
2,000.	Allegheny County bonds, " P. & S. loan " 6%	75	1,500.
512,000.	Alexandria and Fredericksburg Ry. Co. 1st Mtge. bonds, 7%	70	358,400.
3,959,000.	Allegheny Valley R. R. 1st Mtge. 7% Bonds	85	3,365,150.
29,100.	Bald Eagle Valley R. R. 1st Mtge. 6% Bonds	85	24,735.
100,000.	Bald Eagle Valley R. R. 2nd Mtge. 7% bonds	90	90,000.
1,000,000.	Bedford & Bridgeport R. R. 1st Mtge. 7% Bonds	80	800,000.
300,000.	Central Stock Yard & Transit Company 7% Bonds	90	270,000.
50,000.	City of Altoona " Water loan " 7 3/10% Bonds	90	45,000.
4,600.	City of Harrisburg " Water loan " 6% Bonds	90	4,140.
752,000.	Cincinnati & Muskingum Valley R. R. 1st Mtge. 7% Bonds	70	526,400.
1,000,000.	Columbia & Port Deposit R. R. Bonds	60	600,000.
1,258,000.	Columbus, Chicago & Indiana Central Ry. Co., 2nd Mtge., $5,000,000. loan 7% Bonds	70	880,600.
3,504,000.	Columbus, Chicago & Indiana Central Ry. Co. $10,000,000. loan, 7% Income Bonds	50	1,752,000.
15,000.	County of Clark, Illinois, 8% Bonds	75	11,250.
264,000.	Danville, Hazelton and Wilkesbarre R. R. 1st Mtge. 7% Bonds	60	158,400.
112,900.	East Brandywine & Waynesburg R. R., 1st Mtge. 7% Bonds	75	84,675.
3,600.	East Brandywine & Waynesburg R. R., New Holland Extension	75	2,700.
100,000.	Erie & Pittsburgh R. R., 7% Bonds	80	80,000.
20,000.	Holliday's Cove R. R., 2nd Mtge. 7% Bonds	100	20,000.
19,000.	Huntingdon & Broad Top R. R. & Coal Company consolidated Mortgage bonds	40	7,600.
440,000.	Indianapolis & St. Louis R. R. 1st Mtge. 7% Bonds	90	396,000.
50,000.	Indianapolis & St. Louis R. R. equipment Bonds	90	45,000.
350,000.	International Navigation Co. 1st Mtge. Bonds	90	315,000.
271,000.	Jersey City & Bergen R. R. 1st Mtge. 7% Bonds	90	243,900.
9,000.	Lawrence R. R. 1st Mtge. Bonds	90	8,100.
1,500,000.	Lewisburg, Centre & Spruce Creek R. R. 1st Mtge. 7% Bonds	75	1,125,000.
200,000.	Mifflin & Centre County R. R. 1st Mtge. 6% Bonds	50	100,000.

LIST OF BONDS OWNED BY THE PENNSYLVANIA RAILROAD COMPANY ON DECEMBER 31st, 1873
—Continued

Par	*Name of Security*	*Value (Per Cent.)*	*Total Cash Value*
$1,200,000.	Newport & Cincinnati Bridge bonds	85	$1,020,000.
1,000,000.	Northern Central Ry. Co. 7% Income Bonds convertible	85	850,000.
2,000.	Ohio & Pennsylvania Bridge 7% bonds	100	2,000.
18,000.	Pennsylvania Canal Bonds	60	10,800.
3,111,000.	Pennsylvania Company 1st Mortgage 7% Bonds	85	2,644,350.
3,000.	Pennsylvania R. R. 1st mortgage bonds	100	3,000.
1,000.	Pennsylvania R. R. 2nd mortgage bonds	100	1,000.
1,000.	Philadelphia & Erie R. R. 6% bonds currency	80	800.
729,000.	Philadelphia & Erie R. R. 6% bonds	80	583,200.
1,029,000.	Pittsburgh, Cincinnati & St. Louis Ry. consolidated mortgage bonds	65	668,850.
500,000.	Pittsburgh, Virginia & Charleston Ry. 7% Bonds	80	400,000.
770,000.	Pullman Palace Car 8% Bonds	100	770,000.
1,024,000.	Shamokin Valley & Pottsville R. R. 6% Bonds	90	921,600.
6,000.	South Mountain Iron Company bonds	75	4,500.
278,000.	Steubenville & Indiana R. R. 7% bonds	75	208,500.
5,000.	St. Louis & Iron Mountain Ry. 7% Bonds	75	3,750.
225,000.	St. Louis, Vandalia & Terre Haute R. R. 2nd Mortgage convertible Bonds	70	157,500.
700,000.	St. Louis, Vandalia & Terre Haute R. R. 7% Income Bonds	50	350,000.
900,000.	Toledo, Tiffin & Eastern R. R. 7% Bonds	70	630,000.
292,500.	Warren & Franklin R. R. 1st mtge. 7% Bonds	75	219,375.
1,200,000.	Western Pennsylvania R. R. General Mtge. 7% Bonds	90	1,080,000.
10,000.	Western Pennsylvania R. R. 1st Mtge. 6% Bonds	85	8,500.
148,000.	Western Pennsylvania R. R. 6% Branch Bonds Western Pennsylvania R. R. 6% Branch Bonds Western Pennsylvania R. R. 6% Branch Bonds	85	125,800.
15,000.	West Chester & Philadelphia R. R. 1st Mtge. 7% Bonds	100	15,000.
52,000.	Wrightsville, York & Gettysburg R. R. 6% Bonds	100	52,000.
$29,053,200.	Total		$22,054,575.

VALUATIONS PLACED ON SECURITIES

The par value of the Stocks owned was $44,541,240. and Bonds, $29,053,200., or a total of $73,594,440. They were purchased by the Company for the sum of $52,692,419.09, and the Committee placed a cash value on them of $49,662,589., or nearly $3,000,000. below their cost. It should be recalled, however, that this valuation was made shortly after the panic of 1873. A very large part of this reduction was made in the value of the Stocks of the Allegheny Valley Railroad, Philadelphia & Erie Railroad, Pittsburgh, Cincinnati & St. Louis Railway and Baltimore & Potomac Railroad Companies.

ALLEGHENY VALLEY RAILROAD

The 41,500 shares of Allegheny Valley Railroad Stock were carried at cost, viz: $1,100,000., but as a result of the financial difficulties encountered by that Company in the early part of 1874, the Committee stated that the Stock had practically no market value. However, it was felt that it was worth at least $10. per share for the control it gave to the Pennsylvania Railroad Company of that road, and the possibility of a future growth in the territory it served. Therefore, the Committee's estimate of the value of the Company's holdings of this Stock was $415,000.

PHILADELPHIA & ERIE RAILROAD

The ownership in the Philadelphia & Erie Railroad Common Stock consisted of 31,636 shares, purchased at a cost of $779,637.26, and 48,000 shares of the Preferred Special Stock, for which $1,680,000. was paid, or a total investment of $2,459,637.26. The opinion of the Committee was that the Common Stock was valueless, as the road was worth little more than its Bonded debt. It was felt that the Preferred Stock might have some future value, dependent upon the development of the country served by the Philadelphia & Erie Railroad, which, together with the fact that it represented control of the property, led the Committee to give the Preferred Stock a value of $10. per share, or a total of $480,000. for an investment originally costing $2,459,637.26.

PITTSBURGH, CINCINNATI & ST. LOUIS RAILWAY

The cost of the 60,000 shares of Pittsburgh, Cincinnati & St. Louis Railway Second Preferred Stock, namely, $2,250,000., was recommended to be charged off and estimated as lost, as the First Mortgage Consolidated Bonds of that Company were then selling at 65%. The Committee stated that the Second Mortgage Bonds, of which there were $5,000,000., and the First Preferred Stock, had practically no value, and, therefore, the Second Preferred Stock could not be estimated to be worth anything, as its future value depended entirely on the growth of the territory in which that road and its leased lines were located.

BALTIMORE & POTOMAC RAILROAD

The Pennsylvania Railroad Company was also the owner of 36,572 shares of the Capital Stock of the Baltimore & Potomac Railroad Company, which had cost it $876,880., and on which the Committee placed a nominal value of $1. per share. The entire receipts of that road in 1873 were, it was stated, only $381,536.73, and its net earnings $69.93, so that for a number of years it could not be expected to do anything more than pay the interest on its $4,500,000. of 6% Mortgage Bonds. It was pointed out that the entire business of the well established Baltimore & Ohio Railroad between Baltimore and Washington had not reached $500,000. in any one year since the termination of the Civil War.

MANAGEMENT CONDEMNED

The Committee condemned the Management for making what had proven a wasteful outlay of money in financing the needs of companies whose prospects were anything but inviting, especially in the case of the Philadelphia & Erie Railroad, where the Pennsylvania Railroad Company had assumed the double position of landlord and tenant—of landlord in owning so large an interest in the stock of that Company, and of tenant in advancing money to the landlord without adequate security.

GUARANTEES EAST AND WEST OF PITTSBURGH

A whole chapter is devoted by the Committee to the liabilities of the Pennsylvania Railroad Company as endorser, guarantor, lessee or otherwise, with the result of these liabilities in 1873 and an estimate of probable future claims on account of endorsements, etc. The following is a list at that time of the liabilities of the Pennsylvania Railroad Company as endorser or guarantor on the Bonds of other companies East of Pittsburgh:—

EAST OF PITTSBURGH

Principal and Interest Guaranteed

Western Pennsylvania Railroad	$1,158,600.
Connecting Railway	991,000.
Philadelphia & Erie Railroad	10,000,000.
Chartiers Railway	475,000.
Susquehanna Coal Company	1,300,000.
Allegheny Valley Low Grade	9,059,000.
*Allegheny Valley Low Grade	3,500,000.
American Steamship Company	1,500,000.
Pittsburgh, Virginia & Charleston Ry.	700,000.
Baltimore & Potomac Railroad	3,000,000.
†Baltimore & Potomac Tunnel Bonds	1,500,000.
‡Junction Railroad	800,000.
Total amount of bonds, the principal and interest of which are guaranteed	$33,983,600.
Pennsylvania Canal Company,—Interest amounting to $180,000. guaranteed on the $3,000,000. of bonds, but not the principal.	

* Northern Central Ry. and Philadelphia & Erie R. R. Cos. co-guarantors with Pennsylvania R. R. Co.

† Northern Central Ry. Co. co-guarantor with Pennsylvania R. R. Co.

‡ Philadelphia, Wilmington & Baltimore R. R. and Philadelphia & Reading Ry. Co. co-guarantors with Pennsylvania R. R. Co.

WEST OF PITTSBURGH

The following is a statement of the annual liabilities of the Pennsylvania Railroad Company as guarantor for and on account of companies West of Pittsburgh:—

Pittsburgh, Ft. Wayne & Chicago Ry. Co., Total annual rental		$2,617,177.24
Also the following in connection with the lease of above road:		
New Castle & Beaver Valley R. R., Leased for forty per cent. of Gross Earnings, Minimum Rental		140,435.79
Lawrence R. R., Leased for forty per cent. of Gross Earnings, Minimum Rental		75,752.96
Indianapolis & St. Louis R. R., Interest on Debt—		
7% on $3,000,000	$210,000.	
8% on 500,000	40,000.	
One third of minimum Rental of St. Louis, Alton & Terre Haute R. R.	150,000.	
		400,000.00
Grand Rapids & Indiana R. R., Interest on one-half of debt, seven per cent. on $4,000,000. (Gold)		280,000.00
Total liabilities in connection with lease of Pittsburgh, Ft. Wayne & Chicago Ry. Co		$3,513,365.99
Cleveland & Pittsburgh Railroad, Total Annual Rental		1,226,834.47
Erie & Pittsburgh Railroad, Total Annual Rental		380,626.00
Jeffersonville, Madison & Indianapolis Railroad, Total Annual Rental		532,651.70
Little Miami Railroad, Total Annual Rental		723,908.80
Columbus, Chicago & Indiana Central Ry.—Leased for thirty per cent. of gross earnings (but interest at 7% guaranteed on $15,821,000. of debt secured by first mortgages) as shown for 1873		1,343,342.05
St. Louis, Vandalia & Terre Haute Railroad—Leased by Terre Haute & Indianapolis R. R., but Pittsburgh, Cincinnati & St. Louis Ry. is obliged to pay four-fifths of interest on mortgage debt, which is		252,000.00
Newport & Cincinnati Bridge—Guarantee of one-half of $75,000		37,500.00
Indianapolis & Vincennes R. R.—Interest on mortgage debt		206,000.00
Total		$8,216,229.01

The following statement shows the annual liabilities of Pennsylvania Railroad Company as of December 31st, 1873, under leases of roads East of Pittsburgh and Erie; also on account of guarantees on Bonds of leased and controlled companies East of Pittsburgh:—

Western Pennsylvania Railroad—Leased by Pennsylvania R. R. Co. to be operated at cost, balance of receipts turned over to lessor; Pennsylvania R. R. Co. guarantees principal and interest of $800,000. first mortgage main line six per cent. bonds........................	$48,000.	
Also principal and interest of $358,600. first mortgage Pittsburgh Branch six per cent. bonds....	21,600.	
		$69,600.00
Connecting Railway—Leased by Philadelphia & Trenton R. R. Co. at annual rental of six per cent. on its bonds and stock, which amounts to $142,965.90, which sum is included in rental of United Railroads of New Jersey. Pennsylvania R. R. Co. guarantees principal and interest of $991,000. first mortgage six per cent. bonds..........		59,460.00
United Railroads and Canal Company of New Jersey, Leased by Pennsylvania R. R. Co. at annual rental, which amounted in 1873 to.........................		3,117,020.24
Bald Eagle Valley Railroad—Leased by Pennsylvania R. R. Co., which pays lessor forty per cent. of gross receipts, after deducting tonnage taxes......................		
Bedford & Bridgeport Railroad—Leased by Pennsylvania R. R. Co. to be operated at cost, balance of receipts turned over to lessor..		
Danville, Hazleton & Wilkes-Barre Railroad—Leased by Pennsylvania R. R. Co. to be operated at cost, balance of receipts applied to payment of coupons on $1,400,000. bonds; if not sufficient Pennsylvania R. R. Co. purchases coupons and holds them against mortgage; Pennsylvania R. R. Co. guarantees to purchase coupons, seven per cent. on $1,400,000......................................		98,000.00
East Brandywine & Waynesburg Railroad—Leased by Pennsylvania R. R. Co., paying to lessor not less than thirty-three and one-third per cent. of gross earnings to meet interest on bonds..............................		
Ebensburg & Cresson Railroad—Leased by Pennsylvania R. R. Co. to be operated at cost, balance of receipts applied to paying interest on $80,000. mortgage bonds, if sufficient; if not, then pro rata.		
Harrisburg, Portsmouth, Mt. Joy & Lancaster R. R.—Leased by Pennsylvania R. R. Co., rental being six per cent. on bonds, seven per cent. on stock, taxes and organization, or a total of..........................		132,651.46
Lewisburg, Centre & Spruce Creek Railroad—Leased by Pennsylvania R. R. Co. to be operated at cost, balance of gross earnings being devoted to paying interest on bonded debt..		
Mifflin & Centre County Railroad—Leased by Pennsylvania R. R. Co. to be operated at cost, balance of gross receipts being applied to rent ($330.) of Tuscarora Bridge, and to payment of interest on $100,000. Mortgage Bonds, if sufficient; if not, then pro rata.		
Newry Railroad—Leased by Pennsylvania R. R. Co. to be operated at cost; balance applied to paying cost of completion of road and appurtenances,		
Sunbury & Lewistown Railroad—Leased by Pennsylvania R. R. Co. to be operated at cost, paying surplus over to lessor,		

Tyrone & Clearfield Railroad—Leased by Pennsylvania R. R. Co. to be operated at cost, paying surplus over to lessor.

South West Pennsylvania Railroad—Leased by Pennsylvania R. R. Co. to be operated at cost, paying balance over to lessor.

Pennsylvania & Delaware Railroad—Leased by Pennsylvania R. R. Co. to be operated at cost, paying balance over to lessor.

Philadelphia & Erie Railroad—Leased by Pennsylvania R. R. Co. to be operated at cost, balance being devoted to organization, interest on bonds, sinking fund under one of the mortgages, then surplus to lessor, after deducting moneys loaned and advances made by lessee; Pennsylvania R. R. Co. guarantees principal and interest of following issues of said road:

Six per cent. on $2,000,000. Bonds.........	$120,000.	
Six per cent. on 3,000,000. Sterling Bonds..	180,000	
Six per cent. on 5,000,000. Gold Bonds....	300,000.	
		$600,000.00
Chartiers Railway—Leased by Pittsburgh, Cincinnati & St. Louis Ry. for what it costs to operate, paying balance to lessor, Pennsylvania R. R. Co. guarantees principal and interest of $475,000. first mortgage seven per cent. bonds..		33,250.00
Pennsylvania Canal Co.—Pennsylvania R. R. Co. guarantees interest on first and general mortgage bonds, amounting to $3,000,000. at six per cent.....................		180,000.00
Allegheny Valley Railroad—Pennsylvania R. R. Co. guarantees principal and interest of $9,059,000. first mortgage "low grade" seven per cent. bonds..........................	$634,130.	
also $3,500,000. second mortgage "low grade" five per cent. bonds—Northern Central Ry. and Philadelphia & Erie R. R. Cos. joining in this guarantee..............................	175,000.	
		809,130.00
Susquehanna Coal Company—Pennsylvania R. R. Co. guarantees principal and interest of $1,300,000. six per cent. bonds....................................		78,000.00
American Steamship Co.—Pennsylvania R. R. Co. guarantees principal and interest of $1,500,000. of six per cent. bonds..		90,000.00
Pittsburgh, Virginia & Charleston Ry.—Pennsylvania R. R. Co. guarantees principal and interest of $700,000. first mortgage seven per cent. gold bonds.................		49,000.00
Baltimore & Potomac R. R.—Pennsylvania R. R. Co. guarantees principal and interest of $1,500,000. "Tunnel Bonds" at six per cent. gold..	$90,000.	
also $3,000,000. "Main Line Bonds" at six per cent. gold..............................	180,000.	
		270,000.00

(the latter in connection with Northern Central Ry. Co.)

Junction Railroad—Pennsylvania R. R. Co., Philadelphia, Wilmington & Baltimore R. R. Co. and Philadelphia & Reading R. R. Co. guarantee principal and interest on $500,000. first mortgage six per cent. bonds, or	$30,000.	
$300,000. second mortgage six per cent. bonds	18,000.	
		$48,000.00
Grand Total, Lines East		$5,634,111.70

FIXED RENTAL ROADS

In examining the foregoing it will be observed that there are two different kinds of leases, in addition to guarantees, the first, wherein the Pennsylvania Railroad Company agreed to operate the road at cost and turn over to the lessor all surplus profits, and not obligating itself to pay more, and they formed no part of the liabilities of the Company; the second—and most important—are those leases which obligated the Pennsylvania Railroad Company to pay an annual fixed rental, and for the lines East and West of Pittsburgh they were as follows:—

Name of Road	*Yearly Guaranteed Rental*
United Railroads and Canal Co. of New Jersey	$3,117,020.24
Harrisburg, Portsmouth, Mt. Joy & Lancaster R. R. Co.	132,651.46
Pittsburgh, Ft. Wayne & Chicago Ry. Co	2,617,177.24
New Castle & Beaver Valley	140,435.79
Lawrence Railroad	75,752.96
Erie & Pittsburgh	380,626.00
Cleveland & Pittsburgh	1,337,353.51
Jeffersonville, Madison & Indianapolis	535,235.60
Indianapolis and Vincennes	206,000.00
Indianapolis & St. Louis	707,065.46
Columbus, Chicago & Indiana Central	1,343,342.05
Little Miami	710,769.94
St. Louis, Vandalia & Terre Haute	271,395.16
Chartiers Railway	35,000.00
Total Rentals Guaranteed	$11,609,825.41

SYSTEM DIVIDED

The next chapter of the Committee's report was directed to an inquiry into the policy, groups and results of operating the railways and canals owned or controlled by the Pennsylvania Railroad Company. To facilitate the investigation the lines were divided into the Eastern and Western Groups.

The Eastern section included the roads and canals East of Pittsburgh and Erie, and for convenience the interests held South of Baltimore and as far West as Cairo, Ill. The Western Group consisted of the lines West of Pittsburgh, which were subdivided into the Fort Wayne or Northern System, and the Pittsburgh, Cincinnati & St. Louis Railway or Southern System.

WESTERN GROUP

In considering the Western Group the Committee first discussed the reasons for incorporating the Pennsylvania Company, which have already been stated, namely, to use it as a medium for a harmonious and efficient working organization, and to secure a centralization of management for the Lines West of Pittsburgh, which were either owned by or under lease to the Pennsylvania Railroad Company.

PENNSYLVANIA COMPANY

The Committee stated that the Pennsylvania Company was incorporated with a Capital Stock of $11,360,900., of which $8,000,000. was owned by the Pennsylvania Railroad Company, $3,000,000. was used to purchase the Stock of the Union Railroad & Transportation Company (so-called "Union Line"), and $360,900. held by various individuals. Attention was called to the unfortunate transaction by which this $3,000,000. of Pennsylvania Company Common Stock was used for this purpose. It was not felt that an excessive price had been paid, but it meant the introduction of stockholders in the Pennsylvania Company whose views as to the management of its affairs might not always accord with those of the majority stockholder, the Pennsylvania Railroad Company. The latter Company, however, had reacquired this Stock during the course of the Committee's investigation.

NORTHERN SYSTEM

The following is a list of the roads in the Fort Wayne, or Northern System, directly managed or coming under the control of the Pennsylvania Company:—

Pittsburgh, Ft. Wayne & Chicago Ry., Pittsburgh to Chicago		468.3 miles
And under this Company—		
New Castle & Beaver Valley R. R.	14.9 miles	
Lawrence Railroad	20.4 "	
		35.3 "
Erie & Pittsburgh R. R., Extending from a point on New Castle & Beaver Valley R. R. to Girard on Lake Shore R. R.	84 miles	
Branch at Erie	2 "	
		86.0 "
Cleveland & Pittsburgh R. R., extending from Rochester, Pa., by way of Wellsville, O., to Bridgeport and Cleveland, with other branches		202.0 "
Ashtabula, Youngstown and Pittsburgh R.R., Youngstown to Ashtabula		62.5 "
Mansfield, Coldwater & Lake Michigan R. R., was to extend from Mansfield Jc., on Pittsburgh, Ft. Wayne & Chicago Ry., to Allegan, Mich., 216 miles; total track laid on this road at end of 1873		85.5 "
Tiffin, Toledo & Eastern R. R.	24 miles	
Toledo & Woodville R. R., leased by Tiffin, Toledo & Eastern R. R.	18 "	
		42.0 "
Total		981.6 miles

With the lease of the Pittsburgh, Ft. Wayne & Chicago Railway there was also conveyed a contract with the Indianapolis & St. Louis Railroad, by which the Pennsylvania Railroad Company acquired a one-half interest in this line, being the north section of railroad between Indianapolis and St. Louis, which, with a branch four miles long to Alton, had an aggregate mileage of............................265 miles

Pennsylvania Company leased the Jeffersonville, Madison & Indianapolis Railroad, with the guarantees of the Pennsylvania Railroad Company.		
This line extended from Indianapolis to Louisville	110 miles	
Madison to Columbus, Indiana	45 "	
Columbus, Ind., to Cambridge, Ind.	65 "	
		220 "
Pennsylvania Company controlled Indianapolis & Vincennes R. R. by ownership of majority of stock and by paying interest on funded debt, which road was built between Indianapolis and Vincennes		117 "
		602 miles
Which with the Fort Wayne, or Northern System, aggregating		981.6 "
Made the total length of road operated by Pennsylvania Company		1,583.6 miles

SOUTHERN SYSTEM

The lines embraced in the Pittsburgh, Cincinnati & St. Louis Railway, or Southern System, were then shown. The Pennsylvania Company owned a majority of the stock of that Company, which, it was stated, involved no liability on its part other than a loss on the investment, which risk was also taken by the other stockholders in the Pittsburgh, Cincinnati & St. Louis Railway Company. Its owned and leased roads were as follows:—

Road	Miles	Total
Pittsburgh, Cincinnati & St. Louis Ry., extending from Pittsburgh to Columbus:		
Consisting of—		
Section of road between Pittsburgh Union Depot and Washington Turnpike Gate, owned by Pennsylvania Railroad Company, and leased to Pennsylvania Company	1.1 miles	
Steubenville to Newark (Pittsburgh, Cincinnati & St. Louis Proper)	158.9 "	
Newark to Columbus (Jointly owned with Baltimore & Ohio R. R.)	33. "	
Cadiz Branch, built by Springfield & Northwestern Railroad	8. "	
		201 miles
Chartiers Railway, leased to Pittsburgh, Cincinnati & St. Louis Ry. and worked at cost		22.8 "
Cincinnati & Muskingum Valley Railroad, leased to Pittsburgh, Cincinnati & St. Louis Railway, but worked at cost		148.4 "
Little Miami Railroad, leased to Pittsburgh, Cincinnati & St. Louis Ry., and consisting of Cincinnati & Springfield R. R., Dayton & Xenia R. R., Dayton & Richmond R. R. and Columbus & Xenia R. R., in all		196.7 "
Columbus, Chicago & Indiana Central Ry., extending from Columbus to Chicago, through Richmond, Ind., and from Richmond to Indianapolis, and from Bradford Junction to near Logansport, and from Logansport to State Line, Illinois, the whole road also being leased to P., C. & St. L. Ry		581.1 "
		1,150. miles

COMBINED MILEAGE AND CAPITALIZATION—NORTHERN AND SOUTHERN SYSTEMS

The Committee combined the mileage of roads embraced in the Fort Wayne, or Northern System, including the roads leased or controlled directly by the Pennsylvania Company, and those in the Pittsburgh, Cincinnati & St. Louis Railway, or Southern System, the result being given in a statement showing not only the mileage but the total capitalization. There was included in this statement the St. Louis, Vandalia & Terre Haute Railroad, which was almost wholly owned by the Pennsylvania Company, and was operated under a lease by the Terre Haute & Indianapolis Railway Company; also the Cleveland, Mt. Vernon & Delaware Railroad, which was likewise controlled in the interests of Pennsylvania Railroad Company, through the ownership of the majority of its Capital Stock. This road extended from Hudson, O., through Orrville, Millersburg and Mt. Vernon, to Columbus, with a branch to Massillon, a distance of 144 miles. It was also proposed to build a branch of this road from Millersburg to Dresden, O., on the Pittsburgh, Cincinnati & St. Louis Railway, connecting there with the Muskingum Valley Railroad. The statement follows:—

	Length of Roads	*Capitalization*
Northern System	1,583.6 miles	$83,371,901.57
Southern System	1,150.0 "	77,732,383.03
St. Louis, Vandalia & Terre Haute R. R.	168.0 "	8,127,337.49
Cleveland, Mt. Vernon & Delaware R. R.	144.0 "	4,225,435.00
Totals	3,045.6 miles	$173,457,057.09

The Pennsylvania Railroad Company in addition held a majority of the Stock and Bonds of the Newport & Cincinnati Bridge Company, which owned the bridge over the Ohio River at Cincinnati. It was also interested to the extent of holding $375,900. of Capital Stock of the Jeffersonville & Louisville Bridge Company, owners of the bridge over the Ohio River at Louisville, Ky.

OPERATIONS OF WESTERN GROUP

The Committee discussed these Western Lines, and stated as a general proposition the building of railroads in the West had gone far beyond the ability of the Country to make them profitable; that the competition of the Trunk Lines from the East to the West had cut transportation charges below the point of profit; that the Western railroads could not be made to pay on the basis of rates they were then receiving, and referred to the millions of dollars of capital which had already been sunk in them.

The Committee stated, so far as the Western connections of the Pennsylvania Railroad Company were concerned, that paradoxical as it may appear, it would realize more profit from these connections when less tonnage was carried, because of the large volume of farm products handled, on which a profitable freight rate was paid. Reference was made to the profitableness of the Fort Wayne, or Northern System, which was due to the fact that it carried a rapidly increasing local traffic, and was so situated that it handled ore and iron in one direction and coal, cattle and grain in the other, which thus avoided a great deal of empty mileage. In referring to the Pittsburgh, Cincinnati & St. Louis Railway, or Southern System, attention was called to the high rentals paid to several of its leased lines, which were proving a burden to that Company. Its own line, it was stated, would enjoy the benefit of traffic given to it by many roads which joined or intersected it, and it would also be helped by the valuable coal traffic originating on its main line. It was estimated, however, that there would be a future loss of $500,000. a year from the operation of the roads in the Southern System.

The Committee concluded its reference to these Western connections by stating that irrespective of whether or not they paid financially, the true fact was that the Pennsylvania Railroad was built to bring trade and travel through the State of Pennsylvania to the Atlantic Seaboard, which it undoubtedly had done, and, if necessary, a reasonable sacrifice of profit should be made for these objects.

EASTERN GROUP

The Committee then took up and discussed the Eastern Group of railroads and canals in the Pennsylvania Railroad System East of Pittsburgh and Erie, which were divided into seven Divisions, with their mileage, as follows:—

Allegheny Valley Railroad Division		446 miles
Philadelphia & Erie Railroad Division		288 "
Northern Central Railway Division		309 "
Pennsylvania Canal Company Division		347 "
United Railroads of New Jersey Division		344 "
Delaware & Raritan Canal Division		61 "
Pennsylvania Railroad Division		1,021 "
Total		2,816 miles
Total Miles of Railway	2,408	
Total Miles of Canal	408	

ADDITIONAL ROADS

In addition to the foregoing it was considered that the Pittsburgh, Virginia & Charleston Railway might very properly be included in the Pennsylvania Railroad System, this road being completed from South Pittsburgh to Monongahela City in 1873, the object of its construction being to draw travel and trade to Pittsburgh. By the construction of a short piece of road (Port Perry Branch) connecting with the Main Line near Brinton's Station, the Pittsburgh, Virginia & Charleston Railway could be used as a valuable means of passing through freight between the Pennsylvania Railroad and the Pittsburgh, Cincinnati & St. Louis Railway without going through the City of Pittsburgh proper.

The Columbia & Port Deposit Railway might, it was stated, also be considered as part of the Pennsylvania Railroad System, it being a branch 40 miles long, partially graded, between Columbia, Pa., and Port Deposit, Md. When completed it was to make connection with the Philadelphia, Wilmington & Baltimore Railroad at Perryville, and thus open markets for the distribution of coal from the Susquehanna Valley.

ALLEGHENY VALLEY RAILROAD

Taking up the first of the seven Divisions, it was stated that the Allegheny Valley Railroad Division consisted of:—

Allegheny Valley Railroad proper, extending from Pittsburgh to Oil City		132 miles
The Low Grade Extension	110 miles	
Other Branches	37 "	
		147 "
The Oil Creek and Allegheny River Railroad		123 "
The Buffalo, Corry & Pittsburgh Railroad		44 "
Total		446 miles

This road, it was pointed out, traversed one of the most valuable freight producing valleys in the State of Pennsylvania, rich in coal, iron, oil, timber and other products. It was natural to expect that a railroad so favorably located should have been profitable, but unfortunately the Company was not conservatively financed at the inception of the project. This led to embarrassing financial difficulties, which had since been adjusted to the satisfaction of all concerned, and it was felt that the advantages in the location of the road and the connections it made with other lines would sooner or later make it a most valuable property, provided it was properly and economically managed.

REASONS FOR BUILDING LOW GRADE LINE

While on the subject of the Allegheny Valley Railroad, it is interesting to note the views of the Committee on the policy of building the Low Grade Extension of that road from Red Bank to Driftwood, 110 miles in length. They understood the reasons to be that it was a strategic movement to control the valley at the lowest summit of the mountains between the East and the West in Pennsylvania. Further, that, by utilizing 120 miles of the Philadelphia & Erie Railroad and a part of the Northern Central Railway, it could be used as a relief line for the carriage of fourth class freight at slow speed and low rates from the West to the East and vice versa, and in this way add to the earnings of these two roads, in which the Pennsylvania Railroad Company was largely interested.

THE COMMITTEE'S ANSWER

The Committee answered these arguments by stating that it was questionable whether the strategic advantages were worth the cost of nearly $12,900,000., or over $117,000. per mile, to build the line, or whether the traffic tributary to it could not be transported via the Western Pennsylvania Railroad and the Main Line of the Pennsylvania Railroad at as low rates and much faster than by way of the Low

Grade Line; that the Pennsylvania Railroad Company would sustain a loss by sending its freight from Pittsburgh east via that route, and it would be a much better policy to enlarge its existing facilities than to turn the traffic in that direction. As to using the new line for slow freight at low cost for transportation, the Committee questioned whether the difference in time, which was estimated at ten hours, was worth much reduction in rates, having as it would the additional disadvantage of practically limiting the capacity of the road, besides involving a large expenditure for more equipment.

PHILADELPHIA & ERIE RAILROAD

The investigation of the Philadelphia & Erie Railroad Company developed the fact that little could be expected from it, except that it might earn enough to pay the interest on its Funded Debt. The unfortunate location of the road between Driftwood and Warren, with its two summits, one over 2,000 feet and the other nearly 1,700 feet, to overcome, was one important factor against economical operations, and as the road was built north of the territory where oil, coal and heavy timber were abundant, the Committee stated it was small wonder that the outlook for this Company was so discouraging at that time.

NORTHERN CENTRAL RAILWAY

The Northern Central Railway Company was next discussed, its line then consisting of:—

Main Line from Baltimore to Sunbury..........	138	miles
Shamokin Valley & Pottsville Railroad.........	28	"
Elmira & Williamsport R. R. (held by lease)....	78	"
Chemung Railroad (controlled by stk. ownership)	18	"
Elmira, Jefferson & Canandaigua Railroad— (Controlled by stock ownership)............	47	"
Total..............................	309	miles

It was pointed out that it was not difficult to comprehend the importance of this road if its course were followed on a map and its connections noted. At Baltimore it connected with the Baltimore & Potomac Railroad to Washington and the South; thence it passed northwardly through a beautiful and rich agricultural section to Harrisburg, where connection was made with the Main Line of the Pennsylvania Railroad, the Cumberland Valley Railroad, and the roads coming under control of the Philadelphia & Reading Railway; from Harrisburg it extended to Sunbury and there connected with the Philadelphia & Erie Railroad, from which point it had valuable branches to the Lykens Valley coal fields, and through the Shamokin Valley & Pottsville Railroad it reached the fine coal fields of that valley, as well as the large body of coal owned by that Company near Shamokin. The Philadelphia & Erie Railroad was the connecting link between Sunbury and Williamsport, from which latter point the Elmira & Williamsport Railroad (leased to Northern Central Railway) was built to Elmira, and thence via the Elmira, Jefferson & Canandaigua and Chemung Railroads (controlled by Northern Central Railway), the latter's lines were able to reach markets in the centre of New York State.

CLOSER ALLIANCE DESIRABLE

The local trade of the Northern Central Railway and the through traffic given it by the Pennsylvania Railroad required largely increased terminal facilities at Baltimore, that City having built the Union Railroad to connect the Northern Central Railway with the Bay, thus making a complete line to tidewater. The Northern Central Railway Company itself, however, was unable to raise the large sums of money required for these additions to its railroad and naturally looked to the Pennsylvania Railroad Company, its largest stockholder, for financial assistance. It was felt that the latter Company would also profit by the increase in the interchange of traffic between the two Systems as a result of the enlarged terminal facilities. The views of the Committee, therefore, were that if a closer alliance could be had between the two Systems in the form of a lease or otherwise, it would prove of mutual advantage.

PENNSYLVANIA CANALS

A short history of the Pennsylvania Canal Division is given, but as much of it has been set out in earlier pages of this review, it is not repeated here, except to state that the Committee felt the operation of these waterways had been as satisfactory as could be expected. In addition to this, if their control had been in the hands of interests inimical to the Pennsylvania Railroad Company during the period of reduced rates for transportation, the result might have been detrimental to it.

UNITED NEW JERSEY RAILROAD & CANAL COMPANY

The United Railroads of New Jersey Division was discussed at some length by the Committee. The lease of these lines in 1871, it was stated, went a long way toward solving the problem of providing an eastern gateway for the accommodation of the passenger and freight traffic of the Pennsylvania Railroad System to the Metropolis of the Country and New England beyond, for it secured:—

1. A continuous line of railroad between the City of New York and the West under one control.
2. The use of the unrivaled terminal advantages at the City of New York, Jersey City, and South Amboy.
3. The key of the line of southern travel to Baltimore and Washington.
4. The ability to place the products of the mine and the farm on tide-water, at the least expense, nearest to the centre of shipment and consumption.
5. The power to fix through rates.
6. The control of a line of railroads and canal that must continually increase in value and profit.

PENNSYLVANIA RAILROAD DIVISION

The Pennsylvania Railroad Division, consisting of the following Main Line and Branches, was given careful study:—

Pennsylvania Railroad Main Line	358 miles
Columbia Bridge	1 "
York Branch	13 "
Hollidaysburg Branch	42 "
Indiana Branch	19 "
East Brandywine & Waynesburg Railroad	18 "
Bald Eagle Valley Railroad	52 "
Mifflin & Centre County Railroad	13 "
Sunbury & Lewistown Railroad	45 "
Tyrone & Clearfield Railroad	44 "
Ebensburg & Cresson Railroad	11 "
Western Pennsylvania Railroad	85 "
Bedford & Bridgeport Railroad	51 "
South West Pennsylvania Railroad	24 "
Pennsylvania & Delaware Railroad	38 "
Lewisburg, Centre & Spruce Creek Railroad	11 "
Danville, Hazleton & Wilkes-Barre Railroad	44 "
Cumberland Valley Railroad	152 "
Total	1,021 miles

These roads were not discussed in any detail except the Main Line from Philadelphia to Pittsburgh, although mention is made of the fact that the York Branch and Columbia Bridge were consolidated and made part of the Pennsylvania Railroad Company. Further, that the Hollidaysburg Branch, Bald Eagle Valley Railroad, Tyrone & Clearfield Railroad, Western Pennsylvania Railroad, South West Pennsylvania Railway and the Cumberland Valley Railroad were all being profitably operated, and it was expected that the remaining branches would pay the cost of operating them.

PRIDE IN THE MAIN LINE

The Committee pointed with pride to the Main Line of the Pennsylvania Railroad from Philadelphia to Pittsburgh, the trunk line which gave life and support to so many branches, and which in return received strength from them, affecting not only the welfare of the State of Pennsylvania, but directly promoting the happiness and prosperity of a large portion of the people of the United States. The Main Line consisted of four principal parts, the road from Philadelphia to Columbia, purchased from the Commonwealth of Pennsylvania; the Harrisburg, Portsmouth, Mt. Joy & Lancaster Railroad, from Columbia to Harrisburg, leased for 999 years to the Pennsylvania Railroad Company, the line from Harrisburg to Pittsburgh, and the Delaware Extension in Philadelphia, making a direct route from Philadelphia to Pittsburgh 365 miles in length. The Committee placed a value on the Main Line, with equipment, real estate, etc., of approximately $94,398,000., while it stood on the books of the Company at the extremely low cost of $48,571,000., showing a value in excess of cost of about $45,827,000.

IMPROVEMENTS PAID FOR FROM SURPLUS EARNINGS

This favorable condition, it was stated, was brought about through the wise policy inaugurated by the late President Thomson of constructing the original single track road for cash and double tracking and improving it out of surplus earnings, which fortunately was done at a time of exceptionally low wages. In addition the 81 miles of road between Philadelphia and Columbia, acquired from the State of Pennsylvania in 1857, were purchased at a price which in the 70's proved to have been at a very low figure; the lease of the Harrisburg, Portsmouth, Mt. Joy & Lancaster Railroad was not as burdensome as was expected when the contract was signed; and, further, the large amount of real estate purchased by the Company for stations, shops, right of way, etc., at a very early date in its history was worth a price far in excess of the original outlay for it. All of these factors had placed the Pennsylvania Railroad Company at an advantage over its competitors, for while the cost of road and equipment of competing lines was fully represented by the amount of their Stock and Bonded indebtedness, on all of which dividends and interest had to be paid, the Pennsylvania Railroad Company had to pay dividends and interest on securities equal to only a part of the real value of its road and equipment. That, the Committee stated, was the principal reason why it had always been able to pay a fair rate of dividend on its Stock, interest on its Bonded indebtedness, fulfill its obligations to the public and maintain a scale of wages for its employes not exceeded on any other railway system in the Country.

INTERESTS SOUTH OF BALTIMORE

Reference was made to the interests which the Pennsylvania Railroad Company held south of Baltimore, the most important of which was the Baltimore & Potomac Railroad. This road extended from Baltimore to Popes Creek, Md., a distance of 73 miles, with a branch 19 miles in length to Washington, making a single track railroad 92 miles long, with a tunnel through part of the City of Baltimore. The total cost of this road was represented by the issue of securities to the amount of $9,888,736., or over $107,000. per mile including the tunnel, consisting of $3,503,900. of Stock, $4,500,000. of Bonds and a floating debt of $1,884,836., the Pennsylvania Railroad Company owning $1,828,600. of this Stock and jointly guaranteeing the Bonds with the Northern Central Railway Company. The object in constructing this road was, first, to furnish a southern extension for the Northern Central Railway to the City of Washington; second, a better connection with the Pennsylvania Railroad Lines to New York, and lastly to furnish a route northward and eastward for the southern travel from the roads controlled by the Southern Railway Security Company, in which the Pennsylvania Railroad Company was interested.

OTHER INVESTMENTS IN SOUTHERN LINES

In addition to this the Pennsylvania Railroad Company also had the following investments in lines south of Washington, although it was in no way liable for any guarantees, leases or otherwise on account of any railroad in this southern territory:—

Alexandria & Fredericksburg Railway Stock (now part of Rich., Fred. & Pot. R. R.)...	$31,600.00
Alexandria & Washington Railway Stock (now part of Rich., Fred. & Pot. R. R.)........	63,724.00
Southern Railway Security Company........	783,734.33
Richmond & Danville Railroad Stock (now part of Southern Railway System)........	600,000.00
Notes of the Richmond & Danville Railroad, and Bonds of the Atlanta & Richmond Air Line Railroad (now part of Southern Railway System), with collateral of $3,205,691.42	1,164,997.00
Western Railroad of Alabama Stock (now owned by Louisville & Nashville R. R. and Central R. R. of Georgia)..............	60,000.00
	$2,704,055.33

While the cost of these securities had been charged to Profit & Loss in the accounts of 1873, they were given a value of $1,000,000. by the Committee.

CONTROL OF CAIRO-NEW ORLEANS ROUTE

The foregoing investment did not include the $1,300,000. interest taken by the Pennsylvania Railroad Company in the line of railroad from opposite Cairo, Ill., to New Orleans. The Committee was of the opinion that this was not a justifiable investment, though the Company had just begun to receive large returns from the outlay and was able to control for commercial purposes the whole line of railroad from New Orleans to Cairo.

This investment was made in the Bonds of the Mississippi Central Railroad Company, which was built from Cairo, Ill., to Canton, Miss. The road from the latter point to New Orleans was known as the New Orleans, Jackson & Great Northern Railroad Company, and was controlled by the same interests which owned the Mississippi Central Railroad Company. The two roads were subsequently consolidated to form the Chicago, St. Louis & New Orleans Railroad Company. The new Company defaulted in the payment of interest on its Bonds in 1876, was reorganized, and in 1882 leased for 400 years to the Illinois Central Railroad Company, and now constitutes its Main Line between Cairo and New Orleans.

USE OF ROAD BY CARS OF PRIVATE PERSONS OR COMPANIES

A chapter of the Committee's report is devoted to the question of the use of the Pennsylvania Railroad by the freight cars of private individuals and companies, and particularly the so-called fast freight lines. The legal right of any individual or corporation to have their cars transported over the Pennsylvania Railroad was protected by the provisions of the Charter of the Company granting that privilege, and by decisions of the Courts. It was pointed out that in the early days of American railroad transportation, the railway companies furnished the road and motive power, and the shippers provided most of the freight cars. This policy saved the railroads a large investment of capital for equipment, and it had the additional advantage of requiring less cars to carry the same amount of tonnage, as the shippers and transporters by economical loading could get larger train loads with fewer cars than the railroads. So far as the Pennsylvania Railroad Company was concerned, it not only had a large investment in freight equipment, but also handled a great many cars owned by private individuals and companies.

CRITICISM OF UNION AND EMPIRE LINES

There had been for some time a great deal of public criticism of two companies which furnished a fast freight service, namely, the Union Railroad & Transportation Company (then owned by the Pennsylvania Company, but operating under the name of the "Union Line") and the Empire Transportation Company. It had been alleged that the equipment of these companies was too actively used while the cars of the Pennsylvania Railroad Company were lying idle, and that these fast freight lines usually transported the highest paying freight, leaving the lower classes of traffic to be carried in the cars of the Pennsylvania Railroad. The Committee made a thorough investigation and dwelt very largely on the relations with the Empire Transportation Company, because the Union Line was then under the control of the Pennsylvania Railroad Company. As a result, it was stated that the contract with the Empire Company was practically the same as that with other railroads in the East; that no attempt had been made to favor it to the detriment of the interests of the Pennsylvania Railroad Company; that the work of the Empire Company was of a peculiar and special character; that the service it rendered could not be performed in so prompt, economical and satisfactory a manner by any organization which the Pennsylvania Railroad Company might form, and that the Committee did not feel competent to pass upon the matter of rates, preferring to leave this question to the Management to decide.

The Committee felt, however, that there was a tendency

in such companies to go too far in looking after their own interests, and it was generally believed that they had infringed on those of the Pennsylvania Railroad Company. Therefore, it was all the more necessary that its officers and employes should be entirely free of any interest in the fast freight line companies.

RELATIONS WITH PULLMAN COMPANY

The status of the Pullman Palace Car Company and its relations with the Pennsylvania Railroad System received some attention in the report. That Company at that time supplied the Lines East of Pittsburgh with 100 sleeping and drawing room cars and the Lines West with 70 of the same character of cars. The Pennsylvania Railroad Company had the following investment in the securities of this Company:—

$770,000. 8% Bonds (with power to change, in three years into an equal amount of Stock at par), worth..........	$770,000.
1,233 shares Stock at par, paying 12% dividend..................................	123,300.
Total..................................	$893,300.

The opinion of the Committee was that if the Pullman Palace Car Company could earn a dividend of 12% on its Stock, the expenditure of a sum sufficient to provide the necessary equipment for this service on the Pennsylvania Railroad ought to bring it a greater profit than 12%. On the other hand, it was recognized that under the existing contracts with the Pullman Company and the question as to the legal power of the Pennsylvania Railroad Company to make an extra charge for such accommodation, the better policy would probably be to continue the arrangement then in force. The Committee, however, desired to point out that the public who use the Pullman cars should pay more to the railroad company than the small additional sum paid to the Pullman Company.

ANTHRACITE COAL LANDS

The Committee thoroughly investigated the acquisition of the large tract of coal lands in the anthracite region of

Pennsylvania. The coal properties owned wholly or in part by the Pennsylvania Railroad Company were located in the Lykens Valley, at Shamokin, near Hazleton, and at Nanticoke Dam in the Wyoming Valley, and embraced an aggregate of 27,950 acres. A description of these properties and their ownership follows, after which the wisdom of acquiring so large an interest in them is discussed.

LYKENS VALLEY COAL PROPERTY

The Lykens Valley property was situated about 20 miles northeast of Millersburg on the Susquehanna River, and consisted of about 9,200 acres of coal lands and 3,000 acres of farm lands. The ownership of this coal was vested in the Summit Branch Railroad Company, which owned 7,319 shares out of a total of 9,883 shares of the Lykens Valley Coal Company's Stock, in addition to having a credit of $964,889.38 advanced to the latter Company. The Summit Branch Railroad Company was in turn controlled in the interest of the Pennsylvania Railroad Company by a Stock ownership of 43,804 shares out of a total issue of 82,500 shares. The purchase of this stock was stated to be a very wise and prudent policy, assuring to the Northern Central Railway, whose line of road traversed this section, a very large amount of traffic from these fields for shipment to Baltimore and intermediate points.

SHAMOKIN COAL PROPERTY

The ownership of the Shamokin coal fields, which embraced 7,808 acres, was vested in the Northern Central Railway Company (as lessee of the Shamokin Valley & Pottsville Railroad) and in the Pennsylvania Railroad Company, but the property was operated by the Mineral Railroad & Mining Company. Its Stock amounted to 50,000 shares, par value $20. per share, of which one-third was owned by the Pennsylvania Railroad Company and two-thirds by Northern Central Railway Company. The coal in this region was said to be of good quality, but inferior to that found in the Lykens Valley district.

HAZLETON COAL PROPERTY

The Hazleton property, which was owned by the Pennsylvania Railroad Company, consisted of from 2,100 to 2,200 acres, and was then undeveloped. There was a direct route from this property over the Danville, Hazleton & Wilkes-Barre Railroad to the Northern Central Railway and Philadelphia & Erie Railroad, as well as to all lines controlled by the Lehigh Valley Railroad Company and Lehigh Coal & Navigation Company.

SUSQUEHANNA COAL PROPERTY

The Susquehanna Coal Company was organized in 1869, and the area of coal lands it controlled amounted to 5,823 acres, lying on both sides of the Susquehanna River at Nanticoke Dam. The Capital Stock consisted of 15,000 shares, par value $100. per share, amounting to $1,500,000. of which the Pennsylvania Railroad Company owned $1,000,000. and Pennsylvania Canal Company $500,000., the original purpose of the investment being to produce increased tonnage for the canals and at the same time, particularly during the winter months, to provide the Northern Central Railway and other roads associated with the Pennsylvania Railroad, a traffic that might have been diverted to other channels.

The Susquehanna Coal Company had issued $1,283,000. of 6% 40-Year Bonds, to purchase a portion of these lands, the principal and interest of which were guaranteed by the Pennsylvania Railroad Company.

SUMMARY

To summarize the foregoing statements of ownership, the following table shows the acreage and estimated value of all of these coal properties:—

	Number of Acres	*Estimated Value (1874)*
Lykens Valley coal region	12,200	$7,000,000.
Shamokin coal region	7,808	1,300,000.
Hazleton coal property	2,119	2,000,000.
Wyoming Valley coal property	5,823	2,236,884.
Totals	27,950	$12,536,884.

COMMITTEE'S VIEW

While the laws of the State specifically encouraged the ownership and development of its natural resources by railroad companies, there was some question in the minds of the Committee as to the propriety of railroad companies owning and operating coal lands, their view being that a railroad company should only purchase and control coal properties in sections of the State to properly conserve some local interest in which it was concerned. Therefore, it was argued that if this opinion were sound, the Management of the Pennsylvania Railroad Company would seem to have been debarred from acquiring an ownership in any of these coal properties except in the Lykens Valley or Shamokin fields, which were necessary to furnish traffic to the Northern Central Railway and the Pennsylvania Canal. Their judgment was that the purchase, joint ownership or control of coal lands by the Pennsylvania Railroad Company should have begun and ended with the acquisition of the Lykens Valley and Shamokin properties, and that the ownership in the Susquehanna Coal Company and the Hazleton region was injudicious and unwise.

METHOD OF CONTROL OF SUBSIDIARIES

A chapter of the Committee's report is devoted to the finances of the Company and the method of control of the numerous roads in the Pennsylvania Railroad System. Their opinion was that where it was possible to absorb them into the Company, thereby avoiding the expense of a separate organization and securing greater economy in management and uniformity in the accounts, it should be done, but where this plan could not be carried out, the better policy would be to lease these various lines, which might be in three different forms:—

1. By paying a fixed rental;
2. By charging a fixed pro rata rate of receipts;
3. By working the roads at absolute cost and receiving compensation for use of Pennsylvania Railroad Company's engines, machinery, etc.

The first of the three plans was considered the most desirable; the second inadvisable, and the third, while peculiarly adapted to roads of uncertain value and short branches, was not considered satisfactory where the prospective growth and development of a road was a foregone conclusion.

RESTRICTING CAPITAL ISSUES

Great stress was laid by the Committee on the desirability of keeping the amount of Capital Stock and Funded Debt at as low a figure as possible consistent with the best interests of the Company. Two ways of accomplishing this were suggested:—

1. By leasing or absorbing such roads as came in their terms within the range of safety to the Treasury of the Company, and when such roads were leased to dispose of the Stock and Bonds of such companies as may be owned by the Pennsylvania Railroad Company.

2. By the sale of all securities that would bring an approximately fair price, and which could be sold without injury to the Company.

PURCHASE OF STOCKS OF LEASED ROADS

The Pennsylvania Railroad Company had prior to 1873 purchased a very large amount of Stocks and Bonds of companies which had been leased by it or the Pennsylvania Company. The purchases were in most cases made direct from the companies themselves, and the latter used the proceeds to improve and better equip their lines for the transportation service they performed. The largest part of these securities was acquired at low figures, as the policy of the Company had been, first, to take hold of the various roads in poor condition; second, to keep their Stocks and Bonds in its Treasury until they should increase in value and pay a large profit, and, third, to enable the Pennsylvania Railroad Company to purchase such large amounts of Stocks and Bonds in other companies, it was necessary to issue its own securities, thereby increasing the sum required for the semi-annual dividends and the interest on its Funded Debt. This, it was pointed out, was a most dangerous policy, as it led the Management to enter into investments, some of which were non-productive, and which could not be disposed of at a fair price during the period when there was a scarcity of money, as in 1873, at which time the Company had to issue nearly $23,000,000. of Stock and Bonds to meet its requirements, and that it was this policy which finally resulted in the creation of the Consolidated Mortgage, dated July 1st, 1873.

CREATION OF CONSOLIDATED MORTGAGE NOT A NECESSITY

The Stockholders' Committee in referring to the large amount of securities which had been placed under that Mortgage gave its opinion that they were not required to give further security for any Bonds that might be issued thereunder; that some of these securities might have been sold in September, 1873, when the panic came with such force and the Company found its available assets tied up in the Mortgage, which prevented it from paying the regular semi-annual dividend in cash, even though it had been earned; that it was a waste of credit for which the interests of the Company had suffered, as the placing of these securities under the Mortgage had not made the bonds more marketable, nor added to the price received for them; that the holding of the Stocks and Bonds of the numerous companies for a rise, and at the same time borrowing money from the stockholders at high rates to carry them, was most unwise; that the placing of available securities under a Mortgage was of itself an anomalous act, and was contrary to the true policy of the Company in keeping down its capitalization to the lowest amount; and finally that the creation of this Mortgage was not a necessity, for at the time it was executed more money could have been realized from the sale of those securities than from the Bonds issued under and secured by the Mortgage.

RECOMMENDATIONS

The Committee concluded its remarks on the finances of the Company by strongly recommending—

(*a*) "To apply rigidly the provisions of that mortgage as to releases of securities to provide for payment of betterments, etc., made on the different railroads, as therein provided;"

(*b*) "By consolidating with or leasing railroads now in your interest upon favorable terms or at a fair rental, which will relieve you of the necessity of continuing to own these stocks and bonds now necessary to retain the control of such roads."

DISTRUST OF RAILROAD SECURITIES

The Committee devoted a whole chapter to the sources of distrust in the value of railway Stocks and Bonds existing in the early 70's. The prevalent feeling then was that money invested in railway securities was sunk and would ultimately be lost. Therefore, the subject was carefully investigated and an effort made to ascertain the reasons for this want of confidence, and a number of probable causes were suggested. Space will not permit extracting this entire chapter from the report, but it is most interesting and the remarks of the Committee accurately illustrate the skepticism in the public mind at that time with regard to investments in railroad securities. Briefly they were:—

PROBABLE CAUSES

First:—The incomplete reports made by the Directors of railroad companies to their shareholders, which were so meagre that it seemed as if the Directors were being guided by the old adage "the least said is soonest mended." There was then a tendency to limit the annual report to the general results of a year's operations, while the stockholders were left in ignorance as to the value of their own property;

Second:—The managers of railroads were inclined to act as though the property they managed was their own, that is, having become so familiar with all the particulars of their road and never having questioned the infallibility of their own judgment, they looked upon a stockholder as an intermeddler if he should make any inquiry or attempt to criticize the Management, and the assumption of this attitude generally resulted in losing the moral support of the stockholder;

Third:—The fear on the part of the public and stockholders that the railroad might be used by the officers and favored employes for their own benefit. This practice had been followed in different ways, viz: by being interested in companies furnishing materials, such as coal, wood, lumber and iron, to the road and in concerns doing contract work, and also having an ownership in corporations using the road. While the Committee did not accuse anyone, or state that these charges were true in the case of the Pennsylvania Railroad Company, it strongly recommended to the stockholders that such action be taken to prevent any officer or employe in its service from holding any interest in companies furnishing supplies to it, or doing work under contract, or in any company conducting business over the Pennsylvania Railroad, its branches or roads acquired by lease or otherwise.

Fourth:—There had been an unsatisfied doubt in the minds of the stockholders of the Pennsylvania Railroad Company as to its policy with respect to private companies using the road, and as the conclusions of the Committee on this subject were given in preceding pages, they are not repeated here.

Fifth:—The tendency among stockholders of railroad companies to leave decisions on important questions to the Board of Directors. It was pointed out that the stockholders' influence in the Management was almost a nullity so far as matters of policy were concerned, their main utility being to furnish an audience to hear a report and voting for Directors a ticket carefully prepared for them.

Sixth:—The constant desire to extend and expand, as shown in the history of the railroads up to that time. Herein was probably the main cause of the doubt that existed as to the value of railway Stocks and Bonds, and which affected public confidence in them. It was admitted that rivalry between the important lines had produced questions of extensions which were difficult to decide; also that where there was any country beyond the termini of a road or branches, there was an irresistible temptation to go still further in following population and production beyond their limits. The result was the building of extensions far in advance of the needs of the country, and these liabilities became a burden to the guaranteeing corporation. It was stated, so far as the roads controlled by the Pennsylvania Railroad Company were concerned, that they surely covered enough ground and would furnish as large a business as any one corporation could manage, and the Committee urgently recommended that such measures be adopted as would limit the Board of Directors from extending the interests of the Company beyond the then existing bounds.

The Committee in closing this chapter referred to a set of resolutions they had drawn, to which reference is hereinafter made, and which if adopted would, it was felt, favorably influence the public mind and secure a sound administration of the Company's varied interests.

DIRECTORS' RESPONSIBILITY PLACED ON PRESIDENT

The Committee, being impressed with the magnitude of the operations and liabilities of the Company, felt it incumbent to consider the adaptation of the organization then existing to manage such great interests. It was stated that the original theory of a railroad organization was to have a Board of Directors, a President charged with the finances, and a Superintendent in charge of the management of the railroad, the latter being the only one who was either a professional engineer or an expert in railway management. It was pointed out that experience had modified that form of organization by making the President the executive officer, expecting him to be thoroughly qualified and responsible for the entire management of the property; that the Board of Directors of a railroad company were generally chosen for their supposed sound judgment, business knowledge and integrity, but in a number of cases they were unacquainted with the professional side of railroad management. As their whole time and attention was not devoted to the duties of this office, but to a great extent to the direction of their own personal affairs, the Management of the Company was left entirely in the hands of the President, and naturally his views influenced the judgment of the Directors. It was pointed out that the stockholders expected to benefit by the independent action of the Directors, which it was not possible to secure under the foregoing circumstances; that the result of the working of such an organization naturally destroyed the power and influence of the Directors, and placed the responsibility of Management directly upon the shoulders of one man, the President, which power was very often abused, and frequently caused defalcations and numerous cases of bankruptcy.

EFFECT ON PENNSYLVANIA RAILROAD

The thought then arose in the minds of the Committee as to what this centralization of power would mean to a corporation like the Pennsylvania Railroad Company, controlling as it did at that time nearly 6,000 miles of railways and canals, and involving a capitalization of nearly $400,000,000. The question was asked whether it was prudent or wise that this vast interest should be placed under the control of one man, which situation, it was admitted, did exist in the Pennsylvania Railroad Company at that time. It was stated, however, that its growth and prosperity had been entirely due to the inspiration and guidance of a master mind of honest intentions and remarkable ability in the person of John Edgar Thomson, but that changes would have to take place from time to time, and what havoc and destruction of values might be caused by an incompetent or dishonest President.

TOO MUCH FOR ONE MAN

The opinion of the Committee was that the magnitude of the Company's interests had then reached a point where it has passed beyond the mental or physical power of one man to handle the great number of important questions which were ever pressing for decision. The properties then controlled by the Company were located in 11 States, many of which were the largest in the Union, and whose laws and powers, as they affected corporations, required the most devoted attention. Further, there was the necessity for developing the traffic to the highest attainable point, so as to protect the interests of the stockholders, and furnish the public with the greatest facilities at the least cost, all of which, it was pointed out, was a duty which no one person could satisfactorily perform in justice to himself or the interests of the Company. It was felt that the Pennsylvania Railroad Company required in its Management men of the highest type in their respective professions. It took a long time for them to become experienced in the requirements of the service, and when once educated they became a source of wealth to the Company. Further, it was a great mistake to so burden the men with such an amount of duties as would exhaust them mentally and physically after a few years of service.

Briefly summed up the views of the Committee were that under the organization of the Pennsylvania Railroad Company at that time, the Directors' influence in directing the policy of the Company was hardly perceptible, not intentionally so, but from the very necessities of the case. It resulted in placing the control of its immense interests chiefly in the hands of the President, which was unjust, unwise and imprudent; that the Pennsylvania Railroad Company had gotten beyond the ability of one person to properly direct its management, and the time had arrived when this important matter should be carefully considered.

REVISED ORGANIZATION

The first question to be discussed was the basis for a revised organization, and it was evident to the Committee that the principles upon which it should be founded were:—

First:—That the stockholders, under the charter of the Pennsylvania Railroad Company, were the owners of the corporate rights and property, and the original and only source of power and authority;

Second:—That for the more convenient management of their interests, they select a certain number of Directors to represent them in directing the affairs of the Company, these Directors to be guided in their decisions by the general policy laid down and approved from time to time by the stockholders;

Third:—That these executive functions may be most successfully used and developed, it was necessary to provide in the Board of Directors such a variety of talent, experience and character as would make their united opinion approach most nearly to a perfect judgment.

Further, if this were the true conception of the fundamental principles of an organization, it was felt that it plainly required for its harmonious working a plan, which, while it would keep absolute control of the Company in the hands of the stockholders, would also provide for a Board of Directors so constituted as to combine the greatest amount of skilled knowledge with business experience.

STOCKHOLDERS' POWERS

With these views of the true principles of an organization clearly set forth, the Committee took up the powers that should be reserved by the stockholders, which were all of a legislative character, involving the determination of the general policy of the Company and the assumption of obligations, whether in issuing Bonds, leasing railroads, guaranteeing of rentals to other roads, of the interest and principal of Bonds, or of the acts of other companies, or the incurring of any liability outside the ordinary expenses of conducting the operations of the Company, and the approval or acceptance of all acts or laws, general or special, affecting the Company.

DIRECTORS' POWERS

The powers of the Directors, in the opinion of the Committee, should only be such as would enable them to perform those duties, which were embraced under the two general headings of the finances and the road, which it was not thought necessary to elaborate. However, they being placed in such intimate relations with the detailed workings of the road, and studying and watching its growth, development and interests, the Committee stated that the Directors should be the first to detect its wants, and thus be prepared to advise the shareholders, thereby adding to their executive functions those of an advisory character.

PERSONNEL OF BOARD OF DIRECTORS

The personnel of the Board of Directors was then discussed, which, in addition to the President, it was stated, should be composed of a sufficient number of men skilled in the various branches of the railroad profession, the remaining Directors to be men, some possessing a business experience, and others with a knowledge of finance, the value of property, the interests of trade, and the needs of the Country. The Committee's recommendations were that the skilled members of the Board should be elected by the stockholders and be held responsible for their acts in common with other Directors; that of the number of Directors to be elected by the stockholders, three of them should be professional railroad men and one of financial experience and ability; and that of the three trained in railroad practice, one should be chosen as President, another charged with the interests of the Company West of Pittsburgh, and the third with the oversight and care of the roads East of that point.

RESOLUTIONS OFFERED FOR APPROVAL

The Committee in concluding its report stated that it had endeavored to fully and fearlessly investigate questions of policy as to the Company's relations with other roads, the management of its finances, and its organization. It was pointed out that the purpose in doing this had been to enable the stockholders to form an estimate of the value of the property, of the true policy by which the Company should in the future be controlled, and of the character of organization which would most successfully manage the interests of the stockholders. The Committee submitted a number of resolutions, which it believed would to a great extent secure the desired results. Briefly, they were:—

First:—The stockholders, as the source of all authority, reserve to themselves the whole legislative power of the corporation; the acceptance or rejection of all laws of the General Assembly of the State of Pennsylvania affecting its property, and all other powers as to the assumption of liabilities, either in leasing railroads, or guaranteeing the interest or principal of Bonds or other obligations of any Company, not hereinafter committed to the Board of Directors and officers;

Second:—The stockholders confide to the wisdom and discretion of the Directors the executive functions of carrying out the policy established by the stockholders from time to time for properly managing the interests of the Company.

Third:—That to enable the Directors to do this more perfectly, and to secure the necessary intelligence, independence and responsibility in the Board of Directors, the stockholders instruct the Board to procure the passage of a general law by the State of Pennsylvania providing for the election of Directors by the stockholders of a railroad company, who may receive compensation for their services, whenever judicial decisions may have so determined the intent and meaning of the Seventeenth Article of the new Constitution of the State of Pennsylvania (which refers to railroads and canals), that it contains nothing prejudicial to the interest of the Company, or whenever, for other reasons, it may accept any general or special law of the Legislature bringing the Company under and subject to the said Seventeenth Article. Such law, if obtained, to be submitted to the stockholders for their approval at the next following annual meeting.

Fourth:—That if such an Act is obtained and accepted by the stockholders of the Pennsylvania Railroad Company, there shall thereafter be selected from among the Directors four persons, three of whom shall be skilled in the construction and management of railways, and one of distinguished reputation for financial experience and skill, one of the three so selected to be elected President of the Company.

Fifth:—That a Committee of seven stockholders shall be appointed at every annual meeting who shall nominate, after conferring with the President, ten persons for the office of Directors for the ensuing year; that until the passage of an Act, as has been described, it shall be the further duty of said Committee to select, after conference with the President, the proper persons, not exceeding four in number, who shall be recommended for election by the Directors as Vice-Presidents, and that said Committee publish the names of the persons so selected in not less than five daily newspapers in Philadelphia for six days previous to the day of election of such Directors.

Sixth:—That the annual report be published in three daily newspapers in Philadelphia one week prior to each annual meeting, and be a full and complete statement of all facts and results of the business of the Company for the year, so that the stockholders may form a proper estimate of the value of the property and a correct judgment of the ability with which their interests had been taken care of by the Directors.

Seventh:—That it shall be the duty of the Board of Directors at least annually to recommend to the stockholders the adoption of such policy as in their judgment will promote the interests of the Company, with their reasons therefor; also estimates for any extraordinary payments or expenses to be incurred, and how they shall be financed.

Eighth:—That at the time of declaring the semi-annual dividend, or in the middle of their fiscal year, the Directors shall publish a statement showing the operations of the Company for the six months' period, and the amount of net revenue applicable to a dividend.

Ninth:—In order that the credit of the Company may be protected, the Directors to be prohibited from incurring any floating debt, except to meet, and then only for temporary use, expenses for improvements, enlargements or betterments to the Main Line and the railroads of the United Companies of New Jersey; and they were also to be prohibited, except by permission of the stockholders, from loaning the credit of the Company to other companies, except such as may own roads controlled by the Pennsylvania Railroad Company by lease or stock ownership; that all powers heretofore given to the Board so far as they conflict with the language or spirit of this resolution to be revoked and annulled.

SECURITIES PLEDGED UNDER CONSOLIDATED MORTGAGE—FUTURE CORPORATE AND FINANCIAL POLICIES

These nine resolutions were followed by the preamble of another set of resolutions, this preamble stating that the stockholders of the Pennsylvania Railroad Company were convinced that the placing of securities to the value of $50,000,000. in the Consolidated Mortgage was unnecessary to give perfect security to the Bonds to be issued under that Mortgage; that they did not add to the facility of sale, nor to the marketable value of such Bonds; that the Mortgage provided for Bonds largely in excess of the prospective wants of the Company, and the presence of these securities in the Consolidated Mortgage operated as a bar against the true policy of the Pennsylvania Railroad Company, viz: the reduction of the amount of Bonded indebtedness and the payment of the floating debt; therefore, a resolution was submitted stating:—

First:—That the policy of the Company thereafter in its relations with other companies controlled by it should be, in all cases where it was important to the interests of the Pennsylvania Railroad Company to do so, either to consolidate or effect leases on just terms to both parties, giving preference to the plan of leasing the roads to be worked at cost, and thus relieve its Treasury from the necessity of retaining large amounts of securities, which the Company was then compelled to keep in order to continue control of the roads.

Second:—That the Directors be instructed to conform rigidly to the provisions of the Consolidated Mortgage by appropriating the proceeds of such securities as were available for sale to the payment of all betterments, improvements, and real estate purchases, for the benefit of the mortgaged premises.

Third:—That the Directors should, from time to time, sell such available securities as may not be required to pay for betterments, etc., as above, the proceeds thereof to be invested in the Bonds of the Company, so that they may be cancelled and the remaining securities the sooner released from the lien of the mortgage.

Fourth:—That in the opinion of the Committee the policy established in the foregoing resolutions would render unnecessary any further issue of Bonds under the Consolidated Mortgage, without first obtaining the approval of the stockholders, except the £5,000,000. then arranged to be issued, and the Bonds reserved under the Mortgage to pay off existing Bonds as they mature.

The preamble to still another resolution submitted by the Committee stated that as the interests of the Pennsylvania Railroad Company might be unfavorably affected by the presence of other stockholders in the Pennsylvania Company, it was, therefore,

> " *Resolved*, that we recommend to the Directors to adopt such measures as will, in their judgment, secure to the Pennsylvania Railroad Company the absolute and exclusive control of the policy of the Pennsylvania Company."

VALUE OF CAPITAL STOCK—EARNINGS ON CAPITAL INVESTED

The Committee toward the close of their report give a resumé of their investigations, which showed, among other things, that the assets of the Pennsylvania Railroad Company, as of December 31st, 1873, were worth $118,955,405.08 over and above its Bonded and other indebtedness. Deducting the amount of Capital Stock issued to that date, there remained a surplus value of $50,810,930.08, making each share of Stock represent $87.28, excluding any increased value in the anthracite coal fields owned by the Pennsylvania Railroad Company, and that each mile of single track represented a real value of $45,436., while on the books of the Company it showed a cost of but $19,728.59. To better illustrate the influence of the Pennsylvania Railroad over the railways of the United States, it was stated that the railroads and canals directly controlled by it had a length of

5,933.6 miles, or 7.8% of the total railroad mileage of the Country, and represented in Capital $398,267,675.22, or a little less than 13% of the whole sum invested in railways in the United States at that time; that it was encouraging to note that the net earnings of all the lines controlled by the Pennsylvania Railroad Company, including those in which it was directly interested, had averaged 6.39% profit on the whole amount of capital.

PENNSYLVANIA RAILROAD BRINGS PROSPERITY

In concluding its remarks the Committee stated that the Pennsylvania Railroad was wonderfully fulfilling the objects for which it was created; that this was borne out by the comparatively feeble, doubtful and undeveloped condition of the State of Pennsylvania when the road was chartered in 1846, compared with its powerful and prosperous condition at the end of 1873. The Company by its aid to the Western Lines had given Pittsburgh, with its great manufacturing interests, an impetus and growth, which it would have never received had it depended on the waters of the Ohio and other adjacent rivers for its means of transportation. The City of Philadelphia had received new life and sprung into activity, and was rapidly growing from the impulse which the operations of the Pennsylvania Railroad had given it, while the counties reached by its Main Lines and branches were also receiving their full measure of growth and prosperity.

RETURNS TO STOCKHOLDERS

With all these benefits conferred on others, the Company, it was pointed out, had paid to its stockholders from 1853 to 1873, a period of 20 years, an average of 9.9%, the total dividends from its organization to January 1st, 1874, having been 234%. The Company then stood stronger than at any former period, holding a commanding position with respect to rival roads, and the means for the indefinite development and expansion of the inestimable resources with which Providence had blessed the State of Pennsylvania, the only one in the Union which commanded the connections of the sea, the lakes and the Mississippi River, and possessing within her own borders all the elements of material prosperity.

STOCKHOLDERS' ACTION ON REPORT

The resolutions of this Investigating Committee were placed before the stockholders at the annual meeting of the Company on March 9th, 1875. After some discussion a resolution was passed, setting forth that the Board of Directors had already carried out many of the suggestions made by the Investigating Committee, and it was their intention to adopt all of the recommendations that might be found of practical value to the Company. The report of the Committee, together with the resolutions attached thereto, was referred to the incoming Board for that purpose.

QUARTERLY DIVIDENDS

Another resolution was adopted at the Annual Meeting on March 9th, 1875, providing for the payment of dividends quarterly instead of semi-annually, and, as it was found legal and practicable to carry this out, the first quarterly dividend was paid by the Company in August, 1875.

ROADS LEASED TO FREDERICK, MD.

Effective January 1st, 1875, the Pennsylvania Railroad Company leased the Frederick & Pennsylvania and the Littlestown Railroads. It also leased the Hanover & York Railroad, effective July 5th, 1875, the three roads having a total length of 55½ miles, and extending the Pennsylvania Railroad from York, Pa., to Frederick, Md. They were to be operated at cost and compensation for the use of their equipment. These roads promised a very satisfactory traffic for the Pennsylvania Railroad and Northern Central Railway, with which latter the Hanover & York Railroad connected at York, Pa. The three smaller companies were later consolidated to form the York, Hanover & Frederick Railroad Company.

NEW BRIDGE OVER SCHUYLKILL AT WEST PHILADELPHIA

On November 20th, 1875, the Market Street bridge over the Schuylkill River at West Philadelphia, owned by the City was destroyed by fire, and the connection with the Pennsylvania Railroad east of the river was broken. A temporary structure was completed on November 29th, 1875, the traffic in the meantime being handled by drays. The Pennsylvania Railroad Company was subsequently authorized to construct a new bridge, which was completed on December 24th, 1875, the entire work, which included some improvement to the Chestnut Street Bridge, being finished in 207 working hours.

FIRST CAR TRUSTS

To adequately meet the demands of the increased coal trade, arrangements were made, through the issuance of Car Trusts, by which 2,000 eight-wheel coal cars of 15 tons capacity each were placed upon the Pennsylvania Railroad during the year 1875 at very low prices. Under this plan the interest on the cash cost of the cars was paid out of a Car Service Fund, which was made up by an allowance of the same rates per ton theretofore allowed other companies for the use of their cars in transporting a portion of the coal traffic over the Company's lines. The residue of this fund, after payment of interest, was to be applied to extinguish the principal within six years, so that not only would the Company have the use of the equipment in the interim, but would own all of the cars at the expiration of that period without adding to its construction and equipment account.

PAN HANDLE LEASED LINE IN DIFFICULTY

The Columbus, Chicago & Indiana Central Railway, extending from Columbus, O., to Indianapolis, Ind., Chicago, and State Line, Ill., a distance of 581 miles, which was leased to the Pittsburgh, Cincinnati & St. Louis Railway, effective February 1st, 1869, failed to fulfill its obligations thereunder, as the result of which the lease was practically terminated.

Steps were immediately taken, however, by the latter Company to make some adjustment of the financial difficulties of the former which would be fair and equitable to all interests, and also to arrange for the future operation of its lines west of Columbus.

NEW WEST PHILADELPHIA PASSENGER STATION—CENTENNIAL STATION

The West Philadelphia Passenger Station of the Company at 32nd and Market Streets was rebuilt and opened for public use on May 6th, 1876, the cost of reconstructing it being $240,000. Had it not been for the additional facilities which the new station afforded, it would have been impossible to handle the enormous passenger traffic during the Centennial year of 1876. It was believed to be one of the most commodious and convenient passenger stations in the Country, and was capable of accommodating the operation of more trains and traffic within a stated time than probably any other railroad station in America at that time.

In addition to the foregoing, the Company built a large passenger station opposite the Centennial Grounds, and made important changes in the tracks in the West Philadelphia Yards and at the Centennial Station. They were constructed in the form of a circle so that there could be continuous arrival and departure of trains without delay. It was stated that between the period May 10th and November 10th, 1876, the permanent station at West Philadelphia and the temporary Centennial Station handled 42,603 trains, 268,580 cars and 4,955,712 passengers.

CONNECTIONS TO NEW ENGLAND

During the year 1876 an important connection was effected by the Pennsylvania Railroad Company with the New England Lines, by which passengers were carried between Washington, Baltimore, Philadelphia and Boston without change of cars. The arrangement was made by the use on the part of the New York and New England Railroad of a large transfer steamer, on which the passenger and baggage cars were transferred by water route from Jersey City to Harlem Station on the New York, New Haven & Hartford Railroad, and thence were run to Boston by rail.

CREATION OF INSURANCE FUND

The question of insuring the property of the Pennsylvania Railroad Company from loss by fire received special consideration by the Management in 1876, with the result that an arrangement was made whereby it became its own insurer, and to cover any losses which might occur, the following securities were placed with three Trustees, designated "Trustees of the Insurance Fund":—

	Par Value	*Cost*
Western Pennsylvania R. R. Co. Bonds.........	$280,700.	$221,700.00
Steubenville & Indiana R. R. Co. Bonds........	51,000.	40,800.00
Summit Branch R. R. Co. Bonds..............	20,000.	16,238.91
Susquehanna Coal Co. Bonds..................	260,000.	221,261.09
	$611,700.	$500,000.00

The income from the foregoing securities was about $37,000. per annum, which was more than sufficient to meet the average losses occurring during the year. While these securities had cost the Company $500,000., this sum was reduced on its books to the nominal amount of $10,000. by charging the difference to Profit & Loss.

REDUCTION IN WAGES

In consequence of the continued depression in all industries of the Country, causing a material falling off in the revenues of the Pennsylvania Railroad Company and its affiliated lines, a reduction of 10% was made in the wages paid to all its officers and employes, effective as of June 1st, 1877. It was thought at that time that the lower wage scale would not be permanent, and that with a revival in business the Company would be able to restore the previous wage standards.

PITTSBURGH RIOTS

As bearing on the general question of labor and the effects of the reduced wages and depressed conditions existing at that time, it is interesting to read the following remarks of President Scott in the Thirty-first Annual Report of the Company, with respect to the riots in Pittsburgh and vicinity in the Summer of 1877:—

"Your attention has already been directed in this report to the outbreak at Pittsburgh on July 19th, causing the entire suspension of the freight traffic at that point for a period of ten days; in addition to the great loss of revenue thereby sustained by the Company, millions of dollars worth of valuable property were totally destroyed by fire. As soon as the trouble began the authorities of the City of Pittsburgh were notified, and their aid invoked to suppress the disturbance. Their efforts proving unsuccessful, the Sheriff of Allegheny County, in accordance with law, made a requisition upon the Governor of the State for a military force, which was promptly furnished. In endeavoring to restore order a collision occurred between the troops and the mob on the afternoon of July 21st, in which several of the soldiers and a number of the rioters were killed and wounded. The rioters were then joined by large numbers from the various manufactories and mines in the City of Pittsburgh and vicinity, and further reinforced by the idle and vicious classes, which exist in all large communities, and which were attracted to the spot by the opportunity offered for plunder and pillage. On the night of July 21st-22nd the terrible destruction of property occurred, which is particularly stated hereinafter, and the movement of freight trains through Pittsburgh was entirely prevented. This state of things continued practically until the night of the 28th of July. During the interval Governor Hartranft having reached the City, assumed command of the State troops, which had been reinforced by detachments of United States regulars and marines forwarded by the General Government on the Governor's requisition. The Governor at once inaugurated the most energetic measures for the restoration of peace and order, and arrangements were made through which the freight traffic of the road was resumed on the following morning, and many of the ringleaders in the later disturbance were promptly arrested by the civil authorities. By that time the citizens of Pittsburgh, appreciating the responsibility resting upon them, had taken measures to strengthen the hands of the civil authorities; to enforce the law and restore order, and thus enable the public to resume their business without further molestation."

"A large force was immediately put to work to remove the debris of engines, cars, tracks and buildings, which covered the ground from Washington Street to Thirty-third Street, between which points the Company had lost all its shops, engine-houses, offices, depots and all other property capable of being destroyed by fire, including the Union Depot and Hotel; in short, every one of the 39 buildings owned by it except the oil house on 28th Street. In this destruction were included 104 locomotives, 46 passenger cars and 506 freight cars, the whole loss aggregating about $2,000,000. In addition thereto the actual revenue lost by the Company through this stoppage of its traffic, is estimated at $1,000,000. and the value of the merchandise in transit destroyed at from $1,000,000. to $1,500,000. In addition to the above, 20 passenger and 861 freight cars, together with their contents, and valuable buildings belonging to your Western Lines were destroyed, and a large amount of property belonging to outside companies and individuals, including the large grain elevator at Pittsburgh; so that the entire loss will probably exceed $5,000,000."

"In accordance with the laws of Pennsylvania, suits are being instituted against the County of Allegheny to recover the damages thus sustained by your Company and by other Companies and individuals, and no doubt is entertained that the amounts found to be due will be recovered. Pending the settlement of these claims your Board has not deemed it expedient to reduce on your books the value of the property destroyed."

"The same spirit of revolt which prevailed at Pittsburgh existed also at Derry, Johnstown, Altoona, Harrisburg, Columbia and Philadelphia, and at Erie and other points, but no property was destroyed or violence committed at any of those places."

TWO QUARTERLY DIVIDENDS OMITTED

As the result of these disturbances the earning capacity of the Company was temporarily impaired, although it earned over 6% on its Capital Stock in 1877. Cash dividends amounting to 3½% had already been paid in this year, and it was, therefore, deemed advisable not to pay the usual quarterly cash dividends in August and November.

COMPLETION OF COLUMBIA & PORT DEPOSIT RAILROAD

On July 1st, 1877, the Columbia & Port Deposit Railroad, extending from Columbia, Pa., to Port Deposit, Md., a distance of 39.8 miles, was completed and opened for traffic, it being operated as part of the Philadelphia Division at that time.

PURCHASE OF "EMPIRE LINE" AND "GREEN LINE"

On October 17th, 1877, the Pennsylvania Railroad Company purchased the entire equipment, property and franchise rights of the Empire Transportation Company, it paying the latter Company $1,650,000. in Car Trust Certificates for 3,406 freight cars, and $900,000. of the same character of security for 1,308 oil carrying cars, the principal of both issues being due in ten and eight years, respectively. The Pennsylvania Railroad Company also purchased all of the pier and depot property, shops, offices and material for repair and construction of cars belonging to the Empire Transportation Company, for the sum of $450,000., which was paid for in securities owned by the Pennsylvania Railroad Company, making a total of $3,000,000. for the entire property and equipment of the Transportation Company. It was believed that this acquisition would be productive of beneficial results, and that the revenue therefrom would pay for the equipment within the time specified in the obligations issued by the Company therefor. With this purchase, which also included the equipment and property of what was known as the "Green Line," there were no fast freight lines operated on the Lines of the Pennsylvania Railroad not controlled by it.

CONNECTION BETWEEN MAIN LINE AND PITTSBURGH, VIRGINIA & CHARLESTON RAILWAY COMPLETED

The Port Perry Branch connecting the Main Line of the Pennsylvania Railroad near Brinton's station with the Pittsburgh, Virginia & Charleston Railway was laid with double track steel rails from the junction point to the north end of the bridge over the Monongahela River at Port Perry, and the connection completed on November 15th, 1877.

ROCKVILLE BRIDGE COMPLETED

The double track iron bridge, 3,680 feet in length, across the Susquehanna River at Rockville was completed on December 1st, 1877. By the construction of a little more than a mile of second track on this bridge and its approaches, there was made available an entire double track line between Pittsburgh and New York.

OPERATIONS OF AMERICAN STEAMSHIP COMPANY

The Annual Report for 1877 states that the business of the American Steamship Company, in which the Pennsylvania Railroad Company was largely interested, had suffered from the depression which had affected all Trans-Atlantic traffic. The steamers, it was stated, had been maintained in excellent condition; their trips had been made with great regularity and with entire freedom from casualty, and that they were held in high esteem by the traveling public.

PLAN TO PURCHASE GUARANTEED SECURITIES

The Management of the Company had been considering the subject of purchasing over a period of years its guaranteed securities, consisting of the Stocks and Bonds of leased lines and the bonded indebtedness of the Pennsylvania Company, so as to reduce its annual liability to pay dividends and interest thereon. On December 31st, 1877, the par value of these guaranteed securities amounted to slightly more than $180,500,000., on which the Company was paying an average annual guaranteed return of 7.4%, or approximately $13,400,000. It was felt that if these securities could be purchased from time to time, it would not only give them greater freedom from market fluctuations, but that the annual liability to pay interest and dividends on them would be substantially reduced. Therefore, the following plan, referred to in the annual report of 1877, was given consideration, through which it was believed the best interests of the stockholders would be permanently protected and promoted, viz: That there should be appropriated from the net earnings of the Company the sum of $100,000. per month commencing May 1st, 1878, which was to be deposited in a satisfactory Trust Company in Philadelphia, and competent and responsible stockholders appointed as Trustees of this fund. The Trust was to have for its object the purchase from time to time of the Bonds and Stocks of other companies, which were guaranteed by the Pennsylvania Railroad Company, and also Bonds issued by the Pennsylvania Company for which no provision had been made for their retirement.

For the amount of $1,200,000. per annum so appropriated from the net earnings to the Trust, plus such portion of the sum that was expended annually for construction and equipment purposes as would complete the amount of $1,377,404., which was equivalent to 2% per annum upon the Capital Stock, the shareholders were to receive annually scrip equivalent to a dividend of $1. per share (there being 1,377,404 shares then outstanding), redeemable at the option of the Company, bearing interest at 4% per annum, payable semi-annually, and in addition thereto, the balance of the net earnings in cash.

The income of the Trust to be applied:—

1. To the necessary expenses of the Trust;
2. To the payment of interest upon the scrip so issued to the shareholders, and
3. To the purchase from time to time of the outstanding guaranteed and other obligations as before stated.

FINANCIAL RESULT TO COMPANY AND STOCKHOLDERS

Under this plan the ultimate result would be the practical ownership of all the leased lines or their assets and the control of the Company's guaranteed liabilities. As the scrip or debenture proposed to be issued bearing 4% interest would be redeemable at the option of the Company, it would be released from the necessity of raising large sums of money to meet maturing indebtedness. If this plan were further continued, after the liabilities referred to had been reduced, the Company could also follow the same course with its own Bonded debt, and if this were done it would then be enabled, by the same or even a less contribution to the fund, to pay off the scrip indebtedness which it had created. The final result would be that all of the property of the Company would be held by it practically free from Bonded debt and liabilities, and would embrace 3,912 miles of well equipped railroad and 408 miles of canal, controlling a large traffic, upon which it could always earn reliable dividends. It was felt that the Company would be greatly relieved through the operations of the Trust, and the net earnings over the 2% represented by the scrip could be devoted each six months to the payment of cash dividends to the stockholders.

The form of security which it was proposed to give to the shareholders was very similar to that which had been created by many of the English railways as a representation of capital, and was known as a terminable debenture and considered a satisfactory security.

RESOLUTION TO MAKE PLAN EFFECTIVE

To carry out the foregoing arrangement the following resolution was submitted to the stockholders with the annual report for 1877, for their favorable action:—

> "*Resolved,* that the creation of a Trust having for its object the purchase from time to time of the bonds and shares of other companies, which are guaranteed by the Pennsylvania Railroad Company, and also of the bonded debt of the Pennsylvania Company, be, and it is, hereby approved; and that the incoming Board of Directors be, and they are, hereby instructed and authorized to take such action under the advice of counsel, as may, in their judgment, be lawful, necessary and best adapted to create such Trust and to accomplish the objects for which it is designed."

The resolution was discussed at some length at the annual meeting of the Company on March 12th, 1878, and a Committee of seven stockholders appointed to consider the same and report at an adjourned annual meeting on March 25th, 1878. Six members of this Committee reported in favor of the proposed resolution and the other member presented a minority report. The latter, while approving the general principles of the Trust, deferred final action thereon until the next annual meeting of the stockholders in 1879, and required the names of the Trustees, together with the probable annual cost of the Trust, to be submitted at that time for their approval or rejection. Both reports were submitted at the adjourned annual meeting, and it was decided to have the stockholders vote for either the majority or minority reports at the annual election on March 26th, 1878, which resulted in the approval of the majority report.

CREATION OF TRUST OF OCTOBER 9TH, 1878

A Trust was, therefore, created on October 9th, 1878, having for its object the purchase from time to time of Bonds and Stocks of other Companies, the principal, interest, or dividend upon which were guaranteed by the Pennsylvania Railroad Company, and also of the bonded debt of the Pennsylvania Company. The monthly payment was reduced to $50,000., and as the issuance of scrip to the stockholders to represent the sums paid into the Trust was deemed of doubtful legality, the plan of the Trust as finally approved made no provision for issuing this scrip. The more important terms of the resolution creating the Trust were as follows:—

1. Beginning with the first Monday of November, 1878, and the same day of each month thereafter, $50,000. shall be set apart, together with such other sums as may be appropriated by the Company for the same purpose, and placed to the credit of the Managers of this Trust;

2. The Management may set aside such additional sums, after the payment of dividends, as the Company's business will warrant, to be placed in the said Trust, but no appro-

priation shall be made during any year that will, with the monthly payments hereinbefore provided for during the same year, exceed 2% upon the Capital Stock of the Company then outstanding;

3. Trust funds to be under control of five Managers, consisting of the President of the Company, a Vice-President and three members of the Board of Directors.

4. Managers of Trust to be governed by instructions of Board of Directors as to temporary investments in other securities when those contemplated by terms of Trust cannot be purchased at what are regarded as proper prices; such securities temporarily purchased to be held only until those covered by terms of Trust can be acquired at reasonable prices.

DANVILLE, HAZLETON & WILKES-BARRE RAILROAD COMPANY REORGANIZED

On March 20th, 1878, the Danville, Hazleton & Wilkes-Barre Railroad, extending from Sunbury to Tomhicken, Pa., a distance of about 44 miles, and operated at cost under lease to the Pennsylvania Railroad, was sold out under foreclosure proceedings, and reorganized on May 31st, 1878, under the name of the Sunbury, Hazleton & Wilkes-Barre Railway Company. The road was again leased to the Pennsylvania Railroad Company for 50 years from May 1st, 1878, and operated as a branch of the Philadelphia & Erie Railroad.

CONTROL OF ROAD BETWEEN TOLEDO JUNCTION AND TOLEDO, O.

In order to settle the controversy with the City of Toledo with respect to the lease and ownership of the Toledo & Woodville Railroad, extending from Toledo to Woodville, O., a distance of 18 miles, the Northwestern Ohio Railway Company (owned exclusively by the Pennsylvania Company) purchased the interest of the City of Toledo in that railroad for $225,000. The Northwestern Ohio Railway Company had previously acquired the Toledo, Tiffin & Eastern Railroad and the Mansfield, Cold Water & Lake Michigan

Railroad, which extended from Toledo Junction to Woodville. This completed under one organization a first class railroad about 79 miles in length running from Toledo Junction (on the Pittsburgh, Ft. Wayne & Chicago Railway) to Toledo, O.

RESUMPTION OF CASH DIVIDENDS ON SEMI-ANNUAL BASIS

The payment of cash dividends was resumed by the Pennsylvania Railroad Company in November, 1878, at which time 2% was paid. The previous action of the Management providing for the payment of quarterly dividends was also rescinded, and future dividends were to be paid semi-annually in the months of May and November. The last dividend had been paid in May, 1877, the failure to make any payments during the interim being due to the serious losses of the Company in the Pittsburgh riots and the great falling off in the business of the Country. The outlook in the latter part of 1878 was much brighter and the Management felt assured that the strong financial position of the Company warranted the resumption of dividends.

PURCHASE OF PENNSYLVANIA RAILROAD COMPANY STOCK FROM CITY OF PHILADELPHIA

It was deemed advisable in 1879 for the Pennsylvania Railroad Company to purchase at par 59,149 shares of its Capital Stock from the Commissioners of the Sinking Fund of the City of Philadelphia, involving an outlay of $2,957,450., rather than to have this large amount of stock fall into the hands of interests which might be unfriendly to the Management of the Company. Reference is made later to the distribution of practically all of this Stock to the shareholders.

CLAIMS AGAINST ALLEGHENY COUNTY SETTLED

The claims against the County of Allegheny, growing out of the Pittsburgh riots of 1877 were compromised in 1879 and the sum of $1,600,000. was received by the Pennsylvania Railroad Company in full settlement of the loss incurred by it in the destruction of property in that County. The claims of shippers and other corporations against the County were adjusted on practically the same basis as that agreed upon with the Pennsylvania Railroad Company.

LEASE OF PENNSYLVANIA & DELAWARE RAILWAY CANCELLED—POMEROY & NEWARK RAILROAD COMPANY FORMED

The Pennsylvania & Delaware Railway, extending from Pomeroy, on the Main Line of the Pennsylvania Railroad, to Newark, Del., a distance of 38.6 miles, being unable to meet its operating expenses, the lease of that road was cancelled in 1879. The road was foreclosed under its mortgage and that portion of the line in Pennsylvania extending from Pomeroy to the Delaware State Line, was organized as the Pomeroy & State Line Railroad Company. The section of the road in the State of Delaware became known as the Newark & Delaware City Railroad Company. On October 29th, 1881, the latter Company sold that part of its line from a point near Newark, Del., to Delaware City, Del., a distance of 11.8 miles to the Philadelphia, Wilmington & Baltimore Railroad Company. Effective December 29th, 1881, the Pomeroy & State Line Railroad and the Newark & Delaware City Railroad Companies were consolidated to form the Pomeroy & Newark Railroad Company. It extended from Pomeroy, Pa., to Newark, Del., a distance of 26.8 miles and its entire capital stock was owned by the Pennsylvania Railroad Company.

FORMATION OF FREEHOLD & JAMESBURG AGRICULTURAL RAILROAD COMPANY

As it was found desirable to place under one organization the railroad to Sea Girt and other northern New Jersey seacoast resorts, the Freehold & Jamesburg Agricultural Railroad Company, the Squankum & Freehold Marl Company and the Farmingdale & Squan Village Railroad Company were consolidated, effective May 21st, 1879, into the Freehold & Jamesburg Agricultural Railroad Company. A consolidated mortgage for $578,000. was authorized for the purpose of retiring the outstanding bonds and improving the property.

BRANCH FROM WEST CHESTER TO MALVERN PURCHASED

In order to give the Pennsylvania Railroad a proper connection with West Chester, Pa., it purchased in 1879 the West Chester Railroad. This road extended from West Chester to the Main Line of the Pennsylvania Railroad at Malvern, a distance of about 9 miles. It was later found necessary to make considerable change in the alignment of the road, and to provide the connection with the Main Line at Frazer, three miles west of Malvern.

PROPOSED EXTENSION FROM WEST PHILADELPHIA TO CIVIC CENTRE OF CITY

Owing to the great necessity of providing enlarged passenger and other facilities for the Company in Philadelphia, to accommodate its increased traffic, the Management had been considering for several years the question of extending the Pennsylvania Railroad from West Philadelphia to the civic centre of the City. After careful investigation and consideration of the matter, it was decided in 1879 to establish a passenger station near the new public buildings at Broad and Market Streets, and extend the road to that point. In order to avoid the obstruction of traffic upon the streets crossed by the proposed new line, it was necessary to construct the extension above grade and to build a bridge across the Schuylkill River. It was also proposed to utilize the space under the tracks for the storage of coal, lime and other bulky products, and in this way to furnish additional terminal accommodations for the increased business of the Company. The entire cost of the improvements, including the purchase of real estate, freight and passenger depots and other facilities connected therewith, was estimated at $3,000,000.

PROPOSED EXTENSION TO BETHLEHEM, PA.

Another question of importance was also receiving the attention of the Management in 1879, although no definite action was taken, namely, the construction, in connection with the Lehigh Valley Railroad, of a road from a point on the Connecting Railway at or near Ridge Avenue Station in Philadelphia, by way of Germantown, Chestnut Hill, Conshohocken and Norristown, to Bethlehem. It was stated that if the owners of the property along the proposed line would grant the required right of way and depot grounds, and the communities to be benefited by its construction would give proper facilities for passing through their limits, the road could be made an important avenue of transportation both to them and to the City of Philadelphia. By the construction of this new line, the manufacturing and commercial interests in Philadelphia would have access to the valuable coal fields in the Lehigh and Wyoming regions, and, through the action of the Lehigh Valley Railroad and its connecting lines, be able to get their anthracite coal at prices not exceeding those charged in New York City, or other competitive points east of that City. It was proposed to use the depot and other property of the Lehigh Valley Railroad Company for handling the freight business in Bethlehem, the Pennsylvania Railroad merely furnishing the track facilities to and from the same.

FURTHER EXTENSIONS OF SOUTH WEST PENNSYLVANIA RAILWAY

Several extensions of the South West Pennsylvania Railway were constructed from Connellsville southward, and in July, 1880, it was extended to Fairchance, Pa., a distance of about 48 miles from Greensburg, Pa.

NEWPORT AND CINCINNATI BRIDGE

The Newport and Cincinnati Bridge, crossing the Ohio River at Cincinnati, being closely connected with the operations of the Western Lines and coming especially under the supervision of their officers, it was deemed best that the Stock held by the Pennsylvania Railroad Company in the Bridge Company should be transferred to the Pennsylvania Company. This was accordingly done in 1880, and there was received in payment therefor $1,000,000., par value, of Stock of the Pennsylvania Company.

PENNSYLVANIA COMPANY STOCK

During the year 1880, the Pennsylvania Railroad Company had purchased the few remaining shares of Common Stock of the Pennsylvania Company in the hands of the public. This gave it ownership of the entire Capital Stock, both Common and Preferred, and as it was deemed unnecessary to continue the distinction between the two classes of Stock, the Preferred was merged into the Common. The total outstanding Common Capital Stock on December 31st, 1880, amounted to $12,000,000.

SCRIP AND CASH DIVIDENDS

Instead of paying the usual semi-annual dividend in cash in May, 1880, the Pennsylvania Railroad Company declared a 3% dividend payable in scrip, which was redeemable in cash or convertible into Stock when presented in sums of $50., and represented a distribution to the shareholders of a large part of the 59,149 shares of its Stock purchased from the City of Philadelphia on December 4th, 1879, at par. In November of that year (1880), a dividend of 3% in cash was paid, and an additional 1% payable in scrip, redeemable in cash, or convertible into the remaining Stock acquired from the City.

MANAGEMENT WARNS PUBLIC

While at the close of 1880 the earnings of the Pennsylvania Railroad Company had reached the highest mark in the history of the Company, the Management sounded a warning by stating that the prosperity of the Country, combined with the cheap rates for borrowing money, was inducing capital to promote wild railway schemes which were sure to bring loss to their owners and place an additional burden upon the public. The remarks were continued by stating that—

"It is, therefore, proper that all railway companies, like your own, whose shares are so largely and widely distributed, (as an evidence of which we may state that the number of shareholders on your books at the last dividend period was about 13,000), and often held by those mainly dependent upon their dividends, should so manage their affairs as not to depend too strongly upon this seeming prosperity, which must undoubtedly be followed by adverse seasons. Your Management have, therefore, deemed it wise to so conduct the affairs of your Company that while it returns what may be regarded as a reasonable, if not a large, dividend to its shareholders, a proper reserve shall be held to provide against these periods of depression, so that a uniformity can be maintained in its dividends, and your properties at the same time kept up to that full standard of efficiency essential to enable it to meet successfully the schemes of irresponsible competition. It may be noted here that of the 59,149 shares of your stock bought from the City of Philadelphia, and held in trust 47,470 shares have been distributed to the shareholders on account of the dividends declared in May and November last (1880), the premium upon which, added to the cash dividends then paid, makes an aggregate for the past year of nearly 8%. Special allusion is made to this matter from the fact that grave exception has been taken by some of the shareholders to the policy of not dividing at each dividend period the entire net receipts of the Company, the latter being the policy that obtains so strongly in England, where a considerable portion of your shares is held, but which in this Country has never been pursued without weakening a railway company and entailing upon it the necessity of periodical reductions, if not a suspension of its dividends. It is believed by your Management that if this policy were to be applied in this Country, and especially by the Pennsylvania Railroad Company, whose interests are so widely diversified, it could but result in diminishing its efficiency, and eventually returning less dividends to its shareholders. It may be proper at this point to correct the impression, prevailing more strongly abroad than in this Country, that the revenues of your Company, to an unreasonable extent, are devoted to new construction work, and such outlays charged to expenses. This the shareholders may be assured is not the fact.

The cost of all new construction work not properly chargeable to the Expense account is each year added to your Capital Account, the funds for this purpose, for the past 2 years, having been obtained largely by the sale of such securities owned by the Company as it was deemed wise to dispose of."

RESIGNATION AND DEATH OF PRESIDENT SCOTT

On May 1st, 1880, President Scott, upon the advice of his physician and after 30 years of service with the Pennsylvania Railroad Company, tendered his resignation in order to obtain the necessary rest and relaxation for the restoration of his health. It was regretfully accepted, effective June 1st, 1880. Unfortunately, however, the hope that relief from official cares and responsibilities would restore his health and vigor was not realized, and he died at his home on May 21st, 1881.

The following Minute was adopted by the Board of Directors of the Company on May 25th, 1881, in recording his death:—

> "With profound sorrow the Directors of this Company record upon the minutes the death of Thomas A. Scott, which occurred at his country residence on Saturday evening, 21st instant. A little more than a year ago the hope of regaining his failing health constrained him to relinquish his official position, and we then expressed the deep regret felt in recognizing the necessity for his action, and trusted that prolonged life would follow a cessation from his labors. But we are now called to mourn his death, and we feel that the many years devoted to the service of this Company, the inseparable connection of his name with its progress, its trials, and its successes, require that fitting recognition be made of the close of his marvelously active life. We can not here chronicle all that he did; history must do that. The influence of that life will long be felt, not only on the future of this Company, but of the State and Nation. For the latter he accomplished, in what were but episodes in his employments, labors which might well have occupied the whole lives of ordinary men. Looking back upon the scenes in which we have

known him and upon the fruits of his labors, with our tears over his grave we mingle our thanks that he has lived.

To his family we can but express the hope that the sad event which is now to them a bitter anguish may in the fulness of time become a chastened sorrow, softened by the recollections of his greatness, his goodness, and by the contemplation of the works of usefulness and benevolence in which he has borne so distinguished a part. We pass no formal resolves, but express this as our united tribute to the memory of him whom we loved as a friend and honored as an officer, and direct that it be placed upon the minutes of the proceedings of this day, and be certified to his family."

STATISTICAL DATA

The following operating and traffic statistics, and financial statements will indicate the progress made by the Company during his Administration, in the greater part of which he was unfortunately handicapped by the financial and industrial depression, following the panic of 1873, and the serious losses incurred through the labor troubles in the year 1877:—

REVENUE, EXPENSES, OPERATING INCOME, AND RENTALS FROM 1874 TO 1880, INCLUSIVE

All Lines East of Pittsburgh and Erie Operated Directly

Year	Miles	Gross Revenue	Operating Expenses	Operating Income	Rentals Paid	Net Operating Income to Penna. R. R. Co.
1874......	1,599.	$37,386,427.27	$22,357,349.59	$15,029,077.68	$6,230,864.26	$8,798,213.42
1875......	1,631.	34,464,104.38	21,094,461.31	13,369,643.07	6,201,728.53	7,167,914.54
1876......	1,690.	36,891,060.99	22,081,229.34	14,809,831.65	6,308,828.92	8,501,002.73
1877......	1,782.	31,117,146.18	19,028,467.24	12,088,678.94	6,351,242.12	5,737,436.82
1878......	1,782.	31,636,734.58	18,468,993.71	13,167,740.87	5,994,433.17	7,173,307.70
1879......	1,872.	34,620,279.17	20,382,740.15	14,237,539.02	6,245,113.16	7,992,425.86
1880......	1,875.61	41,260,072.49	24,625,047.57	16,635,024.92	7,029,072.53	9,605,952.39

TONNAGE, MILEAGE, REVENUE, EXPENSES, AND AVERAGES ON FREIGHT BUSINESS, 1874 TO 1880, INCLUSIVE

All Lines East of Pittsburgh and Erie Operated Directly

Year	Tons	Tons One Mile	Revenue	Average Revenue per Ton per Mile	Expenses	Average Expenses per Ton per Mile	Average Net Revenue per Ton per Mile
				Cents		Cents	Cents
1874......	15,604,922	1,916,591,690	$24,715,418.15	1.290	$15,554,659.70	0.812	0.478
1875......	15,772,722	2,026,190,425	22,807,660.00	1.126	14,362,136.16	0.709	0.417
1876......	17,064,953	2,221,739,198	21,132,560.23	0.951	14,657,083.29	0.660	0.291
1877......	16,382,268	2,086,659,438	21,149,389.38	1.014	12,834,226.82	0.615	0.399
1878......	17,597,447	2,368,330,428	21,961,447.75	0.927	12,752,696.07	0.538	0.389
1879......	22,867,162	2,974,925,881	24,500,960.21	0.824	14,287,532.62	0.480	0.344
1880......	26,051,091	3,239,482,799	29,750,291.99	0.918	17,490,054.88	0.540	0.378

PASSENGERS, MILEAGE, REVENUE, EXPENSES, AND AVERAGES ON PASSENGER BUSINESS, 1874 TO 1880, INCLUSIVE

All Lines East of Pittsburgh and Erie Operated Directly

Year	Passengers	Passengers One Mile	Revenue	Average Revenue per Passenger per Mile	Expenses	Average Expenses per Passenger per Mile	Average Net Revenue per Passenger per Mile
				Cents		Cents	Cents
1874......	15,020,063	364,532,316	$9,488,968.56	2.603	$6,251,057.94	1.715	0.888
1875......	14,456,864	344,234,876	8,857,619.67	2.573	6,191,289.39	1.799	0.774
1876......	18,363,366	623,208,759	12,817,473.64	2.057	6,572,572.70	1.055	1.002
1877......	13,007,832	298,752,730	6,940,498.97	2.323	5,326,087.97	1.783	0.540
1878......	12,792,305	292,725,524	6,759,426.43	2.309	5,013,723.42	1.713	0.596
1879......	13,602,401	314,260,989	7,085,949.36	2.255	5,370,228.17	1.709	0.546
1880......	16,575,042	382,787,186	8,504,387.22	2.222	6,407,692.10	1.674	0.548

DIVIDENDS AND ALLOTMENTS ON CAPITAL STOCK—THE PENNSYLVANIA RAILROAD COMPANY

DATE	Capital Stock on which Dividend or Allotment was Declared	DIVIDEND				ALLOTMENTS OF STOCK ON SUBSCRIPTION	
		CASH		SCRIP OR STOCK			
		Per Cent.	Amount	Per Cent.	Amount	Per Cent.	Amount
May, 1874.	$67,343,200	5	$3,367,160				
November, "	68,692,350	5	3,434,617 50				
May, 1875.	68,870,200	4	2,754,808				
August, "	68,870,200	2	1,377,404				
November, "	68,870,200	2	1,377,404				
February, 1876.	68,870,200	2	1,377,404				
May, "	68,870,200	2	1,377,404				
August, "	68,870,200	2	1,377,404				
November, "	68,870,200	2	1,377,404				
February, 1877.	68,870,200	2	1,377,404				
May, "	68,870,200	1½	1,033,053				
November, 1878.	68,870,200	2	1,377,404				
May, 1879.	68,870,200	2	1,377,404				
November, "	68,870,200	2½	1,721,755				
May, 1880.	68,870,200	......	....	3	$2,066,106 00	......	Scrip redeemable in cash or convertible into stock when presented in sums of $50, representing the distribution to the stockholders of stock purchased Dec. 4, 1879, by Pennsylvania R. R. Co. from the City of Philadelphia (59,149 shares @ par $50 per share), and not resulting in any increase in the capital stock.
November, "	68,870,200	3	2,066,106	1	688,702 00		

DIRECTORS

The following is a list of the Directors who served during President Scott's Administration, together with the dates of their election and the end of their service:—

Name of Director	*Elected*	*End of Service*
Josiah Bacon................	March 3, 1856,	February 3, 1881;
Wistar Morris...............	January 29, 1858,	March 23, 1891;
John M. Kennedy	February 8, 1860,	March 2, 1863;
"	April 6, 1864,	March 5, 1866;
"	April 4, 1866,	February 25, 1880;
Thomas A. Scott.............	March 21, 1860,	June 1, 1880;
William Anspach.............	March 4, 1867,	March 25, 1879;
G. Morrison Coates..........	"	March 26, 1878;
George B. Roberts...........	May 3, 1869,	January 30, 1897;
Alexander M. Fox...........	March 6, 1871,	October 6, 1907;
John Scott..................	November 2, 1872,	March 26, 1878;
Alexander J. Derbyshire......	December 2, 1850,	February 5, 1855;
"	February 26, 1873,	March 26, 1878;
Samuel M. Felton............	"	September 12, 1883;
Henry M. Phillips...........	March 24, 1874,	August 28, 1884;
N. Parker Shortridge.........	"	January 3, 1915;
Alexander Biddle............	"	May 2, 1899;
Edmund Smith...............	May 3, 1869,	March 1, 1873;
"	August 1, 1874,	June 30, 1888;
A. J. Cassatt................	July 1, 1874,	October 1, 1882;
"	September 12, 1883,	December 28, 1906;
Daniel B. Cummins..........	March 26, 1878,	November 9, 1887;
Henry D. Welsh.............	"	December 19, 1896;
John Price Wetherill.........	March 27, 1878,	September 17, 1888;
William L. Elkins............	March 25, 1879,	November 7, 1903;
James McManus.............	March 23, 1880,	March 22, 1881.

GEORGE BROOKE ROBERTS
Fifth President—June 1st, 1880, to January 30th, 1897.

GEORGE BROOKE ROBERTS

FIFTH PRESIDENT, 1880–1897

ON June 1st, 1880, George Brooke Roberts was elected President to succeed Thomas A. Scott. President Roberts was born on January 15th, 1833, on "Pencoed Farm" (now Bala), Montgomery County, Pennsylvania. He was educated in the schools of the neighborhood and later took a technical course in the Renssalaer Institute at Troy, N. Y., from which he was graduated in 1849. In 1851 at the age of 18 he began his railroad career as a rodman on an engineering corps engaged in constructing the Mountain Division of the Pennsylvania Railroad, and one year later was appointed Assistant Engineer on the Sunbury & Erie Railroad, later reorganized as the Philadelphia & Erie Railroad Company. From that time on he was actively engaged in the construction of numerous roads, including the Sunbury & Erie Railroad, the North Pennsylvania Railroad, the Allentown & Auburn Railroad, the Mahanoy & Broad Mountain Railroad, the West Jersey Railroad and others, many of which he completed as Chief Engineer. In 1862 he re-entered the service of the Pennsylvania Railroad Company as Assistant to John Edgar Thomson, who was then President. Seven years later he was made Fourth Vice-President, then Second Vice-President, and when Thomas A. Scott became President in 1874, he was elected First Vice-President, which position he held at the time of his election to the Presidency.

His familiarity with all questions pertaining to the engineering features of the construction, extension and improvement work on the Company's lines, together with the knowledge and experience gained from the general supervision of the leased and controlled roads of the Pennsylvania Railroad System and their accounting features, enabled him to render valuable services to the Company in the direction of its affairs.

ACQUISITION OF PHILADELPHIA, WILMINGTON & BALTIMORE RAILROAD

At the annual meeting of the Company on March 8th, 1881, President Roberts stated that as it had been learned that the Philadelphia, Wilmington & Baltimore Railroad was about to pass into the hands of parties whose interests were antagonistic to those of the Pennsylvania Railroad Company, the Management was satisfied that the interests of the stockholders of the Pennsylvania Railroad Company required that this road should be controlled by it. The Philadelphia, Wilmington & Baltimore Railroad had the following mileage:—

Main Line:				
Philadelphia to Baltimore	95	miles		
Philadelphia & Baltimore Central Railroad, extending from West Philadelphia to West Chester, and from junction near Lenni to Octoraro Junction, Md., a distance of	46	"		
New Castle & Wilmington Railroad, Delaware Junction to New Castle, Del.	5	"		
New Castle & Frenchtown Railroad, New Castle, Del., to Junction with Delaware Railroad	7	"		
Delaware Railroad, Junction with New Castle & Frenchtown Railroad to Delmar, Del.	84	"		
Queen Anne & Kent Railroad, Massey's to Centreville, Md.	26	"		
Total Main Line			263	miles
Branches:				
Southwark Railroad, Washington Avenue, Philadelphia, to Delaware River	1.37	miles		
Newark & Delaware City Railroad, Newark to Delaware City, Md.	12.56	"		
Port Deposit Branch, Perrysville to Port Deposit, Md.	3.78	"		
Chester Creek Branch, Lamokin to Lenni, Pa.	7.14	"		
West Chester Branch	26.08	"		
Townsend Branch, Townsend, Del., to Massey's, Md.	9.15	"		
Clayton Branch, Clayton to Smyrna, Del.	1.27	"		
Seaford Branch, Seaford to Oak Grove, Del.	5.72	"		
			67.07	"
Total Main Line and Branches about			330	miles

STOCKHOLDERS APPROVE

Accordingly a contract was concluded on behalf of the Pennsylvania Railroad Company with a Committee representing the owners of a majority of the Stock of the Philadelphia, Wilmington & Baltimore Railroad Company for the purchase of not less than 92,000 shares, and any additional amount that might be presented before April 1st, 1881, payment to be made therefor on July 1st, 1881. While the Board of Directors were authorized by the Charter to make this contract, it was deemed desirable to report the matter to the stockholders and secure their approval, and also to obtain authority for the issuance of additional Capital Stock to provide the means of paying for the newly acquired Stock ownership. The stockholders unanimously approved of the purchase and authorized the issuance of 400,000 shares additional of Pennsylvania Railroad Company Stock to finance in part its cost.

METHOD OF PAYMENT

Under the purchase contract there were acquired 217,819 shares out of a total of 235,901 then outstanding. The funds for this purpose were provided in part through the sale at par to the stockholders of 176,000 shares of Capital Stock of the Pennsylvania Railroad Company, and the balance through the sale of $10,000,000. of Trust Certificates, dated July 1st, 1881, maturing July 1st, 1921, and bearing interest at 4% per annum. They were secured by a collateral deposit with the Trustee of 200,000 shares of Philadelphia, Wilmington & Baltimore Railroad Company Stock at its par value of $50. per share. The dividends on the Stock of the acquired road, after providing for the interest upon the then outstanding Trust Certificates, were to be applied as a sinking fund for the purchase and cancellation of the Trust Certificates whenever they could be obtained at a price not exceeding par. The purchase of the majority interest in the Philadelphia, Wilmington & Baltimore Railroad not only furnished the Pennsylvania Railroad with a continuous line between Philadelphia and Washington, but also secured extensive additional terminal facilities at Philadelphia and Baltimore of such a character as could not otherwise be acquired at any reasonable cost, if at all.

PITTSBURGH, VIRGINIA & CHARLESTON RAILWAY EXTENDED

The extension of the Pittsburgh, Virginia & Charleston Railway from Monongahela City to Brownsville, Pa., a distance of 23 miles, was completed and opened for operation on May 15th, 1881.

BROAD STREET STATION OPENED

The construction of Broad Street Station in Philadelphia, and its track approaches from West Philadelphia, was so far advanced that the Station was opened for business on December 5th, 1881. With the transfer of the trains of the Philadelphia, Wilmington & Baltimore Railroad to that Station, it became the central point for the daily arrival and departure of over 200 passenger trains upon the various lines of the Pennsylvania Railroad Company centering in Philadelphia. Its cost to December 31st, 1881, including real estate, was $4,272,268.53.

GIRARD POINT STORAGE COMPANY FORMED

In 1881 a corporation was formed under the name of the Girard Point Storage Company, in which the Pennsylvania Railroad Company had a controlling interest, for the acquisition of the Delaware River waterfront terminal facilities in Philadelphia of the International Navigation Company at Girard Point and Point Breeze. This majority ownership was secured by reason of the fact that the Pennsylvania Railroad Company held a large amount of the obligations of the International Navigation Company, secured upon the grain elevator and other property of the latter Company, which were to be taken over by the new corporation. It was also proposed to construct an additional elevator and otherwise improve the property so as to enable the new company to operate the facilities in the most profitable and economical manner.

TWO ROADS ADDED TO BALD EAGLE VALLEY RAILROAD

On March 17th, 1881, the Bellefonte & Snow Shoe Railroad was purchased by the Pennsylvania Railroad Company and effective April 7th, 1881, it and the Moshannon Railroad Company were consolidated into the Bald Eagle Valley Railroad Company.

INTEREST ACQUIRED IN NORTH & WEST BRANCH RAILWAY

The Management of the Company deemed it advisable to purchase in 1881 a controlling interest in and assume the completion of the North & West Branch Railway. This road extended from a connection with the Sunbury, Hazleton & Wilkes-Barre Railway (controlled by the Pennsylvania Railroad Company) at Catawissa to Wilkes-Barre, a distance of about 43 miles, passing through the latter Company's coal lands and other valuable anthracite coal properties. It was completed and opened for operation on November 23rd, 1882.

MARYSVILLE BRIDGE ABANDONED

The maintenance of the long wooden bridge of the Northern Central Railway Company crossing the Susquehanna River at Marysville had become so expensive as to make it advisable in 1881 to build a road connecting the Main Line of the Pennsylvania Railroad with the Northern Central Railway on the east bank of that river. It was known as the Rockville Branch and was completed on November 1st, 1882. This enabled the latter road to use the substantial iron bridge of the Pennsylvania Railroad just a few miles below, and saved a further expenditure on the old structure to place it in proper condition.

NORTH JERSEY SEASHORE LINES

The Philadelphia & Long Branch Railway, extending from Whitings to the seacoast and thence northwardly along the coast to a connection with the Central Railroad of New Jersey at Bay Head, was completed in 1881, but not in time to accommodate the summer travel. Following the completion of this road, negotiations were opened with the Central Railroad of New Jersey for the use of their leased lines extending from the aforesaid connection to Perth Amboy. The result was a contract between the Pennsylvania Railroad Company, Central Railroad of New Jersey and the New York & Long Branch Railroad Company, by which the first named road secured the joint use of a continuous line from New York to Long Branch, and other prominent seaside resorts in that vicinity, thus making it unnecessary to construct a competing line.

CONTRACT FOR USE OF LINE FROM RED BANK TO MILTON, PA.

The Management of the Company also reported that it had entered into a contract in 1881 with the Wabash, St. Louis & Pacific Railway Company and the Central Railroad of New Jersey, by which the lines controlled by the Pennsylvania Railroad between Red Bank, on the Allegheny Valley Railway, and Milton, on the Philadelphia & Erie Railroad, were to be used by the companies named, for the exchange of through traffic between their respective lines. Under this arrangement the Wabash, St. Louis & Pacific Railway Company and the Central Railroad of New Jersey were to promote the construction of a road between Red Bank and Youngstown, O., and it was expected that if these two railroads availed themselves of this trackage privilege, both the Philadelphia & Erie Railroad and the Low Grade Division of the Allegheny Valley Railroad would be greatly benefited thereby. This construction work, however, was not carried out, and the trackage privilege never exercised.

PENNSYLVANIA COMPANY STOCK INCREASED

For the purpose of providing a large financial basis for the Pennsylvania Company, the Management of the Pennsylvania Railroad Company deemed it advisable in 1881 to transfer the following securities to the Pennsylvania Company:—

Newport & Cincinnati Bridge Co. Bonds, par value	$1,200,000.
19,391 shares of stock of the Jeffersonville, Madison & Indianapolis R. R. Co. at a value of	1,800,000.
$5,000,000. Pennsylvania Company Debenture Bonds	5,000,000.
Total	$8,000,000.

The Pennsylvania Company issued $8,000,000. of its Capital Stock in exchange for the foregoing securities, which made the amount issued and outstanding $20,000,000., all of which was owned by the Pennsylvania Railroad Company.

EXTENSION OF PITTSBURGH, VIRGINIA & CHARLESTON RAILWAY

On September 25th, 1882, the Redstone Extension of the Pittsburgh, Virginia & Charleston Railway, extending from West Brownsville Junction to Redstone Junction on the South West Pennsylvania Railway, a distance of 16½ miles, was completed and placed in operation, giving the former road a through connection with the Connellsville coke fields.

INTEREST IN INDIANAPOLIS & ST. LOUIS RAILROAD SOLD

In 1882 the Pennsylvania Railroad Company, already having a shorter line between Indianapolis and St. Louis, disposed of its one-half interest in the Indianapolis & St. Louis Railroad Company to the Cleveland, Columbus, Cincinnati & Indianapolis Railway Company (part of the New York Central System). Reference has heretofore been made to the fact that this interest in the Indianapolis & St. Louis Railroad Company had been received with the lease of the Pittsburgh, Ft. Wayne & Chicago Railway Company.

CASH AND SCRIP DIVIDENDS

In declaring the regular semi-annual dividend in November, 1882, the Management of the Company, without establishing it as a fixed policy, deemed it advisable that the option should be given to the shareholders of receiving a portion of their dividend in scrip convertible into cash, or Stock at par, and accordingly 2½% was paid in cash and 2% in such scrip. This was done because the Company was compelled to apply a large portion of its current funds for additions and betterments to its railroad and facilities and make advances to branch and auxiliary lines. It was felt that the dividends payable in cash should be limited to such amount as would not seriously interfere with the demands upon the treasury, and that a proper additional portion of the profits should be returned to the stockholders in the Capital Stock of the Company. Nearly all of this scrip was later converted into Stock.

CHESTNUT HILL BRANCH

A Company was organized in 1882 under the name of the Philadelphia, Germantown & Chestnut Hill Railroad Company for the purpose of constructing a branch from a point on the Connecting Railway at North Philadelphia to Chestnut Hill, a distance of about 6¾ miles, the funds therefor having been obtained by a favorable sale of the securities of the new Company. The only liability assumed by the Pennsylvania Railroad Company upon the branch was to provide for any deficit between the net earnings and the interest on the Bonds, amounting to $45,000., and a reasonable Sinking Fund for the redemption of the Bonds at maturity.

CONTROL OF UNION RAILROAD OF BALTIMORE

The Management of the Company reported in 1882 that the Northern Central Railway Company, in which the Pennsylvania Railroad Company had a majority stockholding interest, had, through the pursuance of a conservative policy, been brought into a prosperous condition, and its stockholders could have reasonable assurance that they would receive a fair return on their investment. The Northern Central Railway Company during the year 1882 had obtained control of the Union Railroad of Baltimore, by the purchase of its entire Capital Stock, amounting at par to $600,000. (subject to its funded debt of $1,500,000.), the funds for which were supplied by an allotment and sale of the Capital Stock of the Northern Central Railway Company. It was stated that the acquisition of control of this line had largely tended to strengthen and improve the position of the latter Company in Baltimore, and gave the Pennsylvania Railroad the indirect control of the connecting link in that city between the Philadelphia, Wilmington & Baltimore Railroad, the Northern Central Railway and the Baltimore & Potomac Railroad.

EXTENDING UP THE SCHUYLKILL VALLEY

As the necessity for the construction of a branch from the Main Line of the Pennsylvania Railroad into the Schuylkill Valley to secure coal and other traffic had become evident to the Management, it was determined in 1882 to proceed actively with the building of a line in that direction. Accordingly work was started on the Phoenixville & West Chester Railroad extending from Frazer to Phoenixville, a distance of 11 miles. Surveys had also been made for the development of this valley by a line beginning at 52nd Street Station, Philadelphia, and extending through Manayunk, thence directly up the Schuylkill Valley through Conshohocken, Norristown, Phoenixville, Pottstown, Birdsboro and Reading. A considerable portion of the right of way had been secured and work commenced at some of the more important points.

The companies incorporated for this purpose, namely, the Phoenixville & West Chester Railroad, Philadelphia, Norristown & Phoenixville Railroad and the Phoenixville, Pottstown & Reading Railroad Companies, were, effective June 1st, 1883, consolidated into one Company, under the corporate name of the Pennsylvania Schuylkill Valley Railroad Company. On August 1st, 1883, that section of the road between Frazer and Phoenixville, a distance of 11 miles, was opened for operation.

During the year 1884 the entire road was completed between 52nd Street, Philadelphia, and Reading, a distance of about 54 miles; the various sections of the line being finished and opened for traffic on the following dates, viz: from 52nd Street to Bala on April 1st; to Manayunk on May 12th; to Norristown on June 23rd; to Pottstown on September 22nd, and to Reading on November 24th. The whole line, together with the branch between Phoenixville and Frazer, was leased to the Pennsylvania Railroad Company. It was proposed in the following Spring to make further progress in extending the road through the anthracite coal regions, looking ultimately to a connection with a branch of the Northern Central Railway at Shamokin, and with the North & West Branch Railway near the Susquehanna Coal Company properties, which were controlled in the interest of the Pennsylvania Railroad Company.

COLUMBUS, CHICAGO & INDIANA CENTRAL RAILWAY COMPANY REORGANIZED

On January 10th, 1883, the property of the Columbus, Chicago & Indiana Central Railway Company was sold under foreclosure proceedings, and a reorganization effected on April 1st, 1883, under the name of the Chicago, St. Louis & Pittsburgh Railroad Company. The long and tedious litigation in connection with the lease of that road to the Pittsburgh, Cincinnati & St. Louis Railway Company was thus brought to a close, and the Western Lines relieved of what had been an onerous obligation, and one which, if the final adjudication had sustained the lease, would have seriously affected their revenues. The Management thought it advisable, for the proper protection of the interests of the Pennsylvania Railroad Company, to become, in connection with its Lines West, the owners of a portion of the securities of the new company. Therefore, ownership was secured of $11,500,000. of the First Mortgage 5% Bonds, 117,212½ shares of the Preferred Stock and 14,242½ shares of the Common Stock, with a total par value of $13,145,500., which represented a controlling interest in the Company.

NEW YORK & LONG BRANCH RAILROAD CONTRACT IN COURT

The agreement with the Central Railroad of New Jersey for the joint use of the line between Bay Head and Perth Amboy, known as the New York & Long Branch Railroad, to which reference was made in previous pages, was found to be very satisfactory in furnishing increased facilities to the public, and in promoting the joint interests of all concerned. However, the change in the management of the Central Railroad of New Jersey, which occurred in May, 1883, resulted in a notification from that Company that it would no longer be bound by the agreement, although there was no claim that the Pennsylvania Railroad Company had failed in any manner to carry out the provisions of the contract. The latter Company brought a suit for the protection of its rights, but the matter was amicably adjusted later, and it has since continued its use of the New York & Long Branch Railroad.

PHILADELPHIA & LONG BRANCH RAILROAD MERGER

It was deemed advisable to consolidate the Pemberton & Seashore Railroad with the Philadelphia & Long Branch Railroad, and thus vest in one corporation the ownership of the lines extending from Birmingham, the terminus of the Camden & Burlington County Railroad, to the New York & Long Branch Railroad near Bay Head, N. J., which was effected on November 3rd, 1883, under the title of the Philadelphia & Long Branch Railroad Company. The Capital Stock of the new corporation was fixed at $900,000., with an equal amount of 5% First Mortgage Bonds. Of these securities the Pennsylvania Railroad Company received $750,000. of Capital Stock and $750,000. in Bonds in settlement of its interest in the lines thus consolidated.

RIDGWAY & CLEARFIELD RAILROAD COMPLETED

On November 19th, 1883, the Ridgway & Clearfield Railroad, extending from Ridgway, on the Philadelphia &

Erie Railroad, to Brockwayville, a distance of over 19 miles, was completed and opened for traffic. On September 1st, 1885, this road was extended a further distance of 7½ miles to a connection with the Allegheny Valley Railroad at Falls Creek.

CONTROLLING INTEREST PURCHASED IN CAMDEN & ATLANTIC RAILROAD AND WEST JERSEY FERRY COMPANY

During the year 1883 a controlling interest was secured by the Pennsylvania Railroad Company in the Camden & Atlantic Railroad, extending from Camden to Atlantic City, a distance of 59 miles, and possessing valuable terminal facilities in Camden, and the ferry privileges in connection therewith. A majority of the Capital Stock of the West Jersey Ferry Company was also acquired in the interests of the Pennsylvania Railroad Company. It was felt that these acquisitions would give the public much better accommodations than they had previously enjoyed, and in general promote and protect the position of the Pennsylvania Railroad Company in the State of New Jersey.

NEW ROUTE DELMAR, DEL., TO CAPE CHARLES AND NORFOLK, VA.

In 1883 the Pennsylvania Railroad Company joined with the Philadelphia, Wilmington & Baltimore Railroad Company in a traffic contract to promote the construction of the New York, Philadelphia & Norfolk Railroad, which was to extend from the southern end of the Delaware Railroad at Delmar to the southern extremity of the peninsula of Virginia opposite Norfolk, a distance of nearly 100 miles. There was already in existence a line of railroad from Delmar, Del., to Crisfield, Md., via King's Creek in the latter State, a distance of about 38 miles, which was owned by the Eastern Shore Railroad Company, and also nine miles of railroad between King's Creek and Pocomoke, Md., which had been built by a predecessor of the New York, Philadelphia & Norfolk Railroad Company. The latter Company acquired the Eastern Shore Railroad Company in June, 1884. It, however, used only 29 miles of the existing roads as part of its main line, and early in the Spring of 1884 began constructing 67 miles of railroad from a point about two miles north of Pocomoke to Cape Charles, Va., which was finished October 25th, 1884. It was also necessary to construct a harbor at the latter point to accommodate the car ferry service, which was inaugurated on November 14th, 1884, between Cape Charles and Norfolk, Va., a distance of 36 miles.

It was expected that this route through its directness and ability to shorten the time for the delivery of perishable traffic would secure a large share of this business, which at that time sought the northern ports by water, and thus largely benefit the Philadelphia, Wilmington & Baltimore Railroad Company, as well as other lines in the Pennsylvania Railroad System.

SCRIP DIVIDENDS CONTINUED

The policy adopted by the Management in 1882 of giving the stockholders the option of converting a portion of their cash dividends into Stock, and of making an additional allotment of shares at par, was continued during 1883. Under this plan the Company made use of its current earnings for capital account instead of permitting them to accumulate until the regular dividend periods, while the option thus given enabled the shareholders to acquire additional Stock on favorable terms, and reimbursed the treasury of the Company for the money temporarily used for construction purposes.

Therefore, two semi-annual cash dividends of 2½% and 2% were paid in 1883, and in addition two dividends of 2% each in scrip convertible into cash or Stock at par. Practically all of this scrip was redeemed in Stock.

SUSQUEHANNA & CLEARFIELD RAILROAD COMPLETED

On May 1st, 1884, the Susquehanna & Clearfield Railroad, extending from Keating to Karthaus, a distance of nearly 23 miles, was completed and opened for traffic, it being operated as part of the Middle Division of the Philadelphia & Erie Railroad.

ALLEGHENY VALLEY RAILROAD COMPANY IN FINANCIAL DIFFICULTY

The inability of the Allegheny Valley Railroad Company to meet the interest upon its fixed obligations led its creditors to make application for the appointment of receivers to take charge of the property pending foreclosure, or some proper reorganization of its affairs. Therefore, on May 2nd, 1884, John Scott and William H. Barnes were appointed receivers, and the property placed under their direct control and management.

COMPLETION OF CHESTNUT HILL BRANCH

On June 11th, 1884, the Philadelphia, Germantown & Chestnut Hill Railroad was opened for traffic, this line extending from Germantown Junction (now North Philadelphia) to Chestnut Hill, a distance of about 6¾ miles. It was not thought that the road would be profitable for several years after its completion, its chief value being that of a feeder to the Pennsylvania Railroad.

EXTENSION OF LEWISBURG & TYRONE RAILROAD

On November 3rd, 1884, the extension of the Lewisburg & Tyrone Railroad from Rising Springs to Oak Hall, a distance of about 13 miles, was completed and placed in operation. On May 20th, 1885, this road was extended a further distance of 1½ miles to a connection with the Bellefonte, Nittany & Lemont Railroad south of Lemont. This latter road was being constructed from Bellefonte to this connection with the Lewisburg & Tyrone Railroad, a distance of about 9½ miles, and it was completed and opened for traffic on July 22nd, 1885. The Bellefonte, Nittany & Lemont Railroad was later merged into the Bald Eagle Valley Railroad.

PROPOSED MODIFICATION OF TERMS OF TRUST CREATED OCTOBER 9th, 1878

For some time prior to 1884 the subject of the continued appropriation of $600,000. per annum, as provided in the Trust created October 9th, 1878, had received the careful consideration of the Management. One of the objects in view at the time of the creation of the Trust was to secure an improvement in the market value of all securities, the principal, interest or dividend upon which was guaranteed by the Pennsylvania Railroad Company, and this had been attained. The Management of the Company, was, therefore, of the opinion that the income of the fund as it then stood should continue to be added to the principal, and the monthly appropriation of $50,000. be reduced to an amount equal to 1% of the Net Income of the Company before the payment of dividends to the stockholders. This proposed modification was submitted to the stockholders at the Annual Meeting in 1885, and a stock vote taken, which resulted in its adoption by a very large majority.

SALE OF SHIPS OF AMERICAN STEAMSHIP COMPANY

Owing to the annual loss sustained by the Pennsylvania Railroad Company in its efforts to maintain the line of steamers of the American Steamship Company to and from the port of Philadelphia, it was deemed advisable in 1884 to avail of the opportunity to dispose of the ships upon satisfactory terms to the International Navigation Company.

COURT PROCEEDINGS TO SETTLE FORT WAYNE BETTERMENT ACCOUNT

The Pittsburgh, Ft. Wayne & Chicago Railway Company having declined to issue to the Pennsylvania Railroad Company the form of security theretofore agreed upon, in reimbursement of expenditures made for the improvement and betterment of the property of the Ft. Wayne Company, the Pennsylvania Railroad Company applied to the Courts in 1884 for a judicial determination of the questions at issue, and secured a decision sustaining the position taken by its Management. The officers of the Pittsburgh, Ft. Wayne & Chicago Railway Company thereupon issued a portion of these securities due the Pennsylvania Railroad Company for such improvements, and took the necessary steps toward a settlement of the balance of the account.

CONTROL OF SODUS BAY & SOUTHERN RAILROAD

In order to provide an outlet on Lake Ontario, and obtain valuable connections with important lines of railway, the Northern Central Railway Company in 1884 secured control of the Sodus Bay & Southern Railroad, extending from Stanley, on its Elmira & Canandaigua Division, to Great Sodus Bay, on Lake Ontario, a distance of 34 miles.

ADDITIONAL PARLOR CAR SERVICE

On March 30th, 1885, the Pennsylvania Railroad Company introduced a new system of parlor car service under its own ownership and management. Nine parlor cars and two combined baggage and smoking cars, built in the Company's shops at Altoona, were placed in service in charge of employes of the Pennsylvania Railroad Company, and assigned to through trains running between New York, Philadelphia, Baltimore and Washington. This service was in addition to that supplied by the Pullman Company under its contract with the Pennsylvania Railroad Company.

MARTIN'S CREEK RAILROAD—ENTERPRISE RAILROAD

The Martin's Creek Railroads of Pennsylvania and New Jersey were completed and opened for operation on December 24th, 1885. These roads formed a connection between the Belvidere Delaware Railroad and the Bangor & Portland Railroad, and were built in the interest of the Pennsylvania Railroad to provide facilities for the interchange of traffic between these roads. They extended from a point on the Belvidere Delaware Railroad near Martin's Creek Station, across the Delaware River on a substantial bridge 500 feet in length, connecting with the Bangor & Portland Railroad on the opposite shore, a distance of about three-tenths of a mile. They were operated in connection with the Belvidere Division, as was also the Enterprise Railroad, which was built in 1885 to afford increased trackage facilities for the development of various business enterprises in Trenton, it having a length of about 1½ miles.

WAYNESBURG & WASHINGTON RAILROAD

In 1885, the Chartiers Railway Company, which was then leased to the Pittsburgh, Cincinnati & St. Louis Railway Company, acquired a majority of the Capital Stock of the Waynesburg & Washington Railroad, a narrow gauge road built in 1877 from Washington to Waynesburg, Pa., a distance of about 28 miles. The Chartiers Railway had been built from Carnegie to Washington, Pa., and the purchase of the Stock of the Waynesburg & Washington Railroad Company gave it control of a route extending southward to Waynesburg, Pa.

ESTABLISHMENT OF RELIEF FUND

For a number of years prior to 1886 the attention of the Management had been seriously directed to the establishment of a Relief Fund, with the view of giving assistance to employes when disabled by sickness or accident and making provision for their families in case of death. The details were referred to a Committee of officers of the Company, who, after inquiry into the systems theretofore adopted by other Companies, both in this Country and abroad, finally reported a comprehensive plan for the action of the Board of Directors. After very careful consideration and examination, the plan was approved and resulted in the establishment on February 15th, 1886, of "The Pennsylvania Railroad Voluntary Relief Department." The general features of the plan consisted of monthly contributions by the employes of stated sums, graded according to their rates of wages, which entitled each member to a specified sum per day when disabled by sickness or accident, and, in case of death, the payment of a definite sum to the family or designated beneficiary. The entire expense of conducting the business of the Department was paid by the Pennsylvania Railroad Company. As this Relief Department was established upon an equitable and liberal basis and sought only to provide for the welfare and comfort of the employes, the system commended itself to them and the operations of the Department were successful from the beginning, there being on December 31st, 1886, a total membership of 19,952 on the Pennsylvania Railroad and its affiliated Lines East of Pittsburgh and Erie.

CONSTRUCTION OF ROAD TO BARNEGAT CITY AND BEACH HAVEN

The Long Beach Railroad, extending from a connection with the Tuckerton Railroad at Manahawken, to Barnegat City, a distance of about 13¼ miles, was completed and opened for operation on June 28th, 1886, and a southern extension of this road from Barnegat City to Beach Haven, a distance of nearly seven miles, was completed and opened for traffic on July 24th, 1886.

EXTENSION OF PENNSYLVANIA SCHUYLKILL VALLEY RAILROAD TO POTTSVILLE AND NEW BOSTON COMPLETED

On November 29th, 1886, the Pottsville & Mahanoy Railroad was merged into the Pennsylvania Schuylkill Valley Railroad, by which the latter road was extended to a connection with the Lehigh Valley Railroad at New Boston, 11 miles north of Pottsville. Effective October 29th, 1885, the Reading & Pottsville Railroad, which had been building its line from Reading to Pottsville, was merged with the Pennsylvania Schuylkill Valley Railroad, and the latter completed its construction to Pottsville on November 15th, 1886. An arrangement was also made with the Lehigh Valley Railroad Company under which it undertook to construct a line from New Boston to a connection with the Sunbury, Hazleton & Wilkes-Barre Railway at Tomhicken, a distance of 26 miles, and by which the Pennsylvania Schuylkill Valley Railroad Company secured trackage facilities over that section of railroad and avoided the necessity of building an additional line in that territory.

PROPOSED CONNECTION WITH WEST VIRGINIA ROADS

During the year 1886, the West Virginia Central & Pittsburgh Railway Company arranged for the construction of the Piedmont & Cumberland Railway, 28 miles in length, to connect the latter road with the Bedford & Bridgeport

Railroad, thus giving the Pennsylvania Railroad a direct connection with the railroads extending into West Virginia, via Cumberland and Piedmont.

ELMIRA & LAKE ONTARIO RAILROAD COMPANY FORMED

Effective December 31st, 1886, the Chemung Railroad Company, Sodus Bay & Southern Railroad Company, and the Elmira, Jefferson & Canandaigua Railroad Company were merged to form the Elmira & Lake Ontario Railroad Company, which is one of the subsidiaries of the Northern Central Railway Company, owning the line extending from Chemung Junction to Sodus Point, N. Y., a distance of about 100 miles.

ENACTMENT OF INTERSTATE COMMERCE ACT

The outstanding event in the year 1887, so far as the railroads were concerned, was the enactment of the Interstate Commerce Act, which was approved February 4th, 1887, and became effective on April 5th, 1887. For many years the States had attempted, with little success, to regulate the railroads, but with the rapid growth of the Country and the railroads, and the fact that railroad traffic had largely become interstate in character, it was felt that regulation should be National in its scope and that the jurisdiction of the Federal Government over interstate traffic should be paramount. The more important provisions of the Act were:—

First:—The creation of the Interstate Commerce Commission, to consist of five Commissioners, to be appointed by the President, with the consent of the Senate, each to serve for a term of six years;

Second:—All charges were to be reasonable and just; unjust and unreasonable charges, rebates, discriminations, and pooling of traffic were prohibited;

Third:—Equal facilities were to be provided for the interchange of traffic with connecting lines, with no discriminations in rates, fares and charges between such connecting lines;

Fourth:—No carrier was permitted to make any greater charge in the aggregate, under substantially similar circumstances or conditions, for a shorter than for a longer distance over the same line in the same direction, the shorter being included in the longer distance; but this was not to be construed as authority for any carrier to charge as great a compensation for a shorter as for a longer distance. The Commission, however, was authorized in special cases to permit, after investigation, a less charge for longer than for shorter distances;

Fifth:—The Commission, upon complaint or on its own initiative, to issue order, after making investigation, that carriers cease and desist from any violations of the law;

Sixth:—Power given to the Commission to inquire into the management of the carriers, and to obtain full and complete information required in performance of its duties;

Seventh:—Commission authorized to require annual reports from all railroads engaged in interstate commerce in such form as it prescribed, covering operating and financial details, and regulations concerning passenger and freight rates; the Commission was also authorized to prescribe a uniform system of accounting.

The Management, in commenting on the new law in its Annual Report for 1887, stated that sufficient time had not elapsed to determine what its effect would be upon the transportation interests; that the policy indicated by the law differed so widely from the practices theretofore prevailing that many difficulties had arisen in endeavoring to conform the business of the Country to its requirements. It was also felt that further legislation would be necessary, as a manifest injury was being done to the railroads of this Country by permitting Canadian roads to participate in the carrying trade of the United States without the ability, under the new law, to enforce their observance of its provisions.

REACHING THE ANTHRACITE COAL REGIONS

On April 25th, 1887, the Nescopec Railroad, extending from Nescopec to Rock Glen Junction, a distance of 12 miles, was completed and opened for traffic, and was operated as part of the Sunbury Division. This road in connection with that portion of the Sunbury, Hazleton & Wilkes-Barre Railroad between Rock Glen Junction and Tomhicken, a distance of 15½ miles, and the Pottsville Branch of the Lehigh Valley Railroad, extending from Tomhicken to New Boston, a distance of about 26 miles (which was used in accordance with the arrangement made with that Company), formed a continuous line of railroad nearly 43 miles long between the Pennsylvania Schuylkill Valley Railroad at New Boston and the North & West Branch Railway at Nescopec. As the result of the foregoing railroad development in this general territory, the Pennsylvania Railroad was able to operate a direct through line from Philadelphia, via the Schuylkill Valley, through the Schuylkill and Lehigh coal regions, to the anthracite coal fields in the Susquehanna Valley and to Wilkes-Barre.

SHENANDOAH BRANCH COMPLETED

The Shenandoah Branch of the Pennsylvania Schuylkill Valley Railroad, extending from a connection with the Philadelphia & Reading Railroad at Frackville Junction, to a connection with the Lehigh Valley Railroad at Shenandoah, a distance of about five miles, was completed and opened for traffic on December 19th, 1887, and operated as part of the Schuylkill Division. This branch road in connection with that portion of the Philadelphia & Reading Railroad between Wetherill Junction and Frackville Junction, a distance of about three miles (which was used in accordance with the terms of an agreement made between the two companies on July 19th, 1887), formed a continuous line of railroad between the Pennsylvania Schuylkill Valley Railroad at Wetherill Junction and Shenandoah.

PURCHASE OF ALEXANDRIA & WASHINGTON RAILROAD

In 1887, the Alexandria & Washington Railroad, extending from the south end of the Long Bridge in Washington, D. C., to Alexandria, Va., a distance of about five miles, and connecting the Baltimore & Potomac Railroad with the Alexandria & Fredericksburg Railway, was purchased by the Pennsylvania Railroad Company at judicial sale under proceedings instituted by the City of Washington. Under its reorganization the latter Company became the owner of all its securities.

WEST SHORE RAILROAD OPERATES INTO JERSEY CITY PASSENGER STATION

On June 27th, 1887, the New Jersey Junction Railroad was completed, and as connections had been made with the New York Division of the Pennsylvania Railroad and its Harsimus Branch, the connecting trains of the West Shore Railroad were operated regularly to and from the Jersey City Depot of the Pennsylvania Railroad.

EMPLOYES' SAVING FUND ESTABLISHED

On January 1st, 1888, the Pennsylvania Railroad Company established an Employes' Saving Fund, with the view of enabling the employes to safely and conveniently deposit such portion of their earnings as they might desire to accumulate, the Company assuming responsibility for its safe custody and repayment with reasonable interest on the moneys so deposited.

CRITICISM FROM ABROAD

At the annual meeting of the Company on March 13th, 1888, President Roberts, in response to an inquiry of a stockholder, explained the policy pursued by the Management of the Pennsylvania Railroad Company in the apportionment of expenditures to capital and expenses. The objections made at that time to the method adopted by the Company of charging out expenditures came largely from English stockholders, and arose principally from the fact that they did not comprehend the true condition of the railways of the United States, as compared with their own. It was pointed out that the railroads in England were managed under different circumstances, and if the practices followed over there were applied to any large railway system in this Country, it would soon be placed at a serious disadvantage with its competitors.

THE MANAGEMENT'S ANSWER

The criticism was made that the Pennsylvania Railroad Company did not divide a sufficient amount of net profits in the way of dividends and carried too much to the credit of profit and loss, or else charged too great an amount of what were called "betterments" to expenses, and thus reduced the amount of net profits to be divided among the stockholders. To illustrate that the policy of the Pennsylvania Railroad Company in this respect was no more conservative than it should be as compared with other large transportation systems in the United States, reference was made to a number of important railroad lines, such as the New York Central Railroad Company. This road in 1886 charged every expenditure to expenses, except the sum of $417,000., and only paid a 4% dividend to its shareholders, although the profit and loss account had a credit of over $12,000,000. Attention was called to the fact that the Boston & Albany Railroad, one of the most successful lines in New England, in its annual report for 1886, after charging all improvements to expenses, made the following statement, viz:

> "It is unquestionably the part of wisdom to expend more than enough to simply maintain the property during prosperous years. Improvements should be made and charged to current expenses, so that when the evil days come, as they surely will, the Company will be in good condition to withstand any strain to which it is likely to be put to maintain its dividends and at the same time permit no deterioration of its line."

President Roberts further stated that in the newly developed country beyond Chicago, the Chicago & North Western, one of the largest railroad companies west of that City, operating over 4,000 miles of railroad, charged almost its entire credit balance in the profit and loss account, amounting to over $10,000,000. to the reduction of the value of its property. He concluded by stating that if there was any error in the method of treating the accounts of the Pennsylvania Railroad Company, it was on the side of distributing to the stockholders a greater amount of profits than other competitive companies felt justified in doing, and that any departure from the conservative policy pursued by the Management would be fraught with great danger to the credit and future prosperity of the Company.

EXPLANATION OF PROFIT & LOSS ACCOUNT

President Roberts also desired to correct the wrong impression which had prevailed as to what constituted the Profit & Loss Account. He assumed that the majority of the stockholders of railroad companies thought that it represented just so much cash in bank, being the accumulation of net profits over and above the dividends declared, and which could be divided among the shareholders at any time in cash if the Management deemed it wise to do so. This, it was stated, was an erroneous idea; the Profit & Loss Account being merely the difference between the par value of the share capital and the obligations of the Company on the one side, and the valuation placed upon its assets on the other. To be made available for dividends it must be represented by an increase of the obligations of the Company, upon which it would thereafter have to pay interest or dividends, and this would decrease to just that extent the rate of dividend or interest upon the amount of share capital then existing. Therefore, the stockholders would receive in the aggregate no greater dividend than if the Profit & Loss Account had remained undivided, and the only result would be that the Company would have that amount of increased liabilities for which it would be responsible.

CONSERVATIVE POLICY PURSUED

In closing this statement President Roberts stated that the extracts to which he had referred from the annual reports of other railroad companies were simply for the purpose of explaining the system which prevailed in their accounting departments, and to thus illustrate that the plan which had been adopted by the Pennsylvania Railroad Company was founded upon sound principles. He also desired to correct the erroneous opinion that the Company in paying its dividends was withholding from its shareholders a larger proportion of the net earnings than the necessities of the Company would justify; that if the policy were pursued of dividing up closely the Net Income while its competitors were strengthening themselves, the day was not far distant when it would be placed at a disadvantage with competing lines, and the ability to successfully meet this competition and earn a moderate dividend would be lost.

EAST BRANDYWINE & WAYNESBURG RAILROAD COMPANY REORGANIZED

The East Brandywine & Waynesburg Railroad, extending from the Main Line of the Pennsylvania Railroad at Downingtown to New Holland, a distance of 28 miles, was sold under foreclosure in 1888, and reorganized on July 30th of that year under the name of the Downingtown & Lancaster Railroad Company, all of the securities of which were owned by the Pennsylvania Railroad Company. Arrangements were then made for the extension of this road to a connection with the Main Line at Lancaster, a distance of 10 miles, thus forming an alternate route between Downingtown and Lancaster. This extension was completed on September 15th, 1890.

DISASTROUS FLOODS

President Roberts made the following statement to the stockholders in the annual report of the Company for the year 1889, with respect to the disastrous floods which extended over a greater portion of the State of Pennsylvania from May 30th to June 1st, 1889, inclusive:—

> "On the 31st of May (1889) an extraordinary rainfall began, and following nearly the trend of the mountain range over which your System of lines passes, caused an unparalleled destruction of property, not only upon your Main Line, but many of the other roads forming your System.

In the Juniata Valley three of the largest and most expensive double-tracked bridges, two of which had recently been rebuilt, were entirely destroyed, together with several miles of track. The greatest destruction, both of life and property, took place, however, on the western slope of the mountain in the Conemaugh Valley, where a reservoir (originally constructed by the State of Pennsylvania for its canal system) gave way, and completely destroyed your road for a distance of over 10 miles, including several large bridges, and all the machine shops, roundhouses, and yard facilities at Conemaugh at the foot of the mountain, the destruction being so complete that it was almost impossible to fix the location formerly occupied by your property. Among the property damaged and destroyed were 24 passenger cars, 561 freight cars, 34 locomotives, some of the latter, notwithstanding their weight, being carried more than a mile by the force of the flood. While this loss of property was appalling in its magnitude, yet it was more than overshadowed by the great destruction of life and property in the manufacturing city of Johnstown, a short distance below Conemaugh in the same valley.

In addition to the destruction of property on your Main Line, many of the largest and most important bridges on the Philadelphia and Erie Railroad were entirely destroyed, while on the Elmira & Williamsport line (leased to the Northern Central Railway Company) several miles of railway, including many bridges, were washed away.

The first and second section of the day express East were overtaken by the high waters of the flood while lying at Conemaugh about four o'clock P. M., Friday, May 31st, and 26 passengers are supposed to have been lost from the first section, most of whom were drowned in attempting to escape to the adjacent hillside; the others being lost in one of the passenger cars of the train which was washed away and destroyed. Three passengers and a Pullman car porter were lost from the second section while endeavoring to reach a place of safety. All the other passengers on this section who remained in the cars were saved.

The total amount expended to December 31st, 1889, in repairing the loss caused by the floods to your System was $3,475,425.01, leaving still a considerable sum to be expended to restore its original condition.

This outlay does not include the indirect loss from the suspension of traffic and the serious interruption to the working of your entire system caused thereby."

DAMAGE TO CANALS

The property of the Pennsylvania Canal Company, in which the Pennsylvania Railroad Company was largely interested, both as a shareholder and as a guarantor of the interest upon its Bonds, suffered serious damage from these floods. Many miles of its canals were entirely destroyed, but as they were the most unproductive portions of the property, it was deemed advisable to abandon the destroyed section, rather than to burden the Canal Company with the cost of renewing it. However, repairs were made on some parts of the Canal System which survived the floods, the Pennsylvania Railroad Company advancing the money for this purpose. The valleys occupied by the canals were then traversed with the lines of competing railways, which carried the traffic at very low rates, and it was felt that their value was rapidly passing away; also, that the cost of their maintenance would probably equal the revenue derived from operations, thus necessitating the sum required for the interest on the Canal Company Bonds to be advanced by the Pennsylvania Railroad Company until their maturity on July 1st, 1910.

CONSTRUCTION OF TRENTON CUT-OFF

As the traffic passing through the yards of the Company at West Philadelphia, destined to points east of that city, had become so large as to seriously interfere with the movement of traffic to Philadelphia and adjacent points, a railroad had been located in 1889 and its construction commenced from the Main Line near Downingtown to the New York Division near Trenton (now known as "Trenton Cut-off") a distance of about 45 miles. A very favorable and direct route had been secured through this section of the country on the same maximum grade as that prevailing on the Philadelphia Division. While the line was an expensive one to construct, owing to the general topography of the country and the valuable property through which it passed, it was felt that the economies arising from the saving of distance, which amounted to about 6 miles on through traffic to and from points East of Trenton, and avoidance of delays and overcrowding the yards and tracks at West Philadelphia, would more than repay the Company for the outlay.

COLUMBIA & PORT DEPOSIT RAILROAD COMPANY REORGANIZED

On March 4th, 1890, the Columbia & Port Deposit Railroad, extending from Columbia, on the Philadelphia Division, to Port Deposit, Md., was sold under foreclosure of its mortgages. A new Corporation known as the Port Deposit Railway Company was formed to take over that portion of the road in Maryland while the Columbia & Port Deposit Railroad took over the Pennsylvania section. Effective July 17th, 1890, these two railroads were consolidated to form the Columbia & Port Deposit Railway Company.

NEW YORK BAY RAILROAD

The New York Bay Railroad, which was formed on March 15th, 1890, as the result of the consolidation of the Waverly & Passaic Railroad Company and the Waverly & New York Bay Railroad Company, was completed from a junction with the Main Line of the New York Division two-thirds of a mile east of Waverly, N. J., to a connection with the Central Railroad of New Jersey, at Oak Island Junction, a distance of about two miles. This section of the road was placed in operation on March 20th, 1890, and the interchange of traffic with the Central Railroad of New Jersey transferred from Elizabeth to Oak Island Junction. This road and its branches were being constructed for the purpose of reaching a rapidly improving section of Newark, and ultimately the New York Harbor at Greenville, N. J.

FORMATION OF WASHINGTON SOUTHERN RAILWAY COMPANY

Effective April 1st, 1890, the Alexander & Washington Railroad and Alexandria & Fredericksburg Railway, were consolidated into the Washington Southern Railway Company, the road of the new Company extending from a connection with the Baltimore & Potomac Railroad at the south end of the Long Bridge, Washington, D. C., to Quantico, Va., a distance of 34 miles. The Pennsylvania Railroad Company owned a controlling interest in the new Company.

FORMATION OF PITTSBURGH, CINCINNATI, CHICAGO & ST. LOUIS RAILWAY COMPANY

Effective October 1st, 1890, the principal lines forming the South Western System, viz: the Pittsburgh, Cincinnati & St. Louis Railway, Cincinnati & Richmond Railroad, Jeffersonville, Madison & Indianapolis Railroad, and the Chicago, St. Louis & Pittsburgh Railroad, were merged into one company under the name of Pittsburgh, Cincinnati, Chicago & St. Louis Railway Company. It was believed that through this consolidation a stronger financial basis could be secured upon which to obtain the capital needed for the development of these lines, and that through such unification of the system any conflict of interests that might arise through diverse ownerships would be avoided. The consolidated company controlled an aggregate of 1,516 miles, including leased roads; its Capital Stock amounted to $43,820,650. and the Funded Debt was $41,944,500. It was one of the most important of the controlled Lines West of Pittsburgh, as through it the Pennsylvania Railroad System had direct connection with Cincinnati, Louisville, St. Louis, Indianapolis, Columbus and Chicago, and reached the territory south and southwest of those cities under the most favorable conditions.

FINAL PAYMENT FOR PUBLIC WORKS OF PENNSYLVANIA

On July 31st, 1890, the final payment of $635,654.94, being the principal and accrued interest then due the State of Pennsylvania on account of the purchase of the Public

Works, was made. The entire payments to the State on account of this purchase amounted to $15,565,654.94, of which the principal was $7,500,000., and the interest $8,065,654.94. The contract made with the Commonwealth of Pennsylvania for the acquisition of this property in 1857 had been faithfully carried out by the Company during a period of 33 years, and no default had at any time occurred either in the payment of interest or of any instalment of the principal sum.

CONSTRUCTION OF OHIO CONNECTING RAILWAY

The new bridge and adjoining tracks over the Ohio River, extending from a connection with the Pittsburgh, Cincinnati, Chicago & St. Louis Railway in the vicinity of Point Bridge Station, Pittsburgh, to a junction with the Pittsburgh, Ft. Wayne & Chicago Railway, at Woods Run, were completed and placed in partial operation in October, 1890, and in full service in 1891. The bridge and tracks were constructed by the Ohio Connecting Railway Company, all of the Capital Stock of which is owned by the Pennsylvania Company. The purpose in building the road was to further avoid the expensive transfer of the constantly increasing volume of traffic through the cities of Pittsburgh and Allegheny. It is now leased to the Pennsylvania Railroad Company for 999 years from January 1st, 1921.

TRENTON CUT-OFF COMPLETED

The construction of the Trenton Cut-off (commenced in 1889), which extended from Glen Lock on the Philadelphia Division to Morrisville, Pa., on the New York Division, a distance of 45 miles, was actively prosecuted, with the result that a portion of the new line between Morrisville and Earnest (near Norristown), a distance of 31½ miles, was completed and opened for traffic on June 22nd, 1891. The entire line was finished and placed in service as part of the Philadelphia Division on January 11th, 1892. In 1893 the entire cut-off was double tracked. As the principal portion of the line was constructed under the Charter of the Pennsylvania Railroad Company (the balance under the corporate name of the Trenton Cut-Off Railroad Company, which was later acquired by the Pennsylvania Railroad Company), all but $100,000. of the amount expended thereon was charged to the construction account of the Main Line. The Management saw no reason to change the opinion expressed as to the great value of the road, and steps were then being taken to connect it with the Chestnut Hill Branch, as it was believed that such an extension would be an advantageous one for the Company.

POOLING COST OF FREIGHT CAR REPAIRS

In order to save unnecessary accounting and inspection in connection with the freight equipment of the Pennsylvania Railroad System and secure its more efficient movement, the expenses of repairing same were pooled beginning with August 1st, 1891. Under this arrangement the cost of maintenance of all such rolling stock on the Pennsylvania Railroad and its affiliated lines East and West of Pittsburgh, aggregating 123,340 cars, was consolidated, and apportioned among the various lines on a mileage basis. While it was thought that it might be necessary to modify some of the details of the arrangement, it was felt that the new plan would ultimately tend to more economical maintenance of the Company's equipment.

BRANCHES CONSTRUCTED IN WESTERN PENNSYLVANIA

The South Fork Railroad was constructed and opened for traffic on August 15th, 1891, from South Fork to Dunlo, Pa., a distance of about eight miles. This road and the Scalp Level Railroad, which was formed later, were built for the purpose of developing an important coal producing territory in Western Pennsylvania. The two roads were merged in 1902 under the name of the South Fork Railroad Company, and it owned nearly 45 miles of railroad at the time it was absorbed by the Pennsylvania Railroad Company in 1903.

On September 28th, 1891, the Turtle Creek Valley Railroad, 6½ miles in length, extending from Stewart to Murraysville, Pa., was completed and opened for traffic. The Turtle Creek Branch, extending from Brinton to near Wilmerding, Pa., a distance of over two miles, was also completed during the year 1891. In the following year the road was extended from Murraysville to Export, Pa., a distance of 4.6 miles.

ADDITION TO CAMBRIA & CLEARFIELD RAILROAD

The Ebensburg & Cresson Railroad was sold and reorganized on July 14th, 1891, as the Cresson Railroad Company, and on August 6th, 1891, the latter Company was merged and consolidated into the Cambria & Clearfield Railroad Company. This latter road was projected to develop the territory adjacent thereto in the Allegheny Mountain coal fields. Quite a large amount was expended during the year 1891 in the construction of its main line and branches, which were expected to secure a valuable bituminous coal and miscellaneous traffic for the Pennsylvania Railroad System.

ALLEGHENY VALLEY RAILROAD COMPANY REORGANIZED

The protracted litigation in connection with the Allegheny Valley Railroad, which had extended over a period of seven years, was finally brought to a close by a sale on December 15th, 1891, under a judgment obtained on the coupons of the $10,000,000. Low Grade Division Mortgage, which had been purchased by the Pennsylvania Railroad Company under its guaranty. A reorganization was effected on February 6th, 1892, under the name of the Allegheny Valley *Railway* Company. This sale was made in pursuance of an amicable agreement entered into between the parties in interest, under which the new Company issued $20,000,000. of 50-year 4% General Mortgage Bonds, guaranteed principal and interest by the Pennsylvania Railroad Company. Of these Bonds a sufficient amount was to be retained by the Trustees to meet the then existing mortgage indebtedness of the Allegheny Valley Railroad Company, aggregating $16,800,000., of which the Pennsylvania Railroad Company was practically the guarantor, the balance to be used from time to time as additional capital was required. There were also authorized $18,000,000. of Preferred Stock and $12,000,000. of Common Stock, to be issued in exchange for the outstanding Income Bonds, overdue coupons and other securities of the old Company, and for its general purposes. Under this plan the road was relieved of a large amount of debt, the interest on which it was unable to pay, and with the approaching maturity of a portion of its Bonds and the conversion thereof into securities bearing a lower rate of interest, it was expected that it would prove more profitable with the foregoing changes in its capital structure.

PRESIDENT ROBERTS EXPRESSES COMPANY'S GRATITUDE

It may be of interest to quote the remarks of President Roberts to the stockholders of the Company at the annual meeting on March 8th, 1892, with respect to its moral obligations to the City of Philadelphia, which so generously aided the Company in the time of need, and to the State of Pennsylvania which gave it life. It indicates that the Company was conscientiously endeavoring to show its gratitude, and that it was not unmindful of its duty to the City and State. His remarks were as follows:—

> " The report before us shows that the Company has been in existence for at least forty-five years. It may not be unwise, in view of some recent criticisms upon the manner in which the shareholders have permitted their property to be managed, to explain as far as possible what has been their policy, and what they have accomplished for the City and Commonwealth with which they are so closely and intimately associated.
>
> Before my time, of course, the City of Philadelphia came to the aid of the shareholders in building up its property, and though it may be answered that she, as a corporation, has got back directly all the money and more than she invested, still that is an ungenerous answer to make to a friend who has come to your aid when you needed it badly; and it is well for the shareholders here, probably, to pause a little and see if we

have done our duty to this municipality which helped us so kindly in time of need, and which, together with the Commonwealth that gave us birth, has stood manfully behind us from that day to this, and look to you in your corporate capacity to be their bulwark and protect their interests in the competition that exists between the seaboard cities for the commerce of this great Country.

In looking over the report, there are a few salient points which may be taken as milestones in the progress of this undertaking, and that will indicate, to a certain extent, not only the progress that the corporation has made, but whether or not it has performed its duty to the City of Philadelphia and the State of Pennsylvania. At the same time we must not be unmindful of the fact that the City of Pittsburgh and the County of Allegheny also came to the rescue of this Company in its time of need, that the City of Pittsburgh is a hive of industry, is one of your greatest sources of revenue, and has largely assisted the Company to better dividends for its stockholders. Looking back for a period of ten years only, you may note that the Pennsylvania Railroad Company as a corporation has expended in the City of Philadelphia nearly sixteen millions of money, an average of over one million and a half every year in improvements and facilities within the boundaries of the municipality. That is not an illiberal proportion of the entire amount of money that she has annually expended, standing the foremost, as she does now, among the railways of the Country and the amount which she annually dispersed in additional improvements and in aiding the growth of the industries in the sections which are tributary to her. It is very seldom that this Company expends less than $1,000,000. in each and every calendar month in building up new avenues of trade and traffic and providing increased facilities for the public.

Sometimes our friends on the other side of the water forget that we are a young Country, in which competition is active and where large sums of money have to be expended by individuals and corporations. Now, so far as this expenditure in the City of Philadelphia is concerned, it cannot, of course, be denied that it was done to a certain extent for the purpose of increasing the earnings of the Company; but at the same time it is well to point out that this large sum of money must be expended at the great terminal of this Company every year. Let us see in what way some of this has been expended. It may not be known to all here that until a very recent time there was no pier in the City of Philadelphia at which an ordinary modern steamship could land, except those owned and furnished by this corporation, and today every pier of that description south of Shackamaxon Street has been provided by the shareholders of this Company, and they have provided twelve such piers. In addition to these facilities, what have they done to aid in establishing the foreign commerce of this port? Some years since you established a steamship company—American Steamship Company—fostered by your corporation, in which you took four-sevenths of the original capital, afterwards increasing that from time to time, until you had over $1,000,000. invested in the Capital Stock of that Steamship Company, and in endeavoring to ascertain whether it could be made productive, not only to the interests of the Company, but of the City of Philadelphia. That $1,000,000. has been totally sunk. In addition to that this Company has faithfully paid its obligations as guarantor of the bonds all these years, so that it will have expended finally in the neighborhood of $3,000,000. more as a contribution on the part of your corporation to build up the commerce of this port—not an illiberal sum, and one which has given the Managers of your corporation some anxiety as to whether it was a right and proper policy to pursue. Again, what has been the increase of tonnage to and from the City of Philadelphia over your lines? The tonnage in and out of Philadelphia for a period of ten years has amounted to nearly 60,000,000 tons, so that the tonnage carried to and from the City of Philadelphia averages nearly 7,000,000, showing in all directions a good healthy increase. And at this point it might be well to observe what the City of Baltimore has done in the meantime. In 1865, it is stated by one of her most prominent citizens, the City of Baltimore controlled almost the entire bituminous coal trade to the seaboard; in the year of 1891 she controlled less than twenty-four per cent., and of that twenty-four per cent. one of the roads in your system carried a very large proportion. During the period from 1878 to 1891 this Company increased its coal and coke tonnage from 7,500,000 tons to 32,800,000 tons per annum, an increase in that period of over five hundred per cent. in coal and coke tonnage. You rank now as the largest coal carrying company in the United States, and seem to be destined to take the position of the largest coal carrier in the world. In the year 1864 the Pennsylvania Railroad Company moved in tons a trifle over 3,000,000; in 1891 she moved 5,500,000 per month. In that, gentlemen, is to be found, in a measure, the reason why your Management asked from time to time for an increase of Capital Stock and other obligations of the Company. As before said, we must keep up with the march of progress, and not only keep up, but we must hold our position a little in advance of all other corporations. The moment this Company forgets that its duty is to be at the head of the list of the carrying companies of the United States, and ceases to have the ambition to become the first in the world, that moment do I wish to pass from its Management.

But we started out to see whether or not this corporation has done rightly and properly by the city of Philadelphia. And here let me point out that the Pennsylvania Railroad Company does not occupy a street in the city of Philadelphia for which it has not paid liberally, and that all streets that are occupied by the lines in your system are occupied under rights granted before you became the owners of these corporations, and for which you had to pay roundly to those corporations when you acquired their control. I would cite as an instance the Philadelphia, Wilmington & Baltimore Railroad for which you paid $17,000,000. and the Philadelphia & Trenton Railroad, where you are struggling to earn the ten per cent. per annum which you have to pay on their capital.

The Pennsylvania Railroad with its main line in the city of Philadelphia does not cross an avenue at grade. It has been met generously by the municipality in the endeavor to relieve itself and the public of these dangerous crossings, but it may be well to note the millions of dollars which it has expended for the purpose of relieving the streets of these dangers. It had a permanent right to the surface of Market Street, which it gave up without one penny of consideration, except the privilege of repaving the street, and it then expended nearly $6,000,000. on your Elevated Road in this city, so as to permanently avoid the occupation and obstruction of the city's highways.

In looking over the figures we find that the Pennsylvania Railroad system has in its own capital and obligations and in those of other lines in its system, about $750,000,000. West of Pittsburgh will be found $250,000,000. of this investment, which was made by the Pennsylvania Railroad Company primarily for the interest of its shareholders, but it cannot be gainsaid that it was made likewise for the interests of the Commonwealth of Pennsylvania and of the city of Philadelphia. Through the expenditure of this large amount of money, your Company has secured two of the greatest avenues leading into the West, and reaching all the commercial centres that are worth reaching north of the Ohio and east of the Mississippi River, and brings by means thereof into this Commonwealth a flood of traffic and an interchange of commerce that no other corporation in the United States has pretended to control for the benefit of the city or State which gave it birth.

It is probably wrong to draw comparisons, but the New York Central Railroad Company stands and is entitled to be looked upon as one of the foremost and best railway organizations in the United States, managed, we all understand, honestly and judiciously; and that corporation, as a corporation, has not invested for the State of New York or for itself one dollar of money west of Buffalo.

There is another thing that we might as well refer to here, in connection with the most important industry of the State of Pennsylvania, and that is, that it was through the instrumentality of this Company that the manufacture of Bessemer steel was made possible in the United States. It made the first subscription to the Pennsylvania Steel Company, and a liberal one, to back up that made by individuals, and through the honesty and wise management of that corporation, and the fostering care it has received, it has grown to be a most profitable undertaking. But outside of all that, through these subscriptions it showed that steel rails could be made in the United States, and today nearly all the steel rails that are used in the United States are made here, and the price has been reduced from $125. to $30. per ton. The Bessemer steel that is made in the United States is a prominent feature of its manufacturing industries, and this Company has shown its faith in that which it originally started by purchasing nearly 100,000 tons of steel rails through the past year and using them in construction and repairs, consuming ten and a half tons of steel rails every hour. You held on to your investment in that corporation as long as it seemed necessary to put its success beyond question, and then wisely passed its control over absolutely to the individual shareholders, leaving them to manage it in such a manner as they deemed wise and best.

I think now, probably, I have said all that is necessary. What your Company has done for this Commonwealth and for this city in the past is, perhaps, hardly a measure of what it will do in the future, and the millions of money that are expended every year for the development of the State by building new branch roads and the opening up of new industries and manufactures must go on increasing. In the city of Philadelphia it is today, as it always has been, ready to promote anything that will tend to the industry and prosperity of the community. It will build more wharves, it will invest more money in elevators, it will help the manufacturing industries, it may subsidize other steamship lines for the purpose of promoting the commerce of this city, if the citizens will only respond by coming forward and doing their share. It is disheartening that the investment in the Girard Point Elevators and in the elevators at the foot of Washington Avenue, of between $2,000,000. and $3,000,000. by this Company, should be unproductive. They are there to facilitate and stimulate traffic, but they are not as prosperous as they should be. This Company's interest is in making them prosperous, and with the vigorous co-operation of the community they will be made so.

This Company has stood by the Philadelphia & Erie Road for half a century, until it has finally reached a point where it is self-supporting, and in doing so has built up an important traffic for this city and State; but if anything is lacking let the citizens of Philadelphia point it out, and if it is within reason this Company will, as it has heretofore done, cheerfully join with them and endeavor to promote the prosperity of this city and State, for in their prosperity is to be found the prosperity of this corporation.

Let it not be forgotten that you have contributed within the last ten years $12,000,000. in taxes to this city and State, an average of $1,200,000. a year—a sum of money that ought to go far towards insuring good government in any law-abiding community.

As I said before, I am glad to have this opportunity to point out what the management has done; and if the shareholders, who are so deeply interested think that the management should go forward more rapidly and do more, they will only be too glad to do it. But remember that we are your trustees, and we cannot undertake to go beyond the bounds of what we believe to be good judgment in using the funds of the Company in the direction in which they have been so liberally used heretofore, that is, in the promotion of elevators, steamship lines, and other facilities to build up commerce and stimulate traffic."

KENSINGTON & TACONY RAILROAD

On June 22nd, 1892, the Kensington & Tacony Railroad, extending from a junction with the Philadelphia & Trenton Railroad, at Tioga Street, Philadelphia, to a connection with the same road at Tacony, a distance of over five miles, was completed and opened for traffic.

MINERSVILLE BRANCH

On August 1st, 1892, the Minersville Branch, extending from a junction with the Pennsylvania Schuylkill Valley Railroad at Pottsville to Primrose, 7½ miles in length, was completed and opened for traffic.

CAMBRIA & CLEARFIELD RAILROAD

The Cambria & Clearfield Railroad was so far completed in 1892 that the portion of the line between Cresson and Mehaffey, together with a number of branches, making an aggregate of 80 miles, were opened for traffic at the close of that year. The development of the mining industries on this road had exceeded the most sanguine expectations, and it was believed that it would be one of the most valuable bituminous coal feeders of the Main Line. Further extensions were contemplated in 1893.

CONTROL OF ROAD BETWEEN CRESSON AND IRVONA

On January 2nd, 1893, a lease was made of the Cresson and Clearfield County & New York Short Route Railroad, a local road extending from Cresson, on the Main Line, to Irvona, a distance of 26½ miles. This line was built to develop what was known as the "Mountain Coal District" in the Alleghenies, and under the lease the tonnage of that road was permanently secured to the Pennsylvania Railroad. The latter purchased a majority of its Capital Stock in the year 1893, but in 1894 the road was sold out under foreclosure proceedings. It was reorganized with a reduced capitalization on July 3rd, 1894, as the Irvona & Cresson Railroad Company, in which the Pennsylvania Railroad Company secured a controlling interest.

TOLEDO, WALHONDING VALLEY & OHIO RAILROAD

On the Lines West of Pittsburgh, that portion of the Toledo, Walhonding Valley & Ohio Railroad, 45½ miles in length, lying between Coshocton, on the Pittsburgh, Cincinnati, Chicago & St. Louis Railway, and Loudonville, O., on the Pittsburgh, Ft. Wayne & Chicago Railway, was completed and opened for traffic in the early part of 1893. This line not only formed a connection between the Southwestern and Northwestern Systems of the Pennsylvania Lines West of Pittsburgh, but also afforded one of the most direct routes between the coal fields of Southern Ohio and the Lake ports.

CASH AND SCRIP DIVIDENDS

In May, 1893 (panic year), a dividend of 2% in scrip, redeemable in cash or stock, was paid by the Pennsylvania Railroad Company in addition to the semi-annual cash dividend of 2½%. Practically all of this scrip was later converted into Capital Stock. A cash dividend of 2½% was also paid in November, 1893, making the total dividends for the year 7%.

CRESHEIM BRANCH

On July 30th, 1893, the Cresheim Branch of the Philadelphia, Germantown & Chestnut Hill Railroad, extending from its connection with the foregoing railroad at Cresheim Junction, near Allen Lane Station, to Fort Hill, on the Trenton Cut-off, a distance of nearly six miles, was completed and opened for traffic.

CONTROL OF ROUTE TO ST. LOUIS

The St. Louis, Vandalia & Terre Haute Railroad, which was built in 1868 by the Pennsylvania Railroad Company, in conjunction with the Terre Haute & Indianapolis Railroad Company, for the purpose of extending the Pennsylvania Railroad System to St. Louis, passed at that time by lease under the direct control of the Terre Haute & Indianapolis Railroad Company. The Pennsylvania Railroad Company had no ownership in this latter road so that while a majority of the Capital Stock of the Vandalia line was owned by the Pennsylvania Railroad Company, it had no voice in its management. Therefore, when an opportunity presented itself in 1893, the Pennsylvania Company purchased a large majority of the Capital Stock of the Terre Haute & Indianapolis Railroad Company, and thus finally secured control of the direct line to St. Louis. The latter Company in addition operated through lease or ownership the Terre Haute & Logansport Railroad and the Indiana & Lake Michigan Railway, extending from Terre Haute via Logansport to St. Joseph, Mich., and also the Terre Haute & Peoria Railroad, extending from Farrington to Peoria, Ill., making in all an aggregate of 637 miles coming under control of the Pennsylvania Railroad Company. The Indiana & Lake Michigan Railway, running from South Bend, Ind., to St. Joseph, Mich., was subsequently sold out under foreclosure proceedings, and is now part of the New York Central System.

PURCHASE OF MAJORITY OWNERSHIP OF TOLEDO, PEORIA & WESTERN RAILWAY

In 1893 the Pennsylvania Railroad Company, in order to obtain a more direct connection between its Southwestern Lines and the Chicago, Burlington & Quincy and other western railroads, acquired the ownership of a majority of the Capital

Stock of the Toledo, Peoria & Western Railway, 231 miles in length, and extending from one of the western termini of the Pittsburgh, Cincinnati, Chicago & St. Louis Railway at the Illinois State Line, by way of Peoria, to Warsaw, Ill. This road formed a natural extension of the last mentioned road to the Mississippi River, and traversed a fine belt of farming country, besides reaching the important cities of Peoria, Keokuk and Burlington, and it was believed that its acquisition would be of value to the Pennsylvania Railroad System. Negotiations were being conducted with the Chicago, Burlington & Quincy Railroad Company for such joint ownership and management of this property as would be to the mutual interest of both companies, and enable them to take advantage of its important geographical location. The Burlington road later did take a half interest in the Toledo, Peoria & Western Railway Company. It proved an unprofitable investment for the two Owning Companies and was recently sold out under foreclosure proceedings.

PURCHASE OF CLEVELAND & MARIETTA RAILWAY

With the view of securing a more permanent control of a fair share of the coal traffic destined to Toledo and the State of Michigan than could be obtained through a traffic contract, the Pennsylvania Company purchased in 1893 the Cleveland & Marietta Railway, extending from Canal Dover, its point of connection with the Cleveland & Pittsburgh Railroad, to Marietta, on the Ohio River, a distance of 97 miles, and passing through the extensive Cambridge coal field of Ohio. The line not only secured the coal traffic referred to, but also gave the large iron manufacturing interests in the Mahoning and Shenango Valleys of Ohio a direct connection with the Southwest.

GENERAL OFFICES MOVED TO BROAD STREET STATION

The work of extending Broad Street Station, Philadelphia, and of constructing the new building in connection therewith for the General Offices of the Company, was completed and the removal from No. 233 South Fourth Street to the new location made on July 9th, 1894. The railroad facilities of this Station and the character of the General Office Building made it one of the largest and most important terminal stations in the Country.

EBENSBURG & BLACK LICK RAILROAD

On October 22nd, 1894, the Ebensburg & Black Lick Railroad, 12 miles in length, extending from its junction with the Ebensburg Branch at Ebensburg, to a bridge over Black Lick Creek, east of Vintondale, was completed and placed in service.

LONDON FINANCIAL AGENT

On March 27th, 1895, the London Joint Stock Bank, Ltd., with which the Pennsylvania Railroad Company had for many years maintained intimate business relations, was appointed its financial agent in London. Through the establishment of this agency, the English stockholders were enabled to receive their dividends on the same date as the American shareholders and at their full equivalent in sterling. This is now the Midland Bank, Ltd., has over 2,000 Branches, and is probably the largest Bank in the World.

JOINT TRAFFIC ASSOCIATION FORMED

Reference was made in the annual report for 1895 to the formation of a Joint Traffic Association, through the instrumentality of which it was expected that substantial economies could be enforced in the administration of the Country's transportation service and greater stability and uniformity of rates secured to the public, thus preventing violent fluctuations which tended to disturb values and cause unjust discrimination. It was stated that while sufficient time had not elapsed to thoroughly test its workings, yet enough had been accomplished in the correction of evils to demonstrate its value not only to the railroads, but to the public. The results thus far had justified the belief that the Interstate Commerce Commission would have to look to it, or some like organization, for the potent agency to enable it to enforce the provisions and secure the results sought to be accomplished by the passage of the Interstate Commerce Act.

DELAWARE RIVER BRIDGE

On March 16th, 1896, the Pennsylvania and New Jersey Railroad Companies of Pennsylvania and New Jersey, which were incorporated for the construction of the bridge across the Delaware River east of Frankford Junction, were consolidated to form the Delaware River Railroad & Bridge Company, and $1,300,000. of its 40-year 4% Bonds dated August 1st, 1896, and maturing August 1st, 1936, were issued and sold. The principal of, and interest on, these Bonds were guaranteed by the Pennsylvania Railroad Company, and the proceeds from the sale were used to pay a portion of the cost of the bridge and of branches connecting it with the Pennsylvania Railroad. The bridge was completed on April 19th, 1896, it being 4,397 feet in length; the main river bridge consisting of three spans 1,944 feet in length, with an iron viaduct approach 2,129 feet in length on the Pennsylvania side and one 324 feet in length on the New Jersey side.

FIFTIETH ANNIVERSARY

On April 13th, 1896, a celebration commemorating the 50th Anniversary of the incorporation of the Pennsylvania Railroad Company was held in the General Office Building and the Academy of Music, Philadelphia, to which latter the stockholders were invited. President Roberts delivered the opening address and recalled many incidents in the early history of the Company, presenting statistics showing its remarkable development in mileage, traffic and revenue, and paid a tribute to the fidelity and efficiency of the employes, through whom these gratifying results had been attained. Addresses were also made by Governor Daniel H. Hastings, of Pennsylvania, Mayor Charles F. Warwick, of Philadelphia, Clarence Burleigh, City Attorney of Pittsburgh, J. Twing Brooks, Second-Vice-President of the Pennsylvania Company, and Joseph H. Choate, of New York.

BELVIDERE DELAWARE RAILROAD CONSOLIDATION

On April 14th, 1896, the Martin's Creek Railway Company of Pennsylvania, the Enterprise Railroad Company and Martin's Creek Railway Company of New Jersey were consolidated into and with the Belvidere Delaware Railroad Company.

WEST JERSEY & SEASHORE RAILROAD COMPANY FORMED

On May 4th, 1896, the West Jersey Railroad, Alloway & Quinton Railroad, West Jersey & Atlantic Railroad, the Camden & Atlantic Railroad, Chelsea Branch Railroad and the Philadelphia, Marlton & Medford Railroad Companies, which extended to southern New Jersey seashore points, and all of which were either directly or indirectly controlled by the Pennsylvania Railroad Company, were consolidated into one corporation under the title of the "West Jersey & Seashore Railroad Company." These several railroads had the following mileage:—

		Miles
West Jersey Railroad.	Extending from Camden to Cape May, with branches to Swedesboro, Salem, Bridgeton, Port Norris, Sea Isle City, Ocean City, Stone Harbor and Holly Beach, a total of....................	184.84
Alloway & Quinton Railroad...........	Extending from Alloway Station on West Jersey Railroad, to Quinton, Salem County, N. J........................	4.22
West Jersey & Atlantic Railroad........	Extending from a connection with West Jersey Railroad at Newfield to Atlantic City..............................	32.60
Camden & Atlantic Railroad...........	Extending from Camden to Absecon Inlet, a distance of about 60 miles, with a branch to Longport seven and one-half miles in length, or a total distance of...	67.50
Chelsea Branch Railroad...............	Authorized to construct a railroad from a point in Maine Avenue, Atlantic City, to a point in or near Chelsea, of which there had been constructed...........	1.23
Philadelphia, Marlton & Medford Railroad.	Extending from Haddonfield, on Camden & Atlantic Railroad, to Medford, a distance of about.....................	11.98
	Total............................	302.37

FINANCIAL DETAILS OF CONSOLIDATION

The authorized Capital Stock of the consolidated Company amounted to the aggregate number of shares which the Companies merged were authorized to issue, viz: $8,180,000., par value $50. each, of which $104,000. was to remain as Special Guaranteed Capital Stock as then issued and outstanding by the West Jersey Railroad Company. The right was given to the owners of the latter security to exchange it for Special Guaranteed Capital Stock of the West Jersey & Seashore Railroad Company, or under the terms of the agreement the Directors of the latter Company could offer to the holders of the Special Guaranteed Capital Stock of the West Jersey Railroad Company, in lieu of this Stock, Debenture Certificates of the consolidated Company, bearing 6% interest per annum. The Common Capital Stock of the West Jersey & Seashore Railroad Company was to be issued at par in exchange for the Capital Stock of the consolidated Companies, but not the same number of shares as had been issued by the respective companies before the consolidation, for the reason that the exchange value of the Capital Stock of all the Companies, except one, was less than the par value ($50.) of the Capital Stock of the new Company. The following statement indicates the prices at which the exchange was made:—

	Outstanding Capital Stock	*Price at which exchange was made*
West Jersey Railroad Company	$2,727,100.	$60. per share
Alloway & Quinton Railroad Company	46,500.	$20. per share
West Jersey & Atlantic Railroad Company	1,080,000.	$20. per share
Camden & Atlantic Railroad Company (Com.)	377,900.	$20. per share
Camden & Atlantic Railroad Company (Pfd.)	880,250.	$45. per share
Chelsea Branch Railroad Company	50,000.	$20. per share
Philadelphia, Marlton & Medford Railroad Company	102,900.	$15. per share
Total	$5,264,650.	

In the exchange and conversion provided for in the agreement, the consolidated Company was to issue, for all fractions of shares of Capital Stock, non-interest bearing scrip convertible into Stock when presented in the sums of $50. or multiples thereof on or before January 1st, 1897, after which date the said scrip was to be redeemable in cash.

CAR TRUSTS

At the annual meeting of the stockholders on March 10th, 1896, President Roberts, in explaining the operations of the Company for 1895, among other things clearly set forth the condition of the Car Trusts, stating that 60,000 cars had been built through their instrumentality, which was merely a borrowing of money upon a pledge of the cars until their entire cost was discharged through a series of annual payments; that this system was instituted when the credit of the Company was not quite as good as it was in 1896, and when money commanded a higher rate of interest; that this plan of purchasing cars had been discontinued for the time being, and the necessity would probably not occur again for resorting to that method of financing. The 60,000 cars acquired through the medium of Car Trusts had involved an outlay of approximately $31,000,000., all of which had been paid off with the exception of about $5,500,000., and when that sum was discharged the balance of the cars numbering 27,500 would come into the direct ownership of the Pennsylvania Railroad Company and its allied lines.

GRAND RAPIDS & INDIANA RAILROAD COMPANY REORGANIZED

The foreclosure proceedings instituted by the Pennsylvania Company against the Grand Rapids & Indiana Railroad Company resulted in the sale of that property and its reorganization on August 1st, 1896, as the Grand Rapids & Indiana Railway Company, upon a basis more nearly corresponding to its earning capacity. The main line of this Company extended from a connection with the Pittsburgh, Ft, Wayne & Chicago Railway at Fort Wayne, Ind., to Mackinaw City, Mich., a distance of about 367 miles. It also owned a number of branches and controlled several small railroad companies in Michigan, the total length of line owned and controlled amounting to 589 miles. The Pennsylvania Company continued as the majority stockholder in the new Company.

MANAGERS OF TRUST PAY MATURING OBLIGATIONS

The Bonds of the American Steamship Company, amounting to $1,500,000., the principal and interest of which were guaranteed by the Pennsylvania Railroad Company, matured on October 1st, 1896, and $1,485,000. thereof, which had been presented for payment up to the close of 1896, were paid out of the Managers of the Trust Fund created October 9th, 1878, there being no property held by the Steamship Company for the payment of these obligations. This same action was taken with respect to the interest on the Bonds of the Pennsylvania Canal Company, which was also guaranteed by the Pennsylvania Railroad Company, so that the payment of these large and practically unsecured obligations would not have to be met out of the current revenues of the Company.

DEATH OF PRESIDENT ROBERTS

On January 30th, 1897, President Roberts died at his home in Bala, Montgomery County, Pa., at the age of 64, after a service of 36 years with the Pennsylvania Railroad Company, for nearly 17 of which he was the Chief Executive of the Company. During his Administration many important additions were made to the System, the most important of which were the acquisition of the Philadelphia, Wilmington & Baltimore Railroad Company; the construction of the Pennsylvania Schuylkill Valley Railroad; the Trenton Cut-off; the Philadelphia, Germantown & Chestnut Hill Railroad; the Delaware River Bridge; the Filbert Street Extension, and the building and enlargement of Broad Street Station, Philadelphia. He was also the administrative head of the Pennsylvania Lines West of Pittsburgh during this period.

MINUTE OF BOARD OF DIRECTORS

The following paragraph extracted from the Minute adopted by the Board of Directors of the Pennsylvania Railroad Company on February 1st, 1897, indicates the policy pursued by President Roberts and that of his two predecessors, which emphasizes the statement made in earlier pages of this review that the Pennsylvania Railroad Company has always been fortunate in having as its chief executives men peculiarly fitted to meet the varying business conditions through which the Country was passing during their respective Administrations:—

> " It has been fortunate for the Company that in the period covered by his term of office as President many of the vital questions bound up with its welfare have had to be largely solved. The great system which had its foundation laid by Mr. J. Edgar Thomson, and which had been broadened and strengthened under the active and enterprising administration of Mr. Thomas A. Scott, then needed most of all the strong and conservative policy which marked Mr. Roberts' career to round up and make symmetrical the work of his predecessors. Through his labors many perplexing problems incident to its rapid growth have been disposed of, and the management fortunately left free to meet the new difficulties growing out of the unrestricted competition between the transportation lines and the unsettled condition of our commercial and political affairs.
>
> Careful in reaching a conclusion, and only determining upon a course to be pursued after exhaustive investigation, no one could act more promptly or vigorously when the proper time arrived; and the members of the Board do not need to have recalled to them the many instances where great responsibilities were suddenly assumed by him, and where the outcome of his action was invaluable to the Company's interests.
>
> His official relations with those in the service were marked by the kindliest consideration, and no one could be more patient in listening even when the views expressed might be directly antagonistic to his own. His intercourse with the public in the many business and social phases of life showed the same modest bearing and conscientious discharge of obligation that marked his career

as the President of the Company, and in the home life, to which he was devoted, he found that rest and relaxation which lightened the labors of his busy career."

STATISTICAL DATA

The following operating, traffic and financial statements are of interest as indicating the growth and development of the Company during the administration of President Roberts:—

REVENUE, EXPENSES, OPERATING INCOME, AND RENTALS, 1881 TO 1896, INCLUSIVE

All Lines East of Pittsburgh and Erie Operated Directly

Year	Miles	Gross Revenue	Operating Expenses	Operating Income	Rentals Paid	Net Operating Income to Penna. R. R. Co.
1881......	1,956.	$44,124,182.83	$26,709,809.93	$17,414,372.90	$7,116,391.18	$10,297,981.72
1882......	2,047.06	49,079,833.62	30,647,405.45	18,432,428.17	7,906,169.52	10,526,258.65
1883......	2,102.16	51,083,252.10	31,747,150.44	19,336,101.66	8,417,123.32	10,918,978.34
1884......	2,267.81	48,566,917.84	30,527,016.02	18,039,901.82	8,592,606.66	9,447,295.16
1885......	2,316.41	45,615,033.55	29,479,764.84	16,135,268.71	8,530,931.69	7,604,337.02
1886......	2,387.77	50,379,077.00	32,619,594.61	17,759,482.39	8,935,245.73	8,824,236.66
1887......	2,412.34	55,671,313.13	37,086,584.80	18,584,728.33	9,136,177.95	9,448,550.38
1888......	2,435.72	58,172,077.66	39,331,153.14	18,840,924.52	9,608,649.23	9,232,275.29
1889......	2,456.07	61,514,445.11	41,096,805.64	20,417,639.47	10,042,171.73	10,375,467.74
1890......	2,500.72	66,202,259.83	44,980,554.67	21,221,705.16	10,421,046.18	10,800,658.98
1891......	2,573.46	67,426,840.81	45,947,444.62	21,479,396.19	10,482,132.76	10,997,263.43
1892......	2,657.57	68,841,844.76	48,819,361.30	20,022,483.46	10,228,271.91	9,794,211.55
1893......	2,723.75	66,375,223.83	46,996,017.28	19,379,206.55	9,971,695.64	9,407,510.91
1894......	2,737.07	58,704,284.58	40,363,746.57	18,340,538.01	8,956,440.95	9,384,097.06
1895......	2,741.42	64,627,178.72	44,510,656.31	20,116,522.41	8,896,061.39	11,220,461.02
1896......	2,787.46	62,096,502.66	43,459,326.91	18,637,175.75	8,824,163.09	9,813,012.66

TONNAGE, MILEAGE, REVENUE, EXPENSES, AND AVERAGES ON FREIGHT BUSINESS, 1881 TO 1896, INCLUSIVE

All Lines East of Pittsburgh and Erie Operated Directly

Year	Tons	Tons One Mile	Revenue	Average Revenue per Ton per Mile	Expenses	Average Expenses per Ton per Mile	Average Net Revenue per Ton per Mile
				Cents		Cents	Cents
1881......	30,895,376	3,631,829,468	$31,128,521.00	0.857	$18,773,389.24	0.517	0.340
1882......	34,181,016	3,911,845,087	34,205,596.31	0.874	21,685,852.22	0.554	0.320
1883......	35,684,662	4,059,970,201	35,764,506.82	0.881	22,807,493.84	0.562	0.319
1884......	36,632,571	4,134,657,237	33,242,301.60	0.804	21,399,835.67	0.518	0.286
1885......	39,481,385	4,446,470,651	30,895,747.98	0.695	20,435,253.72	0.460	0.235
1886......	42,833,499	4,584,355,908	34,623,877.39	0.755	22,566,369.73	0.492	0.263
1887......	50,033,297	5,214,900,569	38,080,823.85	0.730	25,912,845.49	0.497	0.233
1888......	55,708,046	5,796,816,928	40,175,773.83	0.693	27,944,386.20	0.482	0.211
1889......	58,373,489	6,170,513,980	42,302,176.16	0.686	29,182,838.01	0.473	0.213
1890......	66,648,730	6,994,332,633	45,783,597.23	0.655	32,404,558.91	0.463	0.192
1891......	66,500,209	7,081,702,979	46,650,184.10	0.659	32,363,057.68	0.457	0.202
1892......	71,120,736	7,582,760,849	47,460,452.77	0.626	34,479,972.67	0.455	0.171
1893......	69,129,790	7,426,109,131	45,606,999.25	0.614	33,211,201.34	0.447	0.167
1894......	63,972,269	6,902,828,482	40,412,551.20	0.585	28,630,373.98	0.415	0.170
1895......	77,598,378	8,152,343,461	45,922,018.18	0.563	32,338,868.22	0.397	0.166
1896......	72,322,609	7,707,883,205	43,500,713.27	0.564	31,521,301.55	0.409	0.155

PASSENGERS, MILEAGE, REVENUE, EXPENSES, AND AVERAGES ON PASSENGER BUSINESS, 1881 TO 1896, INCLUSIVE

All Rail Lines East of Pittsburgh and Erie Directly Operated

Year	Passengers	Passengers One Mile	Revenue	Average Revenue per Passenger per Mile	Expenses	Average Expenses per Passenger per Mile	Average Net Revenue per Passenger per Mile
				Cents		Cents	Cents
1881......	18,985,409	446,316,555	$9,602,768.67	2.152	$7,207,500.69	1.615	0.537
1882......	21,887,992	496,202,927	11,160,816.55	2.249	8,252,581.22	1.663	0.586
1883......	23,081,858	505,180,481	11,605,253.42	2.297	8,215,365.70	1.626	0.671
1884......	25,164,131	512,873,485	11,582,198.17	2.258	8,314,586.21	1.621	0.637
1885......	27,642,018	568,664,914	11,087,445.00	1.950	8,337,776.94	1.466	0.484
1886......	31,090,271	576,906,276	12,194,830.84	2.114	9,292,592.61	1.611	0.503
1887......	35,785,769	657,362,557	13,968,909.51	2.125	10,363,715.40	1.577	0.548
1888......	38,168,374	681,684,854	14,259,507.77	2.092	10,517,506.83	1.543	0.549
1889......	40,189,893	727,312,735	15,140,342.75	2.082	11,106,425.34	1.527	0.555
1890......	43,810,382	778,818,917	16,177,150.55	2.077	11,710,227.29	1.504	0.573
1891......	44,810,727	795,098,618	16,331,444.85	2.054	12,725,352.33	1.600	0.454
1892......	46,648,572	843,819,609	16,709,533.94	1.980	13,332,046.93	1.580	0.400
1893......	44,135,320	813,652,864	16,264,101.22	1.999	12,884,347.53	1.584	0.415
1894......	38,596,160	693,010,056	13,703,799.46	1.977	10,961,541.83	1.582	0.395
1895......	37,452,437	712,072,950	13,909,506.33	1.953	11,331,489.73	1.591	0.362
1896......	36,170,220	699,799,213	13,744,556.70	1.964	11,070,381.51	1.582	0.382

DIVIDENDS AND ALLOTMENTS ON CAPITAL STOCK—THE PENNSYLVANIA RAILROAD COMPANY

DATE	Capital Stock on which Dividend or Allotment was Declared	DIVIDEND				ALLOTMENTS OF STOCK ON SUBSCRIPTION	
		CASH		SCRIP OR STOCK			
		Per Cent.	Amount	Per Cent.	Amount	Per Cent.	Amount
May, 1881.	$68,870,200	4	$2,754,808	......	......	12½	(At par) $8,802,550 00
November, "	77,672,750	4	3,106,910				
May, 1882.	77,672,750	4	3,106,910	......	......	8	(At par) 6,411,800 00
November, "	84,084,550	2½	2,102,113 75	2	Resulting in $1,667,700 00 stock. 13,991 00 cash. (Scrip Redeemable in cash or stock.)		
May, 1883.	85,752,250	2	1,715,045	2	1,703,100 00 stock. 11,945 00 cash.	4	(At par) 3,670,350 00
November, "	91,123,550	2½	2,278,088 75	2	1,810,600 00 stock. 11,871 00 cash.		
May, 1884.	92,936,300	2	1,858,726	2	1,841,550 00 stock. 17,176 00 cash.		
November, "	94,777,850	3	2,843,335 50				
May, 1885.	94,777,850	3	2,843,335 50				
November, "	94,777,850	2	1,895,557				
May, 1886.	94,777,850	2½	2,369,446 25	......	......	4	(At par) 3,744,000 00
November, "	94,777,850	2½	2,369,446 25				
May, 1887.	98,521,850	2½	2,463,046 25	......	......	8	(At par) 8,023,550 00
November, "	98,521,850	3	2,955,655 50				
May, 1888.	106,545,400	2½	2,663,635				
November, "	106,545,400	2½	2,663,635				
May, 1889.	106,545,400	2½	2,663,635	......	......	6	(At par) 6,943,200 00
November, "	106,545,400	2½	2,663,635				
May, 1890.	113,488,600	2½ & ½	3,404,658	......	......	8	(At par) 9,593,450 00
November, "	113,488,600	2½	2,837,215				
May, 1891.	123,082,050	......	......	3	Resulting in $3,692,450 00 stock. 11 50 cash.	......	Scrip redeemable in cash or stock.
November, "	126,771,200	3	3,803,136				
May, 1892.	126,774,050	3	3,803,221 50				
November, "	126,774,500	3	3,803,235				
May, 1893.	126,774,500	2½	3,169,362 50	2	Resulting in 2,531,950 00 stock. 1,796 00 scrip. 1,744 00 cash.	......	Scrip redeemable in cash or stock.
November, "	129,245,800	2½	3,231,145				
May, 1894.	129,289,000	2½	3,232,225				
November, "	129,296,900	2½	3,232,422 50				
May, 1895.	129,299,750	2½	3,232,493 75				
November, "	129,300,700	2½	3,232,517 50				
May, 1896.	129,301,850	2½	3,232,546 25				
November, "	129,303,050	2½	3,232,576 25				

DIRECTORS

The following is a list of the Directors who served during President Roberts' Administration, together with the dates of their election and the end of their service:—

Name of Director	*Elected*	*End of Service*
Josiah Bacon................	March 3, 1856,	February 3, 1881;
Wistar Morris...............	January 29, 1858,	March 23, 1891;
George B. Roberts...........	May 3, 1869,	January 30, 1897;
Edmund Smith.............	"	March 1, 1873;
"	August 1, 1874,	June 30,1888;
Alexander M. Fox...........	March 6, 1871,	October 6, 1907;
Samuel M. Felton............	February 26, 1873,	September 12, 1883;
N. Parker Shortridge.........	March 24, 1874,	January 3, 1915;
Henry M. Phillips...........	"	August 28, 1884;
Alexander Biddle............	"	May 2, 1899;
A. J. Cassatt................	July 1, 1874,	October 1, 1882;
"	September 12, 1883,	December 28, 1906;
Daniel B. Cummins..........	March 26, 1878,	November 9, 1887;
Henry D. Welsh.............	"	December 19, 1896;
John Price Wetherill.........	March 27, 1878,	September 17, 1888;
William L. Elkins............	March 25, 1879,	November 7, 1903;
James McManus............	March 23, 1880,	March 22, 1881;
William Thaw..............	February 9, 1881,	August 17, 1889;
Henry H. Houston...........	March 22, 1881,	June 21, 1895;
Joseph N. DuBarry..........	October 1, 1882,	December 17, 1892;
Frank Thomson............	"	June 5, 1899;
John P. Green..............	"	March 24, 1909;
Clement A. Griscom..........	September 24, 1884,	November 10, 1912;
Benjamin B. Comegys........	November 9, 1887,	March 29, 1900;
Amos R. Little..............	November 28, 1888,	December 16, 1906;
William H. Barnes...........	December 11, 1889,	May 5, 1918;
George Wood................	March 24, 1891,	February 17, 1926;
Charles E. Pugh.............	March 1, 1893,	February 28, 1911;
C. Stuart Patterson..........	July 2, 1895,	November 8, 1924.
Effingham B. Morris.........	December 31, 1896,	....

FRANK THOMSON

SIXTH PRESIDENT, 1897–1899

ON February 3rd, 1897, Frank Thomson was elected President of the Pennsylvania Railroad Company. He was born in Chambersburg, Pa., on July 5th, 1841, and received part of his education in the Chambersburg Academy. In 1858, at the age of 17, he entered the service of the Pennsylvania Railroad Company as an apprentice in the shops at Altoona, Pa., where he remained until the opening of the Civil War, when Col. Thomas A. Scott, then a Vice-President of the Company, selected him as one of his aides in the management of military roads and telegraph lines of the Government. He continued this service until June, 1864, when he resigned to become Superintendent of the Eastern Division of the Philadelphia & Erie Railroad. In March, 1873, he became Superintendent of Motive Power of the Pennsylvania Railroad Company, and on July 1st, 1874, was appointed General Manager of the Lines East of Pittsburgh and Erie. On October 9th, 1882, he was elected Second Vice-President; on June 27th, 1888, First Vice-President; and on February 3rd, 1897, as above stated, he became President.

ADDITIONAL FERRY SERVICE

The Pennsylvania Railroad Company deemed it wise to further increase its ferry facilities across the Hudson River by the establishment of a new uptown ferry service between Jersey City and 23rd Street, New York City, so as to better accommodate the important business and residential centres in that City. This service was begun on May 16th, 1897.

PURCHASE OF BROOKLYN ANNEX

In 1897 the property known as the Brooklyn Annex, comprising the ferryboats operating between the Jersey City piers of the Pennsylvania Railroad and Brooklyn and other

FRANK THOMSON

Sixth President—February 3rd, 1897, to June 5th, 1899.

points in New York Harbor, was purchased by the Company with the view of improving the service and facilities for the passenger traffic to and from those important traffic centres.

TWO WESTERN CONNECTIONS REORGANIZED

On June 29th, 1898, the Cincinnati & Muskingum Valley Railway, extending from Dresden Junction, O., to Morrow, O., a distance of 148 miles, having been sold under foreclosure proceedings, was purchased in the interest of the Pennsylvania Company and reorganized under the name of the Cincinnati & Muskingum Valley Railroad Company.

The Terre Haute & Logansport Railroad, one of the lines embraced in the St. Louis, Vandalia & Terre Haute Railroad System, having been sold under the mortgage securing $1,000,000. of its 6% Extension Bonds, was purchased by the Pennsylvania Company on November 18th, 1898, and reorganized under the name of the Terre Haute & Logansport Railway Company. Its line extended from Rockville, Ind., to South Bend, Ind., a distance of 159 miles, that part of the road from Terre Haute to Rockville having previously been leased to the Chicago & Eastern Illinois Railroad Company.

ADDITIONAL TRACKS ACROSS ALLEGHENY MOUNTAINS

As the double track line operated over the Allegheny Mountains and through the Gallitzin Tunnel had become inadequate to meet the demands of the constantly increasing traffic of the Pennsylvania Railroad System, it was necessary to add materially to the facilities on that portion of the road. For this purpose the Portage Tunnel was rebuilt in 1898 and the Portage Railroad double tracked between Cresson and Bennington on the Main Line, a distance of about five miles. Four tracks were also completed between Altoona and Kittanning Point, so that with the exception of a section about four miles in length between Kittanning Point and Allegrippus, where three tracks were in operation, there was a complete four track system from Altoona, at the foot of the eastern slope, to Lilly, on the western side of the Allegheny Mountains, a distance of about 17 miles.

JOINT TRAFFIC ASSOCIATION DISSOLVED

The Management, in referring to the Joint Traffic Association which had been formed in 1894 for the purpose of securing stability and uniformity of rates to the public and the prevention of violent fluctuation therein, stated that after its formation the legality of the Association was attacked in the courts, and in 1898 the United States Supreme Court held it to be in violation of the Anti-Trust Act, in accordance with which the agreement under which it was formed was cancelled and the Association dissolved. Therefore, as the railroads were not permitted to make agreements for the establishment and maintenance of reasonable rates on traffic, the hope was expressed that legislation would be promptly enacted to enable railroad managements to maintain their roads in the highest state of efficiency for the safety and accommodation of the public, and to protect the interest of their owners as well as the employes.

IMPROVED FERRY AND RAIL SERVICE FOR SEASHORE TRAFFIC

The ferry facilities on the Delaware River were greatly improved in 1898 by the reconstruction of the slips and station at Market Street Wharf, Philadelphia. The passenger travel over the seashore lines controlled by the Pennsylvania Railroad Company was greatly benefited by this improvement, while the double tracking of the West Jersey & Seashore Railroad between Camden and Atlantic City, completed in the early part of 1898, enabled the operation of a much more satisfactory service. Some steel rails 60 feet in length (30 feet was then standard) were used on this double track work, but the results did not at that time justify their general adoption.

CONSOLIDATION OF FERRY COMPANIES

On April 1st, 1899, the Camden & Philadelphia Steamboat Ferry Company and the West Jersey Ferry Company, the owners of the ferries operating between Philadelphia and Camden, were consolidated into the Philadelphia & Camden Ferry Company. The original Ferry Companies held very old Charters, the first named being incorporated on March 5th, 1836, and the second on January 31st, 1849.

DEATH OF PRESIDENT THOMSON

On June 5th, 1899, President Thomson, after a brief illness, died at his home in Merion, Pa. Practically his whole life was spent in the service of the Pennsylvania Railroad Company. Having early familiarized himself with the improvement of motive power and equipment and the structure and maintenance of track, and adding to this the experience gained as General Manager and later as Vice-President in charge of the Transportation and Traffic Departments of the Company's service, he was admirably equipped for the administration of the various departments of the service. The Board of Directors, in recording his death, adopted an appropriate minute on June 7th, 1899, from which the following paragraph has been extracted:—

> "In placing this minute of Mr. Thomson's death on the records of the Company, the Board is but attempting to do justice to the exceptional ability, devotion to duty, keen perception, sound judgment, and prompt execution, which made him so important a factor, not only in our own councils, but in the deliberations of the trunk lines and other important railway assemblages; as well as to the charming traits of personal character that won for him the affection and esteem of his associates, and make his loss one to be deeply and widely deplored."

STATISTICAL DATA

While the Administration of President Thomson covered a period of only slightly over two years, the operating and traffic statistics and financial statements are given so as to preserve the continuity of the information throughout this review:—

REVENUE, EXPENSES, OPERATING INCOME, AND RENTALS FOR 1897 AND 1898

All Lines East of Pittsburgh and Erie Directly Operated

Year	Miles	Gross Revenue	Operating Expenses	Operating Income	Rentals Paid	Net Operating Income to Penna. R. R. Co.
1897......	2,813.35	$64,223,113.15	$43,257,626.59	$20,965,486.56	$9,718,430.42	$11,247,056.14
1898......	2,821.71	65,603,737.95	44,510,015.85	21,093,722.10	10,315,771.90	10,777,950.20

TONNAGE, MILEAGE, REVENUE, EXPENSES, AND AVERAGES ON FREIGHT BUSINESS FOR 1897 AND 1898

All Rail Lines East of Pittsburgh and Erie Directly Operated

Year	Tons	Tons One Mile	Revenue	Average Revenue per Ton per Mile	Expenses	Average Expenses per Ton per Mile	Average Net Revenue per Ton per Mile
				Cents		Cents	Cents
1897......	78,927,656	8,535,158,008	$45,770,174.10	0.536	$31,498,826.46	0.369	0.167
1898......	84,220,747	9,214,565,495	45,939,773.48	0.499	32,744,026.12	0.355	0.144

PASSENGERS, MILEAGE, REVENUE, EXPENSES, AND AVERAGES ON PASSENGER BUSINESS FOR 1897 AND 1898

All Rail Lines East of Pittsburgh and Erie Directly Operated

Year	Passengers	Passengers One Mile	Revenue	Average Revenue per Passenger per Mile	Expenses	Average Expenses per Passenger per Mile	Average Net Revenue per Passenger per Mile
				Cents		Cents	Cents
1897......	34,997,524	693,279,336	$13,506,671.28	1.948	$10,729,968.01	1.548	0.400
1898......	35,962,566	745,962,679	14,410,746.46	1.932	10,688,916.33	1.433	0.499

DIVIDENDS AND ALLOTMENTS ON CAPITAL STOCK—THE PENNSYLVANIA RAILROAD COMPANY

DATE	Capital Stock on which Dividend or Allotment was Declared	DIVIDEND				ALLOTMENTS OF STOCK ON SUBSCRIPTION	
		CASH		SCRIP OR STOCK			
		Per Cent.	Amount	Per Cent.	Amount	Per Cent.	Amount
May, 1897.	$129,303,250	2½	$3,232,581 25				
November, "	129,303,550	2½	3,232,588 75				
May, 1898.	129,304,550	2½	3,232,613 75				
November, "	129,304,900	2½	3,232,622 50				

DIRECTORS

The following is a list of the Directors who served during the Administration of President Frank Thomson, together with the dates of their election and the end of their service:—

Name of Director	*Elected*	*End of Service*
Alexander M. Fox	March 6, 1871,	October 6, 1907;
N. Parker Shortridge	March 24, 1874,	January 3, 1915;
Alexander Biddle	"	May 2, 1899;
William L. Elkins	March 25, 1879,	November 7, 1903;
Frank Thomson	October 1, 1882,	June 5, 1899;
John P. Green	"	March 24, 1909;
A. J. Cassatt	July 1, 1874,	October 1, 1882;
"	September 12, 1883,	December 28, 1906;
Clement A. Griscom	September 24, 1884,	November 10, 1912;
Benjamin B. Comegys	November 9, 1887,	March 29, 1900;
Amos R. Little	November 28, 1888,	December 16, 1906;
William H. Barnes	December 11, 1889,	May 5, 1918;
George Wood	March 24, 1891,	February 17, 1926;
Charles E. Pugh	March 1, 1893,	February 28, 1911;
C. Stuart Patterson	July 2, 1895,	November 8, 1924;
Effingham B. Morris	December 31, 1896,	....
Sutherland M. Prevost	February 10, 1897,	September 30, 1905;
Thomas DeWitt Cuyler	May 10, 1899,	November 2, 1922.

ALEXANDER JOHNSTON CASSATT
Seventh President—June 9th, 1899, to December 28th, 1906.

ALEXANDER JOHNSTON CASSATT

SEVENTH PRESIDENT, 1899–1906

ALEXANDER JOHNSTON CASSATT was elected President of the Pennsylvania Railroad Company on June 9th, 1899. He was born in Pittsburgh, Pa., on December 8th, 1839, and received his early education in the common schools of that City; later when his father resided in Europe, he attended the Continental Schools and Darmstadt University. Upon his return to this country, Mr. Cassatt entered the Rensselaer Polytechnic Institute at Troy, New York, from which he was graduated in 1859 as a Civil Engineer. His first engagement in the railroad profession was as an engineering assistant in the location of a railroad in Georgia, but with the outbreak of the Civil War in 1861 he went to Philadelphia, where he entered the service of the Pennsylvania Railroad Company as a rodman. His knowledge of the technical and other features of railroad operation soon attracted attention and promotions followed rapidly, first, as Assistant Engineer in the construction of the Connecting Railway, linking the Pennsylvania Railroad to the Philadelphia & Trenton Railroad in Philadelphia (1863–1864); then Resident Engineer of the Middle Division of the Philadelphia & Erie Railroad (1864–1866); Superintendent of the Warren & Franklin Railroad, and of Motive Power and Machinery of the Philadelphia and Erie Railroad (1866–1867); Superintendent of Motive Power and Machinery of the Pennsylvania Railroad (1867–1870); General Superintendent of the Pennsylvania Railroad (1870–1871). In December, 1871, as the result of the enlargement of the Pennsylvania Railroad System through the lease of the lines of the United New Jersey Railroad & Canal Company, he was appointed General Manager of the line from Jersey City to Pittsburgh, and in 1873 became the General Manager of the Pennsylvania Lines East of Pittsburgh and Erie. On July 1st, 1874, he was elected Third Vice-President in charge of the Transportation and Traffic Departments of the service; on June 1st, 1880, First Vice-President. In 1882 Mr. Cassatt retired from the Vice-Presidency of the Company, but was elected a Director in 1883. He was also Chairman of the Road Committee of the Board of Directors from 1883 to 1899, which considered operations of, and additions to, the railroad and equipment, and on June 9th of the latter year was elected President.

RUINOUS RATE CUTTING

Grave alarm was expressed by the Management of the Pennsylvania Railroad Company in the annual report for 1899 as to the outcome of the continued decrease in the rates paid the trunk lines for the carriage of freight, due to the ruinous competition resulting from the cutting of rates. On the Pennsylvania Railroad there had been in each year since 1886, with two exceptions, a decrease in the rates over that of the preceding year, the average per ton per mile falling from 0.755 cents in 1886 to 0.473 in 1899. While the railroads made strenuous efforts to stop the downward trend, they met with little success, and although no commercial necessity existed for such reductions, especially in the year 1899 when the industries of the country were overtaxed with business, there was no halt in the fall in rates. Had the railway companies not been able to meet the diminution in the ton mile rate by a corresponding reduction in expenses, disastrous results would have followed, but it was felt that the limit had been reached. The only alternative left was to stop the reduction in rates, which had been largely brought about by the apparently uncontrollable conflict between the various railway companies and between rival communities.

COMMUNITY OF INTEREST PLAN

The problems involved in dealing with the traffic questions covering so large a territory and affecting so many diversified interests were complicated and difficult of solution. It was felt that by united efforts the difficulties could be overcome, and thus restore the credit of those railroad companies whose financial condition had become unsound by reason of the ruinous competition. With this end in view and to establish closer relations between the managers of the trunk lines, it was deemed wise by the Management of the Pennsylvania Railroad Company to join with the New York Central & Hudson River Railroad Company in acquiring an interest in some of the railroads reaching the Atlantic Seaboard, and to unite with other stockholders in supporting a conservative policy, which was commonly known as the "community of interest" plan. In accordance with this decision the Pennsylvania Railroad Company in 1900 acquired an ownership in the Capital Stocks of the Baltimore & Ohio Railroad, Chesapeake & Ohio Railway and Norfolk & Western Railway Companies. This, it was hoped, would result in securing reasonable and stable rates, avoid the unjust discriminations which were the inevitable result of the course theretofore pursued, and enable these Companies to obtain the capital requisite to perform their duties to the public. Aside from the benefits sought to be gained, it was believed that these purchases would ultimately prove profitable from an investment standpoint.

In this connection, and as a continuation of the "community of interest" policy adopted by the Pennsylvania Railroad Company and the New York Central & Hudson River Railroad Company, the former Company arranged early in 1902 for the acquisition of a substantial interest in the Reading Company Stocks, with the understanding that their ownership would be acceptable to, and ultimately be lodged with, the Baltimore & Ohio Railroad Company and the New York Central Company in equal proportions. This action was also taken to prevent control of the Reading passing to adverse or speculative interests which might seriously impair the Trunk Line understanding, and to keep the Reading as an open or terminal railroad for the exchange of traffic with all connecting railroads.

The Pennsylvania Railroad Company at that time had become a large stockholder in the Baltimore & Ohio Railroad Company in furtherance of the "community of interest" plan, and was desirous of perpetuating the connection of the Baltimore & Ohio Railroad via the Reading to New York

City, and continuing it as the preferential route for traffic to and from the Reading lines.

The Pennsylvania Railroad Company had previously (1901), in view of its large financial interest in the Baltimore & Ohio Railroad Company, recommended Mr. L. F. Loree as President of that Company, and he was elected. Previous to his election, he was Fourth Vice-President of the Pennsylvania Lines West of Pittsburgh.

In the early part of 1903, the Lake Shore & Michigan Southern Railway Company (controlled by the New York Central Company) and the Baltimore & Ohio Railroad Company took up and paid for their respective half interests in the Reading Company Stocks, for which the Pennsylvania Railroad Company had arranged, amounting to about 40% of the total then outstanding.

ACQUISITION OF TWO BRANCH ROADS

In 1899 the Pennsylvania Railroad Company purchased the Lancaster & Reading Narrow Gauge Railroad, extending from Lancaster to Quarryville, Pa., a distance of about 15 miles.

The Pennsylvania Railroad Company also purchased, in the same year, the Youghiogheny Railroad, this road extending from its junction with the Main Line at Irwin to Gratztown, Pa., a distance of nearly 10 miles.

NEW JERSEY CITY PASSENGER STATION

The Jersey City Passenger Station of the Pennsylvania Railroad Company, which was destroyed by fire on March 21st, 1898, was rebuilt and placed in service in 1899.

CONTROL OF CLEVELAND, AKRON & COLUMBUS RAILWAY COMPANY

A majority interest in the Cleveland, Akron & Columbus Railway Company, which formed a connection between Hudson, O., on the Cleveland & Pittsburgh Railroad, and Columbus, O., on the Pittsburgh, Cincinnati, Chicago & St. Louis Railway, and also through its Dresden Branch with the latter road at Trinway, O., was purchased in the interest of the Pennsylvania Company in 1899. The traffic of the line being naturally tributary to the Pennsylvania Railroad System, and its construction having for that reason been originally promoted in its interest, it was thought advisable, when an opportunity offered, to acquire control of this road.

PENSION DEPARTMENT ESTABLISHED

The Management of the Company had for a number of years been considering the establishment of a Pension Department, having for its object the retirement from service of all officers and employes who had attained the age of 70 years, or who, being between the ages of 65 and 70 years, and having been 30 years in the service, had become physically incapacitated. Therefore, effective January 1st, 1900, such a Department was created, and the pension allowance was based upon the length of service and average pay during the ten years preceding retirement. A regulation was also adopted that, except in certain cases where the interests of the Company clearly required it, no person who was over 35 years of age (changed to 45 years April 1st, 1907) could be employed in the service of the Company. The purpose of this regulation was to insure as far as practicable that employes should possess the necessary physical qualifications required in the performance of their duties.

PURCHASE OF ERIE & WESTERN TRANSPORTATION COMPANY

In 1900 the Pennsylvania Railroad Company purchased the Capital Stock of the Erie & Western Transportation Company amounting, at par, to $3,000,000. This Company, which operated a line of steamers between Erie and Buffalo and other points on the Great Lakes, for many years had worked in harmony with the Pennsylvania Railroad System. The equipment and organization of this steamship line were such as to attract a fair share of the large lake and rail traffic passing between the West and Atlantic Seaboard points.

SCHUYLKILL & JUNIATA RAILROAD COMPANY FORMED AND ABSORBED

On June 1st, 1900, the Pennsylvania Schuylkill Valley Railroad, Nescopec Railroad, North and West Branch Railway, Sunbury, Hazleton & Wilkes-Barre Railway and Sunbury & Lewistown Railway Companies were consolidated into one Company under the name of the Schuylkill & Juniata Railroad Company for the purpose of simplifying the management of these properties. The line thus formed extended from Philadelphia, via Reading, Pottsville and Tomhicken, to Wilkes-Barre on the north, and via Sunbury to a junction with the Main Line near Lewistown, an aggregate length of 289 miles, and furnished an important highway between the City of Philadelphia and the valleys of the Schuylkill, Susquehanna and Juniata Rivers. The consolidation was made on a conservative basis, and the securities of the new Company held in the Treasury of the Pennsylvania Railroad Company were considered a satisfactory investment. Effective April 1st, 1902, the Schuylkill & Juniata Railroad Company was absorbed by the Pennsylvania Railroad Company.

CONTROL OF WESTERN NEW YORK & PENNSYLVANIA RAILWAY COMPANY

An opportunity having presented itself in 1900, the Pennsylvania Railroad Company acquired a large majority of the Capital Stock and Income Bonds of the Western New York & Pennsylvania Railway Company. Its road formed a direct connection between the Pennsylvania Railroad System and the City of Buffalo at Emporium on the Philadelphia & Erie Railroad; at Oil City on the Allegheny Valley Railway, and at New Castle on the Erie & Ashtabula Division of the Pennsylvania Lines West of Pittsburgh. As Buffalo occupied an exceptional position in connection with the commerce of the Great Lakes, and would undoubtedly become an important center for manufacturing industries, it was deemed wise by the Management to secure this road as a connecting link for the large and increasing traffic which must pass to and from that city over the other lines in the

Pennsylvania Railroad System. The Western New York & Pennsylvania Railway and its subsidiaries had a total mileage of 548.8 miles.

PENNSYLVANIA RAILROAD STOCK LISTED ON NEW YORK STOCK EXCHANGE—TRANSFER OFFICE IN NEW YORK

Owing to the large holdings of the Capital Stock of the Pennsylvania Railroad Company in New York City, as well as its importance as a financial centre, and with the view of facilitating transfers of Stock at that point, it was deemed advisable by the Management to have it listed on the New York Stock Exchange, and to establish a transfer and registry office in that City. This was done on December 1st, 1900, and it has proved to be a great convenience to a large number of stockholders.

FOUR-TRACKING

The four-track system of the Pennsylvania Railroad was further extended west of Coatesville in 1900, so that with the exception of the crossings of the Brandywine and Conestoga Creeks at Coatesville and Lancaster, respectively, it was completed from Jersey City to Harrisburg. Between Jersey City and Pittsburgh, a distance of 440 miles, there were 311 miles four-tracked at the end of 1900, leaving 129 miles to be built to complete the system, which work it was necessary to vigorously prosecute in order to meet the rapid growth of the Main Line traffic.

PETERSBURG BRANCH CONSTRUCTED

The Petersburg Branch was extended in 1900 from Petersburg to a connection with the existing railroad at Aetna Furnace, Pa., thus completing an alternate line between Petersburg and Altoona via Hollidaysburg, and furnishing much needed facilities for the limestone traffic from that territory.

CONTROL OF LONG ISLAND RAILROAD COMPANY

In 1900 the Pennsylvania Railroad Company purchased a controlling interest in the Capital Stock of the Long Island

Railroad Company, which owned the system of lines extending through that island, and reaching many prosperous towns and attractive seashore resorts. The main line extended from Long Island City to Greenport, a distance of about 94 miles, while the Montauk Division was built from Long Island City to Montauk, a distance of about 115 miles, which with numerous branch lines, aggregated a total length of about 379 miles. It was believed that the completion of the bridges and tunnels then projected and under construction between the sections of Greater New York divided by the East River would so increase the business of the Long Island Railroad as to make the investment in its shares profitable. It was also contemplated to use a part of the Long Island Railroad to form a more convenient connection between the Pennsylvania Railroad System and that of the New York, New Haven & Hartford Railroad Company via the proposed New York Connecting Railroad, over which a large traffic was expected to pass to and from New England points.

SUSQUEHANNA & CLEARFIELD RAILROAD SOLD

The Susquehanna & Clearfield Railroad, extending from Karthaus to the Philadelphia & Erie Railroad at Keating, a distance of 23 miles, and originally built to furnish an outlet for the coal tributary thereto, having failed to develop a remunerative traffic, was sold in 1900 to the interests (New York Central) controlling the Beech Creek Railroad. By the use of this line and of trackage rights over the Philadelphia & Erie Railroad between Keating and McElhattan, a distance of 46 miles, the owners of the Beech Creek Railroad secured an economical line for the movement of their traffic, while at the same time the Pennsylvania Railroad Company and the Philadelphia & Erie Railroad Company received an increased return on the capital invested in this portion of the Pennsylvania Railroad System.

ACCEPTANCE OF PENNSYLVANIA CONSTITUTION—CLASSIFICATION OF DIRECTORS

At the annual meeting of the Pennsylvania Railroad Company on March 12th, 1901, two important resolutions were presented to the stockholders:—

First:—The acceptance by the Pennsylvania Railroad Company of all the provisions of the Constitution of Pennsylvania, adopted December 16th, 1873, and in effect January 1st, 1874, particularly the provisions of the Sixteenth and Seventeenth articles thereof (which refer to private corporations and railroads and canals), and approving and consenting to the action of the Board of Directors of the Pennsylvania Railroad Company of December 12th, 1900, to like effect.

Second:—The classification of the Board of Directors of the Company in accordance with the Act of the Legislature of Pennsylvania approved February 9th, 1901, permitting the same. Under this classification it was the intention to divide the 13 Directors of the Pennsylvania Railroad Company, elected by the stockholders, into four classes, the first class to consist of four, and each of the other classes three Directors; those of the first class to be elected for the term of one year, those of the second class for the term of two years, those of the third class for the term of three years, and those of the fourth class for the term of four years, and at each annual election the number of Directors necessary to take the place of those whose terms of office then expire shall be elected for the term of four years.

By resolution of the stockholders a Stock vote was taken on the first resolution on March 26th, 1901, which resulted in its adoption by a large majority vote, while the second was approved without the necessity of a Stock vote.

INCREASE IN AUTHORIZED CAPITAL STOCK

In accordance with the Act of the Pennsylvania Assembly of February 9th, 1901, granting authority to any corporation created by general or special law, to increase its Capital Stock to such amount as it deemed necessary to accomplish, carry on and enlarge its business and purposes, the authorized Capital Stock of the Pennsylvania Railroad Company was increased from 3,034,000 shares, par value, $151,700,000., to 12,000,000 shares, with a total par value of $600,000,000., which is the present amount authorized.

STOCK SOLD AT PREMIUM

In March, 1901, a 33⅓% allotment of Capital Stock was made by the Pennsylvania Railroad Company at $60. per share, resulting in the addition of $50,500,800., par value, to the outstanding Capital Stock. This was the first time in the history of the Company that it sold its Stock at a premium, and it was the largest issue it had made up to that time. The premium realized amounted to over $10,000,000. The proceeds received from this allotment were used for the purpose of meeting maturing obligations, to provide capital for the construction and equipment expenditures on the Company's lines, and for other proper corporate purposes.

ACQUIRING MINORITY STOCKHOLDINGS IN PHILADELPHIA, WILMINGTON & BALTIMORE RAILROAD COMPANY —CONSOLIDATION

A portion of the proceeds from the foregoing sale of Capital Stock of the Pennsylvania Railroad Company was used for the purpose of acquiring the remaining Stock in the Philadelphia, Wilmington & Baltimore Railroad Company not already owned by the former Company. This road formed an important link in the Pennsylvania Railroad System between New York and Washington. The Pennsylvania Railroad Company already held over 90% of its Capital Stock, and, in conjunction with the Northern Central Railway Company, owned all the Stock of the Baltimore & Potomac Railroad Company. The Management, therefore, deemed it wise that the Pennsylvania Railroad Company should become its sole proprietor, and that the Philadelphia, Wilmington & Baltimore Railroad Company and Baltimore & Potomac Railroad Company should later be merged into one corporation. It was felt that this course was all the more desirable as large expenditures were required in connection with the revision of the line and elimination of grade crossings in Washington, D. C., the erection of a new passenger station at that point, and the renewal of the bridge over the Potomac River, which improvements could be better financed by a consolidated Company.

RICHMOND-WASHINGTON COMPANY FORMED

In connection with the reconstruction of the terminal facilities at Washington, it was deemed advisable to unite under one control the Washington Southern Railway and the Richmond, Fredericksburg & Potomac Railroad, the two roads forming the line between Washington and Richmond, Va., and to have this line owned jointly by the Northern and Southern lines reaching the National Capital. This was accomplished through the Pennsylvania Railroad Company selling its Stock and Bond holdings in the Washington Southern Railway Company to the Richmond-Washington Company (a corporation formed for the purpose on September 5th, 1901, under the laws of New Jersey), which latter Company also purchased a majority of the Voting Stock of the Richmond, Fredericksburg & Potomac Railroad Company. The Pennsylvania Railroad Company thereupon became a joint proprietor in the Richmond-Washington Company through the purchase of one-sixth of its Capital Stock, the remaining five-sixths being acquired in equal proportions by the Baltimore & Ohio Railroad, Southern Railway, Seaboard Air Line Railway, Atlantic Coast Line Railroad and Chesapeake & Ohio Railway Companies.

The Richmond-Washington Company financed the purchase of these securities through the sale of its Capital Stock and Bonds, the latter being guaranteed jointly and severally by the six Owning Companies as to principal and interest by endorsement on the Bonds. Subsequently, through further issues and sales of its own Bonds to the public, the Richmond-Washington Company financed, in large part, the purchase of equipment, double track work and other improvements on the railroad between Washington and Richmond. The General Mortgage 3½% Bonds of the Richmond, Fredericksburg & Potomac Railroad Company were issued to reimburse the Richmond-Washington Company for these expenditures, which are pledged with the Trustee of the latter Company's mortgage to further secure its outstanding bonded indebtedness.

NORTH PHILADELPHIA STATION

On June 16th, 1901, a new and commodious passenger station was completed at Germantown Junction (now North Philadelphia Station) for the accommodation of the passenger traffic of the Company, which was rapidly increasing with the growth of that section of the City.

PENNSYLVANIA CANALS FINALLY ABANDONED

In 1901 the remaining 180 miles of canals owned by the Pennsylvania Canal Company, a majority of the Capital Stock of which was owned by the Pennsylvania Railroad Company, were abandoned for operating purposes. These canals had originally formed part of the Public Works of Pennsylvania, but as they could not compete with the railroads occupying the same general territory, it was impossible to operate them at a profit. As a result about one-half of the original system had previously been sold or abandoned, and the same action was to be taken with the remaining canals, the principal part of which extended from Columbia to Nanticoke via Northumberland.

LOGANSPORT & TOLEDO RAILWAY COMPANY FORMED

The Eel River Railroad, extending from Logansport to Butler, Ind., a distance of 94 miles, having been sold under foreclosure proceedings, was purchased on September 12th, 1901, in the interest of the Pennsylvania Company, and reorganized as the Logansport & Toledo Railway. This road furnished a desirable connection between the Vandalia System and the Grand Rapids & Indiana Railway, and greatly facilitated the movement of the passenger traffic between the Southwest and Northern Michigan.

NEW YORK TUNNEL EXTENSION AND STATION

The first definite reference to the construction of the New York Tunnel Extension and Station by the Pennsylvania Railroad Company is contained in the Annual Report for 1901, wherein it is stated that the Management had long felt that its interests, as well as the convenience of the public, required the extension of the Pennsylvania Railroad System into and through New York, and the establishment of a centrally located passenger station in that City, through which the inconvenience and delays of the transfer by ferry would be avoided. Various methods of accomplishing this result had at different times been considered, the great cost of a bridge excluding that plan unless all the railroad companies whose lines terminated on the west bank of the North (or Hudson) River would join in the undertaking. This they had been asked to do, but had declined.

MANY PLANS CONSIDERED

A very full and comprehensive report had been made in 1892 on the subject of a direct entrance into New York City for the railroads, the termini of which were on the New Jersey side, by Samuel Rea (then Assistant to President Roberts and later President of the Pennsylvania Railroad Company), in which attention was called to the fact that many plans had previously been proposed, some for the purpose of reaching a central terminal station in New York similar to the Grand Central Station of the New York Central Lines, or the ideal high-level entrance of the Pennsylvania Railroad into Philadelphia. Others, content with a partial solution, proposed that the termini of the said railroads should remain on the New Jersey side, but be connected with New York by some transit system other than the then existing ferries. By a process of elimination there were only five projects considered worthy of special consideration; three of them furnished an indirect entrance, or, as before stated, a partial solution of the problem, while the remaining two contemplated a direct entrance for solid trains running at express speed to a suitable terminus in New York City, making important connections with other existing steam railroads and with certain proposed lines, and also connecting with the rapid transit systems of both New York and Brooklyn.

FIVE PLANS FINALLY CONSIDERED

The five projects considered by Mr. Rea in 1892 and briefly outlined, were as follows:—

(*a*) An underground system of rapid transit, separate and distinct from the steam railroads, similar to the City and South London Railway, London, connecting Jersey City Station with New York and Brooklyn or with New York alone.

(*b*) The completion of the partially constructed Hudson River Tunnel (for one track) to be followed by the construction of others parallel therewith, the tracks through which were to be connected with the existing steam railroads on the New Jersey side, for the accommodation of passenger traffic only. The steam locomotives were to be detached on the New Jersey side and trains hauled through tunnels by cable power to a terminus in New York south of Washington Square.

(*c*) The establishment in New York on the west side of a suitable railroad terminus connecting with the Eleventh Avenue tracks of the New York Central Lines, the proposed 42nd Street tunnel to Long Island, and reached by the elevated railways; also connecting with the Jersey City Station by means of floating equipment carrying solid trains similar to the steamer "Maryland" service.

(*d*) The establishment of a terminus in New York, fronting on Madison Avenue, and between 37th and 38th Streets, to be reached by a double-track railroad 30½ miles long, extending from a connection with Pennsylvania Railroad at Houtenville, just west of Rahway, N. J., to and over or under Arthur Kill to Staten Island, and thence by subaqueous tunnels 3½ miles long under "The Narrows," between Upper and Lower New York Bay, to a connection with the railroads on Long Island. Thence by the use of those roads and new lines through, or rather around Brooklyn, to Hunter's Point, to a high-level crossing of the East River, the several streets, and the East Side elevated railroads, to the proposed terminus. Said terminus could also be utilized for New England railroads via the proposed line from a connection with the 42nd Street tunnel line and the Long Island Railroad in Long Island City; thence to a high-level crossing of the East River at

Hell Gate via Ward's and Randall's Islands, and thence to the main shore to a connection with the New Haven or New England railroad systems.

(*e*) By a high-level bridge over the Hudson River to a terminus for passenger and freight business, at suitable points between the said river and Broadway, the passenger station to be located on Sixth Avenue in the vicinity of Madison Square. Said bridge and terminus to have ample tracks and to accommodate the regular trains and traffic then running to Jersey City terminus, or as much thereof as might be deemed advantageous to send into New York. The bridge was to accommodate the heaviest trains at express speed and to have assigned tracks for rapid transit, said tracks to connect with all rapid transit systems thereabouts, including Jersey City, Bergen, Staten Island, Newark, etc. The station in New York was to be directly connected with the elevated trains of the Ninth and Sixth Avenue Lines, and with the rapid transit surface lines; also by a spur with the tracks of the New York Central Lines on Eleventh Avenue, and the tracks through the proposed tunnel under 42nd Street; thence with the Long Island Railroad System, the City of Brooklyn, and the proposed "Hell Gate Line" for New England.

BRIDGE PLAN LACKED SUPPORT

Each of these plans was reviewed in detail and the conclusion reached that the bridge project "(e)" for reaching New York and establishing a terminal therein was the best that had been evolved up to that time. It was stated that it would furnish an ideal terminus in the heart of the Country's greatest city for passenger traffic, and in addition would develop freight facilities of inestimable value; that several, if not all, the railroads on the New Jersey side ought to use it and furnish their share of traffic towards meeting the interest on the cost, which was estimated at $100,000,000. Efforts were made to bring this about and the Management of the Pennsylvania Railroad Company offered to co-operate with other railroad companies to that end, but the project failed to receive the necessary support.

TUNNEL SCHEME SUCCESSFUL ABROAD

Therefore, the other alternative, open to the Management of the Company in 1901, was the construction of a tunnel line; but the difficulties incident to steam railroad operation through a tunnel, at the depth and with the gradients required by the topographical conditions, seemed to make that method almost impracticable. Meanwhile, however, the successful operation of a number of tunnels in different parts of the world by electric power, notably the Orleans Railway Extension in Paris, then nearing completion, which President Cassatt examined at the suggestion of Mr. Rea, who was then Fourth Vice-President of the Company, indicated that a satisfactory solution of the problem might be found in the construction of a line, to be operated by electricity, under the North River to a terminal station in New York, and thence under the East River to a connection with the Long Island Railroad; the tunnels to be of such dimensions as to admit of the passage of standard size trains, and electric locomotives to furnish the power for carrying the trains through the tunnels.

WHOLE PROJECT STUDIED BY EMINENT ENGINEERS

It was stated that this plan had a great advantage over the bridge, in that it provided a direct connection between the Pennsylvania Railroad System from a point near Newark, N. J., to a connection with the Long Island Railroad in Long Island City, and also gave to that road the benefit of a central passenger station in the Borough of Manhattan, City of New York. Preliminary investigations having favored its adoption, it was thought best to proceed at once to acquire ground for a central station upon the location selected at Seventh Avenue and 34th Street, New York City. This was done and the greater part of the necessary property purchased at a reasonable price. The importance and cost of this work, however, and the fact that extraordinary engineering questions were involved, made it the duty of the Management before proceeding further, to have the plans for construction, and in fact the whole subject, thoroughly studied by competent engineers. For this purpose a Commission was created, reporting to President Cassatt and Fourth Vice-President Rea, consisting of six civil engineers eminent in their profession, namely, Col. Charles W. Raymond (United States Army), Chairman; Gustav Lindenthal; William H. Brown (Chief Engineer, Pennsylvania Railroad Company); Charles M. Jacobs; Alfred Noble and George Gibbs.

TUNNELS ENTIRELY PRACTICABLE

This Commission supervised the preparation of the plans and specifications of the project. As soon as the problem of building tunnels under the two rivers had been seriously studied, the supposed difficulties largely disappeared, and the Commission had in fact a choice between several feasible plans. Three members of the Commission acted as Chief Engineers of the work, which consisted of three Divisions, the North River Division having been assigned to Mr. Jacobs; the East River Division to Mr. Noble, and the Station Building Division and the electrification of the road to Mr. Gibbs. It was stated that the cost of the work would, of course, be large but the Management was satisfied that the expenditure would eventually be justified.

APPLICATION FOR FRANCHISE

The necessary authority from the States of New Jersey and New York for the prosecution of this enterprise was obtained, but the starting of the work was delayed by the inability to procure the requisite legislation from the municipal authorities of the City of New York. However, under authority of new State legislation, the franchise for this purpose was promptly granted by the Board of Rapid Transit Railroad Commissioners, but some delay was experienced before the Board of Aldermen took affirmative action on December 16th, 1901. The application to the Board of Rapid Transit Railroad Commissioners for a franchise covered—

First:—The construction of a railway consisting of two double-track lines, starting from adjacent points under the

Hudson River, on the line between the States of New York and New Jersey, and running eastwardly through New York City, one under 31st Street and the other under 32nd Street, and thence under the East River and Long Island City to a surface terminus near Thomson Avenue in that City.

Second:—The construction of a passenger station between 31st and 33rd Streets, and Seventh and Ninth Avenues, in New York, and for that purpose the closing and occupancy of 32nd Street between the Avenues named.

Third:—The construction of a third double-track railway from this passenger station under 33rd Street and to and under the East River to the terminus near Thomson Avenue.

Fourth:—The construction of additional tracks under 31st, 32nd and 33rd Streets necessary for the operation of the railway and station.

Fifth:—The occupancy of ground under 33rd Street and east and west of Fourth Avenue for a local station.

Sixth:—The maintenance and operation of the necessary cables, wires, and conduits under and along the route of the railway for power, heating, light, and other necessary purposes.

Seventh:—The right to use private property, lawfully acquired, for its corporate purposes in connection with the construction and operation of the tunnel; and

Eighth:—The right to maintain and operate the railroad in perpetuity.

FRANCHISE GRANTED UNDER CONDITIONS

The conditions under which the franchise was granted were—

(*a*) The Tunnel Company to begin the construction of its road within three months after obtaining the needful municipal and other consents, and complete its construction within five years thereafter, except the portion under 31st Street, as to which an additional ten years was given, with the option to the Company to abandon the construction of that section, or build it in whole or in part during said period; but such period of five years could be extended for a further five years upon reasonable cause shown, and was to be extended so as to cover any delays properly caused by legal proceedings.

(*b*) The Tunnel Company to pay the city a compensation per linear foot for the tracks so laid under the cities of New York and Long Island, and a further compensation for the use, for station purposes, of the underground portions of the streets, other than 32nd, which it so occupies. Such compensation was fixed for the first period of 25 years, and was subject to readjustment at the end of each like period. For the first period of 25 years, it was so adjusted that the Tunnel Company was to pay double the amount per annum for the latter 15 years thereof that it did for the first ten, and on this basis the average for the entire period was about $64,000. per annum.

(*c*) The Tunnel Company was also to pay $36,000. per annum for the portions of 32nd Street vacated between Seventh and Ninth Avenues and occupied by the passenger station, with the right to commute such annual compensation by the payment of $788,600. as soon as the City was authorized to convey the said property to the Tunnel Company in fee.

(*d*) That the power to be used shall be electricity or other approved power not involving combustion in the tunnel.

CONNECTING RAILWAY COMPANY CONSOLIDATION

Effective January 1st, 1902, the Connecting Railway, Philadelphia, Germantown & Chestnut Hill Railroad, Engleside Railroad, Kensington & Tacony Railroad, Fairhill Railroad, Bustleton Railroad and Philadelphia, Bustleton & Trenton Railroad Companies were consolidated with and into the Connecting Railway Company. This simplified the working of these railways and merged into one corporation lines having a common interest and practically covering the local territory between the Main Line and the Philadelphia & Trenton Railroad.

CONVERTIBLE BONDS SOLD

In March, 1902, the privilege was granted to the stockholders of the Company to subscribe, in an amount equal to 25% of their holdings, for $50,000,000. 3½% 10-year Convertible Gold Bonds of the Pennsylvania Railroad Company bearing date November 1st, 1902, and maturing November 1st, 1912. The right was given to the holders of these securities to convert the same into Capital Stock on May 1st, 1904, or at any subsequent semi-annual interest period at $70. per share. Subsequently it was deemed advisable to give them the privilege of an earlier conversion on the same basis, under which they could surrender their Bonds and become shareholders of record May 9th, 1903. The amount received from this issue was used largely to pay for additional equipment estimated to cost $24,000,000., and for construction expenditures on the New York Tunnel Extension, including the purchase of property required for the passenger station in that City.

PENNSYLVANIA & NORTH WESTERN RAILROAD PURCHASED

On March 1st, 1902, the Pennsylvania Railroad Company assumed possession of and commenced to operate the Pennsylvania & North Western Railroad, having acquired the Capital Stock of that Company on satisfactory terms. This road connected with the Main Line at Bellwood, Pa., and extended thence in a northwesterly direction towards the Punxsutawney District and the Low Grade Line of the Allegheny Valley Railway, a distance of about 65 miles, and developed a valuable coal territory tributary to the Pennsylvania Railroad System.

NEW BRIDGE OVER SUSQUEHANNA RIVER AT ROCKVILLE, PA.

On March 30th, 1902, the new four-track stone arch bridge over the Susquehanna River at Rockville, Pa., was completed and placed in service. It was 3,820 feet in length and took the place of the double-track iron bridge previously in use.

LEASE OF WESTERN NEW YORK & PENNSYLVANIA RAILWAY COMPANY

On October 22nd, 1902, the Pennsylvania Railroad Company leased the railroad and property of the Western New York & Pennsylvania Railway Company for 20 years from August 1st, 1903, the lessee agreeing to turn over to the lessor any surplus after the payment of operating expenses and fixed charges. After the expiration of the 20-year term, the lease was to run from year to year thereafter but subject to cancellation by either party on 60 days' notice. This road had been operated under its own organization until August 1st, 1900, on which date the operation was taken over by the Pennsylvania Railroad Company under lease dated July 14th, 1900, for one year, which was subsequently extended from year to year to August 1st, 1903, when the said 20-year lease became effective.

PHILADELPHIA, BALTIMORE & WASHINGTON RAILROAD COMPANY FORMED

On November 1st, 1902, the Philadelphia, Wilmington & Baltimore Railroad and Baltimore & Potomac Railroad Companies, the Capital Stocks of which were practically all owned or controlled by the Pennsylvania Railroad Company, were merged and consolidated into a corporation known as the Philadelphia, Baltimore & Washington Railroad Company, thus placing under one ownership the line between Philadelphia and Washington. That Company was then rebuilding its bridge across the Potomac River at Washington, and upon the passage of the necessary legislation then pending in Congress, work was to proceed on the erection of a new passenger station at the National Capital and the elimination of grade crossings in that City.

WASHINGTON TERMINAL COMPANY

The Station project later developed into the formation of the Washington Terminal Company jointly owned by the Philadelphia, Baltimore & Washington Railroad and Baltimore & Ohio Railroad Companies. The Terminal Company subsequently built a new Union Station, to which reference is later made, in place of the two separately owned Terminals which previously existed.

ROUTE OF NEW YORK TUNNEL EXTENSION

Progress was made during 1902 with the plans for the New York Tunnel Extension, to which reference has heretofore been made. Two Companies had been chartered in 1902 for the purpose, one in New Jersey and the other in New York. It was proposed to commence the Extension at a point on the line of the United New Jersey Railroad & Canal Company about a mile east of Newark, from which point a double track road was to be constructed by the Pennsylvania, New Jersey & New York Railroad Company, (the New Jersey corporation), on an elevated line to Weehawken, and thence by tunnel under Bergen Hill and the North River to a connection on the boundary line between the States of New York and New Jersey with the Pennsylvania, New York & Long Island Railroad. The latter was the New York corporation and it was to complete the line from that point under the North River, the City of New York, the East River and Long Island City, to a junction with the Long Island Railroad near Thomson Avenue in the latter City. Connection was also to be made with the New York Connecting Railroad, and through it with the New York, New Haven & Hartford Railroad, and thus provide an all-rail route between the Pennsylvania Railroad System and New England.

PITTSBURGH STATION

The new Pittsburgh Station and other facilities connected with the passenger service at that point were practically completed and placed in operation in 1902.

CONSTRUCTION OF MONONGAHELA RAILROAD

For the purpose of further developing the coal territory along the Monongahela River, the Monongahela Railroad Company was incorporated in 1901 and was to be constructed from Brownsville Junction to the State Line between Pennsylvania and West Virginia, in the joint interest of the Pennsylvania Railroad and Pittsburgh & Lake Erie Railroad Companies. The road was completed as far south as Martin, Pa., in 1903, a distance of over 26 miles from Brownsville Junction.

IMPORTANT IMPROVEMENT PROGRAM

In conformity with the traditional policy of the Pennsylvania Railroad Company in preparing in advance for the requirements of its traffic, the following estimate was made by the Management in 1902, of the cost of improvements which would have to be made East of Pittsburgh, and which would require from two to three years to complete:—

For the Brilliant Branch, the Sharpsburg, Brilliant, Shire Oaks, Ormsby and other yards, the connection between the Port Perry Branch and the Main Line at Brinton, the elevation of the Western Pennsylvania Railroad, the extension of the elevated railroad along Duquesne Way, and the cost of the new freight station at the Point (Pittsburgh), &c.	$9,500,000.
For the new line between Radebaugh and Derry, and the completion of the four-track system on the Pittsburgh Division	13,000,000.
For the double-tracking of the Western Pennsylvania Railroad and other improvements thereon	2,000,000.
For the new line on the New Portage roadbed, double-tracking the Petersburg Branch, and the building of Hollidaysburg yard	5,000,000.
For completing the four-track system on the Middle Division and other improvements on that Division	3,000,000.
For the new line between York Haven and Parkesburg, and Thorndale and Paoli, and two additional tracks between Paoli and Philadelphia	18,000,000.
For the extension of the West Philadelphia yard, the elevated railroad connecting the Maryland Division and the Delaware Extension with the Main Line and the New York Division, and for other facilities in West Philadelphia	3,000,000.
For reducing the grades on the Trenton Cut-Off	1,500,000.
For two additional tracks, making six running tracks in all, between Trenton and Newark, changes of line at Frankford and Bristol, elevating the road through Rahway, completing the elevation at Newark and New Brunswick and the change at Trenton, and other improvements on the New York Division	12,000,000.
Total	$67,000,000.

While this, it was stated, was a large sum, no less an expenditure would enable the Company to perform its duty to the public. The Management was satisfied that the investment of this amount would result in largely increased net earnings, not only from the greater volume of traffic which could be handled, but through economies resulting from the reduction of grades, the better location and arrangement of yards, the saving in shifting service, and in overtime to train crews.

SMALL CHARGES TO CAPITAL ACCOUNT

Attention was called to the fact in 1902 that the charges to Capital Account for the construction of tracks and roadbed in the five years previous had been comparatively small. From 1897 to 1902, inclusive, the increase in the cost of Road had been only about $6,000,000., or a little over 11%, for improvements of the character referred to, they having been substantially paid for out of Income and not charged to Capital Account. Meanwhile the tonnage of the Main Line and branches had increased during the same time from 47,000,000 to over 77,000,000 tons, or about 64%; Gross Earnings for the same period had increased from about $38,000,000. to $68,000,000., or nearly 80%, and Net Earnings from approximately $14,000,000. to $25,000,000., or over 78%.

SALE OF COLUMBUS, SANDUSKY & HOCKING RAILROAD

The Columbus, Sandusky & Hocking Railroad having been sold under legal proceedings, the portion thereof lying between Columbus and Sandusky, a distance of 110 miles, was purchased in the interest of the Pennsylvania Company in 1902, and made part of the Toledo, Walhonding Valley & Ohio Railroad, which it intersected at Carrothers, and which was controlled by the Pennsylvania Company. The acquisition of this property gave this Toledo line the advantage of another lake terminal at Sandusky, and thus increased its facilities for handling the coal and other traffic interchanged with the Pennsylvania Lines at Columbus.

ACQUISITIONS

Effective April 1st, 1903, the franchises, corporate property, rights and credits of the following Companies were acquired by the Pennsylvania Railroad Company:—

Western Pennsylvania Railroad Company;
South Fork Railroad Company;
West Chester Railroad Company;
Turtle Creek Valley Railroad Company;
Downingtown & Lancaster Railroad Company;
Riverfront Railroad Company.

The Pennsylvania Railroad Company was the owner of the entire Capital Stock of each of these Companies, and their absorption simplified their Management, saved unnecessary accounting and was in the direction of economy and efficiency. The Western Pennsylvania Railroad diverged from the Main Line at a point about two miles west of Johnstown, and also connected therewith further west at Bolivar and Blairsville Intersection. It furnished the low grade line over which a large portion of the through traffic of the Pennsylvania Railroad passed to and from the Pittsburgh, Fort Wayne & Chicago Railway and other roads in the Pennsylvania Railroad System northwest of Pittsburgh. The South Fork Railroad was built to develop a valuable coal territory on the western slope of the Allegheny Mountain. The West Chester Railroad, Turtle Creek Valley Railroad and Downingtown & Lancaster Railroad were branches built to develop local territory. The Riverfront Railroad was a short line, which furnished valuable terminal facilities for traffic of the Company along the Delaware River front in Philadelphia.

STOCK AGAIN SOLD AT A PREMIUM

In order to provide capital for the large construction and equipment expenditures of the Company, a 33⅓% allotment of its Capital Stock was made to the stockholders at $60. per share in March, 1903, which added $75,094,750., par value, to the outstanding Stock. A premium of over $15,000,000. was realized from this allotment, it being the second time within two years that the Company sold its Stock at a premium, the two issues placing over $150,000,000. in the Company's Treasury.

In originating the 1903 issue, the Management had not deemed it necessary to have it underwritten by a banking syndicate, but due to changing market conditions, the price of the Company's Stock declined to a point where the success of the allotment was in jeopardy. This might have adversely affected the credit of the Company, and, therefore, arrangements were promptly made to have the issue underwritten by Kuhn, Loeb & Co. and Speyer & Co., after which the decline in the price of the Stock stopped and the allotment was successful.

REMOVAL OF WESTERN UNION TELEGRAPH LINES

It may be of interest to record the facts in connection with the removal of the poles and wires of the Western Union Telegraph Company from the property of the Pennsylvania Railroad Company in May, 1903, for which the Management of the latter Company was unjustly criticized until the situation was clearly understood. The contract under which the right of way of the Railroad Company was used for the Western Union Telegraph service ran from September 20th, 1881, to September 20th, 1901. With an agreement running for 20 years, it was natural, if it were to be renewed, that with the changing conditions some modifications were necessary, and for more than 18 months prior to its expiration negotiations were conducted with the Western Union Company for the purpose of obtaining a new contract. As no satisfactory progress could be made, and as the contract was to terminate unless a new agreement was executed, the Management of the Pennsylvania Railroad Company reached the conclusion that nothing could be done except to terminate it, and thereupon gave the full six months' notice required by the following terms of the agreement:—

> "If no new agreement is made by the parties hereto, the Telegraph Company shall at the termination of the contract, or at any time thereafter, upon receiving writ-

ten notice from the Railroad Company, remove within six months from the receipt of said notice all of its poles and wires and leave the property of the Railroad Company in good condition and free from the incumbrance thereof to the satisfaction of the general manager, or other proper officer of the Railroad Company, and if not so removed the Railroad Company may remove them at the expense of the Telegraph Company."

The Western Union Company publicly stated at the time that it would not be inconvenienced by the change and could otherwise reach all the principal cities on the Main Line of the Pennsylvania Railroad. Therefore, no trouble or inconvenience to the public was anticipated, and it was assumed that the poles and wires of the Telegraph Company would be removed from the property of the Railroad Company in accordance with the terms of the contract. Further, the Management of the Pennsylvania Railroad Company, in order to save the Western Union Company the expense and loss incident to the removal of the poles and wires, offered to purchase the same at a fair valuation, but the latter Company apparently preferred to allow the Railroad Company to remove them.

Meanwhile, the Pennsylvania Railroad Company, through the inaction of the Western Union Company, was compelled to run the risk of having no commercial telegraph service for its patrons, and, therefore, rather than remain in this position, it entered into a contract with the Postal Telegraph Company on June 25th, 1902, to provide the Railroad Company with its telegraph service. The right of way occupied by the lines of the Western Union Company was required to carry out the terms of the new contract with the Postal Company, and as the former Company made no effort to remove its poles and wires, the Pennsylvania Railroad Company proceeded to take them down in May, 1903. This action was not taken precipitately, but only after extended negotiations for a new contract with the Western Union Company had failed, and no action taken on the offer of the Railroad Company to purchase them. Furthermore, it was not done until the position of the Pennsylvania Railroad Company in the matter had been fully sustained in the United States Court for the Eastern District of Pennsylvania and in the Circuit Court of Appeals for the Third District. After the poles and wires were taken down, the Western Union Company declined to move them away presumably on the assumption that they were not worth removal.

Some years later, upon the expiry of the contract with the Postal Company and when the Management of the Western Union Company had changed, new contracts were entered into with the latter Company and its commercial telegraph service extended over the territory in which the Pennsylvania Railroad System operates.

CAMBRIA & CLEARFIELD RAILWAY COMPANY FORMED

On August 1st, 1903, the Pennsylvania & North Western Railroad, Millersburg Railroad, Tyrone & Clearfield Railway Cambria & Clearfield Railroad, Cresson & Irvona Railroad and Ebensburg & Black Lick Railroad Companies were consolidated into the Cambria & Clearfield Railway Company. As the Pennsylvania Railroad Company was the owner of practically all the Stock of the subsidiary companies, this step was taken for the purpose of simplifying the management of these properties and merging into one organization several roads traversing the bituminous coal territory in the Allegheny Mountain region.

CONSTRUCTION OF CHERRY TREE & DIXONVILLE RAILROAD

The Cherry Tree & Dixonville Railroad Company, which was incorporated and owned jointly by the Pennsylvania Railroad Company and the New York Central & Hudson River Railroad Company, was being constructed in 1903 from Cherry Tree to Dixonville, a distance of about 20 miles. This road was an extension of the Cambria & Clearfield Railway, and was built jointly to avoid a useless duplication of lines in that territory.

ALTERNATE ROUTE PETERSBURG TO ALLEGHENY MOUNTAIN SUMMIT

The construction of a new double-track line about 50 miles in length, via the New Portage Railroad and the Petersburg Branch, between the summit of the Allegheny Mountains and the Main Line at Petersburg in the Juniata Valley was completed in 1903, with the exception of the double tracking of about six miles of the Petersburg Branch at a point where a revision of the location would be necessary in the future. The new line formed an alternate route between the points mentioned for the movement of coal and other heavy traffic.

MONONGAHELA & WASHINGTON RAILROAD ACQUIRED

On July 1st, 1904, the Pittsburgh, Virginia & Charleston Railway Company acquired the Monongahela & Washington Railroad, which extended from a connection with the former road in Monongahela City to a point in West Bethlehem Township, Pa., a distance of about 15 miles.

BRANCH ROAD CONSTRUCTION

On November 10th, 1903, that portion of the Bedford & Hollidaysburg Railroad, extending from its connection with the Bedford Division at Cessna to Imler, a distance of about 12 miles, was completed and placed in service.

On November 27th, 1904, the Brilliant Branch extending from its junction with the Main Line east of East Liberty Station, Pittsburgh, to a connection with the Buffalo & Allegheny Division north of Brilliant and to a junction with the West Penn Division south of Aspinwall, a total distance of nearly four miles, was completed and opened for traffic.

On December 1st, 1904, a portion of the Cherry Tree & Dixonville Railroad, extending from Cherry Tree to Possum Glory Junction, a distance of about 13 miles, was completed and placed in service.

The extension of the Cambria & Clearfield Railway from Dilltown to a junction with the Indiana Branch near Black Lick Station, a distance of about 13 miles, was completed and placed in service on June 1st, 1904. This with the extensions which had previously been constructed furnished a direct connection between the Indiana Branch and the Cambria & Clearfield Railway.

NEW YORK TUNNEL EXTENSION

The construction of the New York Tunnel Extension was actively proceeding in 1904. Contracts had been awarded for the two tunnels under the North River between the Weehawken Shaft in New Jersey and the east side of Tenth Avenue, New York City, for the excavation and retaining walls for the Passenger Station between Seventh and Ninth Avenues in that City, and for the four tunnels under the East River to East Avenue in Long Island City. It was expected that the remaining tunnel work under Bergen Hill on the west side of the North River and in New York City east of the Station as well as the Station in that City would be put under contract during 1905.

Large property purchases had been made for the tunnel line in New York City west of Ninth Avenue, and also in Long Island City and in New Jersey; while a sale of a portion of the property fronting on Eighth Avenue, New York City, opposite the proposed passenger Station, had been arranged with the United States Government for use as a General Post Office Building, the Tunnel Company reserving the subsurface rights for railway purposes.

FORMATION OF VANDALIA RAILROAD COMPANY

Effective January 1st, 1905, the Terre Haute & Indianapolis Railroad, St. Louis, Vandalia & Terre Haute Railroad, Terre Haute & Logansport Railroad, Logansport & Toledo Railroad and Indianapolis & Vincennes Railroad Companies, were merged and consolidated under the title of the Vandalia Railroad Company, the Pennsylvania Company retaining a large controlling interest in the new Company. This consolidation merged into one system the lines which formed a direct connnection via Indianapolis with St. Louis, together with the roads tributary thereto extending to Vincennes on the south and to South Bend and Butler, Ind., on the north, embracing an aggregate of 631 miles of main track.

CONVERTIBLE BOND ISSUE OF 1905

In April, 1905, the privilege was granted to the stockholders of the Company to subscribe, in an amount equal to 33⅓% of their holdings, for $100,000,000. 3½% 10-Year Convertible Gold Bonds of the Pennsylvania Railroad Company, bearing date October 2nd, 1905, and maturing October 1st, 1915. The right was given to the holders of these securities to convert the same into Capital Stock at any time after December 1st, 1905, at $75. per share. The proceeds from the sale of these Bonds were used to pay off over $27,000,000. Consolidated Mortgage Bonds of the Company, which matured on June 15th and July 1st, 1905; to purchase additional equipment and provide increased shop and terminal facilities; also for construction expenditures on the New York Tunnel Extension, and on the Main Line between Pittsburgh and New York. The amount of the issue and the low interest rate led the Company to assure its success against all contingencies through the underwriting thereof by the banking firms of Kuhn, Loeb & Co. and J. P. Morgan & Co.

ACQUISITION OF PITTSBURGH, VIRGINIA & CHARLESTON RAILWAY

On April 1st, 1905, the Pennsylvania Railroad Company acquired the franchises, corporate property, rights and credits of the Pittsburgh, Virginia & Charleston Railway Company. The Main Line of this road extended from a junction with the Pittsburgh, Cincinnati, Chicago & St. Louis Railway, South Side, Pittsburgh, to West Brownsville, Pa., a distance of about 53 miles, which with branches aggregating 45 miles, made a total length of about 98 miles.

WATER SUPPLY

One of the most important matters which received the attention of the Management in 1905 was to provide a sufficient water supply for the existing and future needs of the Company. Owing to the largely increased demand arising from the growth of traffic, the former sources of supply had become inadequate, and on the lines traversing the coal regions, the quality of water was rapidly becoming unfit for locomotive use. Arrangements were accordingly made through contracts with companies organized and owned by the Pennsylvania Railroad Company to secure an adequate supply of good water at all points on the Main Line between Pittsburgh and New York; also on the more important branches, and for the construction of the reservoirs and the piping of the water to the Company's lines, from which it was to be distributed along the right of way to the necessary points of consumption.

This work was carried out and the water supply system now embraces 36 reservoirs and intakes, the largest of which holds one billion gallons, and their total capacity is three billion gallons. The total length of pipe lines in the system is 151 miles, which with those owned by the Pennsylvania Railroad Company on its own right of way, make a total of 441 miles. Eleven pumping and booster stations are operated and maintained, the largest of which has a capacity of 12 million gallons per day. The total number of gallons furnished in 1926 was over 14 billions. The area of mountain land owned in the water supply system on the various water sheds is 27,300 acres, which, in the interest of conservation, are protected and reforested from time to time.

The cost of securing the water supply was large, but the great benefits derived from obtaining water in sufficient quantity and of good quality has made it a valuable investment and more than justified the expenditure, which has amounted to approximately 30 million dollars.

INVESTIGATION BY SPECIAL COMMITTEE OF DIRECTORS

Pursuant to a resolution passed by Congress on March 7th, 1906, the Interstate Commerce Commission was instructed to investigate and report, among other matters, whether common carriers by rail were interested in the ownership of the coal carried over their lines, and whether any officers or employes of such carriers charged with the duty of furnishing cars or other facilities to shippers were interested as owners or otherwise in the coal so carried. As it was alleged during this investigation that employes of the Pennsylvania Railroad Company had not done their duty to the shareholders of the Company or to the public, due to their ownership or interest in corporations doing business with the Pennsylvania Railroad Company, or over its lines, a Special Committee of five Directors was appointed to thoroughly inquire into and report upon the matter. This Committee, after an exhaustive inquiry, reported its findings to the Board of Directors, and a copy thereof, as well as its preliminary report, was sent to each shareholder. The Committee found, as the result of its investigations, that with few exceptions the officers and employes of the companies constituting the Pennsylvania Railroad System had been faithful to their duty. The necessary measures, however, were taken to enforce compliance with a regulation providing that none of the officers or employes of the Company should have any ownership, direct or indirect, in any company, or interest in any firm, or with any individual owning or operating mines located on the Pennsylvania Railroad System, or dealing in coal produced therefrom; or in any other business where such holding might in any way conflict with their duty to the Company, or its duty to the public.

ACQUISITION OF SOUTH WEST PENNSYLVANIA RAILWAY

Effective March 31st, 1906, the franchises, corporate property, rights and credits of the South West Pennsylvania Railway Company were acquired by the Pennsylvania Railroad Company. This road was built as a feeder to the Pennsylvania Railroad System, and extended from the Main Line at Greensburg through the coke region of Pennsylvania to Connellsville and Uniontown to a connection with the Monongahela Division, a distance of about 45 miles. It also owned 86 miles of branch lines.

FRENCH FRANC LOAN

It had been the purpose of the Management to secure a portion of the funds required to provide additional equipment and a permanent water supply through the sale of short term securities to the public. However, the market for investment securities in this Country was such that no large amounts of money could be raised at reasonable rates of interest. Therefore, at the suggestion and with the co-operation of the banking firm of Kuhn, Loeb & Co., arrangements were made to secure a loan on satisfactory terms in France through banking institutions of the highest credit. The result was the entry of the Company into a new field for financing its capital requirements. This was the first time that any American Railroad Bonds had been issued payable in Francs and listed on the Paris Bourse.

The loan took the form of an issue, dated June 15th, 1906, of 250,000,000 francs, or about $48,000,000., of Pennsylvania Company 3¾% Trust Certificates secured by collateral, running for 15 years, but subject to redemption at par and interest on June 15th, 1918, or any interest period thereafter. These obligations were guaranteed by the Pennsylvania Railroad Company, and with their proceeds the Pennsylvania Company purchased the Car Trust and Water Trust Certificates of the Pennsylvania Railroad Company, together with other securities, in an amount substantially equal to the proceeds of this loan. The principal of the Car Trust and Water Trust Certificates was payable in annual installments over a ten year period ending in 1916 and 1917, respectively.

ACQUISITION OF YORK HAVEN & ROWENNA RAILROAD

On March 31st, 1906, the York Haven & Rowenna Railroad, was acquired by the Pennsylvania Railroad Company. This road was a connecting link about 5½ miles long in the Low Grade Freight Line, then nearing completion, from York Haven on the Northern Central Railway on the west side of the Susquehanna River to Glen Lock on the Main Line. As this small stretch of road did not lie in one of the counties through which the Pennsylvania Railroad passed, and, therefore, could not be built under its branching powers, a separate Charter had to be taken out for its construction until it could be absorbed in the manner indicated.

LOW GRADE FREIGHT LINE COMPLETED

On August 10th, 1906, the Atglen & Susquehanna Branch of the new Low Grade Freight Line, extending from Shock's Mills Station to its junction with the Philadelphia Division near Parkesburg Station, a distance of about 45 miles, was completed and placed in service. With the completion of this branch the entire Low Grade Line was opened for traffic between York Haven and Glen Lock. Through its construction a double track relief line 139½ miles in length was placed in operation from Marysville on the west side of the Susquehanna River above Harrisburg to Morrisville on the Delaware River opposite Trenton, with the exception of nine miles between Parkesburg and Thorndale, which formed part of the existing Main Line.

ELECTRIFICATION WORK

The electrification of one of the routes of the West Jersey & Seashore Railroad from Camden via Newfield to Atlantic City, and of its road between Newfield and Millville, was completed and placed in service on September 18th, 1906. Independent terminals and approaches were constructed in Camden and Atlantic City to accommodate this electric service.

NEW YORK TUNNEL EXTENSION

The construction of the New York Tunnel Extension continued in 1906. While the work under the East River was somewhat slower in point of completion, that under the Hudson River was pushed forward so successfully that on September 12th, 1906, one of the iron tubes was completed through from Weehawken to New York City, and on October 9th, 1906, the second tube was in place.

IMPROVEMENT PROGRAM OF 1902 PRACTICALLY COMPLETED

In 1906 the Management called attention to the fact that the improvements referred to in the Annual Report for 1902 as absolutely necessary to enable the traffic of the Company to be promptly and economically handled between Pittsburgh and New York had, with few exceptions, either been actually completed or were rapidly approaching completion. The completed work covered the construction of the Brilliant Branch; the elevated railroad along Duquesne Way, together with the new freight station at Pittsburgh and the terminal yards adjacent to that city; the construction of the double track freight line between Gallitzin and Petersburg and of an important part of the classification yards located thereon at Hollidaysburg; the building of the double track low grade freight line between York Haven and Glen Lock and of the Enola Yard in connection therewith; the construction of the double track elevated freight road through the West Philadelphia Yards between the Main Line and the Delaware Extension and the Philadelphia, Baltimore & Washington Railroad; and the reduction of grades on the Trenton Cut-off.

SALES OF CHESAPEAKE & OHIO, BALTIMORE & OHIO, AND NORFOLK & WESTERN STOCK

As the object sought in purchasing a portion of the securities of the Chesapeake & Ohio Railway Company, the Baltimore & Ohio Railroad Company and Norfolk & Western Railway Company, namely, the promotion of a more conservative policy in their Management and to avoid unjust discrimination between shippers, had been largely accomplished, and through the amendments to the Interstate Commerce Law, the maintenance of tariff rates had been practically secured, it was deemed advisable in 1906 to sell a part of the Company's holdings of these securities. This sale, which was made at a profit, included all of the Stock owned in the Chesapeake & Ohio Railway Company and a majority of the Company's ownership in the Baltimore &

Ohio Railroad and Norfolk & Western Railway Companies. It has since, however, re-purchased an additional interest in the shares of the latter Company.

ACQUIRING BRANCH LINE MINORITY STOCK INTERESTS

The policy of acquiring at the proper time the minority interests in the roads embraced in the Pennsylvania Railroad System had commended itself to the Management, by reason of the fact that the marked development in the traffic of the Main Lines of the Company necessarily increased the business and revenues of the branch and auxiliary roads, and thus created a market value based upon conditions to which they had not contributed. Further, it was in the direction of efficiency and economy of operation that traffic should reach its destination by the most available route, rather than be guided by the question of ownership as between competing lines. For these reasons the Management of the Company in 1906 authorized the purchase of the minority interests in the Philadelphia & Erie and Cumberland Valley Railroads, it having for many years owned a majority of the Capital Stocks of these two Companies, and in the case of the Philadelphia & Erie Railroad was its Lessee and the guarantor upon the greater part of its funded debt. As a result a very large majority of the Stocks of the Philadelphia & Erie Railroad and Cumberland Valley Railroad Companies was acquired on the basis, in the case of the first named Company, of an exchange of Pennsylvania Railroad Company Stock share for share, while three shares of the latter Company's Stock were given for one of the Cumberland Valley Railroad Company.

DEATH OF PRESIDENT CASSATT

On December 28th, 1906, President Cassatt died suddenly at his home. The value of his work not alone to the Pennsylvania Railroad Company, but to the general railway interests of the Country, is well summed up in the following extract from the Minute on his death adopted by the Board of Directors of the Pennsylvania Railroad Company:—

"The events of the years which have elapsed since Mr. Cassatt assumed the responsible duties connected with its (The Pennsylvania Railroad Company) Presidency are too indelibly engraved on the minds of the members of the Board to require anything else than the briefest recital. There never has been a period in the history of American railways so pregnant with possibilities of evil, but, thanks to the genius of Mr. Cassatt and his almost prophetic insight into the future, so fruitful of good not only to the Pennsylvania Railroad but to all the great transportation interests of the country.

When Mr. Frank Thomson's untimely death occurred, the forces that had been steadily disrupting the fabric of railway prosperity had become so controlling that disaster was imminent. The recurrent waves of prosperity and adversity that marked almost every decade in our national life had strewn the path with the wrecks of railway enterprises, and the struggle for competitive traffic had forced down the actual rates paid by shippers to a point where none but the strongest and best equipped lines could earn a living profit. Agreements to maintain rates were not worth the paper upon which they were written, and the rebates extorted by large shippers under a threat to divert their traffic had built up industries whose development often worked injustice to smaller combinations of capital.

It was at this point that Mr. Cassatt announced the policy of the Pennsylvania Railroad to be the abolition of the rebate system and the extension of equal rates and facilities to all shippers.

This meant the observance and enforcement of law, the maintenance of tariff rates, a just recognition of the claims of competitors, and a conscientious and determined effort to secure the adoption of this policy by the other trunk lines.

The records of the Company show what he did. With the cordial support of the Board and the shareholders, he invested nearly ninety millions of dollars in the purchase of securities of the Baltimore & Ohio, Norfolk & Western, and Chesapeake & Ohio Railways, and utilized the influence obtained through these holdings, not for the selfish advantage of the Pennsylvania Railroad, but for the bettering and building up of those lines, with the conviction that in advancing their prosperity, he was advancing the prosperity of the Pennsylvania Railroad and making it strong beyond peradventure. It is certain that nowhere else in railway history can there be found another example of the pursuance of such a broad policy by a powerful company toward its weaker rivals.

Not only did Mr. Cassatt thus aid, far beyond the power of any legal enactment, to destroy the evils that had so long existed, but he was one of the first to recognize that the trend of public opinion, and consequently of legislation, was toward the more complete regulation of interstate traffic by the national government. Instead, therefore, of blindly combating such legislation, he endeavored to so shape it (and it was largely through his unwearying efforts and influence that it was so shaped) as to secure for the railway property of the country, under the recent enactments, the protection of the judicial tribunals, a right never before denied to the humblest citizen, but one which was almost wrested from the industry which has been the most potential in building up our national prosperity. Mr. Cassatt's part in these two great works has certainly not been overstated. Their influence for good stretches over a continent.

While thus broadening and strengthening the foundations of the entire railway system, his work upon the Pennsylvania Railroad has been monumental. Notwithstanding the fact that the policy of the Company for a quarter of a century had been to provide in advance for its traffic, and to apply its surplus revenue toward making the crooked paths straight, Mr. Cassatt saw that the tremendous impulse which had been suddenly given to our national development would require an expenditure far beyond anything that had ever before been dreamed of, and that nothing but heroic measures would put the road in condition to handle the enormous business that would be thrust upon it.

It is not necessary to recall here the increases of Capital Stock, the issues of convertible bonds, the bold financiering, that to the outsider seemed to border on rashness, but which events have proved were absolutely necessary, and without which the road would be today unable to do justice either to its shippers or its shareholders. Immense terminal yards, relief lines almost gigantic in conception and execution, enormous increases in motive power and equipment, have marked the expenditures during Mr. Cassatt's administration. And now, when a new line from the summit of the Alleghenies has almost reached tidewater, when the waters of the Hudson have been tunnelled, when in the near future a great passenger station in New York City will be the sign that the South and the Southwest and Middle West have been united by continuous bands of steel to our great commercial metropolis, when farther south another magnificent station faces, not unworthily, the National Capital, when the work of the last seven years has almost reached fruition, the end has come! and with the close of the year, all that was mortal of Mr. Cassatt has been laid to rest in the quiet churchyard near his country home."

In summarizing the progress made by the Pennsylvania Railroad System during the Administration of President Cassatt, the following paragraphs are extracted from a biographical sketch of his life:—

"To provide necessary terminals at the New York end of the lines, the New York Bay Railroad was extended to Greenville, and an enormous yard laid out at that point; at the western terminus of the road the Union Station at Pittsburgh was rebuilt; a Terminal Station at Camden, N. J., was erected for the Pennsylvania Railroad Company, West Jersey & Seashore Railroad Company, and Philadelphia & Camden Ferry Company; the Rockville Bridge across the Susquehanna River was rebuilt as a four track stone arch bridge 3820 feet in length; a new four track stone arch bridge thrown across the Delaware River near Trenton, the railroad location in that city revised and the grade crossings in Newark and New Brunswick, N. J., in Chester, Pa., and Wilmington, Del., eliminated by elevating the tracks through those cities. To strengthen the position of the Pennsylvania Railroad Company in New York and its vicinity, he acquired a controlling interest in the Long Island Railroad, established terminal facilities on the East River and other New York waters, and built freight stations in various parts of Brooklyn, thus securing a firm hold on the traffic of Greater New York. He also extended the Pennsylvania Railroad Lines into the City of Buffalo through the purchase of the stock of the Western New York & Pennsylvania Railway Company, and to complete the work of binding the lake traffic to the Pennsylvania System, acquired the stock of the Erie & Western Transportation Company. In 1900 he inaugurated the 'community of interest' principle among the several railway lines, and strengthened that principle by the purchase of large blocks of stock in railways leading to the Atlantic Seaboard.

In the year 1901 the principal improvements initiated were the change of line and the building of the new station in West Philadelphia; the construction of the Monongahela Railroad; the Brilliant Cut-Off and other improvements at Pittsburgh, including the Duquesne Way Elevated Railroad; the double-tracking and reduction of grades on the Western Pennsylvania Railroad; the construction of the New Portage Railroad and the double-tracking of the Petersburg Branch, thereby forming a complete alternate double-track road from the summit of the Allegheny Mountains to Petersburg on the Middle Division, and the construction of the freight yards at Hollidaysburg and Enola, Pa. The Richmond-Washington Line was also established as a joint route between these cities for the use of the competitive systems, reaching them from the north and south, in which enterprise the Pennsylvania Railroad acquired a one-sixth interest, and the vast project of a tunnel line to connect New Jersey with New York and Long Island first took definite shape.

The years 1902, 1903, 1904 and 1905 witnessed a steady and vigorous prosecution of this policy in the establishment of a permanent water supply system; the four-tracking of the Main Line; the reduction of grades, the improvement of alignment, and the enlargement of terminals; the building of the Waverly Yards; of the new shops at Trenton, N. J.; of the Mantua tunnel and cut-off for through passenger trains; of the Cherry Tree & Dixonville Railroad; the elevation of the tracks through Camden, N. J.; the electrification and double-tracking of the West Jersey & Seashore Railroad from Camden to Atlantic City; the construction of the remarkable Low Grade Freight Line from the Susquehanna River to Glen Lock on the Philadelphia Division; and the reduction of grades on the Trenton Cut-Off from Glen Lock to Morrisville, opposite Trenton, N. J. In this connection, and as a natural sequence, followed the project to extend the Low Grade Freight Line from Glen Lock to the City of Philadelphia, and construct a further Low Grade Freight Line from Morrisville to Waverly, so that the Pennsylvania Railroad Company would ultimately have the benefit of a through double track freight line independent of the four main tracks, and thus become a six-track system from Pittsburgh to tidewater at New York and Philadelphia.

The year 1906 was noted for the electrification of a portion of the Long Island Railroad; the heavy construction work on the Philadelphia, Baltimore & Washington Railroad, and the building of the new Terminal Station in the City of Washington. During that year the Company, following the policy of acquiring branch or affiliated lines, purchased the minority holdings in the Philadelphia & Erie Railroad and Cumberland Valley Railroad Companies, and made the former railroad, which it had operated under lease for many years, an integral part of the Pennsylvania Railroad."

STATISTICAL DATA

The following operating, traffic and financial statistics will at once indicate the tremendous expansion of the Company's business during President Cassatt's Administration:

REVENUE, EXPENSES, OPERATING INCOME, AND RENTALS, 1899 TO 1906, INCLUSIVE

All Lines East of Pittsburgh and Erie Directly Operated

Year	Miles	Gross Revenue	Operating Expenses	Operating Income	Rentals Paid	Net Operating Income to Penna. R. R. Co.
1899......	2,847.44	$72,922,984.95	$50,344,633.64	$22,578,351.31	$11,320,448.82	$11,257,902.49
1900......	3,715.94	88,539,827.21	58,099,206.02	30,440,621.19	12,224,520.34	18,216,100.85
1901......	3,739.24	101,329,795.22	65,259,543.08	36,070,252.14	14,643,144.34	21,427,107.80
1902......	3,705.70	112,663,330.13	75,051,071.17	37,612,258.96	11,605,948.17	26,006,310.79
1903......	3,723.61	122,626,419.49	84,773,056.09	37,853,363.40	12,097,232.61	25,756,130.79
1904......	3,888.55	118,145,270.06	81,802,988.18	36,342,281.88	11,202,964.15	25,139,317.73
1905......	3,907.08	133,921,992.28	93,390,410.28	40,531.582.00	12,346,754.42	28,184,827.58
1906......	3,964.68	148,239,882.44	101,805,644.25	46,434,238.19	12,552,212.75	33,882,025.44

TONNAGE, MILEAGE, REVENUE, EXPENSES, AND AVERAGES ON FREIGHT BUSINESS, 1899 TO 1906, INCLUSIVE

All Rail Lines East of Pittsburgh and Erie Directly Operated

Year	Tons	Tons One Mile	Revenue	Average Revenue per Ton per Mile	Expenses	Average Expenses per Ton per Mile	Average Net Revenue per Ton per Mile
				Cents		Cents	Cents
1899......	100,054,226	10,875,076,597	$51,395,733.16	0.473	$37,376,428.13	0.344	0.129
1900......	108,847,515	11,922,671,210	64,390,452.51	0.540	43,395,536.62	0.364	0.176
1901......	121,699,340	12,696,352,464	73,899,939.16	0.582	48,391,006.19	0.381	0.201
1902......	133,433,845	14,024,198,051	82,249,169.41	0.586	56,648,712.67	0.404	0.182
1903......	145,558,716	14,846,639,121	89,895,722.67	0.605	63,703,929.02	0.429	0.176
1904......	132,975,037	14,223,451,129	86,014,076.11	0.605	60,250,569.13	0.424	0.181
1905......	107,438,861	16,885,485,241	100,093,828.25	0.593	70,500,600.79	0.418	0.175
1906......	118,438,169	18,478,371,275	109,960,888.10	0.595	76,631,301.86	0.415	0.180

PASSENGERS, MILEAGE, REVENUE, EXPENSES, AND AVERAGES ON PASSENGER BUSINESS, 1899 TO 1906, INCLUSIVE

All Rail Lines East of Pittsburgh and Erie Directly Operated

Year	Passengers	Passengers One Mile	Revenue	Average Revenue per Passenger per Mile	Expenses	Average Expenses per Passenger per Mile	Average Net Revenue per Passenger per Mile
				Cents		Cents	Cents
1899......	38,029,922	823,304,623	$16,010,831.80	1.945	$11,753,978.58	1.428	0.517
1900......	41,922,569	918,198,602	18,181,081.77	1.980	13,453,457.86	1.465	0.515
1901......	46,698,595	1,050,463,693	20,928,395.37	1.992	15,563,611.29	1.482	0.510
1902......	50,287,009	1,165,609,033	23,421,170.86	2.009	16,984,215.63	1.457	0.552
1903......	53,657,638	1,249,805,273	25,345,210.57	2.028	19,596,798.26	1.568	0.460
1904......	51,763,370	1,218,521,705	24,375,018.20	2.000	20,194,259.14	1.657	0.343
1905......	54,701,509	1,305,299,112	26,282,196.28	2.014	21,296,151.76	1.632	0.382
1906......	60,832,313	1,493,393,002	30,074,868.06	2.014	23,695,246.82	1.587	0.427

DIVIDENDS AND ALLOTMENTS ON CAPITAL STOCK—THE PENNSYLVANIA RAILROAD COMPANY

DATE	Capital Stock on which Dividend or Allotment was Declared	DIVIDEND				ALLOTMENTS OF STOCK ON SUBSCRIPTION	
		CASH		SCRIP OR STOCK			
		Per Cent.	Amount	Per Cent.	Amount	Per Cent.	Amount
November, 1899.	$129,305,450	2½	$3,232,636 25				
January, 1900.	129,305,500	......	......	......	......	10	(At par) $12,906,200 00
May, "	139,186,100	2½	3,479,652 50				
November, "	151,471,950	2½ & 1	5,301,518 25				
May, 1901.	151,502,400	2½	3,787,560				
June, "	151,502,400	......	......	......	......	33⅓	(At $60 per share) 60,804,665 00
November, "	202,003,200	2½ & 1	7,070,112				
May, 1902.	204,374,850	3	6,131,245 50				
November, "	204,374,850	3	6,131,245 50				
March, 1903,	225,284,250	......	......	......	......	33⅓	(At $60 per share) 90,113,700 00
May, "	204,380,950	3	6,131,428 50				
November, "	288,716,750	3	8,661,502 50				
May, 1904.	296,483,550	3	8,894,506 50				
November, "	301,284,250	3	9,038,527 50				
May, 1905.	301,285,950	3	9,038,578 50				
November, "	302,513,300	3	9,075,399				
May, 1906.	305,555,650	3	9,166,669 50				
November, "	305,799,750	3½	10,702,991 25				

NUMBER OF STOCKHOLDERS

December 31st

Year	Stockholders
1902	28,408
1903	42,437
1904	42,230
1905	40,385
1906	40,153

DIRECTORS

The following is a list of the Directors who served during President Cassatt's Administration, together with the dates of their election and the end of their service:—

Name of Director	*Elected*	*End of Service*
Alexander M. Fox	March 6, 1871,	October 6, 1907;
N. Parker Shortridge	March 24, 1874,	January 3, 1915;
William L. Elkins	March 25, 1879,	November 7, 1903;
John P. Green	October 1, 1882,	March 24, 1909;
A. J. Cassatt	July 1, 1874,	October 1, 1882;
"	September 12, 1883,	December 28, 1906;
Clement A. Griscom	September 24, 1884,	November 10, 1912;
Benjamin B. Comegys	November 9, 1887,	March 29, 1900;
Amos R. Little	November 28, 1888,	December 16, 1906;
William H. Barnes	December 11, 1889,	May 5, 1918;
George Wood	March 24, 1891,	February 17, 1926;
Charles E. Pugh	March 1, 1893,	February 28, 1911;
C. Stuart Patterson	July 2, 1895,	November 8, 1924;
Effingham B. Morris	December 31, 1896,	....
Sutherland M. Prevost	February 10, 1897,	September 30, 1905;
Thomas De Witt Cuyler	May 10, 1899,	November 2, 1922;
James McCrea	June 9, 1899,	March 28, 1913;
Samuel Rea	June 14, 1899,	....
Lincoln Godfrey	April 11, 1900,	January 12, 1916;
Rudulph Ellis	November 11, 1903,	September 21, 1915;
John B. Thayer	October 10, 1905,	April 14, 1912;
Henry C. Frick	December 26, 1906,	December 2, 1919.

JAMES McCREA

Eighth President—January 2nd, 1907, to January 1st, 1913.

JAMES McCREA

EIGHTH PRESIDENT, 1907–1912

JAMES McCREA, First Vice-President of the Pennsylvania Lines West of Pittsburgh and Erie, and a Director of the Pennsylvania Railroad Company, was elected President of the Company, succeeding Mr. Cassatt, on January 2nd, 1907. President McCrea was born in Philadelphia on May 1st, 1848, and received his civil engineering education in the Pennsylvania Polytechnic College. His railway service began in June, 1865, as rodman and then Assistant Engineer of the Connellsville and Southern Pennsylvania Railroad, in which position he served until December, 1867, when he became rodman on the construction of the Wilmington & Reading Railroad. In September, 1868, he was engaged as Assistant Engineer on the Allegheny Valley Railroad, where he remained until March, 1871. On March 1st, 1871, Mr. McCrea entered the service of the Pennsylvania Railroad as Principal Assistant Engineer in the Construction Department, and on August 1st, 1874, was transferred to the position of Assistant Engineer of Maintenance of Way of the Philadelphia Division, becoming Superintendent of the Middle Division on January 1st, 1875, in which position he remained until October 15th, 1878, at which time he was appointed Superintendent of the New York Division. His long connection with the Lines West of Pittsburgh began on May 1st, 1882, when he was appointed Manager of the Southwest System; on October 10th, 1885, he was promoted to the position of General Manager of all the Pennsylvania Lines West of Pittsburgh; then to Fourth Vice-President, October 19th, 1887; Second Vice-President, March 1st, 1890; and First Vice-President of such Lines on April 23rd, 1891. On January 2nd, 1907, as already stated, be became President of the parent Company.

NEW YORK TUNNEL EXTENSION—SUNNYSIDE YARD

Work was continued on the New York Tunnel Extension and Station during the year 1907, although it was necessarily delayed by the engineering, legal and municipal questions inseparable from so large an undertaking. It was not possible to actively proceed with the construction of Sunnyside Yard, which was an important part of the Tunnel Extension, until June, 1907, when an agreement was reached with the City of New York covering the relocation of certain streets and the construction of highways across this Yard so as to eliminate crossings at grade. The Yard was to be about 5,500 feet long and 1,550 feet across at the widest point, covering an area of 173 acres. It was to contain 53 miles of tracks with a capacity of nearly 1,400 cars. The Long Island Railroad and the New York Connecting Railroad eventually were to be directly connected with the New York Tunnel Extension in the vicinity of this Yard, and through these lines the New York, New Haven & Hartford Railroad and its New England connections would be provided with a direct all-rail route to and from the South and West over the Pennsylvania Railroad System.

On June 26th, 1907, the Companies engaged in the construction of the New York Tunnel Extension, namely, the Pennsylvania, New York & Long Island Railroad Company, a corporation of the State of New York, and the Pennsylvania, New Jersey & New York Railroad Company, a corporation of the State of New Jersey, were consolidated and merged into the Pennsylvania Tunnel & Terminal Railroad Company.

COMPLETION OF UNION STATION, WASHINGTON, D. C.

On November 17th, 1907, the Union Station at Washington, D. C., was opened for operation. The size of the Station was ample for the present and prospective needs of the railroads entering that City, while its architectural appearance was of a character commensurate with its importance and location in the National Capital. The Station and its approaches were constructed by the Washington

Terminal Company, one-half of the Capital Stock of which is owned by the Philadelphia, Baltimore & Washington Railroad Company and the other half by the Baltimore & Ohio Railroad Company. These two Companies jointly and severally guarantee by endorsement $12,000,000. First Mortgage Bonds issued by the Terminal Company to pay in part for the cost of the Station. It contains two levels, there being 20 tracks on the upper level for passengers destined to and from Washington, and 12 on the lower level for through north and southbound traffic. The Station is also used by the Atlantic Coast Line Railroad, Chesapeake & Ohio Railway, Richmond, Fredericksburg & Potomac Railroad, Seaboard Air Line Railway and the Southern Railway, it being the only Station in Washington for steam railroad passenger traffic.

ACQUISITION OF PHILADELPHIA & ERIE RAILROAD

On May 1st, 1907, the franchises, corporate property, rights and credits of the Philadelphia & Erie Railroad Company, the main line of which extended from Sunbury, Pa., to Erie, Pa., a distance of about 287 miles, were acquired by the Pennsylvania Railroad Company.

CHARTIERS RAILWAY ACQUIRED

Under agreement dated November 20th, 1907, the Pittsburgh, Cincinnati, Chicago & St. Louis Railway Company acquired the franchises and corporate property of the Chartiers Railway Company, the road of which extended from Carnegie to Washington, Pa., a distance of about 23 miles.

TWO CENT RATE LAW UNCONSTITUTIONAL

Reference was made by the Management of the Company in the Annual Report for 1907 to the Bill which was passed by the Pennsylvania State Assembly, under which the railroads of the State were forbidden to charge more than 2¢ per mile for passenger transportation within the State. In order to earn the average rate theretofore received, which was only about 2¢ a mile, it would have been necessary to advance the special rates on commutation and excursion business, notwithstanding they had long been in force and had furnished the basis upon which communities had been built up, values fixed and methods of living established, which promoted the health and comfort of the public. If this were not done the rate fixed by this law would have reduced the earnings of the Company below a fair and proper return upon the capital invested. Legal proceedings were, therefore, instituted and after an exhaustive examination of the data and facts submitted to the Court of Common Pleas of the County of Philadelphia to restrain the enforcement of the law, it was decided to be unconstitutional by reason of the fact that under its provisions injustice would be done to the owners of the railways, and this decision was affirmed, on appeal, by the Supreme Court of the State of Pennsylvania.

ACQUISITION OF BALD EAGLE VALLEY AND JUNCTION RAILROADS

Effective March 31st, 1908, the Pennsylvania Railroad Company acquired the franchises, corporate property, rights and credits of the Bald Eagle Valley Railroad Company, which extended from a point on the Main Line of the Pennsylvania Railroad near Tyrone to Lock Haven, a distance of about 54 miles.

Effective March 31st, 1908, the Pennsylvania Railroad Company absorbed the Junction Railroad, three miles in length. It furnished a connection in Philadelphia between the Philadelphia, Baltimore & Washington Railroad, the Main Line and the Philadelphia & Reading Railway.

BRANCH ROAD CONSTRUCTION IN WESTERN PENNSYLVANIA

On January 9th, 1908, the Pennsylvania, Monongahela & Southern Railroad was completed and opened for traffic from Denbo to Rice's Landing, Pa., a distance of about seven miles.

On June 1st, 1908, an extension of the Ellsworth Branch from Ellsworth to Marianna, a distance of about eight miles, was completed and opened for traffic. This branch extended from Monongahela City to Marianna, a distance of nearly 20 miles.

On August 15th, 1908, the Hillman Branch, extending from a point on the Cambria & Clearfield Railway near Hillman Station, to the Clover Run Mine, a distance of about six miles, was completed and placed in service.

SALE OF CONSOLIDATED MORTGAGE BONDS

In 1908 the Company issued and sold $39,400,000. Consolidated Mortgage 4% Bonds, dated May 1st, 1908, and maturing May 1st, 1948, which was a noteworthy transaction in view of the conditions then existing in the investment markets. The financial disturbances of 1907 had been followed by an industrial and business depression, which continued throughout the entire year 1908, and as a result it had been necessary for the railroads to finance largely with short term obligations at high rates of interest. The Management, however, after consultation with its Bankers, decided it was not to the advantage of the Company to meet its capital requirements by temporary financing. Therefore, arrangements were made with Kuhn, Loeb & Co. by which that banking firm and N. M. Rothschild & Sons and Baring Brothers & Co., Ltd., of England, purchased the entire issue of $39,400,000. Consolidated Mortgage 4% Bonds running for a 40-year period. As a result £4,000,000 (equivalent to $19,400,000.) of these Bonds were sold in England and $20,000,000. to American investors, the principal and interest of the former being payable in Sterling and the latter in Dollars.

The satisfactory price received for these Bonds, under such adverse conditions, was an indication of the high credit enjoyed by the Company both in this Country and abroad, and its beneficial effect on the general situation of the railroads was reflected in a restoration of more normal market conditions for their securities.

PURCHASE OF STOCK OF NEW YORK, PHILADELPHIA & NORFOLK RAILROAD COMPANY

Under date of June 24th, 1908, an agreement was made for the acquisition by the Pennsylvania Railroad Company of the Capital Stock of the New York, Philadelphia & Norfolk Railroad, the main line of which extended from Delmar to Cape Charles, Va., a distance of 95 miles, and with the Crisfield Branch, 17 miles in length, it had a total mileage of 112 miles. The Company also owned and operated a ferry service 36 miles in length between Cape Charles and Norfolk, Va. Practically all of the Stock was acquired through the issuance of $7,478,250., 4% Stock Trust Certificates, dated June 30th, 1908, and maturing June 1st, 1948, the principal and interest of which were guaranteed by the Pennsylvania Railroad Company. They were secured through the deposit with the Trustee of the Stock so acquired. The basis for its acquisition was the exchange of every $100. par value thereof for $300., par value, of these Stock Trust Certificates.

This road formed the connecting link between the Philadelphia, Baltimore & Washington Railroad and the railways reaching Norfolk from the South and West, and having, through the growth of Norfolk as a business centre and as a gateway between the Northern and Southern Atlantic States, developed a large interchange traffic with the Pennsylvania Railroad System, it was deemed advisable to acquire the ownership of its Capital Stock.

FIRST SECTION OF HUDSON & MANHATTAN RAILROAD COMPLETED

On July 16th, 1909, the downtown rapid transit tunnels of the Hudson & Manhattan Railroad Company were opened for traffic, and under agreement dated April 18th, 1906, passengers to and from the Pennsylvania Railroad had the option of using these rapid transit tunnels between the Jersey City Passenger Station of the Pennsylvania Railroad Company and the terminal of the Hudson & Manhattan Railroad Company at Church and Cortlandt Streets, New York City. This tunnel system was to be extended westward under the Jersey City Station to a point east of Summit Avenue in that City, where connection was to be made with the Pennsylvania Railroad. From this point the latter road was to be electrified to a new station east of Harrison, N. J. (Manhattan Transfer), and a branch constructed from the latter point into Park Place, Newark, N. J. A joint rapid transit electric service was then to be operated between the Hudson Company's Church Street Terminal, New York City, and Park Place, Newark, while the new station east of Harrison would provide the facilities for passengers desiring to transfer between the rapid transit line and all trains on the Pennsylvania Railroad System.

PAYMENT OF QUARTERLY DIVIDENDS

In view of the large number of investors holding the Stock of the Pennsylvania Railroad Company, the Management deemed it wise to pay its dividends quarterly instead of semi-annually, and this method of payment was begun with the dividend payable in February, 1910. The Company had previously paid quarterly dividends in the period August, 1875, to May, 1877, but after recovering from the effects of the Pittsburgh Riots in the latter year, it began semi-annual payments in May, 1879, which continued until the change made in 1910.

LEASE OF DELAWARE RAILROAD

On March 1st, 1910, the Philadelphia, Baltimore & Washington Railroad Company made a new lease of the railroad and other property of the Delaware Railroad Company for a term of 99 years at a rental equivalent to its fixed charges and 8% on the outstanding Capital Stock. The main line of this road extended from Wilmington to Delmar, Del., a distance of about 95 miles, and with its various branches, the road had a total length of 245 miles.

ACQUISITION OF ALLEGHENY VALLEY RAILWAY

Effective April 7th, 1910, the Allegheny Valley Railway Company was merged into and became a part of the lines directly owned by the Pennsylvania Railroad Company, in accordance with the agreement dated February 15th, 1906, for the acquisition of the franchises, corporate property, rights and credits of that Company. The Pennsylvania Railroad Company agreed to pay $1.00 per share for the Common Stock of the acquired Company and $40.00 per share for its Preferred Stock, or at the option of the holder of the latter, two shares of this Preferred Stock were exchangeable for 1⅛ shares of Pennsylvania Railroad Company Stock. The Allegheny Valley Railway formed the connection, through its river and low grade divisions, between the Main Line at Pittsburgh and the former Philadelphia & Erie Railroad at Driftwood, and also furnished through its line to Oil City and the Western New York & Pennsylvania Railway, which was also controlled by the Pennsylvania Railroad Company, a direct route to Buffalo, Rochester and other important traffic centres. Its terminals at Pittsburgh were of great value and its location along the Allegheny River made tributary to it a territory already largely devoted to steel and other manufacturing industries, and capable of increased development in the future.

BEDFORD & HOLLIDAYSBURG RAILROAD EXTENSION

On May 29th, 1910, the extension of the Bedford & Hollidaysburg Railroad from Imler to Brookes Mills, a distance of about 11 miles, was completed and opened for traffic. The new line formed the connecting link between the Main Line and the Bedford & Bridgeport Railway, and was an improvement long desired by the communities served by these two branch roads.

LEASE OF LYKENS VALLEY RAILROAD & COAL COMPANY

Effective July 1st, 1910, the Northern Central Railway Company leased the railroad and other property of the Lykens Valley Railroad & Coal Company for a term of 99 years at a rental equivalent to 4% on the outstanding Capital Stock of that Company, and the short term agreement under which the Northern Central Railway Company had previously operated that line was cancelled. The leased road extended from Millersburg to Williamstown, Pa., a distance of about 19 miles.

NEW YORK TUNNEL EXTENSION COMPLETED—UNVEILING OF STATUE OF PRESIDENT CASSATT

It was deemed appropriate that the completion of the important extension of the Pennsylvania Railroad System into the heart of New York City should be commemorated by a fitting tribute to the former President, in whose Administration the work was undertaken. A statue of Mr. Cassatt was, therefore, erected in the main waiting room of Pennsylvania Station in that City, which bears the inscription:—

> "Alexander Johnston Cassatt, President, Pennsylvania Railroad Company 1899–1906, whose foresight, courage and ability achieved the extension of the Pennsylvania Railroad System into New York City."

This statue was unveiled on August 1st, 1910. Vice-President Rea opened the ceremony with the following remarks:—

> "We are here today to honor the memory of the late President of the Pennsylvania Railroad Company, Mr. A. J. Cassatt, and to unveil a statue as a tribute to his genius. Mr. Cuyler, Chairman of the Memorial Committee, will now present the statue to the Company, and Mr. McCrea, President, will, on its behalf, accept the same."

The remarks of Mr. Thomas DeWitt Cuyler, Chairman of the Memorial Committee, follow:—

> "We are gathered here today to take part in an event which marks one of the most important epochs in the history of the Pennsylvania Railroad. With the unveiling of the statue before which we stand, it is proposed, sir, that you should officially declare the Station opened for the purpose for which it was built.
>
> The occasion calls for no ostentatious ceremony or elaborate words. These massive walls and columns speak in their severe simplicity and majestic silence far more eloquently than human tongue could give utterance to. And so too this splendid statue which we are now to look upon, in the greatness of the genius and the simplicity of the character of the man, finds a fitting resting place amid these surroundings.
>
> It has been at once the privilege and duty of the

Directors to have here placed this portrait of Mr. Cassatt and how well the artist has done his work all will admit.

We ask you as the head of this great corporation to take this statue into your keeping and to unveil it to the public eye so that all men may know as the inscription so aptly tells us 'whose foresight, courage and ability achieved the extension of the Pennsylvania Railroad system into New York City.' "

President McCrea's remarks were:—

"On behalf of the Board of Directors of The Pennsylvania Railroad Company, I accept this noble statue of Mr. Cassatt. It is fitting and proper that its unveiling should be coincident with official opening of the great terminal which The Pennsylvania Railroad Company has, prompted by his foresight and courage, builded for itself in this, America's greatest city.

As the years roll round the greater will be the tribute paid to the genius of Mr. Cassatt—and it is the source of the greatest pleasure to those of us who had the privilege of knowing him, to feel that there has been erected to his memory in so fitting a place a statue that will so truly express to those who follow, the manner of man he was.

As the fitting conclusion of these ceremonies, I now declare this Station officially opened."

The Board of Directors also authorized the erection of two panels on each side of the main entrance to the Station on Seventh Avenue. The panel on the north side bears the following historic record:—

" This tablet is erected by the Board of Directors of the Pennsylvania Railroad Company to commemorate the extension of its Railroad System into New York City by the completion and opening on the Eighth day of September, A. D. 1910, of the tunnels and Station, and to record the names of the Directors and Officers who shared the responsibility of authorizing and constructing the undertaking.

The tunnels and Station were planned and constructed under the executive direction and supervision of Alexander Johnston Cassatt, President, and Samuel Rea, Vice-President, of the Companies, incorporated in 1902 in the States of New York and New Jersey, and later merged constituting the Pennsylvania Tunnel and Terminal Railroad Company.

General Counsel, George V. Massey.

BOARD OF ENGINEERS AND CHIEF ENGINEERS

Chairman, General Charles W. Raymond.

Gustav Lindenthal, resigned December 15, 1903.

Chief Engineer, North River Division, Charles M. Jacobs.

Chief Engineer, East River Division, Alfred Noble.

Chief Engineer, Electric Traction and Station Construction, George Gibbs.

Chief Engineer, Meadows Division, William H. Brown, retired March 1, 1906, succeeded as Chief Engineer by Alexander C. Shand.

Architects, New York Station, McKim, Mead & White.

BOARD OF DIRECTORS OF THE PENNSYLVANIA RAILROAD COMPANY

Alexander Johnston Cassatt, President, died December 28, 1906.

Sutherland M. Prevost, Vice-President, died September 30, 1905.

William L. Elkins, died November 7, 1903.

Amos R. Little, died December 16, 1906.

Alexander M. Fox, died October 6, 1907.

John P. Green, Vice-President, retired March 24, 1909.

N. Parker Shortridge,
Clement A. Griscom,
William H. Barnes,
George Wood,
C. Stuart Patterson,
Effingham B. Morris,
Thomas DeWitt Cuyler,
Lincoln Godfrey,
Rudulph Ellis,
Henry C. Frick,
Charles E. Ingersoll,
Percival Roberts, Jr.

W. W. Atterbury, Fifth Vice-President.
Henry Tatnall, Fourth Vice-President.
John B. Thayer, Third Vice-President.
Samuel Rea, Second Vice-President.
Charles E. Pugh, First Vice-President.
James McCrea, President."

The panel on the south side contains the following historic inscription:—

"PENNSYLVANIA TUNNEL AND TERMINAL RAILROAD COMPANY

The franchise from the City of New York authorizing the construction, maintenance and operation of the Tunnel Extension and Station of The Pennsylvania Railroad System was granted October 9, 1902, by the Board of Rapid Transit Railroad Commissioners

Alexander E. Orr, Chairman.

John Claflin, Edward M. Grout,
Morris K. Jesup, Woodbury Langdon,
Charles Stewart Smith, John H. Starin,

Mayor, Seth Low.

The construction of the Tunnel Extension was begun June 10, 1903. The two tunnels under the North River and the four tunnels under the East River were built by shields driven from each side of the respective rivers, and union was completed by the junction of the last tube on the following dates:

North River Tunnels, October 9, 1906.
East River Tunnels, March 18, 1908.

These were the first tunnels for standard railroad trains constructed under these rivers.

The construction of the New York Station building was begun May 1, 1904, and trains were first operated from it on regular schedule September 8, 1910.

The principal contractors were:

North River Tunnels
O'Rourke Engineering Construction Company.

East River Tunnels
S. Pearson & Son, Inc.

Crosstown Tunnels—East River to New York Station
United Engineering and Contracting Company.

New York Station
Engineers, Steel Structure and Machinery: Westinghouse, Church, Kerr & Co.
Excavation: New York Contracting Company.
Erection: George A. Fuller Company.

Bergen Hill Tunnels
William Bradley.

Meadows Division
McMullen & McDermott.—H. S. Kerbaugh.
Henry Steers, Inc.
Sunnyside Yard and Approaches
Degnon Realty and Terminal Improvement Company.
Naughton Company and Arthur McMullen.
Erected by the Board of Directors of The Pennsylvania Railroad Company on the Eighth day of September, 1910."

TUNNEL EXTENSION AND STATION OPENED

On September 8th, 1910, the East River Division of the New York Tunnel Extension was completed from Pennsylvania Station, New York City, into Long Island, and was opened for the operation of trains of the Long Island Railroad under trackage rights granted by the Pennsylvania Railroad Company and the Pennsylvania Tunnel & Terminal Railroad Company.

The western portion of the Tunnel Extension from the Station in New York City, under the Hudson River to Harrison (Manhattan Transfer), N. J., was completed and opened for traffic on November 27th, 1910, from which date the entire electrified road from that point to a connection with the Long Island Railroad in Sunnyside Yard, a distance of about 13 miles, has been in operation.

CONSTRUCTING THE TUNNELS

The length of the railroad in tunnels is 5.1 miles, of which 1.5 miles are under the Hudson and East Rivers. There are two single track, cast-iron, reinforced, concrete-lined tunnels under the Hudson River and four under the East River. The construction of these river tunnels exemplifies the skill of modern engineering. They were driven by the shield method under compressed air through the mud, sand and rock 70 feet below the surface of the river. As the shields progressed the rings of the tubes, 23 feet in diameter, were fitted in place, the borings started from each side of the river, and the calculations were so accurate that in every case the tunnels met within a fraction of an inch.

THE STATION

The Station covers an area of 28 acres, in which there are 16 miles of tracks, and it contains 21 running tracks with 11 separate island platforms. It was anticipated when the Station was opened that it would serve the needs of the Pennsylvania Railroad System for many years to come, but the remarkable growth of traffic, particularly that of the Long Island Railroad, has already made it necessary to enlarge the space allocated to that road.

COST OF NEW YORK TUNNEL EXTENSION AND STATION

The Annual Report for 1910 stated that the cost of the New York Tunnel Extension and Station, including real estate not permanently required for its use, to December 31st, 1910, was $112,965,415. This expenditure was carried on the books of the Pennsylvania Railroad Company at a cost of $55,565,415., while of the difference, $47,400,000. had been charged against the Surplus Income and Profit & Loss Accounts of previous years, and $10,000,000. was borne by the Pennsylvania Company, because this important work was constructed for the benefit of the entire Pennsylvania Railroad System. As the Lines West of Pittsburgh would unquestionably reap a direct advantage therefrom, it was pointed out that it was only fair that they should participate in the cost thereof.

FERRY SERVICE DISCONTINUED

On November 30th, 1910, the ferries from Jersey City to 23rd Street, New York, and also to Brooklyn, were discontinued, because with the inauguration of direct rail service into New York City and Brooklyn via the Tunnel Extension, it was no longer necessary to furnish this ferry service.

STUDIES FOR PHILADELPHIA PASSENGER TERMINAL IMPROVEMENTS

While the approaches to Broad Street Station, Philadelphia, had previously been enlarged and improved, it became evident to the Management in 1910, in view of the constant increase in the number of passenger trains, which, based on track capacity, was not exceeded in any other large terminal in this Country, that further extensions and improvements to properly accommodate the passenger traffic in and out of Philadelphia would have to be undertaken on a large scale. The proposed Parkway planned by the City of Philadelphia made it difficult to enlarge the Station on its present location, as had previously been contemplated, and this led the Management to appoint a Board of Engineers to devote their time to assembling and studying the several plans and suggestions for the improvement of the passenger terminal facilities, and obtaining all information bearing on the subject, and submit their conclusions to an Advisory Board, consisting of the Executive, Engineering and Operating Officers of the Company. The final recommendation of the Advisory Board, and plans and estimates for carrying the same into effect, were to be submitted to the President and Board of Directors of the Company for consideration and to authorize such improvements as the situation required.

LEASE OF NORTHERN CENTRAL RAILWAY

In the Annual Report for 1910 reference was made to the fact that many minority stockholders of the Northern Central Railway Company, representing substantial holdings, requested the Pennsylvania Railroad Company to consider whether a more permanent operating arrangement or lease of its property to that Company could be made on a basis equitable to all interests, and a special committee of the Board of the Northern Central Railway Company, and also a Minority Stockholders' Committee, were appointed to consider the subject. After a careful analysis and study of the whole situation, these Committees united in a recommendation that the lease of the railroad, franchises, equipment and all other property of the Northern Central Railway Company be made to the Pennsylvania Railroad Company for 999 years from January 1st, 1911, upon the following general basis: (*a*) Dividends of 8%, payable on the outstanding Capital Stock of the Company after it had been increased by a 40% Stock dividend; (*b*) the payment of a 10% cash dividend on the Stock outstanding before the 40% increase; (*c*) a further sum sufficient to preserve and maintain that Company's corporate existence and organization; (*d*) the Lessee to also pay all fixed charges and taxes. The 40% Stock dividend represented a part of the capital expenditures previously made, but paid for out of income and surplus.

COURT PROCEEDINGS BLOCK LEASE

The proposed lease stating in detail the full terms and conditions was submitted to the stockholders of the Northern Central Railway Company, and approved by the vote and consent of shareholders representing over 93% of the whole stock, which included over 85% of shares owned by others than the Pennsylvania Railroad Company. The lease, and consequent increase of Capital Stock were submitted to the Public Service Commission of Maryland for its approval as required by law. Upon such approval, the lease could become effective, but by reason of two suits instituted by dissatisfied minority stockholders, one in the United States Circuit Court of the District of Maryland and the other in the same court for the Eastern District of Pennsylvania, the Pennsylvania Railroad Company Management deemed it prudent to declare that it should not be required to execute and effectuate the said lease, if approved by the Public Service Commission of Maryland. Further, it would not take possession of the railway and property of the Northern Central Railway Company, until each of the two suits against the latter Company and the Pennsylvania Railroad Company were decided, or until the latter Company was advised by Counsel that it was proper to consummate the same prior to such decision.

ADVANTAGES OF LEASE

The Northern Central Railway Company had been affiliated with the Pennsylvania Railroad Company for almost 50 years. In that time it had received the full benefit of the latter Company's experience in railroad operation and management, and although several previous attempts to lease that property to the Pennsylvania Railroad Company were unsuccessful, because of the lack of unanimity among the Northern Central Railway Company stockholders, it was believed that the time had come when it was desirable and proper for it to be leased. Both Companies, by reason of this long affiliation, their mutual trackage agreements, and terminal grants, had become so essential in their operations to each other, and the Northern Central Railway Company being dependent upon the traffic interchanged with the Pennsylvania Railroad for about 85% of its gross revenues, it was evident that a lease would be a natural result. It was felt that the closer operating relationship which would be thereby effected could not fail to be beneficial to the two Companies, and to the territory served by the Northern Central Railway.

RIDGWAY & CLEARFIELD RAILROAD ACQUIRED

Effective March 31st, 1911, the Ridgway & Clearfield Railroad Company was absorbed by the Pennsylvania Railroad Company. This road extended from Ridgway, on the Erie Division, to Falls Creek, on the Allegheny Valley Low Grade Division, a distance of about 27 miles, and had been owned and operated by the Pennsylvania Railroad as one of its subsidiaries for over 25 years.

HOLLIDAYSBURG, BEDFORD & CUMBERLAND RAILROAD FORMED

Effective May 1st, 1911, the Bedford & Hollidaysburg Railroad Company and the Bedford & Bridgeport Railway Company were consolidated under the corporate name of the Hollidaysburg, Bedford & Cumberland Railroad Company. The consolidated Company extended from Brookes Mills to a junction with the Cumberland & Pennsylvania Railroad at the Pennsylvania-Maryland State Line, a distance of about 62 miles, which with the Holderbaum and Mt. Dallas branches, gave it a total length of nearly 72 miles. On May 20th, 1914, the new Company was acquired by the Pennsylvania Railroad Company.

WESTERN CONSOLIDATIONS

Under agreements effective July 1st, 1911, two important consolidations were effected on the Pennsylvania Lines West of Pittsburgh. The first was the merger of the Toledo, Walhonding Valley & Ohio Railroad Company and the Cleveland & Marietta Railway Company into the Toledo, Columbus & Ohio River Railroad Company, which the Pennsylvania Company was to continue to operate. The consolidated company had a total mileage of 341 miles, consisting principally of the line from Mansfield to Toledo, O., 80 miles; the Sandusky Branch, extending from Sandusky to Columbus, O., 108 miles; the road from Canal Dover to Marietta, O., 103 miles, and the line from Coshocton to Loudonville, O., 45 miles.

The second consolidation, effective July 1st, 1911, was the Cleveland, Akron & Columbus Railway Company and the Cincinnati & Muskingum Valley Railroad Company into the Cleveland, Akron & Cincinnati Railway Company, which was also to be operated by the Pennsylvania Company. The consolidated company had a total mileage of 335 miles, consisting principally of the line from Hudson to Columbus, O., nearly 144 miles, the Dresden Branch extending from Killbuck to Trinway, O., 33 miles, and the road from Trinway to Morrow, O., 148 miles.

NORTHUMBERLAND YARD COMPLETED

On August 6th, 1911, the Northumberland Classification Yard, Northumberland, Pa., was completed and placed in operation. This yard covered an area of 700 acres and contained 70 miles of new track, it having been constructed to replace the two yards at Sunbury, to relieve the congestion at Harrisburg Yard, and to facilitate the handling of traffic over the Northern Central Railway and the Erie Division of the Pennsylvania Railroad. It was also necessary to construct a new line between the Williamsport and Sunbury Divisions in order to properly accommodate the traffic to and from the yard. The expenditure involved was to be divided between the Northern Central Railway Company and Pennsylvania Railroad Company in proportion to their respective use of the facilities.

RAPID TRANSIT LINE COMPLETED TO NEWARK, N. J.

On November 26th, 1911, the Newark Rapid Transit Line, which provided a frequent multiple unit electric service to and from the Terminal of the Hudson & Manhattan Railroad at Cortlandt and Church Streets, New York City, via Manhattan Transfer Station, to Park Place, Newark, N. J., was completed and placed in operation.

CONSTRUCTION OF NEW YORK CONNECTING RAILROAD

The New York Connecting Railroad Company, the Capital Stock of which had been owned for many years one-half each by the Pennsylvania Railroad Company and the New York, New Haven & Hartford Railroad Company, was constructing its railroad in 1911 from a connection with the Long Island Railroad, near the boundary line between the Boroughs of Brooklyn and Queens, New York City, through the latter Borough to and over the East River and Randall's and Wards Islands, to a connection with the New York, New Haven & Hartford Railroad near Port Morris, in the Borough of Bronx; also a connection from said main line to the New York Tunnel Extension in Sunnyside Yard, Long Island City. A franchise had been obtained to carry out this work from the City of New York after several years' delay. Contracts had been awarded for the steel work for the bridge over the East River known as "Hell Gate Bridge," and its viaducts and approaches, on the north into Bronx Borough, and on the south into the Borough of Queens, Long Island.

Upon the completion of this railroad, and the exercise of trackage rights to be obtained from the Long Island Railroad Company between the said connection and its Bay Ridge Terminals on New York Harbor, the freight traffic interchanged between the Pennsylvania and New Haven Systems, which was then transported by floats between the

Pennsylvania terminals on the west side of the Hudson River and the New York, New Haven & Hartford Railroad Company's lines at Port Morris, a distance of about 14 miles, would be floated from Greenville, N. J., to Bay Ridge, Long Island, a distance of about 3½ miles, and thence moved by rail to Port Morris. Further, the connection with the New York Tunnel Extension would permit a direct all-rail movement via the Pennsylvania Station, New York City, for the passenger traffic interchanged between the two Systems. It was also felt that the New York Connecting Route would materially expedite the movement of passenger and freight traffic to and from New England and avoid congestion and delays in New York Harbor, which frequently occurred by reason of fog, ice, tides and the crowded condition of the Hudson and East Rivers.

ESTIMATED COST

It was stated that about three years would be required to construct the New York Connecting Railroad, including its East River Bridge and Viaducts, and the cost thereof, estimated at about $15,000,000. (in addition to the $5,000,000. previously advanced in equal amounts by the two owning Companies and represented by its Capital Stock and Notes) was to be provided for through an issue of its Bonds. The principal and interest of these securities were to be guaranteed by the Pennsylvania Railroad Company and the New York, New Haven and Hartford Railroad Company, and the line was to be operated pursuant to an agreement between the two Companies, under which they were to participate in its profits, or meet its deficits.

WILKES-BARRE CONNECTING RAILROAD

The Wilkes-Barre Connecting Railroad Company was incorporated on November 18th, 1912, jointly by the Pennsylvania Railroad Company and the Delaware & Hudson Company, to construct a line seven miles in length from Buttonwood Yard, on the Pennsylvania Railroad, west of the City of Wilkes-Barre, to Hudson, on the Delaware & Hudson Company's road. This was done in order to facilitate the interchange of traffic between the two roads and avoid its movement through the business centre of that City, and via the tracks of other railroads. The road was completed and opened for traffic in 1915.

PHILADELPHIA PASSENGER TERMINAL IMPROVEMENTS

The improvements of the passengers facilities in Philadelphia, to which reference has heretofore been made, continued to receive consideration by the various departments in the service, and also by the Consulting Electrical Engineers of the Company in the year 1912. From the studies that had been made it was evident that it would necessitate an increase in the tracks and platforms, and the enlargement and improvement of the station facilities at Broad Street Station and its approaches as far as West Philadelphia Station and Yard; the widening of the bridge, and its approaches, over the Schuylkill River and the adjoining entrances to Fairmount Park at Girard Avenue, by the construction of three additional tracks and a revision of the signals and interlocking; the enlargement of North Philadelphia passenger station and its approaches by the addition of four new tracks with high level island platforms, and other improvements including the relocation of the junction of the Chestnut Hill Branch with the New York Division at that point.

CAMBRIA & CLEARFIELD RAILWAY ABSORBED

Effective March 31st, 1913, the Cambria & Clearfield Railway Company was absorbed by the Pennsylvania Railroad Company. It was made up of a great many branch roads, the most important and largest of which were the line from Bellwood to Fordham, a distance of nearly 65 miles; the branch from Cresson to Glen Campbell, 50 miles; the Black Lick Branch extending from Kaylor to a connection with the Conemaugh Division at Black Lick Station, 37 miles; the line from Cresson to Irvona, 26 miles, and the Susquehanna Branch, which was built from Bradley Junction to Cherry Tree, 18 miles. The Cambria & Clearfield Railway had been owned and operated by the Pennsylvania Railroad Company in connection with its Main Line for many years, the construction of the former road and its several constituents having been promoted by it for the development of the bituminous coal traffic in the Clearfield region.

IMPROVEMENTS BETWEEN PITTSBURGH AND BUFFALO

It became evident to the Management in 1912 that to more expeditiously and economically handle the increasing traffic between Pittsburgh and Buffalo via the Allegheny Division and the Western New York & Pennsylvania Railway, it was necessary to construct three tunnels, reduce the grades and make other improvements on the Allegheny Division between Pittsburgh and Oil City; also to make reduction of grades and otherwise improve the railroad and yard facilities between Oil City and Buffalo via Brocton and the Chautauqua Branch, and thus more fully utilize it as the principal route for passenger and freight traffic between these cities. This work was authorized and when completed the objectionable heavy grades would be restricted to relatively short distances between the said cities, and this route made 58 miles shorter than the existing line via Oil City, the Salamanca Branch and Olean. It would not only have this advantage in distance, but its use would postpone for several years the double tracking and other expenditures on the route then used.

PURCHASE OF OHIO RIVER & WESTERN RAILWAY COMPANY

During the year 1912 the Pennsylvania Company purchased practically the entire outstanding Capital Stock and all the Bonds of the Ohio River & Western Railway Company, a narrow gauge road extending from Bellaire to Zanesville, O., a distance of about 110 miles.

RESIGNATION AND DEATH OF PRESIDENT McCREA

On November 13th, 1912, Mr. McCrea tendered his resignation as President, effective January 1st, 1913, expressing a desire to be relieved from the arduous duties and responsibilities so inseparably connected with that office, and thus endeavor to secure the rest and relaxation necessary for the preservation of his health. The Minute of the Board of Directors in accepting his resignation paid a splendid tribute to the valuable, efficient and untiring services rendered by Mr. McCrea, which concluded with an expression of keen regret at the severance of his official relations with the Company. He, however, consented to continue as a Director of the Company, and served until his death on March 28th, 1913.

The Board of Directors, in recording his death, adopted an appropriate Minute, in which the stockholders joined, expressing their deep sorrow and keen sense of personal and official loss, and calling attention to his 48 years of devoted service, during which time he had risen from the humble post of rodman to the Presidency of the Company. The following paragraphs, extracted from the Minute, indicate the value of his service to the Company and the esteem in which he was held by his associates:—

> " As an officer his sole aim was the betterment of the service, as a Director and Chief Executive the advancement of the interest of the Company and its Stockholders, and the preservation of its prestige and integrity.
>
> James McCrea has come to the inevitable end of man, but his achievements are of lasting importance, and his name and memory are indelibly and worthily inscribed, with those of his distinguished predecessors, high in the hall of fame, and deep in the hearts of those whose privilege it was to know and labor with him."

STATISTICAL DATA

The following operating and traffic statistics and financial data will indicate the growth of the Company during the Administration of President McCrea, 1907 to 1912, inclusive:—

REVENUE, EXPENSES, OPERATING INCOME, AND RENTALS, 1907 TO 1912, INCLUSIVE

All Lines East of Pittsburgh and Erie Directly Operated

Year	Miles	Gross Revenue	Operating Expenses	Operating Income	Rentals Paid	Net Operating Income to Penna. R. R. Co.
1907......	3,970.79	$164,812,825.64	$119,607,348.28	$45,205,477.36	$10,837,864.27	$34,367,613.09
1908......	4,048.30	136,296,871.03	101,400,992.90	34,895,878.13	6,437,357.42	28,458,520.71
1909......	4,015.18	153,564,527.49	111,903,160.24	41,661,367.25	7,656,936.37	34,004,430.88
1910......	4,044.69	166,433,683.16	128,473,137.10	37,960,546.06	5,652,272.49	32,308,273.57
1911......	4,084.79	163,118,139.61	127,210,391.43	35,907,748.18	4,919,204.86	30,988,543.32
1912......	4,091.83	181,023,693.30	141,330,559.92	39,693,133.38	5,301,473.35	34,391,660.03

Taxes are included in Operating Expenses commencing with the year 1908.

TONNAGE, MILEAGE, REVENUE, EXPENSES, AND AVERAGES ON FREIGHT BUSINESS, 1907 TO 1912, INCLUSIVE

All Rail Lines East of Pittsburgh and Erie Directly Operated

Year	Tons	Tons One Mile	Revenue	Average Revenue per Ton per Mile	Expenses	Average Expenses per Ton per Mile	Average Net Revenue per Ton per Mile
				Cents		Cents	Cents
1907......	132,284,515	21,473,176,903	$123,816,999.03	0.577	$88,699,264.83	0.413	0.164
1908......	101,296,504	16,993,748,017	96,711,869.79	0.569	69,391,361.01	0.408	0.161
1909......	120,418,380	19,107,965,601	110,748,978.04	0.580	72,658,908.94	0.380	0.200
1910......	129,858,353	20,279,992,323	118,203,016.73	0.583	83,537,518.56	0.412	0.171
1911......	125,175,068	19,419,779,983	114,069,932.34	0.587	78,959,056.93	0.407	0.180
1912......	143,480,431	22,012,606,175	128,346,181.60	0.583	90,280,848.81	0.410	0.173

Taxes are included in expenses commencing with the year 1908.

PASSENGERS, MILEAGE, REVENUE, EXPENSES, AND AVERAGES ON PASSENGER BUSINESS, 1907 TO 1912, INCLUSIVE

All Rail Lines East of Pittsburgh and Erie Directly Operated

Year	Passengers	Passengers One Mile	Revenue	Average Revenue per Passenger per Mile	Expenses	Average Expenses per Passenger per Mile	Average Net Revenue per Passenger per Mile
				Cents		Cents	Cents
1907......	65,568,699	1,629,769,525	31,353,613.69	1.924	$23,346,511.93	1.433	0.491
1908......	59,666,292	1,466,109,092	28,951,656.23	1.975	22,880,319.70	1.561	0.414
1909......	62,392,136	1,548,180,263	30,410,788,39	1.964	26,330,572.84	1.701	0.263
1910......	69,979,457	1,693,943,849	33,185,030.96	1.959	28,581,547.86	1.687	0.272
1911......	67,445,714	1,722,734,924	34,113,529.48	1.980	31,087,215.24	1.805	0.175
1912......	72,452,887	1,838,352,119	36,067,012.71	1.962	33,614,731.69	1.829	0.133

NOTE.—Commencing with 1907 the figures are made up on a different basis from those for the preceding years, the expenses applicable to mail and express traffic having been eliminated from the passenger train expenses in subsequent years.

Taxes are included in expenses commencing with the year 1908.

DIVIDENDS AND ALLOTMENTS ON CAPITAL STOCK—THE PENNSYLVANIA RAILROAD COMPANY

DATE	Capital Stock on which Dividend or Allotment was Declared	DIVIDEND				ALLOTMENTS OF STOCK ON SUBSCRIPTION	
		CASH		SCRIP OR STOCK			
		Per Cent.	Amount	Per Cent.	Amount	Per Cent.	Amount
May, 1907.	$311,622,400	3½	$10,906,784				
November, "	314,332,900	3½	11,001,651 50				
May, 1908.	314,594,650	3	9,437,839 50				
November, "	314,594,700	3	9,437,841				
May, 1909.	314,607,800	3	9,438,234				
November, "	324,516,950	3	9,735,508 50				
" "	330,071,350					25	(At par) $82,517,800 00
February, 1910.	401,086,000	1½	6,016,290				
May, "	401,102,250	1½	6,016,533 75				
August, "	412,591,700	1½	6,188,875 50				
November, "	412,610,700	1½	6,189,160 50				
February, 1911.	412,610,850	1½	6,189,162 75				
May, "	412,616,200	1½	6,189,243			10	(At par) 41,261,600 00
August, "	450,974,050	1½	6,764,610 75				
November, "	453,856,050	1½	6,807,840 75				
February, 1912.	453,877,850	1½	6,808,167 75				
May, "	453,877,900	1½	6,808,168 50				
August, "	453,877,900	1½	6,808,168 50				
November, "	453,877,900	1½	6,808,168 50				

NUMBER OF STOCKHOLDERS

December 31st

Year	Number	Year	Number
1907	57,226	1910	65,283
1908	58,273	1911	73,165
1909	56,809	1912	75,155

DIRECTORS

The following is a list of the Directors who served during President McCrea's Administration, together with the dates of their election and the end of their service:—

Name of Director	*Elected*	*End of Service*
Alexander M. Fox	March 6, 1871,	October 6, 1907;
N. Parker Shortridge	March 24, 1874,	January 3, 1915;
John P. Green	October 1, 1882,	March 24, 1909;
Clement A. Griscom	September 24, 1884,	November 10, 1912;
William H. Barnes	December 11, 1889,	May 5, 1918;
George Wood	March 24, 1891,	February 17, 1926;
Charles E. Pugh	March 1, 1893,	February 28, 1911;
C. Stuart Patterson	July 2, 1895,	November 8, 1924;
Effingham B. Morris	December 31, 1896,	....
Thomas DeWitt Cuyler	May 10, 1899,	November 2, 1922;
James McCrea	June 9, 1899,	March 28, 1913;
Samuel Rea	June 14, 1899,	....
Lincoln Godfrey	April 11, 1900,	January 12, 1916;
Rudulph Ellis	November 11, 1903,	September 21, 1915;
John B. Thayer	October 10, 1905,	April 14, 1912;
Henry C. Frick	December 26, 1906,	December 2, 1919;
Charles E. Ingersoll	January 23, 1907,	....
Percival Roberts, Jr	October 23, 1907,	April 14, 1920;
"	April 9, 1926,	....
Henry Tatnall	March 24, 1909,	May 1, 1925;
W. W. Atterbury	March 3, 1911,	....
George D. Dixon	September 16, 1912,	August 1, 1925.

SAMUEL REA

NINTH PRESIDENT, 1913-1925

FOLLOWING the resignation of President McCrea, the Board of Directors on November 13th, 1912, elected Samuel Rea as President, effective January 1st, 1913. Mr. Rea was born in Hollidaysburg, Pa., on September 21st, 1855. His first connection with the Pennsylvania Railroad Company was in the Engineering Department in 1871, as a chainman and rodman on the Morrison's Cove, Williamsburg and Bloomfield Branches. Early in 1874, he left the service of the Pennsylvania Railroad Company, but returned to it in the Spring of 1875, and was stationed at Connellsville, Pa., with an engineering corps. From 1875 to 1877 Mr. Rea was Assistant Engineer in the construction of the chain suspension bridge over the Monongahela River in Pittsburgh, and upon its completion was appointed Assistant Engineer of the Pittsburgh and Lake Erie Railroad, then in course of construction, with which Company he remained until the completion of that road. In 1879 he again returned to the Pennsylvania Railroad in the capacity of Assistant Engineer in charge of the construction of the extension of the Pittsburgh, Virginia & Charleston Railway; from 1879 to 1883, he was Engineer in charge of surveys in Westmoreland County and of the re-building of the Western Pennsylvania Railroad, to make it a low-grade freight line; in 1883 he was transferred to Philadelphia as Assistant to Vice-President DuBarry, with title of Principal Assistant Engineer, which he held until his appointment in 1888 as Assistant to the Second Vice-President. He retained this office until 1889, when he resigned to go to Baltimore as Vice-President of the Maryland Central Railway Company, and Chief Engineer of the Baltimore Belt Railroad Company.

In 1891, on account of ill health, Mr. Rea resigned and left Baltimore, doing no active work for a year, after which he resumed the practice of his profession. After an absence of three years from the service of the Pennsylvania Railroad

SAMUEL REA
Ninth President—January 1st, 1913, to October 1st, 1925.

Company he was appointed Assistant to the President of that Company on May 25th, 1892. On February 10th, 1897, he was appointed First Assistant to the President, and on June 14th, 1899, was elected Fourth Vice-President of the Company; on October 10th, 1905, Third Vice-President, and on March 24th, 1909, Second Vice-President. In addition to his former duties he was placed in charge of the Engineering and Accounting Departments. On March 3rd, 1911, he was elected First Vice-President, and on May 8th, 1912, when the practice of designating the Vice-Presidents numerically was discontinued, Mr. Rea was elected Vice-President, which position he held at the time of his election to the Presidency.

He actively supervised the locating, planning, and construction of the Pennsylvania Railroad's Tunnel Extension into and through New York City and the large station in that City, as well as the New York Connecting Railroad, and its "Hell Gate Bridge," which is the connecting line of railroad between the Pennsylvania and New Haven Systems on Long Island. He was also a member of the Railroads' War Board, which was voluntarily formed in 1917 to co-ordinate, for the period of the World War, the operations of all the railroads of the United States into a single railroad system, which was placed unreservedly at the service of the Government.

ELECTRIFICATION BETWEEN ALTOONA AND CONEMAUGH

The Management stated to the stockholders in the Annual Report for 1913 that, in keeping with its policy to promote efficiency and economy of operations, it had been considering the advisability of electrifying that portion of its Main Line between Altoona, at the foot of the eastern slope, and Conemaugh on the western slope of the Allegheny Mountains, a distance of about 35 miles. Preliminary estimates had been made which indicated that a saving could be effected which would compensate for the outlay, but that the work would not be actively taken up until there was an improvement in the earnings of the Company.

PROPOSED LEASE OF WEST JERSEY & SEASHORE RAILROAD

The Pennsylvania Railroad Company concluded negotiations in 1913 for a lease of the West Jersey and Seashore Railroad Company for 999 years on the basis of guaranteeing the payment of 6% dividends upon its Stock and all fixed charges and taxes. The lease, however, failed to receive the approval of the New Jersey Public Utilities Commission and no further effort was made to lease the property.

FLOODS IN OHIO AND INDIANA

In March, 1913, the Company's Lines West of Pittsburgh suffered very severely from an unprecedented rainfall in Ohio and Indiana, especially in the valleys of the Muskingum, Scioto and Miami Rivers. All of them overflowed their banks, causing great loss of life and hundreds of millions of dollars in property damage. Commencing on March 23rd, there fell in less than three days more than three months' rainfall, submerging stations, bridges and roadbed, and causing hundreds of miles of track to be swept away. The cities of Dayton, Hamilton, Piqua and Zanesville, O., were almost completely submerged, and great damage was also caused in certain districts of Columbus and Cincinnati. The city of Dayton, in which 98 lives were known to have been lost, was the greatest sufferer. The Lines of the Pennsylvania Company, Pittsburgh, Cincinnati, Chicago & St. Louis Railway and Vandalia Railroad Companies were the most seriously affected, it having cost over $3,500,000. to restore them to their normal condition.

DISPOSITION OF ANTHRACITE COAL PROPERTIES

On September 26th, 1913, the Pennsylvania Railroad Company announced that it had decided to dispose of its security holdings in the anthracite coal companies owning properties served by its System, namely: the Susquehanna Coal Company, Mineral Railroad & Mining Company and Summit Branch Mining Company. It was, however, deemed advisable to first compact the ownership of these securities and properties into the Susquehanna Coal Company, and steps were accordingly taken to sell to that Company the Stock of the Summit Branch Mining Company, upon the consummation of which the latter Company was to be dissolved. The Mineral Railroad & Mining Company, one-third of the Capital Stock of which was owned by the Pennsylvania Railroad Company and two-thirds by the Northern Central Railway Company, operated coal lands leased from the latter Company and the Manor Real Estate & Trust Company. However, being unable to pay the prescribed royalties, it transferred its 999 year leases to the Susquehanna Coal Company. The lands of the Manor Real Estate & Trust Company operated by the Mineral Railroad & Mining Company were sold to the Susquehanna Coal Company, and negotiations concluded for the sale to the latter Company of other lands operated by the Mineral Company for the Northern Central Railway Company. The Susquehanna Coal Company subsequently issued its 5% 5-Year Gold Bonds, due January 1st, 1919, to pay for these lands. The purpose of vesting the ownership of these properties in the Susquehanna Coal Company was to insure a continuation of the policy of operating the mines in the interest of conserving the coal supply, so that should a purchaser be found for the securities of the Susquehanna Coal Company, the new owners would obtain possession of the properties subject to these mining obligations.

FEDERAL VALUATION OF RAILROADS

Under the Act of Congress approved March 1st, 1913, providing for the Federal Valuation of property owned or used for railroad purposes, the railroads were required to co-operate with the Interstate Commerce Commission under whose direction the valuation was to be made. As this was a very important subject from the standpoint of the railroads of the Country, they appointed on April 24th, 1913, a Presidents' Conference Committee on Federal Valuation, for the purpose of acting in an advisory capacity on behalf of the railroads with a view to promoting co-operation with the

Commission. President Rea was elected General Chairman of this Committee in 1913, and up to the present time has continued to serve in that capacity.

The Pennsylvania Railroad Company also appointed for this purpose a Valuation Committee, consisting of officers from various Departments of the service, so as to facilitate the preparation of the necessary data and give the subject the consideration which its importance required.

EXCHANGE OF BALTIMORE & OHIO FOR SOUTHERN PACIFIC STOCK

Reference was made in the Annual Report for 1913 to the exchange of 57,250 shares of Common Stock and 142,736 shares of Preferred Stock of the Baltimore & Ohio Railroad Company for 171,438 shares of Capital Stock of the Southern Pacific Company. In consummating this transaction, the Southern Pacific Company Stock was valued at its par value of $100. per share and the Common Stock of the Baltimore & Ohio Railroad Company at the same figure, while the 4% Preferred Stock of the latter Company was valued at $80. per share, which was its approximate market value. It was stated that the Pennsylvania Railroad Company would receive greater dividend returns from the Southern Pacific Company Stock, and that it could be held either as an investment or sold when conditions permitted.

CORNWALL & LEBANON RAILROAD COMPANY STOCK PURCHASED

In 1913 the Pennsylvania Railroad Company acquired a majority of the Capital Stock of the Cornwall and Lebanon Railroad Company, whose road connected with the Main Line of the former Company at Conewago, Pa., and extended to the manufacturing town of Lebanon, Pa., a distance of about 22 miles.

CHICAGO UNION STATION

The Pennsylvania Company, Pittsburgh, Cincinnati, Chicago & St. Louis Railway, Chicago, Burlington & Quincy Railroad, and the Chicago, Milwaukee & St. Paul Railway

Companies, having made large expenditures for the purchase of real estate in the City of Chicago for a new Union Passenger Station, incorporated the Chicago Union Station Company in 1913 to carry out this work. It was to be erected adjacent to the then existing Union Station, which had become inadequate to meet the demands of the traffic, and when the necessary franchise rights had been obtained, work on the new Station was to begin. The cost was to be financed largely through the issuance and sale of Bonds of the Station Company, which were to be guaranteed principal and interest by the Owning Companies.

SOUTH PHILADELPHIA IMPROVEMENTS

On March 23rd, 1914, an agreement was executed between the City of Philadelphia and the Pennsylvania Railroad Company, Philadelphia, Baltimore and Washington Railroad Company and the Baltimore & Ohio Railroad Company, under which nearly all grade crossings of the foregoing railroads were to be eliminated in the southern part of Philadelphia. Under this agreement the City agreed to bear an equitable portion of the cost of the work.

SUGGESTING NEW RAILROAD LEGISLATION

In 1914 the Management of the Pennsylvania Railroad Company in its Annual Report suggested that the increased scope and great burden of the duties and responsibilities imposed upon the Interstate Commerce Commission should be followed by the amendment of the Federal Laws from which its authority is derived; that the Commission should be enlarged and definitely empowered by specific provisions in the laws to strengthen the railroads, upon which the welfare of the Country was largely dependent; that the position of a Commissioner should be placed beyond political influence by a long tenure of office and the compensation should be sufficient to attract and retain men of the widest experience and greatest ability; that the regulatory power of the Commission should be clearly extended to the supervision and control of all rates and practices, which directly or remotely affect interstate transportation; that the services of the Commission should be made available to remedy the concededly inadequate revenues of the railroads for the transportation of mails and parcel post and the power of Commissions, State and Federal, to suspend increases in rates should be limited so as to prevent loss of revenue to the railroads during the suspension of rates subsequently determined to be reasonable.

LEASE OF NORTHERN CENTRAL RAILWAY

On July 29th, 1914, the lease of the Northern Central Railway to the Pennsylvania Railroad Company was executed and the lines of that Company were made a part of the Central Division of the Pennsylvania Railroad. The necessary rental payments and other adjustments between the lessor and lessee were made effective as of January 1st, 1911.

YORK, HANOVER & FREDERICK RAILWAY FORMED

During the year 1914 the Central Railroad of Maryland, which had commenced the building of a railroad extending from Keymar, Md., to Union Bridge, Md., a distance of 5½ miles was, effective July 6th, 1914, consolidated with the York, Hanover & Frederick Railroad Company, forming a new corporation known as the York, Hanover & Frederick Railway Company, which was entirely owned by the Pennsylvania Railroad Company. The new Company completed in 1914 the construction of what then became a branch between Keymar and Union Bridge, which, with its main line from York, Pa., to Frederick, Md., gave it a total length of 61 miles.

SCHUYLKILL RIVER BRIDGE COMPLETED

The five-track re-enforced concrete and stone arch bridge over the Schuylkill River at the Girard Avenue entrance to Fairmount Park, Philadelphia, was completed and placed in operation in 1914 and the old double track bridge removed.

PURCHASE OF ROADS TO DAYTON, O.

The Pennsylvania Company acquired in 1914 by purchase all of the outstanding stock of the Dayton, Lebanon & Cincinnati Railroad & Terminal Company, which owned a line 23.27 miles long, connecting with the Cincinnati, Lebanon & Northern Railway (also owned by Pennsylvania Company) at Dodds, O., and extending into Dayton, O., in which City it owned an extensive and valuable terminal property.

FINAL ISSUE OF CONSOLIDATED MORTGAGE BONDS

The Pennsylvania Railroad Company sold, in the early part of 1915, $49,000,000. Consolidated Mortgage 4½% Bonds, bearing date February 1st, 1915, and maturing August 1st, 1960. With this issue, the total amount of Bonds outstanding under the Consolidated Mortgage was almost $100,000,000., which was the maximum amount that could at any time be issued and outstanding. In view of the creation of the new General Mortgage, to which reference is later made, it was deemed advisable to close the Consolidated Mortgage and issue no more Bonds thereunder.

CREATION OF GENERAL MORTGAGE

With the continued growth of the Pennsylvania Railroad System and the great expansion of the Country's commerce and industry, the capital requirements for the improvement of the property were constantly increasing. It was, therefore, realized that the Company would have to create a mortgage which would provide a broad basis for financing capital expenditures for some years to come, just as the Consolidated Mortgage had been created in the early 70's for a similar purpose, and a General Mortgage was created and dated June 1st, 1915. Its principal provisions were:—

1. The aggregate amount of General Mortgage Bonds, at any time outstanding, could not exceed the par value of the outstanding Capital Stock of the Company.
2. At no time was the total issue of General Mortgage Bonds, together with other outstanding prior debts

of the Company, to exceed three times the outstanding par value of Capital Stock. This was inserted to meet the laws of some States governing investments by Savings Banks and Insurance Companies.

3. A sufficient margin of General Mortgage Bonds was reserved to refund the outstanding issue of Consolidated Mortgage Bonds and other underlying Bonds when they matured. At the maturity of such prior lien Bonds no further issues could be made under their respective mortgages.

4. That subject to the Consolidated Mortgage and mortgages of acquired companies, the General Mortgage was a first lien on the Main Line and branches of the Pennsylvania Railroad between Philadelphia and Pittsburgh, its equipment, appurtenances, etc., as well as certain leaseholds East of Pittsburgh and Erie.

FIRST SALE OF GENERAL MORTGAGE BONDS

The Company sold in May, 1915, $65,000,000. of these General Mortgage 4½% Bonds, Series "A," dated June 1st, 1915, and maturing June 1st, 1965, this being the first issue and sale of Bonds under that Mortgage. The proceeds, together with the funds derived from the sale of $49,000,000. Consolidated Mortgage 4½% Bonds, were used to pay off $86,827,000. of 3½% Convertible Bonds which matured October 1st, 1915, and to meet other maturing obligations of the Company, as well as provide the capital required to make necessary additions and betterments to its railroad and equipment.

It may be of interest to record that the day following the sale of these Bonds, the sinking of the "Lusitania" by a German submarine was announced. The Company obtained the proceeds from the sale, but the Bankers had the serious responsibility of disposing of a $65,000,000. issue in the face of the disturbed financial conditions which immediately followed the announcement.

PANAMA CANAL ACT—STEAMSHIP OPERATIONS

In the enforcements of the provisions of the Panama Canal Act, the Interstate Commerce Commission, acting under its discretion conferred by that Act, declined to permit the further operation of certain steamer lines operated by, or in connection with, the various railroad lines. The Commission accordingly issued an order which in effect required the Erie & Western Transportation Company, the Stock of which was owned by the Pennsylvania Railroad Company, to discontinue operation of its steamer lines on the Great Lakes, effective December 15th, 1915, and this was done. The Erie & Western Transportation Company accordingly sold its steamers and expected to dispose of its remaining property when satisfactory offers were obtained. The Commission also issued an order requiring the Baltimore, Chesapeake & Atlantic Railway Company, in which the Pennsylvania Railroad Company was interested, to discontinue the operation of nearly all of its steamers on the Chesapeake Bay, effective April 1st, 1916, and the Maryland, Delaware and Virginia Railway Company, which was affiliated in interest with the Baltimore, Chesapeake & Atlantic Railway Company, to discontinue the operation of its Chester River steamers on the Eastern shore of Chesapeake Bay. The continued operation of the steamer lines of both Companies on the Western shore of the Bay was left subject to further orders of the Commission.

As a discontinuance of the service to and from the Eastern shore would have seriously and detrimentally affected the communities served, the shippers and commercial organizations of Baltimore and the Eastern shore of Maryland and Virginia joined in a petition to the Commission, to which these two Companies were parties, for a postponement of the effective date of the Order and a re-opening of the case. This was granted and the two Companies have since continued to operate their steamer lines, although unprofitable, pending final disposition of the question.

CONGRESSIONAL INQUIRY INTO RAILROAD REGULATION

Reference was made in the Annual Report for 1915 to the fact that the President of the United States had recommended a Congressional inquiry into the transportation problem and regulation affecting the common carriers. The Management of the Company, it was stated, would render all reasonable assistance desired in connection with such an important National inquiry, and attention was called to the fact that public regulation had served many useful purposes, which it was desirable to continue, but that there had been a notable lack of a definite business policy and co-operation between the Federal and State Governments as to railroad legislation and regulation. Further, that the time for complaint and destructive criticism had passed, and that through this inquiry an opportunity was presented for formulating a constructive policy and insuring equitable treatment for the railroads, which were very essential factors in creating and continuing National prosperity.

BRANCH LINE ACQUISITIONS

Effective April 30th, 1915, the Pennsylvania Railroad Company absorbed the Lancaster & Quarryville Railroad, Pennsylvania, Monongahela & Southern Railroad and the Lewisburg & Tyrone Railway Companies, which were owned and operated by the Pennsylvania Railroad Company in connection with its Main Line. The first named road extended from Lancaster to Quarryville, a distance of 15.21 miles; the second from Denbo to Crucible, 9.65 miles, and the third from Tyrone to Fairbrook and from Lemont to Montandon, a distance, with branches, of 84.93 miles, all three being constructed within the State of Pennsylvania.

MONONGAHELA RAILWAY COMPANY FORMED

Effective July 1st, 1915, the Monongahela Railroad and Buckhannon & Northern Railroad Companies were consolidated to form the Monongahela Railway Company. The first named Company had constructed its road from Brownsville Junction to the Pennsylvania-West Virginia State Line, a distance of nearly 36 miles, while the Buckhannon & Northern Railroad was built from that point to Fairmont, W. Va., a distance of about 34 miles. The consolidated Company was owned jointly by the Pennsylvania Railroad and Pittsburgh & Lake Erie Railroad Companies, and its road had a total length with branches of over 82 miles.

PHILADELPHIA SUBURBAN ELECTRIFICATION

In order to relieve congestion by increasing the yard and track capacity at Broad Street Station, Philadelphia, the Main Line of the Pennsylvania Railroad was electrified from that point to Paoli, a distance of 20 miles, for suburban passenger trains, and the electric service inaugurated on September 4th, 1915.

SIX TRACK WORK

The six track system on the New York Division between Colonia and Bay Way (west of Elizabeth, N. J.) was completed in 1915, the work including the elimination of 15 grade crossings through the elevation of the four existing main tracks, the building of two additional elevated tracks, and the construction of a new passenger station at Rahway, and new undergrade connections with the Perth Amboy & Woodbridge Railroad east of Rahway.

70th ANNIVERSARY

The stockholders' attention was called to the fact that April 13th, 1916, marked the 70th Anniversary of the enactment by the State of Pennsylvania of the Act incorporating The Pennsylvania Railroad Company. The Annual Report for 1915 pointed out that, notwithstanding the many financial and business vicissitudes in that long period, the Company had endeavored to discharge its duty to the public by maintaining an adequate, safe and high standard of transportation service; by encouraging the development of the territory served by its lines and connections; and by safeguarding the interests of the stockholders and bondholders and the welfare of its employes; that since its incorporation the Company had paid a cash return upon its Capital Stock in every calendar year and had pursued the sound financial policy of devoting many millions of dollars of its income to provide betterments and improvements to the railroad and equipment, instead of issuing Capital Stock or Bonds to procure funds therefor.

PURCHASE OF STERLING BONDS

During the World War period the Pennsylvania Railroad Company took advantage of the fall in Sterling exchange by purchasing during the years 1915 and 1916 a large amount of its 3½% and 4% Sterling Bonds, due July 1st, 1945, and May 1st, 1948, respectively. At the normal rate of exchange the 3½% Bonds purchased were equivalent, in American dollars, to $866,210., and the 4% Bonds, $14,132,900. When these Bonds were acquired they were stamped payable in dollars, and $385,000. of the 3½% Bonds and $14,570,000. of the 4% Bonds were sold in this Country, which resulted in a considerable profit to the Company. The increased par amount of Stamped 4% Bonds sold compared with the par of those purchased was offset by a cancellation of sufficient 3½% Stamped Bonds to equalize the increase.

PURCHASE OF PENNSYLVANIA COMPANY FRENCH FRANC CERTIFICATES

The Pennsylvania Company carried out similar transactions during the period 1915 to 1918 in connection with its $48,262,548. 3¾% French Franc Loan, issued June 15th, 1906, and maturing June 15th, 1921 (but called for redemption June 15th, 1920). With the depreciation in the value of the Franc, there were purchased French Franc 3¾% Certificates to the extent, under normal rates of exchange, of $37,531,140. These Certificates were deposited with the Girard Trust Company as collateral for a newly created issue of $37,531,140. Pennsylvania Company 4½% Gold Loan Bonds, dated June 15th, 1915, and maturing June 15th, 1921. The increased interest rate on the new issue was more than offset by the large profit realized by reason of being able to purchase the foregoing amount of 3¾% Franc Certificates and calling the balance of them for redemption during a period when the French Franc was selling considerably below its normal value.

The foregoing transactions were also of benefit to the Allied Governments and to American industry in making dollar balances available, which were so much needed then for the purchase of materials in the United States during the War period. The French Government encouraged the purchase of the French Franc Bonds by agreeing to exempt all Bonds so purchased from the French Stamp Transfer and Revenue taxes, which by previous agreement would have been paid thereon for the life of the Bonds.

PENNSYLVANIA CANAL COMPANY BONDS

There was charged against the Profit & Loss Account of the Pennsylvania Railroad Company in the year 1916 the sum of $1,923,408.16, which was paid by that Company to the Trustee of the Mortgage securing an issue of 6% Bonds of the Pennsylvania Canal Company, pursuant to a decree handed down by the United States District Court for the Eastern District of Pennsylvania. These Bonds, of which there were then outstanding $1,948,000. matured July 1st, 1910, and as the sale of the Canal Company's property did not yield sufficient proceeds to pay the outstanding coupons, which by the terms of the Mortgage had priority over the principal of the Bonds, nothing remained available for the payment of the principal.

Certain bondholders thereupon instituted legal proceedings claiming that the Canal Company had failed to make all of the Sinking Fund payments provided for by the Mortgage. The terms of the latter were that Sinking Fund payments should be made out of the Net Earnings of the Canal Company, and from the time the Mortgage was created it had been assumed that the term "Net Earnings" meant the amount remaining after the payment of operating expenses and interest on the Bonds. The Courts held, however, that in determining whether Net Earnings were available for Sinking Fund payments, the interest on the Bonds should not be taken into account. Based upon this interpretation, the Court directed the Pennsylvania Railroad Company to pay to the Trustee of the Mortgage $1,379,941.28, together with interest thereon from July 1st, 1910, which payment amounting to $1,923,408.16 had been made. The distribution of this amount was to be made by the Trustee, and the Pennsylvania Railroad Company, as the holder of $384,000., par value, of the Bonds of the Canal Company, would receive its proportionate share thereof.

ADAMSON EIGHT HOUR LAW

During the year 1916 the employes in the train service on most of the railroads in the United States submitted demands through their labor organizations for an Eight-Hour basic day at the existing rates of pay, and time and one-half time payments for all overtime in freight and yard service. Although many of the men in the train service did not work eight hours per day, this reduction in the time, constituting a basic work day meant in effect an unjustifiable increase of pay for most of these employes. Conferences were held between the railroads' representatives and the trainmen's organizations, but the latter would not consent to arbitration or other investigation, and orders for a strike were given in case the railroads refused to comply with their demands. It was questionable whether many of the men, especially those in the service of the Pennsylvania Railroad System, would finally have deserted their positions, yet the suffering and disruption of business that would have resulted from the strike were so evident that the so-called Adamson Eight Hour Law was enacted by Congress (approved September 3rd, 1916) in the brief period of a few days. The threatened strike was averted, but in the hasty proceedings leading to its enactment, the principle of arbitration, as the paramount and equitable method of settling labor disputes, was sacrificed, not in the public interest, nor for the benefit of a majority of railroad employes, but for a group of men constituting only a small percentage of the total number, and no action was taken by Congress to prevent or settle future strikes.

This law provided that beginning January 1st, 1917, eight hours shall in contracts for labor and service be deemed a day's work and the measure or standard of a day's work for the purpose of reckoning compensation of employes engaged in the operation of interstate trains. It established a Commission of three to observe the effects of the law for a period of from six to nine months, and report its findings to the President and Congress; but it also required that, pending the report of the Commission and for thirty days thereafter, the existing standard day's wage should be paid for an eight-hour day, and for overtime the employes should be paid not less than the pro rata rate for such standard eight-hour day. While wages were increased by its provisions, there was apparently nothing to prevent an employe working more or less than eight hours per day. The Management of the Company, being unable to satisfactorily interpret the provisions of the law, and having grave doubts as to its constitutionality, instituted proceedings to test its validity in the Federal Courts, but the law was later held to be constitutional by the Supreme Court of the United States.

NEWLANDS COMMITTEE ON RAILROAD REGULATION

In accordance with the recommendation of the President of the United States, a Joint Congressional Committee was appointed, pursuant to a resolution of the House and Senate approved July 20th, 1916 (known as the Newlands Committee), to investigate, so far as the railroads were concerned, the efficiency of the existing system of public regulation in protecting the rights of shippers and carriers, and promoting the public interest. The Chief Executives of a number of important railroad companies submitted evidence to show that the system of Federal and State regulation under which the railroads were then conducting their business was inconsistent, confusing and wasteful, and requested consideration of a program which, in substance, covered:—

1. Federal supervision of the issue of railroad securities;
2. Federal incorporation of interstate railroads;
3. Exclusive Federal regulation of rates;
4. A regional and functional division of the work of the Interstate Commerce Commission;

5. Restricting rate suspensions by the Commission to not more than 60 days;

6. Giving the Interstate Commerce Commission the power to prescribe minimum as well as maximum rates.

The Management stated that a serious responsibility rested upon this Congressional Committee to make a thorough, prompt and impartial investigation of the entire transportation problem; that the aim of constructive legislation should be to allow the railroads to conduct the transportation service under such conditions as would preserve their credit, so that they could at all times carry the commerce of the Country efficiently and economically; that new legislation should be recommended to replace the then existing conflicting regulation, insure reasonable rates and adequate service to the public, and permit the railroads to earn a fair return on the capital invested in their properties.

CONSOLIDATION FORMING THE PHILADELPHIA, BALTIMORE & WASHINGTON RAILROAD COMPANY

Effective September 15th, 1916, the Columbia and Port Deposit Railway Company, the Philadelphia & Baltimore Central Railroad Company, the Elkton & Middletown Railroad Company of Cecil County, and Philadelphia, Baltimore & Washington Railroad Company were consolidated and merged so as to form The Philadelphia, Baltimore & Washington Railroad Company. Practically all of the Capital Stock of the latter Company was owned by the Pennsylvania Railroad Company.

PENNSYLVANIA HOTEL PROJECT

During the year 1916 the Pennsylvania Terminal Real Estate Company, the owner of the valuable property fronting on Seventh Avenue between 32nd and 33rd Streets (opposite Pennsylvania Station) in New York City, contracted, with the approval of the Pennsylvania Railroad Company, which owns all its Stock, for the construction of a 2,000 room hotel thereon, at a cost of approximately

$9,500,000., exclusive of the land, and arrangements were made for the furnishing and operation of the hotel by an experienced and responsible lessee at a satisfactory rental. The Pennsylvania Railroad Company, it was stated, would have preferred to sell the property for development by others, but it had been unable to do so at a satisfactory price for a number of years. It was, therefore, deemed advisable to improve the property and the funds necessary to construct the hotel were to be advanced by the Pennsylvania Railroad Company to the Real Estate Company, to be repaid by the latter company through a mortgage on its property if that course were found desirable.

PITTSBURGH, CINCINNATI, CHICAGO & ST. LOUIS *RAILROAD* COMPANY FORMED

Effective December 31st, 1916, the Pittsburgh, Cincinnati, Chicago & St. Louis Railway, Vandalia Railroad, Chicago, Indiana & Eastern Railway, Pittsburgh, Wheeling & Kentucky Railroad, and the Anderson Belt Railway Companies were consolidated to form a new corporation under the title of The Pittsburgh, Cincinnati, Chicago & St. Louis *Railroad* Company. The new company assumed the lease of the Little Miami Railroad to The Pittsburgh, Cincinnati, Chicago & St. Louis Railway Company; also the lease of the Terre Haute & Peoria Railroad to the Vandalia Railroad Company.

PROPOSED EXTENSION TO DETROIT

The project of extending the Pennsylvania Railroad System from the City of Toledo into the City of Detroit had been under consideration for some years, but the unprecedented development of that district had been such as to make it essential to promptly undertake the construction of this extension. For that purpose, the Pennsylvania-Detroit Railroad Company had been incorporated on February 27th, 1917, to which the Pennsylvania Company had advanced $2,754,473., it being the owner of the entire Capital Stock of the newly created Company. The necessary contracts were made for a joint and equal use of a portion of the Pere Marquette Railway as part of this extension, and also the right of joint and equal use of facilities furnished by the Wabash Railway and the Pere Marquette Railway at Detroit, these companies being granted similar rights of joint and equal use of facilities to be provided by the Pennsylvania Railroad. This was done so that by a moderate expenditure the Pennsylvania Railroad would be enabled to operate its own passenger and freight trains to and from the City of Detroit, and also join with the existing Companies in providing increased facilities and improved service for the public. The purchase of necessary right of way and real estate for main tracks, yards and terminal freight station purposes was completed to a large extent, and construction work was commenced in 1917 on various parts of the project.

ACQUIRING LONG ISLAND RAILROAD COMPANY MINORITY STOCK

On February 13th, 1917, the Pennsylvania Railroad Company, as a majority stockholder of the Long Island Railroad Company, and with the view of obtaining the shares which it did not then hold, amounting at par to $5,202,100., offered the minority holders for their Stock a like amount of 5% Twenty Year Debenture Bonds of the Long Island Railroad Company, dated May 1st, 1917, and maturing May 1st, 1937. The Pennsylvania Railroad Company had received these Debenture Bonds in part payment for surrendering $26,500,000. of 4% Debenture Certificates and in settlement of advances amounting to $812,350., a total of $27,312,350.; it also agreed to accept $22,110,250. additional Common Stock of the Long Island Railroad Company, at par, for the balance of this indebtedness. By this action the fixed charges of the Long Island Railroad Company were reduced more than $800,000., and its credit improved to that extent.

OPENING OF NEW YORK CONNECTING RAILROAD

On March 9th, 1917, the first passenger train was operated over the New York Connecting Railroad between

Pennsylvania Station, New York City, and a connection with the New York, New Haven & Hartford Railroad near Port Morris in that City. The dedicating ceremonies, in which the Directors and Officers of the Pennsylvania and New Haven Systems participated, marked the completion of the most important part of that road, viz: The Hell Gate Bridge over the East River, which has a span of 1,000 feet. The top of the arch of the bridge is 310 feet and the bridge floor 140 feet above high water, while the towers on each side of the bridge are 250 feet high. It is a four-track bridge, which, with the viaduct approaches, is three miles in length, the whole road being nearly 9 miles long. Mr. Gustav Lindenthal, the Chief Engineer and Designer of the bridge, formally turned the bridge and railroad over to Mr. Rea, as President of the New York Connecting Railroad Company, on the above date with the following remarks:—

> "Acting under your authority, the engineers have finished the work on this bridge and railroad, and in its design of rugged strength and beauty, have endeavored to express the stability of the two great railroad systems that are its sponsors.
>
> I now ask you to accept it for public use."

In accepting the property from the hands of Mr. Lindenthal, Mr. Rea said:—

> "The New York Connecting Railroad Company was incorporated a quarter of a century ago, and its Railroad and Bridge have taken four years to construct. It exemplifies great engineering skill in its design and construction, and has cost over $27,000,000. of money, provided by the public on the guarantee of the Pennsylvania and New Haven Systems.
>
> I congratulate the Chief Engineer and Designer, Gustav Lindenthal, and the other engineers connected with this work, upon the completion of one of the notable projects of the world.
>
> This railroad, with its East River bridge, on which we stand, is transferred to the New York, New Haven & Hartford Railroad Company, for operation as part of its System, to replace the river service over the Hudson

and East Rivers. It completes the direct rail connection, via New York City, between the Pennsylvania and New Haven Systems, and between the New England States and the States lying West and South of the Hudson and East Rivers.

Informally, and yet with a deep sense of the increased obligation and responsibility of this act to the owners, the Management and the Officers of the Pennsylvania and New Haven Systems, it is my duty and pleasure to dedicate this Railroad and Bridge to the transportation service of the country.

May it prove a further link to bind our citizens and the railroad systems in closer ties of friendship, and bring increased unity of effort and service in promoting the best interest of our country, and insure greater prosperity and happiness to us all."

The road was accepted by the officers of the New York, New Haven & Hartford Railroad Company to operate on behalf of both Companies. The portion of the main line from Hell Gate Bridge to a connection with the Long Island Railroad near Fresh Pond Junction, to be used chiefly for freight traffic, was not expected to be completed until the close of 1917.

HARRISBURG, PORTSMOUTH, MT. JOY & LANCASTER RAILROAD ACQUIRED

Effective April 25th, 1917, the Pennsylvania Railroad Company acquired the Harrisburg, Portsmouth, Mt. Joy & Lancaster Railroad, which extended from Harrisburg to Dillerville, and from Royalton to Columbia, all in the State of Pennsylvania, a distance of approximately 52½ miles. This road was one of the original links in the Main Line of the Pennsylvania Railroad from Philadelphia to Pittsburgh, and was built some years before the latter road was constructed. It had been controlled through Stock ownership and lease for many years by the Pennsylvania Railroad Company.

SALE OF GENERAL MORTGAGE BONDS

The funded debt of the Pennsylvania Railroad Company was increased by the issue and sale in April, 1917, of $60,000,000. additional of its General Mortgage 4½% Bonds, Series "A," dated June 1st, 1915, and maturing June 1st, 1965. The proceeds were used largely for capital expenditures, the great industrial activity, due to War conditions, making it necessary to provide additional equipment, tracks, larger yards and terminals, and other facilities.

ACQUISITION OF GRAIN ELEVATORS, ETC., PHILADELPHIA AND BALTIMORE

During the year 1917, the Pennsylvania Railroad Company acquired, and operated, the grain elevator, piers, tracks and other property of the Girard Point Storage Company in Philadelphia. It also, as Lessee of the Northern Central Railway Company, assumed the operation of grain elevators in Baltimore, formerly operated by the Central Elevator Company of Baltimore City. Both of these subsidiary companies were later dissolved.

SALE OF ANTHRACITE COAL PROPERTIES

The Susquehanna Coal Company, all of the Capital Stock of which was owned by the Pennsylvania Railroad Company, disposed of its mining properties to the Susquehanna Collieries Company in 1917, and discontinued mining and selling coal. The remaining assets were to be disposed of and the Company gradually liquidated. The Pennsylvania Railroad Company received $9,315,000. of 5% bonds of the Susquehanna Collieries Company, in exchange for a like amount of other obligations of the Susquehanna Coal Company, which bonds will eventually be retired through Sinking Fund provisions.

RESTORING IMPROVEMENT EXPENDITURES TO ROAD AND EQUIPMENT ACCOUNTS

To give a more complete record of expenditures on the Pennsylvania Railroad, and also to be in accord with the accounting requirements of the Interstate Commerce Commission, the improvements made on the property and charged to Income or Profit & Loss between January 1st, 1887, and June 30th, 1907, amounting to $128,907,201., were during the year 1917 restored to the Road and Equipment Accounts in the General Balance Sheet. The off-setting entries on the liability side of the General Balance Sheet were shown under "Accrued Depreciation" and "Additions to Property through Income and Surplus." Such expenditures subsequent to June 30th, 1907, had been included in the Road and Equipment Accounts.

THE RAILROADS IN THE WORLD WAR

The railroads of the United States occupied such a prominent place in the great World War that extensive references are made in the Annual Reports to the important events which took place in the year 1917, when the United States entered the conflict, and the following year when the railroads were taken over for operation by the Government.

THE RAILROADS' WAR BOARD

It was on April 6th, 1917, that the United States declared War on Germany. Five days later, on April 11th, 1917, the Chief Executives of most of the important railways of the Country assembled in Washington, and by voluntary action pledged themselves with the Federal and State Governments, and with each other, that during the War they would merge their individual competitive activities, co-ordinate their operations and operate their properties as a continental railway system, so as to produce the maximum of national transportation efficiency.

For this purpose an Executive Committee on National Defense of the American Railway Association was appointed, consisting of Fairfax Harrison (Chairman), President, Southern Railway Company; Samuel Rea, then President, Pennsylvania Railroad Company; Howard Elliott, Chairman, Executive Committee, Northern Pacific Railway Company; the late J. Kruttschnitt, Chairman, Executive Committee, Southern Pacific Company, and Hale Holden, President, Chicago, Burlington & Quincy Railroad Company. In addition, Daniel Willard, President, Baltimore & Ohio Railroad Company, who was a member of the Council of National Defense, and Hon. E. E. Clark, a member of the Interstate Commerce Commission, were ex-officio members of this Executive Committee, which became generally known as the "Railroads' War Board."

In this manner over $17,500,000,000. of railroad property, represented by 260,000 miles of railroad with their terminals and facilities; 2,500,000 freight cars; 56,000 passenger cars; and over 66,000 locomotives; operated by over 1,750,000 officers and employes were, with their experienced managements, unitedly placed at the service of the Government, and through various Departments and Committees co-ordinating with the Governmental Departments, all the railroads of the Country were in effect united to carry out the instructions of the Railroads' War Board.

CURTAILING THROUGH PASSENGER SERVICE

Subsequently when traffic became so congested in the Fall of 1917, President Rea notified the Railroads' War Board that the Pennsylvania Railroad Company was ready and willing to curtail its through passenger train service to any extent deemed desirable by the Board, so as to permit of a more expeditious movement of freight traffic. As a result a number of through trains were withdrawn from service, among which was the popular "Broadway Limited." It was taken off the schedule on December 1st, 1917, and not restored until May 25th, 1919.

OPERATING UNDER DIFFICULTIES

The Annual Report for 1917 points out that the transportation service rendered under the direction of the War Board by the railroads, with the co-operation of the public, was so extensive that the Country should feel gratified at the results obtained in the face of serious difficulties. Over 2,000,000 troops were moved; many cantonments, which were really military cities, were constructed; new mines were opened; new shipbuilding plants and industries of all kinds were established all over the Country; and the existing industries, plants, and mines, were greatly enlarged, so that the United States and its Allies could be furnished with large quantities of equipment, materials, supplies and munitions to meet the most destructive conditions of War the world had ever known. The Pennsylvania Railroad System, serving the largest centers of population and industry east of the Mississippi River, and the chief sources of coal, coke, iron and steel, and reaching the Atlantic Ports and the Great Lakes, was called upon to carry an unprecedented freight, passenger, mail and express traffic. It was impossible to properly accommodate and co-ordinate the very heavily increased flow of traffic for home and foreign consumption, and, naturally, congestion followed. The situation was made worse by the precedence given to various kinds of traffic to facilitate Government work required at home and abroad; by continued severe winter weather; by insufficient motive power and other equipment due to manufacturing priority granted to the Government for the Allied Nations; and the loss of thousands of trained men, who entered the Government service, or went into other occupations because of higher wages, and had to be replaced by a large number of inexperienced men. So large was the labor turn-over, it was estimated that during 1917 approximately 278,000 persons were employed from all parts of the Country and distributed over the Pennsylvania Railroad System. The employment and training of these men were costly, and seriously hampered operations, because many of them remained only a short time in the service.

REPORT OF INTERSTATE COMMERCE COMMISSION

This was the situation as the year 1917 drew to a close, and with constant public pressure for a greater output of transportation, the Interstate Commerce Commission on December 5th, 1917, transmitted a special report to Congress outlining the necessity for further unification of railroad operations during the War period as indispensable to the National defense and welfare. The Commission indicated alternative methods for accomplishing this unification, namely, through operation as a unit by the carriers themselves, relieved from embarrassing restrictions of certain State and Federal Laws, or through unified operation by the Government under which the President of the United States, under the Act of August 29th, 1916, should take over the railroads as a War measure, and guarantee an adequate compensation to their owners.

PRESIDENT REA URGES CONSTRUCTIVE ACTION

Several weeks after the Commission had submitted its report, the Government announced its policy with respect to the railroads. In the meantime, however, the President of the Company, in an effort to secure some constructive Governmental action that would restore confidence in railroad securities, which had suffered from the depressing effects of steadily declining net earnings, addressed the following letter to the President of the United States under date of December 20th, 1917:—

"Dear Mr. President:—

The Nation is in a financial depression, leading to a crisis. Let us not stop to discuss the cause, but instantly try to restore confidence. Railroad securities have been favorites for the investments of savings banks, insurance companies and estates, as well as individuals, but since regulation has for the time broken down, the uncertainty respecting their financial status has caused people to sacrifice their holdings, and the reserves of their financial institutions are greatly reduced. Over 97,000 stockholders own the entire $500,000,000. of Pennsylvania Railroad Company stock, all full paid in cash and considerable of it at a premium. One-half of these are women, and thousands of them largely dependent on their dividends for their living. You can imagine their fears. They feel the high cost of living for themselves. Many of them know of the reduced net earnings of the railroads, and that the latter, instead of being accorded adequate rates to earn a reasonable return, are the subject of recommendations, which are now unnecessarily making speculations of the soundest railroad investments. The price of Pennsylvania Railroad stock is the lowest in 40 years, when the property was being destroyed by rioters.

This Company and 122,000 of its employes subscribed over $20,000,000. to the last Liberty Loan. We are now solidly supporting the War Savings Certificates. But how much can they and other railroad investors, with values seriously reduced, subscribe for the next loan, which must be imminent and in much larger amount?

Therefore, unless the credit of the railroads is strengthened, the credit of the Nation will be impaired. Appreciation of the railroads in this War has been expressed by unbiased authorities, including the Interstate Commerce Commission and the Secretary of War. If you could publicly indicate that you have the matter under consideration, and that the railroad employes and the security holders would be protected, and the former aided and supported in their great War work for the Nation, I can assure you it would restore confidence, and prevent what may become a panic, and impair the usefulness of many railroads to the Government.

I respectfully request you to consider the suggestion.

Yours respectfully,

SAMUEL REA,
President."

To Hon. Woodrow Wilson,
President of the United States,
Washington, D. C.

to which he received the following reply:—

"The White House
Washington

20th December, 1917.

My dear Mr. Rea:

The matter referred to in your letter of today, which has just been handed to me, has been giving me, you may be sure, a great deal of very serious and anxious thought. I am obliged to you for your suggestion and can assure you that I shall presently attempt to do something to steady the situation.

Cordially and sincerely yours,

WOODROW WILSON"

Mr. Samuel Rea, President,
Pennsylvania Railroad Company,
Philadelphia, Pennsylvania.

GOVERNMENT TAKES OVER OPERATIONS

It was apparent that the situation required constructive action on the part of the Government, and, therefore, the President of the United States, on December 26th, 1917, issued a Proclamation taking over the railroads as a War measure on December 28th, 1917, but effective from an accounting standpoint on January 1st, 1918. As this action was of far-reaching importance in its effect on the American railroads, the Proclamation is quoted in full, together with the accompanying statement issued by the President at the same time:—

"BY THE PRESIDENT OF THE UNITED STATES OF AMERICA.

A PROCLAMATION.

Whereas the Congress of the United States, in the exercise of the constitutional authority vested in them, by joint resolution of the Senate and House of Representatives bearing date April 6, 1917, *resolved:*

'That the state of war between the United States and the Imperial German Government which has thus been thrust upon the United States is hereby formally declared; and that the President be, and he is hereby authorized and directed to employ the entire naval and military forces of the United States and the resources of the Government to carry on war against the Imperial German Government; and to bring the conflict to a successful termination all of the resources of the country are hereby pledged by the Congress of the United States.'

And by joint resolution bearing date of December 7, 1917, *resolved:*

'That a state of war is hereby declared to exist between the United States of America and the Imperial and Royal Austro-Hungarian Government; and that the President be, and he is hereby authorized and directed to employ the entire naval and military forces of the United States and the resources of the Government to carry on war against the Imperial and Royal Austro-Hungarian Government; and to bring the conflict to a successful termination all the resources of the Country are hereby pledged by the Congress of the United States.'

And whereas it is provided by section 1 of the act approved August 29, 1916, entitled 'An act making appropriations for the support of the Army for the fiscal year ending June 30, 1917, and for other purposes,' as follows:

'The President in time of war is empowered, through the Secretary of War, to take possession and assume control of any system or systems of transportation, or any part thereof, and to utilize the same, to the exclusion, as far as may be necessary, of all other traffic thereon, for the transfer or transportation of troops, war material, and equipment, or for such other purposes connected with the emergency as may be needful or desirable.'

And whereas it has become necessary in the national defense to take possession and assume control of certain systems of transportation and to utilize the same, to the exclusion, as far as may be necessary, of other than war traffic thereon, for the transportation of troops, war material, and equipment therefor, and for other needful and desirable purposes connected with the prosecution of the war;

Now, therefore, I, Woodrow Wilson, President of the United States, under and by virtue of the powers vested in me by the foregoing resolutions and statute, and by virtue of all other powers thereto me enabling, do hereby, through Newton D. Baker, Secretary of War, take possession and assume control at 12 o'clock noon on the 28th day of December, 1917, of each and every system of transportation and the appurtenances thereof located wholly or in part within the boundaries of the continental United States and consisting of railroads and owned or controlled systems of coastwise and inland transportation engaged in general transportation, whether operated by steam or by electric power, including also terminals, terminal companies, and terminal associations, sleeping and parlor cars, private cars and private car lines, elevators, warehouses, telegraph and telephone lines, and all other equipment and appurtenances commonly used upon or operated as a part of such rail or combined rail-and-water systems of transportation; to the end that such systems of transportation be utilized for the transfer and transportation of troops, war material, and equipment, to the exclusion so far as may be necessary of all other traffic thereon; and that so far as such exclusive use be not necessary or desirable such systems of transportation be operated and utilized in the performance of such other services as the national interest may require and of the usual and ordinary business and duties of common carriers.

It is hereby directed that the possession, control, operation, and utilization of such transportation systems, hereby by me undertaken, shall be exercised by and through William G. McAdoo, who is hereby appointed and designated Director General of Railroads. Said director may perform the duties imposed upon him, so long and to such extent as he shall determine, through the boards of directors, receivers, officers, and employes of said systems of transportation. Until and except so far as said director shall from time to time by general or special orders otherwise provide, the boards of directors, receivers, officers, and employes of the various transportation systems shall continue the operation thereof in the usual and ordinary course of the business of common carriers, in the names of their respective companies.

Until and except so far as said director shall from time to time otherwise by general or special orders determine, such systems of transportation shall remain subject to all existing statutes and orders of the Interstate Commerce Commission and to all statutes and orders of regulating commissions of the various States in which said systems or any part thereof may be situated. But any orders, general or special, hereafter made by said director shall have paramount authority and be obeyed as such.

Nothing herein shall be construed as now affecting the possession, operation, and control of street electric passenger railways, including railways commonly called interurbans, whether such railways be or be not owned or controlled by such railroad companies or systems. By subsequent order and proclamation, if and when it shall be found necessary or desirable, possession, control, or operation may be taken of all or any part of such street railway systems, including subways and tunnels; and by subsequent order and proclamation possession, control and operation in whole or in part may also be relinquished to the owners thereof of any part of the railroad systems or rail and water systems, possession and control of which are hereby assumed.

The director shall, as soon as may be after having assumed such possession and control, enter upon negotiations with the several companies looking to agreements for just and reasonable compensation for the possession, use, and control of their respective properties on the basis of an annual guaranteed compensation above accruing depreciation and the maintenance of their properties equivalent, as nearly as may be, to the average of the net operating income thereof for the three-year period ending June 30, 1917, the results of such negotiations to be reported to me for such action as may be appropriate and lawful.

But nothing herein contained, expressed or implied, or hereafter done or suffered hereunder, shall be deemed in any way to impair the rights of the stockholders, bondholders, creditors, and other persons having interests in said systems of transportation or in the profits thereof to receive just and adequate compensation for the use and control and operation of their property hereby assumed.

Regular dividends hitherto declared and maturing interest upon bonds, debentures, and other obligations may be paid in due course; and such regular dividends and interest may continue to be paid until and unless the said director shall from time to time otherwise by general or special orders determine; and, subject to the approval of the director, the various carriers may agree upon and arrange for the renewal and extension of maturing obligations.

Except with the prior written assent of said director, no attachment by mesne process or on execution shall be levied on or against any of the property used by any of said transportation systems in the conduct of their business as common carriers; but suits may be brought by and against said carriers and judgments rendered as hitherto until and except so far as said director may, by general or special orders, otherwise determine.

From and after 12 o'clock on said 28th day of December, 1917, all transportation systems included in this order and proclamation shall conclusively be deemed within the possession and control of said director without further act or notice. But for the purpose of accounting said possession and control shall date from 12 o'clock midnight on December 31, 1917.

In witness whereof I have hereunto set my hand and caused the seal of the United States to be affixed.

Done by the President, through Newton D. Baker, Secretary of War, in the District of Columbia, this 26th day of December, in the year of our Lord one thousand nine hundred and seventeen, and of the independence of the United States the one hundred and forty-second.

WOODROW WILSON.

By the President:

Robert Lansing,
Secretary of State.

Newton D. Baker,
Secretary of War."

"STATEMENT OF THE PRESIDENT.

I have exercised the powers over the transportation systems of the country which were granted me by the Act of Congress of last August because it has become imperatively necessary for me to do so. This is a war of resources no less than of men, perhaps even more than of men, and it is necessary for the complete mobilization of our resources that the transportation systems of the country should be organized and employed under a single authority and a simplified method of coordination which have not proved possible under private management and control. The Committee of railway executives who have been cooperating with the Government in this all-important matter have done the utmost that it was possible for them to do; have done it with patriotic zeal and with great ability; but there were difficulties that they could neither escape nor neutralize. Complete unity of administration in the present circumstances involves upon occasion and at many points a serious dislocation of earnings, and the committee was, of course, without power or authority to rearrange charges or effect proper compensations and adjustments of earnings. Several roads which were willingly and with admirable public spirit accepting the orders of the committee have already suffered from these circumstances and should not be required to suffer further. In mere fairness to them the full authority of the Government must be substituted. The Government itself will thereby gain an immense increase of efficiency in the conduct of the war and of the innumerable activities upon which its successful conduct depends.

The public interest must be first served and, in addition, the financial interests of the Government and the financial interests of the railways must be brought under a common direction. The financial operations of the railways need not then interfere with the borrowings of the Government, and they themselves can be conducted at a greater advantage. Investors in railway securities may rest assured that their rights and interests will be as scrupulously looked after by the Government as they could be by the directors of the several railway systems. Immediately upon the reassembling of Congress I shall recommend that these definite guarantees be given: First, of course, that the railway properties will be maintained during the period of Federal control in as good repair and as complete equipment as when taken over by the Government; and, second, that the roads shall receive a net operating income equal in each case to the average net income of the three years preceding June 30, 1917; and I am entirely confident that the Congress will be disposed in this case, as in others, to see that justice is done and full security assured to the owners and creditors of the great systems which the Government must now use under its own direction or else suffer serious embarrassment.

The Secretary of War and I are agreed that, all the circumstances being taken into consideration, the best results can be obtained under the immediate executive direction of the Hon. William G. McAdoo, whose practical experience peculiarly fits him for the service and whose authority as Secretary of the Treasury will enable him to coordinate as no other man could the many financial interests which will be involved and which might, unless systematically directed, suffer very embarrassing entanglements.

The Government of the United States is the only great Government now engaged in the war which has not already assumed control of this sort. It was thought to be in the spirit of American institutions to attempt to do everything that was necessary through private management, and if zeal and ability and patriotic motive could have accomplished the necessary unification of administration it would certainly have been accomplished; but no zeal or ability could overcome insuperable obstacles, and I have deemed it my duty to recognize that fact in all candor, now that it is demonstrated, and to use without reserve the great authority reposed in me. A great national necessity dictated the action, and I was therefore not at liberty to abstain from it.

WOODROW WILSON."

RAILROADS TAKEN OVER AND DIVIDED INTO OPERATING REGIONS

The railroads were, therefore, taken over by the Government at noon on December 28th, 1917, and Hon. William G. McAdoo was appointed Director General of Railroads. They were divided into Operating Regions, the Pennsylvania Railroad System up to June 1st, 1918, being included in the Eastern Region, but on that date the number of Regions was increased and the Pennsylvania Railroad Lines East of Pittsburgh, were, for operating purposes, included in the Allegheny Region. Those West of Pittsburgh remained in the Eastern Region until December 1st, 1918, when the entire Pennsylvania Railroad System was placed in the Allegheny Region. Mr. C. H. Markham, who had been President of the Illinois Central System prior to Federal Control, was appointed Regional Director of the Allegheny Region, effective June 1st, 1918.

SEPARATION OF OPERATING AND CORPORATE RELATIONS

Shortly after his appointment, Director General McAdoo issued instructions that all railroad officers and employes were to perform their customary duties, which seemed to contemplate the same plan adopted in England for the operation of their railroads during the War. This arrangement, however, continued only until June 1st, 1918, at which time Federal Managers were appointed by the United States Railroad Administration to operate the railroads, thus relieving the executive heads from this duty. The responsibility of the Federal Managers was made directly to the Regional Directors and not to the Boards of Directors of the railroad companies owning the properties. Under this policy, the Regional Directors and Federal Managers were required to sever their official relations with their respective companies, and become exclusive representatives of the Railroad Administration. This meant that officers of the Pennsylvania Railroad System performing transportation duties could act in no capacity whatever for the corporation, which necessitated the appointment of separate officers to protect the corporate interests. The Director General of Railroads also issued instructions that all expenses incident to the maintenance and preservation of the corporation and its offices and official staff were to be paid by the corporation without any allowance in its standard compensation to cover such expenses.

While relieved of the duty of operating their properties, the corporate management had the important responsibility of negotiating contracts with the Government for their use, and to see that the agreements were carried out, especially with respect to the maintenance, renewal and replacement of the railroad facilities and equipment; also to pass upon, and assume the financial responsibility for, the huge capital expenditures recommended by the Federal Railroad Administration, and generally to see that their properties were returned in substantially as good repair and complete equipment as when taken over by the Government.

With a centralized authority in Washington directing the operations of the railroads entirely independent of their owners, and issuing orders, which, in the judgment of those representing the owners, did not always fully recognize their rights, there were possibilities of constant differences of opinion and controversy. However, the cordial relations which Regional Director Markham at once established and continued were of material assistance not only to the Government, but to the Corporate Officers during Federal Control.

USE OF PENNSYLVANIA STATION, NEW YORK, BY OTHER ROADS

At the close of 1917, President Rea had voluntarily tendered the use of Pennsylvania Station, New York City, to all of the lines terminating on the New Jersey side of the Hudson River. This action was taken so as to provide, if found desirable, for enlarged use of the terminals of these roads for freight traffic, and thus tend to relieve the congestion in the New York Harbor District. As a result, the Baltimore & Ohio Railroad began to use Pennsylvania Station for its through passenger traffic on April 28th, 1918, which terminated on September 1st, 1926. The Lehigh Valley Railroad also took advantage of this offer, and it began using the Station for its through passenger trains on September 15th, 1918, under a ten year contract.

COMPENSATION UNDER FEDERAL CONTROL CONTRACTS

Under the Federal Control Act, which was approved on March 21st, 1918, the President of the United States was authorized to enter into contracts with the Companies owning the railroads, for their possession and use, including maintenance and up-keep, during the period of Federal Control; also for the determination of the rights and obligations of the parties to the agreements arising out of Federal Control, including the just and reasonable compensation to be received, which was to be equivalent, as nearly as may be, to the average of the Net Railway Operating Income earned by the railroads for the three-year period ending June 30th, 1917. On March 29th, 1918, the President, by a Proclamation, authorized the Director General of Railroads, either personally or through his representative, to agree with the carriers upon the amount of compensation to be paid to each of them, but which was to be first certified to by the Interstate Commerce Commission. The policy of the Federal Railroad Administration was to have a standard form of contract, but it was not until December 31st, 1918, that the agreement between the Director General of Railroads and the Pennsylvania Railroad Company was executed. This agreement covered a number of other Companies in its System, while separate contracts were also executed for some of its affiliated lines, the total compensation to be paid annually to each being as follows:—

		Standard Compensation Per Annum
Pennsylvania Railroad Company—Eastern Lines......		$49,598,874.08
Pennsylvania Railroad Company—Western Lines......		15,207,217.88
Baltimore, Chesapeake & Atlantic Railway Company..		71,320.73
Baltimore & Sparrows Point Railroad Company.......		55,520.12
Barnegat Railroad Company........................	Dr.	8,888.76
Cincinnati, Lebanon & Northern Railway Company....		116,422.56
Connecting Terminal Railroad Company..............		58,038.45
Cumberland Valley Railroad Company................		1,243,120.04
Grand Rapids & Indiana Railway Company...........		909,274.57
Long Island Railroad Company......................		3,258,000.00
Louisville Bridge and Terminal Railway Company.....		132,739.74
Manufacturers Railway Company.....................	Dr.	38,504.21
Maryland, Delaware & Virginia Railway Company.....		42,536.22
New York, Philadelphia & Norfolk Railroad Company.		996,050.76
Ohio River & Western Railway Company.............	Dr.	17,967.18
Philadelphia & Beach Haven Railroad Company.......	Dr.	22,905.36
Philadelphia & Camden Ferry Company..............		401,556.86
Pittsburgh, Cincinnati, Chicago & St. Louis Railroad Company..		11,256,340.10
Rosslyn Connecting Railroad Company..............	Dr.	6,598.83
Union Railroad Company of Baltimore...............		1,387,766.97
West Jersey & Seashore Railroad Company...........		952,878.22
Wheeling Terminal Railway Company................		111,195.80
Total for entire Pennsylvania Railroad System....		$85,703,988.76

LESSONS FROM THE WAR

The close of the War came with the announcement of the Armistice on November 11th, 1918, and the Annual Report for that year points out that one of the outstanding facts developed during the War was the absolute dependence of the Country upon the great transportation systems, especially the Eastern Railroads, which reach the chief sources of raw and manufactured materials required for the conduct of the War. Federal Control likewise forcefully demonstrated that the Government could not operate the railroads to the best advantage without freedom from the restrictive and confusing Federal and State regulations and laws, which theretofore had prevented the railroads from co-operating with each other to the fullest extent to produce the most efficient and economic transportation. Furthermore, the Federal Government found it was not possible to operate the railroads and meet the increased cost of material and labor, and higher taxes and expenses of all kinds, without substantial increases in transportation charges.

SUPPORTING THE GOVERNMENT

The Management of the Pennsylvania Railroad Company most earnestly supported the Government in all measures essential to win the War. Large capital expenditures were made to increase the transportation facilities; officers and employes of the Pennsylvania Railroad System numbering 26,286 entered the National service, of whom 443 died while on active duty, and it not only co-operated in every action and order issued by the Railroads' War Board and the United States Railroad Administration, but gave the assistance and advice of its experienced organization in carrying on the War. It also released a number of its officers for important transportation duties abroad, among whom was Mr. W. W. Atterbury, then Operating Vice-President, who was appointed Director General of Transportation, and later Brigadier General, in charge of transportation service for the American Expeditionary Force in France. Over 700,000 subscriptions to the various Government Bond issues were made by the officers and employes of the Pennsylvania Railroad System, the amount thus subscribed being over $56,000,000., and in addition the various corporations in the System subscribed to over $15,000,000. of these Bonds.

Further, when Congress delayed action on the appropriation of $750,000,000. requested by the Director General of Railroads in 1919, which was necessary for the continued Governmental operation of the railroads during the year, it left the United States Railroad Administration temporarily without adequate funds; whereupon the Pennsylvania Railroad Company, in order to relieve the embarrassed situation of the industries along its lines, borrowed, on its own credit, $22,000,000. in March, 1919, which it advanced to the Railroad Administration. This was done so that the latter could pay overdue vouchers for expenditures incurred in the Governmental operation of the Pennsylvania Railroad lines, including purchases of fuel, materials and supplies, and expenditures for improvement and betterment work. The money was used exclusively in paying these overdue vouchers and greatly relieved many manufacturers and others doing business on the Pennsylvania Railroad System. The Company was reimbursed through the Government crediting that sum to the amount due it as compensation for the use of its railroad.

LEASE OF PHILADELPHIA, BALTIMORE & WASHINGTON RAILROAD

In order to more closely unite the Philadelphia, Baltimore & Washington Railroad Company with the operations of the Pennsylvania Railroad Company, the former Company was leased to the latter for a term of 999 years from January 1st, 1918, on a rental basis equivalent to the fixed charges, taxes and 6% dividends upon the Capital Stock of the Philadelphia, Baltimore and Washington Railroad Company. Almost all of this Capital Stock is owned by the Pennsylvania Railroad Company, which operates the Main Line of the Lessor Company from Philadelphia to Washington, and the various branch and leased roads, including the lines of the former Chester Creek Railroad Company and Pomeroy & Newark Railroad Company, which the Lessor Company acquired during 1917.

ASSUMING PENNSYLVANIA COMPANY CONTRACTS AND OBLIGATIONS

To effect a closer unity of the interests of the Pennsylvania Lines West of Pittsburgh, the Pennsylvania Railroad Company entered into an agreement to take over the leases and operating contracts of the Pennsylvania Company, and assume its obligations and liabilities to the lines and properties in which it had an interest, effective as of January 1st, 1918. The Pennsylvania Company was created, as before stated, to promote and operate various lines West of Pittsburgh in the general interests of the Pennsylvania Railroad Company, which owns its entire Capital Stock and guarantees the payment of its outstanding Bonds. This further unification was in pursuance of the policy followed of eliminating corporations which were no longer necessary, and at the same time giving these Western Lines the direct strength and credit of the Pennsylvania Railroad Company.

LEASE OF UNION RAILROAD OF BALTIMORE

On April 1st, 1918, the Union Railroad Company of Baltimore, Md., the Capital Stock of which is owned by the Philadelphia, Baltimore & Washington Railroad Company and the Northern Central Railway Company, was leased for 999 years to the Pennsylvania Railroad Company on the basis of guaranteeing payment of 8% dividends upon its Capital Stock. This road connected the lines of the Northern Central Railway and the Philadelphia, Baltimore & Washington Railroad in Baltimore. These two roads had already been leased to the Pennsylvania Railroad Company, and the lease of the Union Railroad Company enabled all three roads to be more closely united with the Lessee Company in their operations, and eliminated the separate accounting for the use of each other's facilities.

ELECTRIFICATION—WEST PHILADELPHIA TO CHESTNUT HILL

The electrification work on the Pennsylvania Railroad from West Philadelphia to Chestnut Hill, a distance of 10.9 miles, was completed and the operation of multiple-unit electric trains started on April 1st, 1918.

ROADS TO CONEWAGO AND BERWICK, PA., ACQUIRED

The Pennsylvania Railroad Company acquired the properties and franchises of the Cornwall & Lebanon Railroad Company, effective April 15th, 1918, and the Susquehanna, Bloomsburg & Berwick Railroad Company on the same date. Both of these small roads connected with its Main Line, the first named extending from Conewago, Pa., to Lebanon, Pa., 26.44 miles, and the second from Watsontown, Pa., to Berwick, Pa., 41.83 miles. As the Pennsylvania

Railroad Company owned all the Capital Stock of both companies, the necessity for maintaining these separate corporations no longer existed.

INDIANAPOLIS & FRANKFORT RAILROAD COMPLETED

In 1918 the Indianapolis & Frankfort Railroad Company, which was owned by the Pennsylvania Company, completed the construction of its line between Ben Davis, Ind., on the St. Louis Division of the Pittsburgh, Cincinnati, Chicago & St. Louis Railroad, to Frankfort, Ind., on the Michigan Division of that road, a distance of 41 miles. It was expected that this new line would afford a more direct route for the movement of the rapidly growing traffic from the bituminous coal region of southern Indiana to Chicago, Ill., and other western points.

PHILADELPHIA, BALTIMORE & WASHINGTON RAILROAD COMPANY ACQUISITIONS

The Philadelphia, Baltimore & Washington Railroad Company acquired on January 3rd, 1919, the Baltimore and Sparrow's Point Railroad Company, a line about 5.43 miles long, which, in connection with the Union Railroad Company of Baltimore, extended the railroad of the Philadelphia, Baltimore & Washington Railroad Company to Sparrow's Point, Md., and the adjacent works of the Bethlehem Steel Company and other industries. The line of the acquired Company, and also the industrial railroad known as the Eddystone & Delaware River Railroad Company, became subject to the lease of the Philadelphia, Baltimore & Washington Railroad to the Pennsylvania Railroad Company.

SALE OF GENERAL MORTGAGE BONDS

On January 15th, 1919, the Pennsylvania Railroad Company sold $50,000,000. of its General Mortgage 5% Bonds, series "B," dated December 1st, 1918, and maturing December 1st, 1968. The proceeds were used to pay for additions and betterments, to meet maturing obligations, and for other proper corporate purposes.

HOTEL PENNSYLVANIA COMPLETED AND LEASED

The construction of the Hotel Pennsylvania, between 32nd and 33rd Streets, fronting on Seventh Avenue, New York City, adjoining Pennsylvania Station and the City's four-track subway, was completed in 1919. The Pennsylvania Terminal Real Estate Company, the Stock of which is all owned by the Pennsylvania Railroad Company, is the owner of the Hotel building. It was opened on January 25th, 1919, and leased for operation to an experienced hotel management. It has satisfactorily fulfilled the purposes for which it was constructed, and has also proven a great convenience to Pennsylvania Railroad passengers and those of other roads which use the Pennsylvania Station.

CUMBERLAND VALLEY RAILROAD ACQUIRED

Effective June 2nd, 1919, the Pennsylvania Railroad Company acquired the Cumberland Valley Railroad which extended from a connection with its road in the City of Harrisburg to the Potomac River, at Powells Bend, Md., a distance, including branches, of about 108 miles. This line also exchanged traffic and connected with the Western Maryland Railway, Baltimore & Ohio Railroad and the Norfolk & Western Railway, at Hagerstown, Md., and with the Baltimore & Ohio Railroad, at Martinsburg, W. Va., and Winchester, Va., through its controlled line the Cumberland Valley & Martinsburg Railroad. The Pennsylvania Railroad Company owned practically all of the Capital Stock of the Cumberland Valley Railroad, which for many years had formed a part of its System.

EQUIPMENT TRUSTS ISSUED TO UNITED STATES RAILROAD ADMINISTRATION

On January 15th, 1920, the Pennsylvania Railroad Company issued to the United States Railroad Administration, at par, $58,412,000. 6% Equipment Trust Certificates in payment for 16,450 freight cars and 165 locomotives which were allocated to it by the Railroad Administration. The Certificates matured at the rate of $3,894,000. annually beginning January 15th, 1921, and ending January 15th, 1935.

TRANSPORTATION ACT OF 1920

The sudden cessation of the War had brought about serious reconstruction questions, and none more important than the future relations and policy of the Government to the railroads which were still under Federal Control. The Railroad Executives, as a result of their long experience and study of this important question, gave exhaustive testimony before Congressional Committees in Washington, which finally resulted in the enactment on February 28th, 1920, of what was known as the "Transportation Act, 1920," the important features of which were: The termination of Federal Control on March 1st, 1920, with a continuance for the six months ending August 31st, 1920, of the Government guarantee of compensation on the same basis as that paid during the Federal Control period under the terms of the Federal Control Act to such carriers as desired this protection; empowering the Interstate Commerce Commission to make such rates so that the carriers as a whole (or as a whole in each of such rate groups or territories as the Commission may designate) will, under honest, efficient and economical management, earn an aggregate annual Net Railway Operating Income equal, as nearly as may be, to a fair return upon the aggregate value, as determined by the Commission, of the railroad property held for and used in the transportation service. It was also provided in this Act that the Commission was to take as such fair return for two years beginning March 1st, 1920, a sum equal to 5½% of such aggregate value, but in its discretion could add thereto one-half of 1% per annum to provide for improvements, betterments and equipment chargeable to Capital Account. If the Net Railway Operating Income of any single carrier, or system, exceeded 6% per annum of the value of the railway property so held and used, one-half of the excess was to be placed in the carrier's reserve fund until it reached 5% of the value of its property, and this fund could be used by the carriers only for the purpose of paying dividends, interest and rents for leased roads to the extent that its Net Railway Operating Income was less than 6% on its property valuation. After the reserve fund amounts to this figure of 5% of the value of the carrier's property, it may be used for any lawful purpose. The remaining one-half of such excess income was annually to be paid to the Interstate Commerce Commission for the purpose of establishing a general railroad contingent fund, to be used by the Commission in furtherance of the public interest in transportation, either in making loans to the carriers, or by purchasing transportation equipment and facilities and leasing same to the railroads.

OTHER PROVISIONS

After March 1st, 1922, the Commission was to determine, and make public, what percentage of such aggregate value constituted a fair return thereon (5¾% was fixed by the Commission, which is the present rate), and in making such determination was required to give due consideration to the transportation needs of the Country, and the necessity for enlarging its facilities to provide adequate transportation. The membership of the Commission was increased from nine to eleven; the compensation of the Commissioners was fixed at $12,000. per annum, and their term of office seven years. The powers of the Commission were also materially enlarged to cover the regulation of rates, security issues, new construction and improvement work, and abandonment of railroad mileage. Provision was also made for the settlement of matters arising out of Federal Control, and the funding of carriers' indebtedness to the United States for ten years at 6% interest. Several far-reaching amendments were made to the Interstate Commerce Act of 1887, including the authority to effect railroad consolidations when approved by the Interstate Commerce Commission, and delegating to the Commission the preparation and adoption of a plan for the consolidation of the railway properties of the Continental United States into a limited number of Systems. The Act also recognized the necessity for temporary loans to railroads, payable within 15 years, and at 6% interest, to enable them to serve the public during the transition period immediately following Federal Control, and an appropriation of $300,000,000. was made for that purpose. Disputes between carriers and their employes as to wages and working conditions were to be dealt with by Railroad Boards of Labor Adjustment established by agreement between the carriers and their employes; and by a Labor Board of nine members appointed by the President of the United States, of which three members were to represent the employes, three the management, and three the public.

REVISING OPERATING ORGANIZATION

In accordance with this legislation, the properties of Companies in the Pennsylvania Railroad System were returned to its Management on March 1st, 1920. However, for the subsequent six months, they (excepting West Jersey & Seashore Railroad Company and Philadelphia & Camden Ferry Company, which did not accept the six months' guaranty of compensation) continued to receive Government compensation on the same basis as that paid during the Federal Control Period, as provided in the Transportation Act. In view of the changed conditions, and the fact that it was not deemed advisable to divide the System at Pittsburgh for operating purposes, the Organization was revised and the System divided into four Operating Regions. The large manufacturing and repair shops of the Company at Altoona were also separated from regular railroad operations and placed under the supervision of one officer to devote his whole time and attention to the manufacture, repair and renewal of equipment and to the motive power and shop problems of the System.

The Eastern Region comprised generally the territory between New York City on the east, Sodus Point on the north, Renovo and Altoona on the west, and Washington and Norfolk on the south; with Headquarters at Philadelphia.

The Central Region comprised generally the territory between Altoona and Renovo on the east, Rochester, Buffalo, Erie, Ashtabula, Cleveland and Lorain on the north, Mansfield, Columbus and Zanesville on the west, and Marietta,

Powhatan, Wheeling, Waynesburg, West Brownsville and Uniontown on the south; with Headquarters at Pittsburgh, Pa.

The Northwestern Region comprised generally the territory between Sandusky and Mansfield on the east, Mackinaw City on the north, Chicago and Effner on the west, and Columbus, Bradford and Logansport on the south; with Headquarters at Chicago, Ill.

The Southwestern Region comprised generally the territory between Columbus on the east, Logansport and Adams on the north, Peoria and St. Louis on the west, and Vincennes, Louisville and Cincinnati on the south, including the line from Trinway to Cincinnati; with Headquarters at St. Louis, Mo.

SALE OF $50,000,000. 7% BONDS

The Pennsylvania Railroad Company, in May, 1920, sold $50,000,000. of Ten-Year 7% Secured Gold Bonds, dated April 1st, 1920, and maturing April 1st, 1930. They were secured by the deposit as collateral of $50,000,000. General Mortgage, Series "C," 6% Bonds of the Pennsylvania Railroad Company, dated April 1st, 1920, and maturing April 1st, 1970, and $5,000,000. Philadelphia, Baltimore & Washington Railroad Company General Mortgage, Series "A," 6% Bonds, dated April 1st, 1920, and maturing April 1st, 1960. The Company required about $31,000,000. to meet maturities in that year, and the balance of the proceeds from the sale of these Bonds were needed to provide for its addition and betterment expenditures. A number of reasons made it necessary to sell Bonds bearing a 7% interest rate in 1920, the chief of which were, so far as the railroads were concerned, that 1920 was the year in which they were released from Federal Control and returned to their owners with no final settlement for Federal Control in sight; their physical condition was poor; wages and material costs were still rising even above the War level, and the average price of 40 corporation bonds had fallen from 96.25% in 1917 to 71.96% in May, 1920. The Company also had to compete with large foreign loans and security issues of industrial companies which were paying as high as 8% for capital, and there were also large amounts of Government issues—Federal, State and Municipal, the United States Government itself at the end of 1920 paying as high as 6% interest on a one year loan. This was really the first large railroad financing following the enactment of the Transportation Act, and broke the deadlock which had been existing so far as railroad borrowing was concerned. A long term issue of General Mortgage Bonds could have been sold at a somewhat lower rate, but not sufficiently attractive to warrant their sale.

INCREASED FREIGHT AND PASSENGER RATES

In August, 1920, the Interstate Commerce Commission approved of increases in rates in the Eastern territory amounting to 40% on freight traffic (except that interchanged with roads in other territories on which the increase was 33⅓%); 20% in passenger rates, and an extra charge for passengers carried in Pullman cars equal to about 50% of the usual Pullman transportation charge. Many of the State Commissions also permitted similar increases on intrastate passenger and freight traffic, but others declined which deprived the Company of this additional revenue. The increased revenues derived from the higher rates were, however, offset to a large extent by increases in wages granted to railroad employes which were made retroactive to May 1st, 1920, and by the continuance of the wasteful working rules imposed on the railroads during the period of Federal Control, so that the beneficial effects expected to be secured from the higher rates were not realized. In addition, the railroads had the "outlaw strikes" in April of that year to contend with, which retarded movement of traffic and otherwise interfered with the plans of the Management to recover as quickly as possible from the effects of the Federal Control Period.

EMPLOYES' REPRESENTATION PLAN

The Annual Report for 1920 points out that the Management, in an effort to improve the relations with its employes, had for several months been in conference with them in an effort to arrive at a basis by which, through mutual understandings, future adjustments could be made in the War period working conditions and standards of employment, which would increase efficiency and economy, reduce the extent of non-employment, and provide a method for the settlement of differences without having to resort to interruptions of the transportation service, and the consequent hardship upon the public, the employes and the railroad companies. As a result of these conferences, a Memorandum of Understanding was signed on December 29th, 1920, between the Pennsylvania Railroad System Management and its employes in engine and train service, covering the method to be followed in the handling of various questions in controversy. Similar memoranda were later signed on behalf of employes in other branches of the service, which became known as the Pennsylvania Railroad Employes' Representation Plan.

The essential features of this Plan, as set forth in a pamphlet published by the Company, are:—

The Management deals collectively with the men through employe representatives.

These representatives must be bona fide employes. They are nominated by the employes themselves. They are elected by secret ballot by the votes of the employes.

Every employe, regardless of his membership or non-membership in any organization, is entitled to vote. Every employe, regardless of his membership or non-membership in any organization, is eligible to election.

Any employe can belong to any union he desires. No employe is disqualified to vote, to be nominated, or to be elected because he happens to be a member or officer of any organization.

The Management simply insists upon dealing with the employes themselves through employe representatives and not with representatives of absentee organizations to which they may belong.

Every important question affecting the employes' wages and working conditions is settled by joint action of Management and men.

The highest authority on the railroad in the settlement of any question, whether it is between an individual employe and his immediate supervisory official or between any group of employes and the Management as a whole, is a joint reviewing committee in each of the various departments of the service, equally representative of management and men. In these committees all members are on equal terms and a two-thirds vote is necessary to decide any question.

In order that the questions which inevitably arise in such a large organization may be settled promptly and justly, regular monthly meetings are held between committees of employe representatives and representatives of the management, from the local supervisory official on up through division superintendents, general superintendents, general managers and the reviewing committees.

The whole plan thus enables any individual employe to get a fair hearing and a prompt decision by responsible officers, and if necessary a review and decision by a joint board of officers and duly elected representatives of the employes, which has final authority to dispose of the case without interference or veto by any executive officer of the company.

ACQUIRING MINORITY STOCKS

In 1920, the Pennsylvania Company, which then owned over 75% of the Capital Stock of the Pittsburgh, Cincinnati, Chicago & St. Louis Railroad Company, made an offer to the minority stockholders to exchange their holdings, par for par, for the General Mortgage 5% Bonds of that Company (guaranteed principal and interest by the Pennsylvania Railroad Company) which it held in its Treasury. As a result of this offer, the Pennsylvania Company acquired additional shares of the Capital Stock of the Pittsburgh, Cincinnati, Chicago & St. Louis Railroad Company, and at the close of 1920, owned about 98% of the total outstanding Stock.

In the same year the Pennsylvania Company, which then owned a majority of the Capital Stock of the Grand Rapids & Indiana Railway Company, made an offer to exchange the balance of this Stock owned by the public, par for par, for the Second Mortgage 4% Bonds of that Company which it held in its Treasury. A great many stockholders accepted the offer and it resulted in giving the Pennsylvania Company a 97% ownership in the Capital Stock of the Grand Rapids & Indiana Railway Company.

COMPACTING THE SYSTEM BY LEASES

During the year 1921, the Pennsylvania Railroad continued its policy of compacting the various Companies in the System, so as to secure greater efficiency and economy in operation and administration, and permit the parent company to route traffic and use the terminals and facilities of the subsidiary companies in the interest of the System as a whole without regard to the separate ownership and results to each of these smaller companies. Therefore, leases were executed with the following Companies on the dates and terms shown, all of which were effective from January 1st, 1921:—

The Cincinnati, Lebanon & Northern Railway Company: March 26, 1921;
999 years; 4% dividends on Stock, interest on Bonds and organization expenses.

The Cleveland, Akron & Cincinnati Railway Company: March 26, 1921;
999 years; 4% dividends on Stock, interest on Bonds and organization expenses.

Cumberland Valley & Martinsburg Railroad Company: March 15, 1921;
999 years; 6% dividends on Stock and organization expenses.

The Englewood Connecting Railway Company: March 26, 1921;
999 years; 4% dividends on Stock and organization expenses.

Grand Rapids & Indiana Railway Company: March 26, 1921;
999 years; 4% dividends on Stock, interest on Bonds and organization expenses.

Indianapolis & Frankfort Railroad Company: March 26, 1921;
999 years; 4% dividends on Stock and organization expenses.

Louisville Bridge & Terminal Railway Company: March 26, 1921;
999 years; 4% dividends on Stock and organization expenses.

The New York Bay Railroad Company: April 4, 1921;
949 years; 4% dividends on Stock, interest on Bonds and organization expenses.

New York, Philadelphia & Norfolk Railroad Company: December 14, 1920;
999 years; 12% dividends on Stock, interest on Bonds and organization expenses.
The Ohio Connecting Railway Company: March 26, 1921;
999 years; 4% dividends on Stock, interest on Bonds and organization expenses.
Perth Amboy & Woodbridge Railroad Company: April 4, 1921;
949 years; 6% dividends on Stock and organization expenses.
The Pittsburgh, Cincinnati, Chicago & St. Louis Railroad Company: March 26, 1921;
999 years; 4% dividends on Stock (5% beginning with January 1, 1926), interest on Bonds and organization expenses.
The Pittsburgh, Ohio Valley & Cincinnati Railroad Company: March 26, 1921;
999 years; 4% dividends on Stock, interest on Bonds and organization expenses.
The South Chicago & Southern Railroad Company: March 26, 1921;
999 years; 4% dividends on Stock and organization expenses.
The Toledo, Columbus & Ohio River Railroad Company: March 26, 1921;
999 years; 4% dividends on Stock, interest on Bonds and organization expenses.
The Wheeling Terminal Railway Company: March 26, 1921;
999 years; 4% dividends on Stock, interest on Bonds and organization expenses.

The Stocks of most of these Companies were owned almost entirely by The Pennsylvania Railroad Company or other Companies in the System with which they had been affiliated for many years, and, therefore, that part of the rental covering dividends would be returned to the Companies owning the Stocks of such leased roads.

DATES OF ANNUAL MEETING AND ELECTION CHANGED

At the Annual Meeting of the stockholders held on March 8th, 1921, there was submitted the question of changing the dates of the Annual Meeting from the second Tuesday in March to the second Tuesday in April, and the Annual Election of Directors from the fourth Tuesday of March to the fourth Tuesday of April. This change was necessary because, with the growth of the Company and its many ramifications, it was difficult to close and audit the accounts and furnish financial data and operating and maintenance statistics between the close of the year and the date when the Annual Report must be in printed form for circulation. Therefore, a resolution to make the changes effective was adopted by the stockholders to become effective beginning with the year 1922.

SALE OF $60,000,000. 6½% BONDS

In March, 1921, the Pennsylvania Railroad Company sold $60,000,000. of its 6½% 15-Year Secured Gold Bonds, dated February 1st, 1921, and maturing February 1st, 1936. They were secured by the deposit of $60,000,000. of its General Mortgage, Series "C," 6% Bonds dated April 1st, 1920, and maturing April 1st, 1970, and $6,000,000. of General Mortgage, Series "A," 6% Bonds of the Philadelphia, Baltimore & Washington Railroad Company, dated April 1st, 1920, and maturing April 1st, 1960. The proceeds from the sale of these Bonds were used in part to purchase from the Pennsylvania Company the locomotives, cars and other equipment it owned at an approximate cost of $20,000,000.; also shares of Common and Special Guaranteed Stock of the Pittsburgh, Ft. Wayne & Chicago Railway Company, the dividends on which, under a 999 year lease, were guaranteed by the Pennsylvania Railroad Company; and also Stocks of other Companies embraced in the System. The Pennsylvania Company having transferred its leasehold interests in various Companies to the Pennsylvania Railroad Company, there was no longer any necessity for it to own this rolling stock which had been originally acquired for its various leased lines. The Pennsylvania Company utilized the proceeds from these sales to pay off nearly $50,000,000. of funded debt maturing in June and July, 1921.

This was the first issue of Bonds made by the Company which required authorization by the Interstate Commerce Commission under the provisions of the Transportation Act of 1920.

OPERATING RESULTS IN 1921—DIVIDEND REDUCED

The Management in presenting the results for 1921, which was the first full year of operation following the Federal Control and Guaranty Periods, referred to the extraordinary conditions under which the System was operated in that year, which affected both the revenues and expenses, and resulted in the reduction of the quarterly dividend paid by the Pennsylvania Railroad Company from 1½% to 1% beginning with the dividend paid in May, 1921. It had been a year of deflation and economic readjustments, with the Country experiencing a most severe business depression, and as a result the ton mileage of the System was reduced 30% below the previous peak year of 1917, and 23% below the year 1920. This was reflected in a reduction of $82,000,000. in total Operating Revenues in 1921 compared with the previous year, notwithstanding the rate increases in effect in 1921, and as operating costs and taxes continued at a high level, it was necessary to resort to enforced retrenchments in Expenses. The monthly pay roll of the Pennsylvania Railroad System for December, 1920, carried 280,733 employes, while for December, 1921, the number was reduced to 218,859, a decrease of 22%. As a result of this policy, the total Operating Expenses of the Pennsylvania Railroad System were reduced about $190,000,000. in 1921, of which over $98,000,000. was in Transportation Expenses, and the balance in Maintenance and other Expenses.

Some part of the reduction, it was pointed out, was due to wage reductions of about 12% in July, 1921, and to modifications of working conditions effected by negotiations with employes, and by orders of the United States Railroad Labor Board. But in addition there was increased efficiency in the personnel; a reduction in overtime; savings from the closing down of shops; restrictions placed upon the use of materials and supplies; and curtailment of the transportation service to offset the loss in traffic, so that the Net Railway Operating Income in 1921 was over $40,815,000. compared with a deficit of $62,622,000. in 1920, or an improvement of over $103,000,000. in the operating results, compared with the previous year. Notwithstanding these improved results the Net Railway Operating Income of 1921 was equal to only about 2% upon the Investment in Road and Equipment of the System, and the Management stated that this rigorous retrenchment policy was to be continued until the net returns showed substantial and permanent improvement.

PENNSYLVANIA COMPANY OBLIGATIONS ASSUMED

The Pennsylvania Railroad Company assumed as of June 14th, 1921, the obligations of the Pennsylvania Company with respect to the issuance by the latter Company of its Guaranteed Trust Certificates, of which there were then outstanding $33,167,000. as a consideration for the purchase of $34,000,000., par value, of Special Guaranteed Stock of the Pittsburgh, Ft. Wayne & Chicago Railway Company, which Stock, to the amount mentioned, was pledged as security for the Guaranteed Trust Certificates. It also assumed the Pennsylvania Company's obligations with respect to that portion of the Equipment Trust Certificates of 1920 issued to the United States Railroad Administration, which represented the equipment allocated to the Pennsylvania Company and other of its subsidiary Companies West of Pittsburgh.

CLAIMS AGAINST THE GOVERNMENT

The 1921 Annual Report points out that final settlement had not been made with the United States Railroad Administration for matters growing out of Federal Control. A statement of accounts between the Railroad Administration and the Railroad Companies included in the Pennsylvania Railroad System had been submitted to the Director General, which included not only amounts due to the Government for Additions and Betterments, but also the balance due to the Pennsylvania Railroad System for compensation, depreciation reserves, interest, undermaintenance, materials and supplies taken over by the Railroad Administration and not replaced, and miscellaneous open accounts. The largest item due these Companies had been for undermaintenance and depreciation. It was stated that the maintenance provisions of the contract with the Government, covering the upkeep of the property during Federal Control, had been given various interpretations, and there was consequently a difference of opinion as to the exact amount due for the failure on the part of the Railroad Administration to return the property in as good condition as when taken over by the Government. So far as maintenance was concerned, the Company had taken the position that the Railroad Administration should have performed actual maintenance equal to the average of the Test Period of three years ending June 30th, 1917; and to the extent that it failed to do so the Government should reimburse the Company. During Federal Control the deficiency in applying track material on the Pennsylvania Railroad System was equivalent to 5,500,000 cross ties, 160,000 tons of new rail, 60,000 tons of second-hand rail, and 530,000 cubic yards of stone ballast and the cost of labor to apply this material.

It was also pointed out that there had been deferred maintenance on bridges, buildings, signals and other structures; also for deferred maintenance, replacements and depreciation of equipment and claims for the destruction of property without replacement. Further, the condition of the locomotives, freight cars and passenger cars owned by the Company at the termination of Federal Control was not as good as at the beginning of that period, and consequently there was also included in the claim against the Government an amount representing the deficiency in making proper repairs.

While the magnitude and difficulties of the task of effecting a settlement with the Government were fully appreciated, the long delay had been a great disappointment to the Management, in view of its belief that a large sum was due to it, which could have been used for maintenance, replacement and other necessities in 1921, and which would have assisted in mitigating the effects of the business depression and unemployment following the period of Federal Control.

WAGES AND WORKING CONDITIONS MORE DIFFICULT QUESTION TO SETTLE

The Management not only referred to these claims, but also called attention to other serious obstacles in the way of successfully operating the property, which militated against earning a fair return thereon. Deficiencies in maintenance, it was stated, might be supplied by equitable monetary settlements of claims by the Government, but the other serious obstacles alluded to, which had been forced upon the Company, arose chiefly from the wages and working conditions established as the result of War conditions and Federal Control. They impaired discipline, disrupted the harmonious co-operative arrangements between the employes and the Management, and produced waste, inefficiency and controversy, to the detriment of the old-time high standards of service, characterized by courtesy and mutual confidence.

RESULTS FOR 1922 BETTER DESPITE STRIKES

The Annual Report for 1922 refers to marked improvement in general industrial and financial conditions, notwithstanding the serious effects of strikes in the anthracite and bituminous coal mining industries for a period of about five months; also the country-wide railroad shopmen's strike, beginning in July, 1922, which resulted in traffic congestion, temporarily increased the number of unserviceable cars and locomotives, and, like the mining strikes, added to the losses and disorder, which are inseparable from serious industrial and transportation interruptions. Fortunately, on the Pennsylvania Railroad System, its loyal supervisory and working forces enabled it to continue an active transportation service during the strike period, and the year closed with 90% of its total locomotives and 93% of its freight cars in serviceable condition, which was a distinct improvement compared with 1921.

The Management stated that public opinion was strongly expressed against these strikes, and that it should be understood that force and intimidation would not induce the American people to acquiesce in the paralysis of their transportation service or industries, especially when the questions at issue could be impartially decided through available mediation or arbitration proceedings.

EQUIPMENT ORDERED

To enable the Company to handle the existing and prospective traffic on its lines, and to retire smaller capacity locomotives and cars, the following new equipment, and improvements to existing equipment, were ordered in 1922 and the early part of 1923, a portion of it having been put in service in 1922, and the balance was to be delivered in 1923:—

475 freight locomotives;
97 passenger locomotives;
43 switching locomotives;
3 electric locomotives;
3 gasoline rail motor cars;
100 cabin cars;
250 steel passenger cars;
20 steel dining cars;

also equipping 15 passenger cars with electric apparatus for electrified suburban service, and increasing the carrying capacity of 10,118 coal cars by the substitution of 70-ton trucks for 50-ton trucks. Funds to pay for a portion of this equipment were to be provided through the sale of $31,500,000. of Pennsylvania Railroad General Equipment Trust 5% Certificates, to which reference is later made.

DETROIT EXTENSION COMPLETED

The Pennsylvania-Detroit Railroad, to which reference has been made, was opened for traffic December 30th, 1922, from Carleton, Mich., to the City of Detroit, a distance of about 20 miles. By its use and the joint use of connecting portions of the Ann Arbor and Pere Marquette Railroads from Carleton south to Toledo, O., and of certain tracks and terminals of the Pere Marquette and Wabash Railroads in and near the City of Detroit, the Pennsylvania Railroad System had obtained a direct entrance from Toledo into Detroit for passenger and freight traffic.

EMPLOYES' REPRESENTATION PLAN UPHELD BY COURT

In referring to relations with its employes, the Management stated in the Annual Report for 1922 that the year had been marked by a further test of the method by which representatives of the employes in the service of the Pennsylvania Railroad Company and the Management could, in mutual conference, discuss various questions and make amicable settlements of differences affecting their wages and working conditions. It was pointed out that to protect that common-sense method of dealing with these important matters the aid of the Federal Courts had to be invoked, and under an opinion of the United States Supreme Court the Company and its employes retained the right to select representatives and decide controversies as to wages and working conditions, according to such orderly process as they may agree upon. The United States Labor Board was likewise free to make such recommendations as it desired, so that an uninterrupted transportation service could be assured.

IMPROVEMENT PROGRAM OF THE RAILROADS

At the Annual Meeting of the Company on April 10th, 1923, President Rea, among other remarks on the general railroad situation, called attention to the huge program of improvements on which the railroads of the Country had embarked to meet the anticipated growth in traffic and to rehabilitate their properties. He said, in part:—

> "Your Company has joined with other railroads in the adoption of a program by which the railroads of the country, in full realization of the necessity for a greater improvement and expansion of the country's transportation facilities, to meet the growing demands of commerce, have authorized since January, 1922, for cars, locomotives, tracks and other facilities, expenditures of over One and a half billion Dollars, of which Four hundred and forty million Dollars were expended during the year 1922. For this purpose large amounts of new capital must be borrowed by the railroads in the abiding faith in the further progress and prosperity of our country, in the fairness of the American people, and relying on the enforcement by the Government of the constructive rail-

road policy in the Federal Transportation Act of 1920, under which reasonable protection to the investment in the railroad property is assured, and just returns permitted to be earned thereon. From January 1st, 1922, to the middle of March, 1923, the railroads purchased over 223,000 new freight cars and 4,219 new locomotives. Of these, 117,280 freight cars and 2,106 locomotives have been delivered and placed in service, and the balance will be delivered by the Fall, when the traffic is usually the heaviest. Furthermore, the railroads are unitedly urging the active prosecution of their new construction work in the early part of the season to increase the existing facilities; that locomotives and cars awaiting heavy repairs be reduced to a normal basis as quickly as possible; that a reasonable supply of coal for railroad purposes be stored by September First, so that after that date the equipment and other facilities may be used to the greatest extent for commercial purposes. The railroads are likewise stressing upon all interested, the necessity for the movement of coal and ore via the Lakes, and the prompt purchase of coal supply for consumption at inland points, in the largest possible quantities early in the season. The railroads of the country have, through the American Railroad Association, established an effective organization in the car-service division for the central control and distribution of freight cars to the best possible advantage of the country."

SALE OF EQUIPMENT TRUSTS

In April, 1923, the Pennsylvania Railroad Company sold $31,500,000. General Equipment 5% Trust Certificates, Series "A," which were dated March 1st, 1923, and matured at the rate of $2,100,000. annually for 15 years beginning March 1st, 1924, and ending March 1st, 1938. These Equipment Trust Certificates were sold to pay, in part, for equipment ordered in the years 1922 and 1923, to which reference has been made.

BROAD STREET STATION FIRE

On June 11th, 1923, the train shed of Broad Street Station, Philadelphia, was destroyed by fire. The Station accommodated daily 530 inbound and outbound passenger trains, carrying about 80,000 passengers. The day following the fire every scheduled train, in and out of Philadelphia, was resumed by using temporary platforms and stairways leading from the elevated structure at the west end of the train shed to the street, and terminating other trains at West Philadelphia and North Philadelphia Stations. Five working days after the fire had been extinguished, all sixteen tracks in Broad Street Station had been rebuilt and platform facilities restored, so that approximately 70% of all trains were brought back into the Station, the remainder being handled at other stations in order that the work of removing the damaged framework of the train shed might proceed.

PLANS FOR NEW STATION AND GENERAL OFFICES

This loss, it was stated, emphasized the already existing necessity for the enlargement and reconstruction of the passenger terminal facilities in Philadelphia. Arrangements were, therefore, made for the preparation of plans to properly accommodate the local and through passenger service, and to discuss the entire project with the authorities of the City of Philadelphia, so as to reach some mutually satisfactory understanding respecting new passenger facilities and their relation to the present and future transit lines and streets of the City. The General Office of the Company, at Broad and Market Streets, had not afforded sufficient accommodation for the official and clerical forces for several years, and the plans for the reconstruction of passenger facilities were also to include provision for new General Offices. Having in mind the rapid transit and street developments essential to the growth of the population, industry and commerce of the City, it was felt that the situation would probably require the construction of a main Station on the west side of the Schuylkill River, and suitable accommodation for the suburban traffic near 15th Street, Filbert Street and the Parkway, and the widening of Filbert Street westward to the Schuylkill River.

P. R. R. EMPLOYES' PROVIDENT AND LOAN ASSOCIATION ESTABLISHED

In July, 1923, the Pennsylvania Railroad Employes' Provident and Loan Association was established by co-operation of the officers and employes for their mutual benefit. The Pennsylvania Railroad Company has no financial or other relation thereto, except to give every reasonable assistance to enable the officers and employes to make it a success. The various features of the Association are a savings fund; a plan for the purchase of homes; provision for obtaining moderate emergency loans, the purchase of increased pension allowances, and also securities of Companies in the Pennsylvania Railroad System on the installment plan. As a result of the formation of this Association, it was no longer necessary to continue the Pennsylvania Railroad Employes' Saving Fund, which had been established since 1888. At the close of 1923 the Association had a total enrollment of 18,434 members, of whom 13,978 had availed themselves of the saving fund feature, and 19,666 shares of Pennsylvania Railroad Company stock had been purchased in addition to other securities in the System. A number of loans had been made for the purchase of homes, as well as for emergency purposes, and 555 employes had purchased increased pension allowances.

SETTLEMENT FOR FEDERAL CONTROL PERIOD

On June 12th, 1923, final settlement was effected between the United States Railroad Administration and the Pennsylvania Railroad Company and the leased, operated and controlled lines embraced in its System, covering all claims arising out of the possession, use and operation of these properties by the United States Government during the period of Federal control, from January 1st, 1918, to February 29th, 1920. It was a net settlement of the amounts due either to, or by, the United States, or the System Companies. It included balances due the latter on account of the standard return, or compensation, for the use of their properties; for assets collected, depreciation, retirement of property and equipment not replaced, interest and under-maintenance. The settlement likewise included balances due to the Government for additions and betterments made to the properties, for liabilities paid, for interest, and for materials and supplies returned to the System Companies in excess of those turned over to the United States Railroad Administration.

The terms of such net settlement required the payment of $90,000,000. to the Government for the entire System. The Pennsylvania Railroad Company issued its Note to the Government for $70,225,000., and the Pittsburgh, Cincinnati, Chicago & St. Louis Railroad Company issued its Note for $18,250,000., the balance having been paid in cash. These Notes, in accordance with the provisions of the Transportation Act of 1920, were secured by collateral, bore interest at 6% per annum, and were due March 1st, 1930. Payments on account of these Notes were made in 1924, and both were paid off in full in 1925.

The expenditures made for additions and betterments on the lines embraced in the Pennsylvania Railroad System during the 26 months of Federal Control amounted to $159,264,226. This did not include equipment purchased by the Director General of Railroads and allocated to the System Companies, costing $58,442,161., so that the total expenditures during this period amounted to $217,700,000. Reference has heretofore been made to the fact that the cost of the assigned equipment was financed through the issuance of $58,412,000. Pennsylvania Railroad 6% Equipment Trust Certificates in 1920.

1917 OPERATING RESULTS COMPARED WITH FEDERAL CONTROL PERIOD

It was recognized that in the operation of the railroads for most of the Federal Control period, unusual conditions at home and abroad had to be faced, which forced a character of operation and range of expenditure, as well as a sacrifice of public convenience and service, that would not be tolerated in times of peace, and could not be justified from an economic standpoint. The Management pointed out that the Net Railway Operating Income of the Pennsylvania Railroad System for the year 1917, at the close of which the Government assumed the operation of the property, was $77,800,000., while the result for 1918 was a Net Railway Operating Income of $27,018,000.; for 1919 it was $10,034,000., and for 1920 a Net Railway Operating *Deficit* of $62,742,000. The number of employes at the close of 1917 was 235,000, and on March 1st, 1920, 273,000. The monthly payroll for 1917 averaged $20,770,000., and for 1920, $43,950,000., the latter year including an increase of wages and changed working conditions for the greater part of the year, while the higher rates on traffic did not become effective until August 26th, 1920.

MANAGEMENT'S VIEWS

The following paragraph has been extracted from the concluding reference of the Management to the Federal Control Period in the Annual Report for 1923:—

> "Without any desire to unduly criticize Governmental operations, or to minimize the responsibilities resulting from political and economic difficulties growing out of the great World War, it must be clearly stated that the lines were returned to the Company with wages and working conditions largely increased and fixed not only during the War period but after the War had ended, and entirely out of line with the rates and net operating results; with the efficiency and loyalty of the working forces seriously demoralized, and with the physical condition of the property inferior to that which existed at the beginning of Federal control. This was the result of War conditions and of a system of centralized management at Washington, under which the policies, expenditures, wages, classification and organization of employes, working conditions and other features were dictated to meet the varying conditions as they appealed to the Railroad Administration. The responsibility for rectifying that situation at the end of Federal control had to be assumed by your Management. This was accomplished by increasing operating efficiency, enforcing economy and by getting co-operation from the public through the payment of increased rates. Notwithstanding the

higher rates paid by the public, these unfavorable conditions, accentuated by the fall of traffic in 1921 and the strikes in the anthracite and bituminous coal mining industries, and the country-wide strike of the railroads' shopcrafts in 1922, entailed considerable sacrifice by the shareholders through the reduction in the rate of dividends. Prompt and reasonable settlements for the Federal control period, such as those made by Great Britain with her railroads, probably would largely have averted such results. Fortunately, the improved results for 1923 have materially helped in adjusting the situation. With no disposition to cavil respecting a closed transaction, nor to suggest any lack of courtesy by the Government officials in dealing with this important transaction, it is, nevertheless, the opinion of the Management of your Company that the interpretations of the provisions of the Federal Control Act and Contract by the Government prevented the payment of an amount sufficient to properly reimburse your System Companies for the taking of their property and equipment, and their necessary restoration to a condition equal to that when possession was assumed by the Government. It is also felt that the 6% rate of interest charged by the Government on the Collateral Notes issued to effect final settlement for the balance due on improvements by the Government to assist in winning the War, and charged at their high war costs against your System, might justly be reduced to a rate that more closely corresponds to the cost of money to the Government."

HEROIC SERVICE MEDALS

In accordance with the policy adopted by the Management to award Heroic Service Medals to employes who performed unusual acts of heroism in connection with their regular duties, or while on the Company's property, 27 of such Medals were awarded to employes on May 28th, 1924. The Company has since continued this policy, 24 medals being awarded in 1925 and 8 in 1926.

NEW EQUIPMENT

During the year 1924 the following new equipment was placed in service:—

1,000 stock cars,
3,000 automobile cars,
10,716 box cars (100,000 pounds capacity),
50 heavy passenger locomotives (for through passenger service),
45 ten-wheel passenger locomotives (for suburban service),
23 six-wheel shifting locomotives,
6 four-wheel shifting locomotives,
2 electric locomotives,
12 all-steel dining cars,
3 rail gasoline motor cars,
1 Diesel-electric tug-boat,
6 car floats.

All of the locomotives, as well as the dining cars, were constructed in the Company's Altoona Shops.

SALE OF EQUIPMENT TRUST CERTIFICATES

A portion of the money required to pay for this equipment was raised through the sale in May, 1924, of $20,100,000. General Equipment 5% Trust Certificates, Series "B," which were dated April 1st, 1924, and matured at the rate of $1,340,000. annually for 15 years beginning April 1st, 1925, and ending April 1st, 1939.

In order to finance the cost of additional box cars, the Company in October, 1924, issued and sold $15,750,000. General Equipment 4½% Trust Certificates, Series "C," which were dated October 1st, 1924, and matured at the rate of $1,050,000. per annum over a period of 15 years, starting October 1st, 1925, and ending October 1st, 1939.

SALE OF $50,000,000. 5% SECURED BONDS

In November, 1924, the Pennsylvania Railroad Company also sold $50,000,000. 40-Year 5% Secured Gold Bonds, dated November 1st, 1924, and maturing November 1st, 1964. The proceeds from the sale of these Bonds were used to reduce the 6% Collateral Note of the Pennsylvania Railroad Company held by the United States Government, which had been given in connection with the settlement for the Federal Control period.

PENNSYLVANIA, OHIO & DETROIT RAILROAD COMPANY FORMED

Effective July 1st, 1924, The Cincinnati, Lebanon & Northern Railway Company, The Cleveland, Akron & Cincinnati Railway Company, The Toledo, Columbus & Ohio River Railroad Company, The Manufacturers Railway Company and Pennsylvania-Detroit Railroad Company entered into an agreement for the consolidation of such Companies into The Pennsylvania, Ohio & Detroit Railroad Company. The total owned mileage of the consolidated road was about 783 miles, extending from Cincinnati, Columbus and Marietta, on the south, to Akron and to Sandusky and Toledo on Lake Erie, on the north, and (partly by trackage) from Toledo to Detroit. All of the Capital Stock of the constituent Companies was owned or controlled by the Pennsylvania Railroad Company, which operated their lines. This consolidation became effective from an accounting standpoint on January 1st, 1926.

PITTSBURGH IMPROVEMENTS

The 1924 Annual Report refers to the urgent necessity for the enlargement and improvement of passenger and freight terminals of the Company in the City of Pittsburgh, which had been apparent for several years, but which could not be undertaken during the War period. Since then negotiations had been actively resumed with the City of Pittsburgh, and had resulted in reaching an agreement providing for the vacation, relocation and widening of certain streets in the vicinity of Pennsylvania Station, Pittsburgh, and its eastern and western approaches. The plans contemplated the removal of the then existing Grant Street freight station facilities, and the utilization of the property for street improvement and building purposes, including a General Post Office Building to be constructed by the Government.

It was stated that final plans for the complete railroad improvements had not yet been made, but they contemplated additional tracks both eastwardly and westwardly from the Pennsylvania Station; the enlargement of the Station Building itself so as to provide adequate ticket offices, waiting rooms, baggage and other facilities, as well as subways to enable passengers to pass to and from the Station without crossing the street and tracks at grade.

NORFOLK & WESTERN RAILWAY LEASE NEGOTIATIONS TERMINATED

Reference was made in the Annual Report for 1924 to the fact that negotiations in connection with the suggested lease of the Norfolk & Western Railway by the Pennsylvania Railroad Company had been terminated, because it could not negotiate a lease on a mutually advantageous basis. A large volume of traffic was being exchanged with the Norfolk & Western Railway, and it was stated that the close working relations, and the active policy of co-operation which had existed for over twenty-five years, would continue.

TENTATIVE RAILROAD CONSOLIDATION PLAN

Reference has already been made to the provisions of the Transportation Act of 1920, under Section 5 of which the Interstate Commerce Commission was to prepare and adopt a plan for the consolidation of the railway properties of the Continental United States into a limited number of systems. The Commission employed Prof. William Z. Ripley, of Harvard University, to prepare, under its direction, a report on the subject. This he did and it formed the basis of a tentative plan which the Commission served upon the carriers in August, 1921. Under this tentative plan, there were allocated to the Pennsylvania Railroad System, which was designated as "System No. 2," the following roads:—

Pennsylvania R. R.
West Jersey & Seashore R. R.
Long Island R. R.
Baltimore, Chesapeake & Atlantic Ry.
Cumberland Valley R. R.
Maryland, Delaware & Virginia Ry.
New York, Philadelphia & Norfolk R. R.
Pittsburgh, Cincinnati, Chicago & St. Louis R. R.
Waynesburg & Washington R. R.

Grand Rapids & Indiana Ry.
Cincinnati, Lebanon & Northern Ry.
Ohio River & Western Ry.
Louisville Bridge & Terminal Ry.
Wheeling Terminal Ry.
Toledo, Peoria & Western Ry.
Lorain, Ashland & Southern R. R.
Lake Erie & Pittsburgh Ry.
Central Indiana Ry.
Pittsburgh, Chartiers & Youghiogheny Ry.
Monongahela Ry.

and all other railway properties controlled by any of the above carriers under lease, stock ownership, or otherwise, except the Norfolk & Western Railway and railway properties controlled by it, which, it was stated, may be included in a separate System,

The Commission made some reservations which were that the Lorain, Ashland & Southern Railway may be included in System No. 4, Erie Railroad, which owns one-half the stock, the Pennsylvania Railroad owning the other half. The Lake Erie & Pittsburgh Railway, Central Indiana Railway, Pittsburgh, Chartiers & Youghiogheny Railway and Monongahela Railway may be included in System No. 1, New York Central Railroad, which controls one-half the Stock of each road, the Pennsylvania Railroad controlling the other half.

NEW LEGISLATION REQUIRED

The Interstate Commerce Commission subsequently held hearings on consolidations in various cities throughout the Country at which voluminous testimony was taken, but it has never adopted a plan of consolidation as prescribed by the terms of the Transportation Act. The Commission has on the other hand asked to be relieved of this duty, and has recommended that it be given broad powers to approve or disapprove such consolidations as may be proposed, and to make such modifications and attach such terms and conditions prior to approval as it may find just and reasonable. It is generally agreed that if a complete plan of consolidation were imposed on the railroads, it could not be carried out largely because of the lack of the necessary machinery in the present Federal law and in the laws of many of the States. For this reason, Congressional Committees have been at work on amendatory legislation for some time, which would permit of voluntary consolidations on the general lines recommended by the Interstate Commerce Commission.

CONFERENCES IN THE EASTERN DISTRICT

Meanwhile, the Management reported to the stockholders in the Annual Report for 1924 that the officers of the Company had participated in conferences with representatives of the larger Systems operating in the Eastern District of the Country in an effort to bring about some general agreement on the part of all interested as to the consolidations that should be effected in that section. This was, of course, to be subject to the requirements of the Transportation Act, which provided that competition was to be preserved as fully as possible, and wherever practicable the existing routes and channels of trade were to be maintained. Further, the several Systems were to be so arranged that the cost of transportation as between competitive Systems, and as related to the value of the properties through which the service is rendered, shall be the same, so that, as far as practicable, these Systems can employ uniform rates in the movement of competitive traffic, and under efficient management earn substantially the same rate of return upon the value of their respective properties.

SO-CALLED FOUR SYSTEM PLAN

These conferences resulted in the informal presentation to the Consolidation Committee of the Interstate Commerce Commission by the Presidents of the New York Central, the Baltimore & Ohio, and the Nickel Plate Systems of a suggested consolidation of the railroads of the Eastern District into four Systems. The consolidation thus suggested was not in the judgment of the officers of the Pennsylvania Railroad Company a fair one to the latter Company, nor would its adoption accomplish the purposes and objects of the consolidation provisions of the Transportation Act. This plan provided for the grouping of all the large railroads in the Eastern District of the Country into four Systems, one being the Pennsylvania Railroad System, but made no disposition of the New England roads and of terminal and short lines. It treated the Pennsylvania Railroad System, including therein the Norfolk & Western Railway, as already practically complete, largely because of its size, and accordingly assigned to the other three Systems all of the important roads in the Eastern District and the principal gateways to the New York District and Harbor not then embraced in the Pennsylvania Railroad System.

PENNSYLVANIA PROTESTS AND MAKES SUGGESTIONS

This plan, it was pointed out, failed to allocate to the Pennsylvania Railroad System the roads necessary to enable it to adequately and economically transport its existing traffic and that which it would undoubtedly be called upon to transport in the future; and its adoption would result in the diversion from its lines of traffic then being handled by it, and would seriously disrupt and destroy existing routes and channels of trade and commerce. Therefore, the Management felt impelled to indicate to the Interstate Commerce Commission its dissatisfaction with the plan as proposed, and its belief that its adoption or acceptance by the Commission would be detrimental to its stockholders, to its shippers and to the territory served by it. In doing this the Management made certain suggestions, the chief of which were that in the grouping and allocation of the Eastern railroads there should be included in the Pennsylvania Railroad System, not only the Norfolk & Western Railway, which had been affiliated with it for over 25 years, and the Virginian Railway, which was operated in conjunction with the Norfolk & Western Railway during the period of Federal Control, but also the Lehigh Valley Railroad, whose inclusion in the Pennsylvania Railroad System would provide an additional and important gateway to and from the New York

City District. It would also continue a large local and through traffic exchange, and would furnish a shorter and less congested route for business which concentrated in the Sunbury, Williamsport and Wilkes-Barre district, and better terminals and connections in the Buffalo-Rochester territory.

The suggested plan, together with the recommendations made upon behalf of the Pennsylvania Railroad System, were taken under consideration by the Consolidation Committee of the Interstate Commerce Commission, time being granted to the Companies interested for further consideration of the whole subject in the hope that some more acceptable plan might be evolved.

PHILADELPHIA TERMINAL IMPROVEMENTS

Further progress was made in 1924 in preparing plans for improved passenger terminal facilities in Philadelphia. They contemplated the removal of the elevated railroad structure between Broad Street Station and West Philadelphia, and the erection of a new Station on the west bank of the Schuylkill River, to contain about eighteen tracks, each having 1500-foot platforms for through and local trains, and eight additional tracks for suburban electric trains, a total of twenty-six tracks. The Station when completed was to have two levels of tracks, the lower one for the through and long distance trains and the upper level for the suburban traffic. Electrically operated suburban trains were to reach the business center of the city by means of a new bridge across the Schuylkill River, south of Arch Street, leading into a subway of four or more tracks beginning near Twentieth or Twenty-first Street, and terminating in an underground terminal between Fifteenth and Seventeenth Streets, north of the Filbert Street elevated structure. This, it was stated, would eventually eliminate the operation of steam trains into the center of the city from West Philadelphia. The plans also provided for the erection of a General Office Building adjacent to the new Station to accommodate official and clerical forces, which had been scattered in various office buildings throughout the City.

PRESIDENT REA SPEAKS TO THE STOCKHOLDERS

President Rea presided at the Annual Meeting of the Company on April 14th, 1925, and as he made some very interesting remarks with respect to his prospective retirement as President, under the Pension Regulations, in the Fall of that year, and also as to the general position of the Company, a part of them are quoted below:—

> "At this Annual Meeting you will be asked to approve the Seventy-eighth Annual Report of your Company, and although individuals come and go, the Company continues as one of the great national systems of transportation. The Company is a permanent and self-perpetuating institution, although the personnel of its executives and management does change. As most of you know, I will reach the age of seventy next Fall, and under the regulations of the Company I will retire from active service. It may not be out of place, therefore, for me to extend a word of special greeting to the stockholders at this meeting.
>
> I am the first of your Presidents to reach that age, and, as it is fifty-four years ago since I first entered the service, my term of active service is probably the longest. As an engineer I obtained a close grasp on the physical features of the Pennsylvania Railroad in the great coal and steel traffic producing territory. This was followed by service which gave me charge of the location, promotion and construction of the many branch lines and subsidiaries on various parts of the Pennsylvania System in my capacity as Principal Assistant Engineer, Assistant to the Vice-President, later as Assistant to the President, and afterwards as Vice-President. So that the work which started as a rodman in the fields of Pennsylvania, culminated with the corporate and engineering work in extending the Pennsylvania System into and through New York City, including a connection with the New Haven Railroad System known as the New York Connecting Railroad and its Hell Gate Bridge, and in the acquisition through lease, contract or stock ownership of other roads and interests.
>
> My Vice-Presidential duties also put me in charge, for several years, of the Engineering Department, the Accounting Department, and through assisting a former Vice-President, the late John P. Green, I was brought into close touch with the administration of the Treasury

Department. I have been a Director of the Company for twenty-six years, and over twelve years ago I was honored with one of the most important positions of trust and responsibility in this Country through my election as President of The Pennsylvania Railroad Company and the important lines in its System.

The administration of each of your Presidents has had to meet its own serious problems. The Company keeps pace with the Country—in periods of expansion and periods of depression. Aside from regular administration questions, my administration may be characterized by at least two far-reaching influences—the first, the Company had to meet the crest of the long continued period of destructive legislation and regulation, and a hostile attitude of the public generally towards the railroads; and the second, the far-reaching consequences of the World War which began to be seriously felt about eight years ago and are not yet concluded.

We have had a continuous struggle to prevent the confiscation of the railroad investment and service by unwise, wasteful and hostile legislation and regulation which, happily, a fully informed public opinion has tempered, so that at present there is a closer understanding of the necessity of strong railroads and ample transportation facilities and a desire to allow railroads to earn fair returns.

As contradistinguished from the destructive standpoint, the clearer view is that their properties represent real value and efficient service, and are not overcapitalized or enfeebled institutions, but effective instruments of national prosperity. We must not overlook the fact that while railroads always desire to do a large part of their financing through the sale of capital stock, yet the result of unwise regulation, hostile legislation, and restricted earnings has been to make sales of capital stock at par practically impossible, except for a very few companies in the last ten years. Under the laws of Pennsylvania capital stock cannot be sold for less than par. The last occasion on which The Pennsylvania Railroad Company sold its stock at par was in the year 1913, but we are in no different position from that of most of the large railroad companies.

The Management appreciates the confidence imposed in it by the stockholders. Your railroad system is very conservatively capitalized because, while it represents an investment of over $2,250,000,000., the total capital obligations held by the public only slightly exceed $1,545,000,000.

It will need at all times the continuing support and strength of public opinion, and fair legislation and regulation, and it is sure to have the continued confidence of its stockholders who have reached the number of over 146,000, which includes practically all of our officers and large numbers of the employes. This ownership represents citizens in all classes of life, and their financial, educational, religious and charitable institutions.

I close my active career with the deepest confidence in the basic earning power of the property which has paid a return on the capital stock in every year since it was incorporated. It has done its duty by its owners and probably out-ranks every large corporation in the Country in the total amount of dividends it has paid to its stockholders and at reasonably fair rates. Its employes have always received as good wages as the Company could afford to pay, and notwithstanding wars and panics they have always been paid in cash and on the date due.

The Company will have to meet its periods of prosperity and adversity that will test the skill and ability of the Management, but so long as we conserve and maintain the solid foundations of a solvent Company, with fair returns to the stockholders, with capable Directors to manage its affairs, and with well trained and loyal officers and employes, the stockholders have no need to fear for the future or to feel that The Pennsylvania Railroad Company will not hold its rightful place with other railroads."

FINAL SETTLEMENT WITH GOVERNMENT

Final settlement with the United States Government for the Guaranty Period (the six months succeeding Federal Control, March 1st to August 31st, 1920), was concluded during the year 1925. The net book loss sustained for the Federal Control and Guaranty Periods, amounting to $8,415,976., was charged to Profit & Loss Account, and the accounts with the Government were then closed. It was stated that this figure by no means represented the total losses caused by the War, but under the contract interpretations and the settlement basis established by the Government, the Company's claims against it were not allowed to the extent of the foregoing amount, even though they had been presented on a reasonable basis.

NEW EQUIPMENT

During the year 1925, the following new equipment was placed in service:—

7,284 box cars (100,000 pounds capacity),
6 poling cars,
5 ten-wheel passenger locomotives (for suburban service),
50 eight-wheel shifting locomotives,
1 electric locomotive,
28 baggage-express cars,
10 passenger-baggage cars,
4 gas motor rail cars, together with 1 trailer for use with gas motor cars,
1 gas-electric motor rail car,
5 covered barges,
4 harbor floats,
2 grain barges,
6 150-ton wrecking derricks.

All of the foregoing equipment was paid for without the issuance of new securities.

PHILADELPHIA TERMINAL IMPROVEMENTS

Reference was again made in the 1925 Annual Report to the necessity for the reconstruction of the passenger terminals and tracks to properly accommodate the through and local passenger service in and adjacent to the City of Philadelphia, the elimination of the Filbert Street elevated railroad structure east of the Schuylkill River, and provision for General Office accommodations in that City for official and clerical forces. However, it was not until the plan for passenger terminal improvements in Philadelphia was fully developed that the location for a new office building could be determined upon. Therefore, in the Autumn of 1925, the construction of a modern fire-proof office building at the junction of 32nd Street, Market Street and Lancaster Avenue was commenced.

The plans covering these important improvements have heretofore been described, and during the year 1925 the necessary enabling ordinances, prepared in collaboration with the Mayor and the Council of the City, were passed, and an agreement dated July 13th, 1925, entered into covering the improvement program. In addition to the proposed changes in railroad facilities and improvements, the plans contemplated the creation of a new central avenue, 90 feet in width, to be called "Pennsylvania Boulevard," on the location of Filbert Street, extending from City Hall to the main Passenger Station on the west bank of the Schuylkill River; also the electrification of additional local lines radiating from Philadelphia in order to handle the suburban traffic through the proposed subway terminating in an underground station between Fifteenth and Seventeenth Streets, north of the Filbert Street elevated structure. The electrification of the lines between Philadelphia and Wilmington and between Philadelphia and West Chester, via Media, had also been authorized.

The total cost of the improvements under the plan agreed to with the City was estimated at approximately $60,000,000., of which the City was to pay its fair proportion for street and other municipal improvements, which would develop and improve the central section of the City and that part lying west of the Schuylkill River. It was stated that the Company would be able to release considerable property in the heart of the business section of Philadelphia, which could be sold for commercial purposes, and thus reimburse itself for a large part of the cost of the improvements.

CHICAGO UNION STATION OPENED

The new station of the Chicago Union Station Company, which also included an Office Building, was formally opened and dedicated to public use on July 23rd, 1925. This Station was designed and constructed to furnish the maximum of convenience to the traveling public, and expeditiously handle the large volume of passenger traffic going to and coming from the great commercial center of Chicago, and to and from the many connecting railroads entering that City. A seven-story Mail Building, which had been leased to the United States Government, was built adjoining the Station and was connected with it by a tunnel under the concourse. Other important work carried out in connection with the construction of the Station included the relocation of the freight facilities of the Pennsylvania Railroad Company, the Chicago, Burlington & Quincy Railroad and Chicago & Alton Railroad Companies, the relocation and rebuilding of approach and Station tracks on concrete foundations; the installation of an interlocking signal system; the extending and widening of twelve streets which were carried across the Station layout on concrete viaducts, and the widening and grading of Canal Street for nine city blocks.

The cost of this work was financed through the issuance and sale of First Mortgage and Guaranteed Gold Bonds of the Chicago Union Station Company and advances made by the four Owning Companies. The Capital Stock of the Station Company was owned one-half by the Pennsylvania Railroad Company and its leased line, the Pittsburgh, Cincinnati, Chicago & St. Louis Railroad Company, one-quarter by the Chicago, Burlington & Quincy Railroad Company and one-quarter by the Chicago, Milwaukee & St. Paul Railway Company. These four Companies also guaranteed the principal and interest of these Bonds, the rentals from the use of the Station, the Office Building and Mail Building being more than sufficient to pay the fixed charges of the Station Company. The Chicago & Alton Railroad Company also uses the Station as a tenant.

PURCHASE OF WESTERN ALLEGHENY RAILROAD

For several years, plans had been under consideration to construct a 60-mile connecting link north of Pittsburgh between Red Bank, Pa., and a point near Enon, Pa., on the Fort Wayne road, to relieve the Pittsburgh terminals of part of the through eastbound and westbound train movements. As the Western Allegheny Railroad occupied a large part of the proposed route between those points, the Pennsylvania Railroad Company purchased its Capital Stock, amounting at par to $1,511,100. The road was to be improved and ultimately used to expedite and increase the movement of through traffic, and thus greatly relieve the Pittsburgh Gateway.

MOTOR COMPETITION

The Pennsylvania Railroad Company, like all other railroads, had felt for several years the serious inroads upon its traffic, and particularly in passenger business, arising out of the general use of public bus lines and motor trucks and private automobiles. It, therefore, deemed it wise to reduce or abandon service on certain of its branch lines having rather light traffic, and to substitute therefor a gasoline motor rail service, so as to fully meet the transportation requirements and prove more economical. It was also deemed advisable in other cases to substitute motors on the highways for ordinary rail service, and in order to be in a position to utilize this form of service where it could be done in the interest of both public convenience and economical operation, an application was made for a charter for a Company through which such operations could be conducted in those Counties of the State of Pennsylvania reached by its rail lines. It was not the purpose of the Company, it was stated, to enter the general business of transportation by motor bus or truck, but to engage in such service insofar as it might be necessary to protect existing traffic, or to provide further convenience in handling the business.

NORTHWESTERN-SOUTHWESTERN REGIONS CONSOLIDATED

On June 1st, 1925, the operation of the Company's lines in the Northwestern and Southwestern Regions were consolidated to form the Western Region, with headquarters at Chicago, Ill.

RETIREMENT OF PRESIDENT REA

On October 1st, 1925, Mr. Samuel Rea, who had been President of the Pennsylvania Railroad Company and of its principal affiliated Companies since January 1st, 1913, having, after many years of service, reached the age of 70 years, was retired under the Pension Regulations. Mr. Rea was the first President to attain that age in active service, and as an indication of the esteem in which he was held by the Board of Directors, the following Minute was adopted at a meeting held on September 30th, 1925:—

"Fifty-four years ago Samuel Rea began his career as a rodman doing the bidding of the engineers constructing a part of what has become one of the great railroad systems of the world; today he commits to other hands the leadership of its forces and the responsibility of shaping its destinies, which have been his for the past thirteen years.

Born in the State of Pennsylvania seventy years ago, his career of accomplishment has been within its borders, and in the development of its resources and transportation facilities.

To tell the story of his life and achievements, interwoven as they are with the growth of the Pennsylvania Railroad System and the advancement of the science of railroad management, is the province of the biographer and the historian.

It is for us to record, upon this day, our personal and official testimony to his skill and fidelity in the great trust in his keeping; his unremitting devotion to the interests of the great property and its owners; the ample justification of the confidence reposed in him, and the regrets inseparable from the termination of his leadership,—a leadership so executed in harmony with, and consideration for, his associates as to inspire and assure their lasting regard and affection.

In the life of this Company, each administration has been confronted, from time to time, with difficult problems growing out of the development of the country and the rise and fall of the tide of National prosperity, but his,—exceeded in length by only two of his eight predecessors,—has virtually been beset by difficulties throughout. Beginning when the country was emerging from a period of financial depression, which had necessitated a policy of restricted expenditure upon the property, the greatest upheaval in history, fittingly known as the world War, shortly ensued, with its extraordinary demands upon many of the resources of this Country,—upon none more than transportation.

Realizing the importance of meeting these demands, the railroad presidents organized a 'War Board' to provide more effective transportation service through closer co-operation, and upon this Mr. Rea rendered signal service.

When, by proclamation of the President of the United States, the operation of the railroads was assumed by the Federal Administration, upon him devolved the duty and burden of protecting the interests of the stockholders and securing from the Government adequate compensation for the use of the property and for its preservation and maintenance.

When Federal Control ended, he was confronted with the problem of re-establishing the equilibrium and standard of the service and of restoring its earning power in the face of high costs and wages on the one hand, and demoralized traffic arrangements and disorganized forces on the other.

Lastly came the intricate and still unsolved problem of consolidating the railroads of the country into what have been termed 'Major Systems,' to the proper solution of which he has given the same cautious thought and skillful attention which has characterized his care of this Company's interests throughout his years of service.

Mr. Rea has lived to a greater age than any of his predecessors, and today reaches the time appointed by the Company for relief from the cares and exactions of daily routine, and receives the reward of freedom.

An eminent engineer and honored by the profession, an authority in the art of accounting, clear of vision and sound in judgment in the realm of finance, Samuel Rea holds a place as pre-eminent in the science of railroad management as in the affections not merely of those who have been closely associated with him, but as well of the army of which he has been the distinguished commander.

It is the good fortune of the Company, as well as a source of gratification to his fellow directors, that he remains a member of this Board. Released from the exactions of the Presidency, may he enjoy many years of health and happiness, and may his usefulness to the Company long continue."

STATISTICAL DATA

The following operating and traffic statistics and financial data will be of interest as indicating the progress made by the Company during President Rea's Administration:—

REVENUE, EXPENSES, OPERATING INCOME, AND RENTALS, 1913 TO 1925, INCLUSIVE

All Lines Directly Operated

Year	Miles	Gross Revenue	Operating Expenses Including Taxes	Operating Income	Rentals Paid	Net Operating Income to Penna. R. R. Co.
1913......	4,110.82	$191,501,490.29	$153,319,007.12	$38,182,483.17	$3,974,987 33	$34,207,495.84
1914.....	4,578.70	181,184,822.32	* 146,089,877.83	35,094,944.49	5,566,867.52	29,528,076.97
1915.....	4,608.04	196,628,170.10	* 150,377,245.42	46,250,924.68	8,574,859.59	37,676,065.09
1916.....	4,603.28	230,278,533.33	* 175,222,522.01	55,056,011.32	9,462,294.54	45,593,716.78
1917.....	4,608.19	255,093,494.85	* 210,829,087.29	44,264,407.56	7,365,604.32	36,898,803.24
#1918.....	5,427.57	367,414,694.70	* 347,325,756.20	20,088,938.50	⊙ 10,921,884.39	⊙ 9,167,054.11
1919.....	5,376.93	378,091,498.79	* 369,151,612.11	8,939,886.68	⊙ 10,819,350.06	Def. ⊙ 1,879,463.38
1920.....	7,389.04	566,860,758.34	* 609,121,730.92	Def. 42,260,972.58	⊙ 22,741,978.72	Def. ⊙ 65,002,951.30
1921.....	7,406.01	500,175,083.80	* 451,538,564.34	48,636,519.46	15,617,100.55	33,019,418.91
1922.....	10,600.94	646,352,107.78	* 563,316,336.25	83,035,771.53	34,290,803.91	48,744,967.62
1923.....	10,576.92	721,397,408.68	* 623,333,150.52	98,064,258.16	35,246,256.30	62,818,001.86
1924.....	10,575.00	645,299,176.22	* 548,121,589.82	97,177,586.40	38,291,126.38	58,886,460.02
1925.....	10,582.34	672,136,962.08	* 559,119,998.57	113,016,963.51	44,385,948.62	68,631,014.89

* Includes Uncollectible Railway Revenues.

⊙ The figures for 1918, 1919 and 1920 shown in these columns are based on the actual results of operation by the United States Railroad Administration from January 1, 1918, to February 29, 1920, and during the Guaranty period from March 1st to August 31, 1920, except those under "Rentals Paid," which represent the Rental obligations of the Pennsylvania Railroad Company. The amount shown under "Net Operating Income to the Pennsylvania Railroad Company" is the difference between the actual result of operations during the Federal Control and Guaranty periods and the Rental Obligations and War Taxes of the Corporation.

The operation of the Delaware & Raritan Canal (66 miles) is excluded from the 1919 figures on account of same being operated by the New York and New Jersey Canal Section of the United States Railroad Administration.

Beginning with the year 1918, the Pennsylvania Railroad Company leased a number of important railroads in its System, the operating results of which had not theretofore been included with the lines it directly operates. Therefore, the figures for the period 1918 to 1925 inclusive, reflect the inclusion of the operating results of these leased lines, as well as the normal growth in traffic.

TONNAGE, MILEAGE, REVENUE, EXPENSES AND AVERAGES ON FREIGHT BUSINESS, 1913 TO 1925, INCLUSIVE

All Rail Lines Directly Operated

Year	Tons	Tons One Mile	Revenue	Average Revenue per Ton per Mile	Expenses Including Taxes	Average Expenses per Ton per Mile	Average Net Revenue per Ton per Mile
				Cents		Cents	Cents
1913.....	155,208,778	25,025,219,387	$145,951,051.97	0.583	$108,766,444.42	0.435	0.148
1914.....	135,296,035	22,104,102,693	130,095,698.91	0.589	96,017,268.30	0.434	0.155
1915.....	142,826,993	22,849,758,469	139,442,177.84	0.610	97,448,135.02	0.426	0.184
1916.....	166,245,104	26,966,806,131	162,518,994.87	0.603	117,619,240.29	0.436	0.167
1917.....	169,647,278	27,790,944,860	175,365,902.62	0.631	142,203,469.66	0.512	0.119
#1918.....	177,304,522	29,741,407,863	238,317,645.27	0.801	229,694,055.97	0.772	0.029
1919.....	155,606,274	26,984,225,153	237,304,970.62	0.879	232,932,107.84	0.863	0.016
1920.....	196,046,777	36,151,383,535	384,372,253.81	1.063	449,272,107.34	1 243	Loss0.180
1921.....	151,416,202	28,298,672,521	328,932,913.78	1.162	315,957,093.00	1.117	0.045
1922.....	194,856,802	40,346,569,722	439,528,929.11	1.089	400,084,661.73	0.992	0.097
1923.....	246,206,544	48,444,210,243	502,698,605.90	1.038	457,367,005.61	0.944	0.094
1924.....	214,636,127	41,587,072,190	440,567,310.38	1.059	392,031,236.82	0.943	0.116
1925.....	228,889,365	44,842,971,253	465,013,723.60	1.037	401,021,481.99	0.894	0.143

The Operation of the Delaware & Raritan Canal (66 miles) is excluded from the 1919 figures on account of same being operated by the New York and New Jersey Canal Section of the United States Railroad Administration.

Beginning with the year 1918, the Pennsylvania Railroad Company leased a number of important railroads in its System, the operating results of which had not theretofore been included with the lines it directly operates. Therefore, the figures for the period 1918 to 1925, inclusive, reflect the inclusion of the operating results of these leased lines, as well as the normal growth in traffic.

PASSENGERS, MILEAGE, REVENUE, EXPENSES AND AVERAGES ON PASSENGER BUSINESS, 1913 TO 1925, INCLUSIVE

All Rail Lines Directly Operated

Year	Passengers	Passengers One Mile	Revenue	Average Revenue per Passenger per Mile	Expenses Including Taxes	Average Expenses per Passenger per Mile	Average Net Revenue per Passenger per Mile
				Cents		Cents	Cents
1913.....	82,777,232	2,108,358,924	$41,141,762.74	1.951	$38,248,964.06	1.814	0.137
1914.....	80,873,281	2,017,389,251	39,359,698.76	1.951	37,625,553.69	1.865	0.086
1915.....	73,555,230	1,881,057,582	38,687,713.21	2.057	34,268,746.97	1.822	0.235
1916.....	85,420,573	2,168,833,089	44,989,746.80	2.074	36,119,219.30	1.665	0.409
1917.....	95,622,472	2,524,340,952	53,042,546.27	2.101	42,987,222.42	1.703	0.398
#1918.....	141,423,586	4,018,607,927	95,363,405.03	2.373	78,843,113.75	1.962	0.411
1919.....	147,696,895	4,079,632,918	102,218,862.73	2.506	90,987,178.97	2.230	0.276
1920.....	164,766,666	4,877,375,349	133,241,548.16	2.732	117,276,657.82	2.405	0.327
1921.....	135,381,182	4,064,960,198	129,324,479.99	3.181	98,537,772.00	2.424	0.757
1922.....	135,927,255	4,597,645,876	147,424,246.61	3.207	116,229,107.65	2.528	0.679
1923.....	139,330,905	4,847,822,366	155,516,003.42	3.208	118,535,794.86	2.445	0.763
1924.....	132,883,492	4,600,403,131	147,523,905.30	3.207	110,882,585.71	2.410	0.797
1925.....	128,701,385	4,517,916,335	144,969,963.21	3.209	112,448,307.90	2.489	0.720

The operation of the Delaware & Raritan Canal (66 miles) is excluded from the 1919 figures on account of same being operated by the New York and New Jersey Canal Section of the United States Railroad Administration.

Beginning with the year 1918, the Pennsylvania Railroad Company leased a number of important railroads in its System, the operating results of which had not theretofore been included with the lines it directly operates. Therefore, the figures for the period 1918 to 1925, inclusive, reflect the inclusion of the operating results of these leased lines, as well as the normal growth in traffic.

DIVIDENDS AND ALLOTMENTS ON CAPITAL STOCK—THE PENNSYLVANIA RAILROAD COMPANY

DATE	Capital Stock on which Dividend or Allotment was Declared	DIVIDEND				ALLOTMENTS OF STOCK ON SUBSCRIPTION	
		CASH		SCRIP OR STOCK			
		Per Cent.	Amount	Per Cent.	Amount	Per Cent.	Amount
February, 1913.	$453,877,950	1½	$6,808,169 25				
May, "	453,877,950	1½	6,808,169 25	....	....	10	(At par) $45,387,750 00
August, "	493,872,150	1½	7,408,082 25				
November, "	493,882,350	1½	7,408,235 25				
Feb., 1914, to Feb., 1921, inclusive.......	499,265,700	1½	7,488,985 50 Feb., May, Aug. and Nov. of each year.				
May, 1921, to Aug., 1922, inclusive.......	499,265,700	1	4,992,657 May, Aug., Nov. 1921; Feb., May, Aug. 1922				
Nov., 1922, to Nov., 1925, inclusive.......	499,265,700	1½	7,488,985 50 Feb., May, Aug. and Nov. of each year........				

NUMBER OF STOCKHOLDERS
December 31st

Year	Number	Year	Number
1913	88,586	1919	117,725
1914	91,571	1920	133,068
1915	93,768	1921	141,699
1916	90,388	1922	137,429
1917	100,038	1923	144,228
1918	106,911	1924	145,174
1925	140,578		

DIRECTORS

The following is a list of the Directors who served during President Rea's Administration, together with the dates of their election and the end of their service:—

Name of Director	*Elected*	*End of Service*
N. Parker Shortridge	March 24, 1874,	January 3, 1915;
William H. Barnes	December 11, 1889,	May 5, 1918;
George Wood	March 24, 1891,	February 17, 1926;
C. Stuart Patterson	July 2, 1895,	November 8, 1924;
Effingham B. Morris	December 31, 1896,	....
Thomas DeWitt Cuyler	May 10, 1899,	November 2, 1922;
James McCrea	June 9, 1899,	March 28, 1913;
Samuel Rea	June 14, 1899,	....
Lincoln Godfrey	April 11, 1900,	January 12, 1916;
Rudulph Ellis	November 11, 1903,	September 21, 1915;
Henry C. Frick	December 26, 1906,	December 2, 1919;
Charles E. Ingersoll	January 23, 1907,	....
Percival Roberts, Jr.	October 23, 1907,	April 14, 1920;
"	April 9, 1926,	....
Henry Tatnall	March 24, 1909,	May 1, 1925;
W. W. Atterbury	March 3, 1911,	....
George D. Dixon	September 16, 1912,	August 1, 1925;
W. Heyward Myers	January 1, 1913,	March 1, 1920;
Joseph Wood	April 9, 1913,	March 4, 1922;
Bayard Henry	January 13, 1915,	September 17, 1926;
George H. McFadden	October 13, 1915,	October 16, 1926;
Levi L. Rue	January 12, 1916,	....
Clement B. Newbold	May 22, 1918,	March 30, 1926;
Andrew W. Mellon	February 25, 1920,	January 12, 1921;
A. J. County	March 1, 1920,	....
Howard Heinz	September 22, 1920,	....
Edgar C. Felton	March 7, 1921,	....
Spencer C. Gilbert	April 3, 1922,	January 24, 1924;
Arthur W. Thompson	November 22, 1922,	....
Jay Cooke	February 13, 1924,	....
Elisha Lee	January 28, 1925,	....

WILLIAM WALLACE ATTERBURY
Tenth President—October 1st, 1925, to date.

WILLIAM WALLACE ATTERBURY

TENTH PRESIDENT, 1925 TO DATE.

WILLIAM WALLACE ATTERBURY was elected President of the Pennsylvania Railroad Company, effective October 1st, 1925. He was born at New Albany, Ind., on January 31st, 1866, and after receiving a liberal preparatory education, was graduated from Yale University in 1886 with the degree of Bachelor of Philosophy. He entered the service of the Pennsylvania Railroad Company on October 11th, 1886, as an apprentice in the Altoona shops. From 1889 to 1892 he served as Assistant Road Foreman of Engines on various Divisions of the Pennsylvania Railroad and Philadelphia, Wilmington & Baltimore Railroad. In 1892 he was promoted to Assistant Engineer of Motive Power of the Pennsylvania Company's Northwest System, and, in 1893, to Master Mechanic for the Pennsylvania Company at Fort Wayne, Ind.

On October 26th, 1896, Mr. Atterbury was appointed Superintendent of Motive Power of the Pennsylvania Lines East of Pittsburgh and Erie, and on October 1st, 1901, he was advanced to General Superintendent of Motive Power. He was appointed General Manager of the Pennsylvania Lines East of Pittsburgh and Erie on January 1st, 1903; Fifth Vice-President, in charge of Transportation, on March 24th, 1909, and Fourth Vice-President on March 3rd, 1911.

On May 8th, 1912, when the practice of designating the Vice-Presidents numerically was discontinued, Mr. Atterbury's title was changed to Vice-President in charge of Operation, which title he retained when the practice of dividing the System at Pittsburgh for operating purposes was discontinued on March 1st, 1920. On November 15th, 1924, he was elected Vice-President, from which position he was advanced to the Presidency.

On May 17th, 1916, Mr. Atterbury was unanimously elected President of the American Railway Association. As the head of that Association, he rendered invaluable service to the United States Government in connection with the transportation of troops and war supplies to the Mexican Border, as well as to the Atlantic Seaboard.

Shortly after the United States entered the war against Germany, Mr. Atterbury was requested by the Secretary of War to go to France and assume charge, as Director General of Transportation of the American Expeditionary Forces, of the details of organization for the construction and operation of the United States transportation requirements there, as well as to harmonize them with those of our Allies in France.

He sailed for Europe in August, 1917, and on October 5th, 1917, was commissioned Brigadier General of the United States Army, which, three days later, was confirmed by the United States Senate. He returned to America on May 31st, 1919, and on the following day received his discharge from the Army.

In recognition of his work with the American Expeditionary Forces, General Atterbury received the following decorations:—

United States....Distinguished Service Medal.
France..........Legion of Honor, rank of Commander.
Great Britain....Companion of the Most Honorable Order of the Bath.
Belgium.........Commander of the Order of the Crown.
Serbia...........Royal Order of the White Eagle.

IMPROVED OPERATING RESULTS—INCREASED DIVIDEND

The first full year (1926) of President Atterbury's Administration was noteworthy by reason of the fact that the Company enjoyed one of the best years in its history, the Net Income being equal to 13.53% on its Capital Stock. This gratifying result was due largely to greater operating efficiency, favorable business and financial conditions, and the large expenditures which have been made in rehabilitating the property since the period of Federal Control. The Management, therefore, felt justified in increasing the quarterly dividend paid to the stockholders in November, 1926, from 1½% to 1¾%, or at the rate of 7% per annum.

The Annual Report for 1926 referred to the great improvement which had taken place in operating the property since the period of Federal Control, as evidenced by the following statement showing the Operating Ratio of the Pennsylvania Railroad System (which is the percentage of Operating Revenues used to pay Operating Expenses), beginning with the year 1921, the first full year of operation following the Federal Control and Guaranty periods:—

1921	87.56%	1924	80.16%
1922	82.35%	1925	78.32%
1923	81.77%	1926	77.52%

Based on the Operating Revenues of the System for the year 1926, a reduction of 1% in the Operating Ratio was equal to saving over $7,000,000. This, it was stated, readily explained the continued efforts of the Management to produce the maximum amount of transportation with the greatest efficiency and economy.

GROWTH AND MAGNITUDE OF OPERATIONS

The first full year in which the Pennsylvania Railroad operated with its own completed line between Harrisburg and Pittsburgh was 1855, and in that year its Operating Revenues amounted to slightly more than $3,500,000. In 1926, the Operating Revenues of the System, which sprung from such modest beginnings, were nearly $767,000,000. The Operating Expenses in 1855 were approximately $1,500,000., while in 1926, they were more than $594,000,000. Such has been the growth of the System in this 71-year period.

Some idea of the magnitude of the present operations, and the great mass of people, the industries and communities which are dependent on the steady earning power of the System, may be gained from the fact that in 1926 it paid out about $390,000,000. in wages to over 200,000 persons; approximately $260,000,000. were spent for material and supplies and for improvement work; nearly $89,000,000. were paid in fixed charges and dividends, and about $40,500,000. in taxes.

LEASE OF PENNSYLVANIA, OHIO & DETROIT RAILROAD

On April 29th, 1926, the Pennsylvania Railroad Company leased the Pennsylvania, Ohio & Detroit Railroad, to which reference has been made, for 999 years from January 1st, 1926, and agreed to guarantee the payment of all fixed charges and 5% dividends per annum on the Capital Stock of the leased Company.

OFFICE BUILDING COMPLETED

The new office building of fireproof construction at West Philadelphia, the necessity for which has been previously explained, was practically completed at the close of 1926. Early in 1927 it was occupied by forces theretofore located in various parts of the City, which, in addition to effecting increased efficiency and economy in carrying on the work through the concentration of forces, will result in a large saving in rentals.

NEW EQUIPMENT

The Company continued its policy of adding to its equipment, and in the year 1926, the principal units placed in service were as follows:—

2,000 automobile box cars (100,000 pounds capacity),
500 box cars (100,000 pounds capacity),
61 steel cabin cars,
200 mountain type freight or passenger locomotives,
58 shifting locomotives,
13 electric locomotives,
100 13,000-gallon capacity freight service tenders,
176 steam service passenger cars,
28 electric service coaches,
34 dining cars,
319 combined baggage-express cars,
10 combined baggage-mail cars,
5 combined passenger-baggage cars,
6 combined passenger-baggage-mail cars,
5 tug boats,
2 covered barges,
8 car floats.

SALE OF EQUIPMENT TRUST CERTIFICATES

To pay, in part, for the cost of this equipment, the Company issued and sold in May, 1926, $17,030,000. General Equipment 4½% Trust Certificates, Series "D," which were dated May 15th, 1926, and matured at the rate of $1,310,000. annually, starting May 15th, 1929, and ending May 15th, 1941.

As the Company made such notable progress in rehabilitating and adding to the tractive power and capacity of its equipment beginning with the year 1919, it may be of interest to briefly summarize in statement form the cost of same, the amount of Equipment Trust Certificates issued against it, and the equipment covered, viz:—

DETAIL OF EQUIPMENT ACQUIRED AND FINANCED 1919-1926, INCLUSIVE

	Original Cost of Equipment	Amount Originally Issued	Amount Outstanding Dec. 31, 1926	Principal Payable Annually	Date of Final Maturity	Equipment Covered
P. R. R. 6% Equipment Certificates of 1920, dated 1/15/1920	$58,442,161.	$58,412,000.	$35,048,000.	$3,894,000.	1/15/1935.	Freight Cars.. 16,450 Locomotives.. 165
P. R. R. 5% General Equipment Trust, Series "A," dated 3/1/1923..................	39,254,099.	31,500,000.	25,200,000.	2,100,000.	3/1/1938..	Passenger Cars 250 Locomotives.. 475
P. R. R. 5% General Equipment Trust, Series "B," dated 4/1/1924..................	25,501,215.	20,100,000.	17,420,000.	1,340,000.	4/1/1939..	Freight Cars.. 12,000
P. R. R. 4½% General Equipment Trust, Series "C," dated 10/1/1924............	21,018,786.	15,750,000.	13,650,000.	1,050,000.	10/1/1939.	Freight Cars.. 10,000
P. R. R. 4½% General Equipment Trust, Series "D," dated 5/15/1926............	24,354,270.	17,030,000.	17,030,000.	1,310,000. (Begins 5/15/1929)	5/15/1941.	Passenger Cars 109 Baggage Cars. 125 Freight Cars.. 2,000 Locomotives.. 200
	$168,570,531.	$142,792,000.	$108,348,000.	$8,384,000.	....	Passenger Cars 359 Baggage Cars. 125 Freight Cars.. 40,450 Locomotives.. 840

The foregoing does not represent the cost of all equipment acquired in the period 1919–1926, because additional equipment, valued at many millions of dollars, was purchased or built at the Altoona Works of the Company, for which no Equipment Trust Certificates were issued.

CHANGES IN SECURITIES OWNED

The Annual Report for 1926 stated that the Pennsylvania Railroad Company had purchased additional shares of Common and Preferred Stocks of the Norfolk & Western Railway Company, and as a result it was then the owner of $56,823,200., par value, of Common and $12,098,000., par value, of Preferred Stocks of the Norfolk & Western Railway Company. The balance of the Company's holdings of stock of the Southern Pacific Company were also sold in 1926. It will be recalled that this stock had been received in 1913 in exchange for the Pennsylvania Railroad Company's holdings of Baltimore & Ohio Railroad Company Common and Preferred Stocks.

PROGRESS ON LITTLE CREEK EXTENSION

The New York, Philadelphia & Norfolk Railroad, one of the Company's leased roads, began the construction of its Little Creek Extension in 1926. The purpose was to expand the terminal facilities in and near Norfolk, Va., and expedite the movement of traffic between Cape Charles and Norfolk by reducing the water haul from 36 miles to 24 miles, thus providing more dependable freight service between a large and important producing and consuming area in the South and Southeast and the leading northern centers of population and industry.

NEW LONG ISLAND CITY EXPRESS TERMINAL

The Pennsylvania Tunnel & Terminal Railroad, which furnishes the entrance of the Pennsylvania Railroad System into and through New York City, completed and placed in service in December, 1926, a new express building in Long

Island City, which was the largest plant of its kind in the Country, and was operated by the American Railway Express Company under lease. It contained all modern devices for the handling of express traffic, covered approximately 750,000 square feet of ground, and permitted the loading or unloading of nearly 300 vehicles at one time. Upon the completion of this improvement the handling of express traffic was transferred from Pennsylvania Station, New York City, which released track and platform space in that Station for passenger traffic, and at Pier "D," Jersey City, N. J., for commercial purposes.

CANTON-BAYARD LINE COMPLETED

A new double track low grade line, approximately 15 miles in length, between Canton and Bayard on the Pittsburgh, Ft. Wayne & Chicago Railway, which was leased to the Pennsylvania Railroad Company, was completed and placed in operation in 1926. This furnished a cut-off between Canton, O., and Rochester, Pa., with grades in both directions of 0.3% except for one helper grade, compared with maximum ruling grades of 1% on the route formerly used. The purpose in building it was to expedite the movement of the through eastbound and westbound traffic; permit the operation of a greater number of train units; increase the tonnage per train, and produce other operating economies.

MOTOR SERVICE

As the application for a charter to operate a motor service in the various Counties of Pennsylvania served by the Company's rail lines was denied, the Management stated that the matter would continue to receive careful consideration and proper steps would be taken to protect the interests of the Company. It was recognized that the private motor car, the motor bus and motor truck furnished a very flexible instrument of transportation, being especially adapted to light loads and short distance, and to service demanding prompt changes to meet the varying conditions and character of traffic. It was for that reason that the Company had co-operated with various concerns specializing in this form of transportation, and had made an application for the charter.

RELATIONS WITH EMPLOYES

In referring to the Company's relations with its employes, it was stated in the Annual Report for 1926 that the Employes' Representation Plan continued to function successfully, and had contributed to the satisfactory operating results obtained during that year. The essential aim of this plan, as previously explained, was to promote the welfare of the employes, to assure them adequate representation in discussing with the Management questions of wages and working conditions, and eventually to develop relations of such confidence that the Management might be able to mobilize effectively the results, not merely of the effort but of the observation, experience and wisdom of all employes in the improvement of every phase of the Company's operation. It was, therefore, gratifying to the Management that recognition had been given to the desirability of just such methods of handling labor questions through the passage by Congress of the Watson-Parker Bill, and its approval by the President on May 20th, 1926.

WATSON-PARKER BILL

The Watson-Parker Bill repealed existing railroad labor legislation, as expressed in the Transportation Act, and substituted for it a method of dealing with labor questions which held promise of far more satisfactory results than anything which had yet been realized. It provided for the creation on each railroad, or groups of railroads, of Boards of Adjustment similar to the joint reviewing committees on the Pennsylvania Railroad. If these local Adjustment Boards were unable to settle differences, the services could be invoked of a permanent Mediation Board, consisting of five commissioners appointed by the President of the United States. This Board would seek to settle the dispute through the exercise of its good offices or effect an agreement to arbitrate the controversy. The decision of such arbitrators would be final, would be filed with the United States District Court, and, unless successfully impeached, would become a judgment of the Court. It was also provided, in the event that the local Boards of Adjustment failed to agree, that mediation and conciliation also prove unavailing, that arbitration was unacceptable to both parties and that, as a consequence, a substantial interruption to interstate commerce was threatened, the President of the United States had the right to create a Board to investigate and report to the public within thirty days the facts respecting the dispute. During the Board's investigation and for thirty days after the filing of its report, no change could be made, unless by agreement of the parties to the controversy, in the conditions out of which the dispute arose.

This Bill, it was stated, had been presented to Congress with the approval of an overwhelming number of the principal railroad executives of the Country, and with the approval of the representatives of the employes. It had been well described as providing "machinery for the arrangement of peace; not a manual of war." The whole purpose of the legislation was to encourage and provide for the settlement of disputes by mutual consent and in the interest of all parties. Above all things the Bill represented expressed recognition on the part of both railroad Management and railroad employes that uninterrupted transportation was of paramount importance to the public, and that both Management and employes had a primary duty to compose their differences fairly, without inconvenience to, or undue burden on, the public.

PUBLIC INTEREST PROTECTED

The public interest was thoroughly protected in the Bill, for in the event of any dispute going to arbitration, the arbitrators may be regarded as representing the public, and, in case arbitration should be declined, the report of the fact-finding commission appointed by the President would bring the full force of public opinion to bear in the direction of settling the dispute on its real merits. It took away from the Interstate Commerce Commission none of its power to review proposals for increased freight rates or to take any other measures for the protection of the public interest against burdensome charges or conditions of any kind. The Bill, in brief, protected the public interest in every practicable way.

EMPLOYE REPRESENTATION PLAN NOT AFFECTED

The enactment of this legislation, it was pointed out, required no modification of the Employe Representation Plan of the Pennsylvania Railroad Company, because the intent of the Watson-Parker Bill was that disputed questions should, as far as possible, be settled in conference in a spirit of mutual understanding between representatives designated respectively by the carriers and the employes, which was the basis of the Pennsylvania Railroad Employe Representation Plan. Therefore, the Management of the Company had joined with its own employes and with the Managements and the representatives of employes of other railroads in urging its enactment.

RELIEF DEPARTMENT

At the close of 1926, the Pennsylvania Railroad Employes' Relief Department had a membership of 199,406 officers and employes, and $5,189,000. were distributed to the members in payment of death, sickness, accident and disablement benefits, and for superannuation allowances in the year 1926. The Relief Fund since its organization in 1886, has disbursed in benefits over $89,700,000., which were provided through contributions from the officers and employes and income from assets in the Fund, while over $16,000,000. have been contributed by the Company to meet the Operating Expenses in carrying on this work.

PENSION DEPARTMENT

The Pension Department, established in 1900, was at the close of 1926, paying pensions to 8,561 officers and employes retired from active service, of whom 32 had reached the age of ninety years or more, while the average age of the pensioners was 72 years and 7 months. Over $46,300,000. have been disbursed in pensions since 1900, in addition to the Operating Expenses of the Department, all of which were paid by the various Companies in the System.

OTHER CO-OPERATIVE ASSOCIATIONS

There are other co-operative associations maintained by the officers and employes for which the Company assumes no responsibility, one of which, the Employes' Provident & Loan Association, had on December 31st, 1926, a membership of 79,248. Of this number, 67,674 had saving fund accounts with total deposits of $7,263,078. Officers and employes numbering 14,315 had purchased 69,681 shares of Pennsylvania Railroad Company Stock as well as other securities of companies in the System, and 1,394 had purchased additional pension allowances to supplement those paid by the Company. A great many members of the Association also availed themselves of the privilege of purchasing their homes through building loans made to them, aggregating $3,269,069., and emergency loans in the sum of $453,080. had been granted. Another organization maintained solely by the officers and employes is the Mutual Beneficial Association, which has a membership of over 18,000 and, in addition to paying death and disability benefits, has been the means of purchasing over 27,000 shares of Pennsylvania Railroad Company Stock for officers and employes. Over $10,000,000. of insurance is carried in this Association for the benefit of its members and their families, and since its organization death and disability benefits to members and their beneficiaries amounting to $380,000. have been paid.

TENTATIVE VALUATION OF PENNSYLVANIA RAILROAD SYSTEM

In December, 1926, the Interstate Commerce Commission served its tentative valuation of the property of the Pennsylvania Railroad Company and its leased lines as of June 30th, 1918, which was required under the Valuation Act of Congress passed in March, 1913. The Company had co-operated in this extensive work which cost the Pennsylvania Railroad System $5,426,774. to December 31st, 1926.

The respective dates of valuation of the Companies in the System were as of June 30th in the various years between 1915 and 1918, but the Commission uniformly used prices in the inventories which it considered as representing conditions as of June 30th, 1914, and valued the lands as of the respective dates of valuation. The findings of the Commission did not, of course, reflect what the properties were worth at the end of 1926, because at least $500,000,000. had been expended for additions thereto and improvements thereof since the valuations were made.

The total assets so found for the entire 80 Companies comprising the Pennsylvania Railroad System were as follows:—

The total of the Commission's cost of reproduction new was	$1,790,460,568.00
Its value of lands	425,635,077.00
But in addition the Companies had:	
Materials and supplies	69,664,112.64
Working Capital (including special deposits)	44,747,259.80
Securities of corporations not operated as a portion of its System, which cost	157,628,474.47
Making a total of	$2,488,135,491.91

Against the foregoing figures of the System must be placed the total par value of Stock, Bonds and other securities of the 80 Companies outstanding on the dates at which the respective valuations were made, which amounted to $1,793,240,093. Of this total, $471,275,607. were owned by Companies comprising the Pennsylvania Railroad System, either directly or through sinking funds, insurance or trust funds, leaving capital issues in the hands of the public of $1,321,964,486. as against total assets of $2,488,135,491. As several legal questions and some differences as to facts were involved in the making of these valuations, protests had been filed, and the various Companies in the System were to be given an opportunity to present their arguments before the Interstate Commerce Commission.

FOREIGN PASSENGER AND FREIGHT AGENCIES

Arrangements were made in 1926 to give the Company's passenger service world-wide representation by the appointment of Thomas Cook & Son, a well-known and experienced travel organization, as General Foreign Passenger Agents. This arrangement, it was stated, would benefit not only foreign travelers coming to this Country, but also American tourists going abroad. This firm was to represent the Pennsylvania Railroad Company in Europe, Australia, New Zealand, Tasmania, India, Burma, Ceylon, the Straits Settlements, Palestine, Syria, Mesopotamia, Egypt, the Sudan, Algeria, Tunisia, China, Japan, South Africa and the Belgian Congo. Their individual offices were to perform all the functions of a Pennsylvania Railroad passenger agency, advising travelers about the Company's passenger facilities and points of interest on its lines, and arranging accommodations, reservations and tickets for travel to points on or reached via its railroad.

Arrangements were also completed for the establishment of freight agencies in the principal cities and ports of Europe to facilitate and expedite the through movement of freight from abroad to points reached by the Pennsylvania Railroad System, and also to aid in the handling of export business.

STATISTICAL DATA—ALTOONA WORKS

As this recital of the growth and development of the Company closes with the first full year of President Atterbury's Administration, the operating and traffic statistics and financial data for 1926 will be found in the concluding chapter and in the addenda, which expresses in facts and figures the accumulated growth of the Company since its incorporation over 80 years ago. Furthermore, this work would not be complete without reference to the great Altoona Works of the Company, and a brief description of this important producing unit in the System will be found on subsequent pages.

DIRECTORS

The following is a list of the Directors who have so far served as Directors during the Administration of President Atterbury:—

Name of Director	*Elected*	*End of Service*
George Wood................	March 24, 1891,	February 17, 1926;
Effingham B. Morris.........	December 31, 1896,	....
Samuel Rea..................	June 14, 1899,	....
Charles E. Ingersoll..........	January 23, 1907,	....
W. W. Atterbury.............	March 3, 1911,	....
Bayard Henry...............	January 13, 1915,	September 17, 1926;
Geo. H. McFadden..........	October 13, 1915,	October 16, 1926;
Levi L. Rue.................	January 12, 1916,	....
Clement B. Newbold.........	May 22, 1918,	March 30, 1926;
A. J. County................	March 1, 1920,	....
Howard Heinz...............	September 22, 1920,	....
Edgar C. Felton.............	March 7, 1921,	....
Arthur W. Thompson........	November 22, 1922,	....
Jay Cooke..................	February 13, 1924,	....
Elisha Lee..................	January 28, 1925,	....
J. L. Eysmans..............	March 10, 1926,	....
M. C. Kennedy.............	"	....
Charles Day................	March 24, 1926,	....
Percival Roberts, Jr..........	October 23, 1907,	April 14, 1920;
"	April 9, 1926,	....
John T. Dorrance............	October 13, 1926,	....
Richard B. Mellon..........	December 8, 1926,	....

It will be noted from the foregoing that the present Directors of the Company, listed in accordance with their seniority of service as Directors, are as follows:—

Effingham B. Morris,
Samuel Rea,
Charles E. Ingersoll,
W. W. Atterbury,
Levi L. Rue,
A. J. County,
Howard Heinz,
Edgar C. Felton,
Arthur W. Thompson,
Jay Cooke,
Elisha Lee,
M. C. Kennedy,
J. L. Eysmans,
Charles Day,
*Percival Roberts, Jr.,
John T. Dorrance,
Richard B. Mellon.

* Also served as Director from October 23rd, 1907, to April 14th, 1920.

ALTOONA WORKS

The Company has located in the City of Altoona, Pa., the most extensive group of railroad shops in the World, which are the result of over 76 years of development. Little was it realized that a new City was to be born when the construction of the Pennsylvania Railroad was approaching the eastern base of the Allegheny Mountains, but from a modest beginning it has grown to be one of the greatest railroad centers in the Country. The prosperity and adversity of the Pennsylvania Railroad System mirrors itself in the life and activities of Altoona perhaps more than in any other City on its Lines. As early as 1849 (when the present City of Altoona was occupied by a few farms), the site was selected and plans made for the erection of an enginehouse, a machine shop and an erecting shop. Work was begun on these buildings in the early part of 1850, and as the System grew so did the Altoona Works until at the present time there are, for operating purposes, four separate and distinct units. They comprise the following shops, the description of which was furnished by the Motive Power Department of the Company, viz:—

Altoona Machine Shops,
Altoona Car Shops,
Juniata Shops,
South Altoona Foundries.

Each of the four large units is complete in itself and is handled by an operating organization reporting to the Works Manager.

ALTOONA MACHINE SHOPS

The Altoona Machine Shops had their origin in several small buildings erected in 1850, of which practically nothing remains today. These shops now comprise the following buildings:—

Hammer Shop,
Brass Foundry,
Miscellaneous Department,
Smith Shop,
Spring Shop,
Flue Shop,
Cab and Pilot Shop,
Tank and Automatic Shop,
Frame Shop,
Wheel Shop,
Boiler Shop,
3 Erecting Shops,
Machine and Air Brake Shop,
Bolt Shop.

These shops are used in the repairing of locomotives, the manufacture of standard locomotive repair parts, and the production of non-ferrous castings, which are supplied to the entire System. The plant employs 5,500 men, who, with the exception of the brass foundry force, are engaged in locomotive work. The normal output is 4 locomotives given heavy repairs per day. The first locomotive built at Altoona Machine Shops was in 1866 for passenger service, it weighing with tender 137,700 pounds, which is about equal to the weight on two pairs of driving wheels of the present standard passenger locomotives.

ALTOONA CAR SHOPS

The Altoona Car Shops were the first to separate from the original installation at Twelfth Street, they having been built in 1869. From a small beginning the plant has expanded until it covers a space of 82.46 acres, stretching, with material yards, over a length of about one mile, normally employing 3,000 men. It consists of the following units:—

Passenger Car Paint Shop,
Freight Car Paint Shop,
Planing Mill and Cabinet Shop,
Trimming Shop,
Bolt Shop,
Machine Shop,
Smith Shop,
2 Passenger Shops,
Truck Shop,
Steel Car Shop,
Sheet Metal Shop.

A portion of the Company's passenger and freight car equipment is built here and it was at this plant that the steel car industry had its origin. The first all-steel passenger car was completed in these shops on June 11th, 1906; the first all-steel baggage car on November 27th, 1906, and the first all-steel postal car on February 4th, 1907. Heavy repairs are also made to both passenger and freight cars, the latter being practically rebuilt.

The Steel Shop is an important feature of this plant. It is occupied with heavy repair work and the manufacturing of standard repair parts, employing presses up to 2,200 tons capacity, multiple punches, spacing tables and other necessary tools, to insure the interchangeability of parts and maintenance of standards.

Heavy repairs to open top steel cars are about to be discontinued at this shop and the space devoted to the preparation of standard car parts. A lateral extension of the shop is about completed, in which will be located all locomotive tender construction and repair work for Altoona Machine and Juniata Shops.

The original Car Shop building, erected as a freight car construction and repair shop, is now used as a Finishing Shop for locomotives repaired at the Altoona Machine and Juniata Shops. The building is equipped as a modern enginehouse where locomotives are given their finishing touches, are prepared for the road and receive necessary attention during the trial period. This department, while located on Car Shop territory, is operated under the direct supervision of the Works Manager.

The normal output from these Shops is ten open freight cars repaired per day; three passenger cars given heavy and five light repairs per day.

JUNIATA SHOPS

The growing business of the Company and crowding at Altoona Machine Shops led to the construction, in 1889, of the Juniata Shops. They comprise the following buildings:—

2 Smith Shops,
Boiler Shop,
2 Machine Shops,
Storehouse and Office,
Tank Shop,
Erecting and Machine Shop,
2 Welfare Buildings.

Originally constructed to build new locomotives, this plant is now devoted in the main to repair work with a limited amount of new construction, normally employing 4,200 men.

The rated output of these Shops is four locomotives receiving heavy classified repairs per day and the building of twelve new heavy type locomotives a month. Some of the largest and most powerful locomotives in the world, both steam and electric, are built at the Juniata Shops.

SOUTH ALTOONA FOUNDRIES

In 1903 the need of more space in Altoona Machine Shops rendered further expansion necessary and the plant known as the South Altoona Foundries, located two miles south of the City and employing 700 men, was erected in 1904. It is made up of the following units:—

2 Foundries,
Power Plant,
Oil Mixing Plant,
Machine Shop,
Pattern Shop and Storage.

The Wheel Foundry was designed to make all cast iron wheels required for the System and had a capacity of 1,000 wheels per day. Shrinkage in the number of cast iron wheels required, owing to increased use of steel wheels, has made it possible to utilize this foundry to a large extent for gray iron castings.

TEST DEPARTMENT

The Test Department, while located in Altoona Works territory, is a distinct organization, devoted to physical and chemical tests of materials and apparatus purchased and also to research work. It is housed in four buildings at the West end of Altoona Machine Shop Yard—the Physical and Chemical Laboratory, the Locomotive Test Plant, the Manufacturing Laboratory and the Brake Shoe Test Building. These departments are concerned chiefly with research work required for the preparation of specifications, with tests necessary for the maintenance of standards and safe-guarding the health of employes and public, and with the testing of locomotives, both steam and electric.

SUMMARY

The entire Shop Yards occupy an area of 217.82 acres and the shops contain 38.96 acres of floor space; 122 buildings are occupied; 4,391 machine tools are used; 94 overhead traveling cranes, ranging in capacity from 2 tons to 250 tons, and numerous power jib cranes, are required for the handling of material and equipment.

Eleven reservoirs with a total storage capacity of 802,895,000 gallons supply pure water for drinking and industrial purposes to the Works and local enginehouses through 54 miles of main distributing pipes. Daily water consumption is approximately 10,000,000 gallons.

The seven boiler plants have a total capacity of 32,000 horse power. These supply steam for air compressors of 30,670 cubic feet per minute, electric generators of 12,975 K.W. and hydraulic pumps of 1,416 gallons per minute.

The approximate number of men employed under normal conditions, including supervisory forces, is 14,800, requiring a monthly pay roll of approximately $1,800,000.

CONCLUSION

IT may be of interest to summarize some of the outstanding facts and figures connected with the growth of the Company during the last eighty years. In this period, the Country passed through cycles of prosperity and depression, financial panics, labor disturbances, destructive wars, hostile railroad regulation and finally Governmental operation of the railroads. A number of the large roads, particularly in the South and West, sought refuge in Courts of Bankruptcy in the panics of 1873 and 1893, but the Pennsylvania Railroad Company weathered the storms, paid cash dividends in both years, and its proud record is that it has never in all its history failed to meet a financial obligation when due.

PHYSICAL GROWTH

From a Company chartered to build a railroad from Harrisburg to Pittsburgh with a branch to the Great Lakes at Erie, a distance of about 372 miles, all located within the confines of the State of Pennsylvania, and with an authorized Capital Stock of $7,500,000., it has grown into a System with a Property Investment on December 31st, 1926, of over $2,375,000,000. It operates over 11,640 miles of first main track and 28,040 miles of all tracks, which extend through the States of Pennsylvania, New Jersey, New York, Ohio, Indiana, Illinois, Missouri, Michigan, Kentucky, West Virginia, Virginia, Maryland, Delaware and the District of Columbia. The System directly reaches most of the important cities between the Mississippi River and the Atlantic Seaboard and those between the Potomac and Ohio Rivers and the Great Lakes, in which reside about one-half of the Country's population. Its lines traverse a highly developed territory, rich in natural resources, and with great industrial activity and heavy traffic density. This has made it necessary, in order to keep abreast of traffic growth, to make large expenditures for the intensive development of the System, such as additional running tracks, larger terminals, yards and shops, more powerful locomotives, etc. It is a noteworthy fact that the greater part of the expenditures in the last fifty years have been for internal improvements, because with few exceptions the System has not been extended to any important points which were not embraced within the territory it served at the close of President John Edgar Thomson's Administration in 1874. This is a great tribute to the vision and courage of the Management, who so early in the history of American railroads planned and established the Pennsylvania Railroad System in a territory in which there has subsequently been such tremendous industrial expansion and growth of population.

CORPORATE STATUS

The Pennsylvania Railroad System originally consisted of over 600 constituent railroad, bridge, ferry, water supply, real estate, warehouse and electric railway companies, but through consolidations and acquisitions, the number has been reduced to 63 active transportation companies. It also has a stock ownership in 95 additional active and inactive companies, some of which, however, are jointly owned and used with other railroad systems, making a total of 158 companies embraced in the System. A great deal more could have been accomplished in further reducing this total had the consolidation provisions of the Transportation Act permitted, and if the law is modified in a broad way, there is no doubt that much greater progress will be made. The Pennsylvania Railroad Company since its incorporation, and as the parent of many of these companies, has remained solely a corporation of the State of Pennsylvania, but through lease or stock ownership it has been able to extend its operations into other States.

FINANCIAL

The great physical growth of the System has placed it at the head of all American railroads, with a gross investment in Road and Equipment at the end of 1926, of over $2,375,000,000., which with the ownership of securities of other railroads not in its System, amounting to $192,000,000., results in a total investment of over $2,500,000,000. This huge asset was represented by outstanding securities on December 31st, 1926, amounting at par to $2,109,533,891., of which $1,098,900,910., or 52.09% was in Capital Stock, and $1,010,632,981., or 47.91% in Funded Debt. However, various Companies within the System own over $577,000,000., par value, of these securities, leaving only slightly more than $1,500,000,000. held by the public, divided between Capital Stock and Funded Debt as follows:—

Total Capital Stock held by public (par value)...................	$595,656,195.	38.87%
Total Funded Debt held by public (par value)...................	936,674,101.	61.13%
Total....................	$1,532,330,296.	100.00%

It will be noted from the foregoing that at the close of 1926 the securities of the System owned by the public were divided 38.87% in Capital Stock and 61.13% in Funded Debt. In 1916 the ratios were about even, but due to the uncertain conditions existing during these 10 years, which covered the War and Federal Control periods, the parent Company could not continue its policy of selling additional Stock at par to its stockholders. The Management has, therefore, had to resort to sales of Bonds and Equipment Trust Obligations to meet its financial requirements, but it has been most conservative in thus adding to its Funded Debt. This is illustrated by the fact that the average expenditures for Road and Equipment purposes of the System has been nearly $58,000,000. *per annum* in the period 1916 to 1926, and investments in securities of other railroads also increased on an average of over $2,000,000. per annum, making a total increased investment *annually* of approximately $60,000,000. In this same period, there has been an average *annual* increase of about $30,000,000. in Funded Debt held by the public, and an average *decrease* in the Capital Stock so held, amounting to over $3,000,000. per annum (due largely to exchange of Bonds for Stock), so that the average net increase of capital liabilities in the hands of the public was only $27,000,000. *per annum* in the ten-year period from December 31st, 1916, to the close of 1926. This compares with an average *annual* increase of $60,000,000. in the investment in physical property and securities of corporations not in the System. The point of the comparison is that the capital liabilities of the System held by the public have increased less than fifty cents for every dollar of increased investment during this ten-year period.

The large excess of capital assets over capital liabilities is due largely to the policy established by the Management shortly after the road was opened, and since continued, of utilizing a large portion of its surplus earnings and income for additions and betterments to the property rather than to issue securities therefor. This has been of great assistance to the Company in carrying it through business depressions, and particularly during the period of hostile railroad regulation and for several years following the return of the railroads to their owners in 1920.

STOCKHOLDERS

The stockholders have shared in the prosperity of the Company, having received a cash dividend in every calendar year beginning with 1856, and prior to that time (1847 to 1855, inclusive) interest was paid at the rate of 6% per annum on paid-in installments on Capital Stock subscriptions. In addition, a number of Stock and Scrip dividends were paid representing a part of the expenditures made on the property out of surplus income. The average cash dividends paid have been slightly in excess of 6% per annum over this long period, and if the Stock and Scrip dividends were included the average return paid to the stockholders would be about 7½% per annum. Cash dividends paid have ranged from as high as 10% in the 60's and early 70's to 2% in 1878 (following the Pittsburgh Riots of 1877), and they are now being paid at the rate of 7% per annum.

As indicating how highly the Stock of the Pennsylvania Railroad Company is regarded by investors, the books of the Company show that at the end of 1926, there were 141,202 registered stockholders residing in every State in the Union and nearly all foreign Countries, of whom 49.85% were women, whose holdings amounted to 32.93% of the entire amount of Stock outstanding. A majority of the stockholders (55.53%) are residents of the State of Pennsylvania, where 51.43% of the outstanding Stock is held, and a large part of the balance is owned in the territory served by the Company's lines. The ownership of the Stock is so widely held by citizens in all walks of life, as well as their financial, insurance, educational, religious and charitable institutions, that a great responsibility is imposed on the Management to so shape the policies of the Company as to protect these interests, as well as those of the public and employes.

EMPLOYES

The Management has always been mindful of the interests of its employes, and it has not only paid fair wages, but has been a leader in seeking to improve their working conditions and providing agencies to serve as a practical means of relief in times of sickness, accident, old age and death. In line with this policy the Company established more than forty years ago a Relief Fund and later a Pension Department.

There are other co-operative associations maintained by the officers and employes for which the Company assumes no responsibility, the two largest of which are the Employes Provident & Loan Association and the Mutual Beneficial Association, and their activities have already been mentioned. All of these organizations serve to promote the esprit de corps of the service, and in order to establish even a closer relationship between the Management and its employes, the Company was the pioneer among railroads in adopting the so-called Employes' Representation Plan. The details of this plan have already been referred to in this review, but the experience since it was established has more than justified the belief of the Management that when a spirit of mutual understanding is reached in reviewing disputed labor questions, the representatives of the employes and the Management, each having equal power, can be expected to deal fairly with each other. This is the aim of the plan and it is becoming increasingly evident that it is a sound and common sense method of insuring industrial peace.

THE MANAGEMENT

One basic factor closely interwoven with the growth and prosperity of the Company, upon which comment is rarely made, is that it has had an experienced and progressive Board of Directors, composed of stockholders, whose advice and counsel have been of inestimable value in directing the affairs of the Company. The Directors, other than the officers who serve on the Board, have not as a rule been trained railroad men, but leaders of great ability and prominence in other fields of business activity, and possessing the confidence of the stockholders and the public. The President and four Vice-Presidents, who are Directors, have risen from the ranks, are experienced railroad men, and have an intimate knowledge of the property. The framework of the Organization was laid over 75 years ago by President John Edgar Thomson, but it has been enlarged from time to time to meet the growth of the Company and the changing conditions. However, the policy then adopted of selecting for higher positions men who had been trained on the railroad, and who had won promotion through hard work and conspicuous service, has been continued. It is the knowledge of this traditional policy which has inspired many employes to strive for official recognition.

MODERN PRACTICES

The adoption of modern practices is a necessary part of the growth of any large corporation, and the Pennsylvania Railroad System has been a leader in this respect, particularly in the field of electrification and motive power developments. As early as 1901, when there had been little experience in this Country with the construction and operation of standard sized railroad subaqueous tunnels to accommodate heavy and high speed passenger traffic, it embarked on its New York Tunnel Extension with electrified motive power to haul the trains. The extension of the Orleans Railway in Paris and its electrification proved that trunk line electric operation was feasible. This work was examined and seemed to offer the solution of the problem to extend the Pennsylvania Railroad System directly into and through New York by tunnels. A careful study and investigation were, therefore, made which developed that it was entirely practicable, so the work was begun and completed, and it has since been regarded as an outstanding engineering achievement. In 1902 it began the work of electrifying the Long Island Railroad; over twenty years ago the electrification of one of the Company's routes between Camden and Atlantic City, N. J., was completed; a number of its suburban lines radiating from Philadelphia have also been electrified for some years, and plans are now under way to electrify all of its local lines running from Philadelphia. Studies have also been made of other electrification projects, notably the crossing of the Allegheny Mountains between Altoona and Conemaugh, a distance of about 35 miles.

Similarly, it has kept pace with motive power developments, the tractive effort of its locomotives having increased from less than 10,000 pounds in the 50's to 90,000 pounds for the large freight locomotives. It has built at its Altoona Works a number of large electric locomotives for passenger and freight service and a smaller type for shifting purposes, and it has also under construction several Diesel-Electric shifting locomotives, so that as the lines in the System are electrified, there will be available for service electric locomotives of proven efficiency and adaptability. It was the first steam railroad to adopt the all-steel type of passenger car for its service, and was among the pioneers in the use of the all-steel freight car. More than 4,300 miles of its main track are laid with 130-pound steel rail, and it has in its service the latest type of signal devices. Its shop machinery and tools are of the most modern type, and experiments and tests are continually being made to develop the most scientific appliances which human ingenuity can design, all for the purpose of providing the American public with a transportation machine which will be as efficient and safe as it is humanly possible to make it.

THE FUTURE

The Pennsylvania Railroad System is today established as one of the strongest and most efficient agencies of transportation in the Country, but this enviable position was not won without going through the usual vicissitudes which beset the growth of every great enterprise. It, however, has survived them all, and is now enjoying one of the most prosperous periods in its history. With the experience of the past as a guide, it can look forward with confidence to the future, and while from a physical standpoint its growth will probably continue for some years to be intensive, because of the rapid industrial expansion in the vast territory it already serves, it must also be prepared, in any consolidation plans adopted for the railroads of the Country, to protect its well established traffic routes and provide for future growth. Further progress will also be made in varied forms of transportation, but whether it be by electrification, motorized transport, or aircraft, it can safely be assumed that the Pennsylvania Railroad System will be in the forefront in providing its patrons with the most modern transportation service.

The future is full of promise for this great transportation System, subject, of course, to such limitations as may be placed on its earning power by the legislative or regulatory authorities, but with a vigilant and progressive Management, an efficient staff of officers and employes, and a loyal body of stockholders, there is every reason to expect that it will rise to even greater heights in the field of American railway transportation.

This review concludes with the following interesting operating, traffic, and financial statements, viz:—

THE PENNSYLVANIA RAILROAD COMPANY

A—Mileage operated;
B—Income Statement for 1926;
C—Return on Property Investment, 1910 to 1926, inclusive;
D—Percentage earned on Capital Stock, 1890 to 1926, inclusive;
E—Cash, Stock and Scrip Dividends paid since Incorporation;
F—Record of Market Prices of Stock, 1876–1926, inclusive.
G—General Balance Sheet for year ending December 31st, 1926;
H—Classification of Freight Traffic.

THE PENNSYLVANIA RAILROAD SYSTEM

I—Combined Operating Results of all Transportation Companies for 1926;
J—Return on Property Investment, 1910 to 1926, inclusive;
K—Comparative Data, 1916–1926;
L—Comparisons with Class I Railroads in United States for 1925;
M—Various Classes of Equipment Owned;
N—Number and Kind of Companies;
Map.

ADDENDA "A"

MILEAGE OPERATED BY THE PENNSYLVANIA RAILROAD COMPANY

LINES OWNED—PENNSYLVANIA RAILROAD COMPANY		Miles Dec. 31st, 1926
Broad Street Station, Philadelphia, Pa., to Pittsburgh, Pa., with extensions and branches		2,174.27
Sunbury, Pa., to Erie, Pa., with extensions and branches		632.99
Kiskiminetas Junction, Pa., to Oil City, Pa., and Red Bank, Pa., to Driftwood, Pa., with extensions and branches		226.33
Total Lines Owned		3,033.59
LINES OPERATED UNDER LEASE OR CONTRACT		
Belvidere Delaware Railroad	Trenton, N. J., to Manunka Chunk, N. J., and branches	80.35
Bradford Railroad	Bradford, Pa.	0.66
Camden and Burlington County Railway	Pavonia, N. J., to Pemberton, N. J., and branches	31.28
Cincinnati, Richmond and Fort Wayne Railroad	Adams, Ind., to Richmond, Ind.	85.67
Cleveland and Pittsburgh Railroad	Rochester, Pa., to Cleveland, O., and branches	205.45
Connecting Railway	North Philadelphia, Pa., to Chestnut Hill, Pa., and branches	35.74
Cumberland Valley and Martinsburg Railroad	Powell's Bend (State Line), to Winchester, Va.	33.73
Delaware Railroad	Shellpot Crossing, Del., to Delmar, Del., and branches	245.22
Delaware, Maryland and Virginia Railroad	Harrington, Del., to Rehoboth, Del., and Georgetown, Del., to Franklin City, Va.	97.64
Delaware River Railroad and Bridge Co.	Philadelphia, Pa. (Frankford Junction), to Haddonfield, N. J., and branches	9.52
Elmira and Lake Ontario Railroad	Chemung Junction, N. Y., to Canandaigua, N. Y., and branches	99.91
Elmira and Williamsport Railroad	Williamsport, Pa., to Elmira, N. Y.	73.49
Englewood Connecting Railway	Chicago, Ill.	2.34
Erie and Pittsburgh Railroad	New Castle, Pa., to Girard Junction, Pa., and branch	83.01

ADDENDA "A"—Continued

MILEAGE OPERATED BY THE PENNSYLVANIA RAILROAD COMPANY—Continued

LINES OPERATED UNDER LEASE OR CONTRACT		Miles Dec. 31st, 1926
Freehold and Jamesburg Agricultural Railroad	Jamesburg Junction, N. J., to Sea Girt, N. J.	27.32
Grand Rapids and Indiana Railway	Fort Wayne, Ind., to Mackinaw City, Mich., and branches	476.69
Harrison and East Newark Connecting Railroad	Harrison, N. J.	.21
Indianapolis and Frankfort Railroad	Ben Davis, Ind., to Frankfort, Ind.	40.94
Johnsonburg Railroad	Johnsonburg, Pa., to Clermont, Pa.	19.62
Little Miami Railroad	Columbus, O., to Cincinnati, O., and branches	195.41
Louisville Bridge and Terminal Railway	Clarksville, Ind., to Louisville, Ky.	4.15
Lykens Valley Railroad and Coal Company's Railroad	Millersburg, Pa., to near Williamstown, Pa.	20.43
Massillon and Cleveland Railroad	Massillon Junction, O., to Clinton, O.	12.16
New York Bay Railroad	Waverly, N. J., to Greenville, N. J., and branches	12.94
New York, Philadelphia and Norfolk Railroad	Delmar, Del., to Cape Charles, Va., and branches	122.28
Northern Central Railway	Dauphin, Pa., to Sunbury, Pa., and Baltimore, Md., to Marysville, Pa., and branch	142.13
Ohio Connecting Railway	Pittsburgh, Pa.	9.11
Pennsylvania, Ohio & Detroit Railroad	Cincinnati, O., to Dayton, O.; Morrow, O., to Trinway, O.; Columbus, O., to Hudson, O.; Columbus, O., to Sandusky, O.; Carleton, Mich., to Ecorse Jct., Mich., and branches	793.06
Pennsylvania Tunnel and Terminal Railroad	Manhattan Transfer Station, N. J., to Woodside Avenue, Long Island City, N. Y., and branches	13.68
Perth Amboy and Woodbridge Railroad	Near Rahway, N. J., to Perth Amboy, N. J.	6.33
Philadelphia, Baltimore and Washington Railroad	Philadelphia, Pa., to Washington, D. C., and branches	416.29
Philadelphia and Trenton Railroad	Kensington, Philadelphia, Pa., to New Jersey and Pennsylvania State Line in Delaware River at Trenton, N. J.	30.66

ADDENDA "A"—Continued

MILEAGE OPERATED BY THE PENNSYLVANIA RAILROAD COMPANY—Continued

LINES OPERATED UNDER LEASE OR CONTRACT		Miles Dec. 31st, 1926
Pittsburgh, Cincinnati, Chicago and St. Louis Railroad	Pittsburgh, Pa., to East St. Louis, Ill., and branches	1,874.79
Pittsburgh, Fort Wayne and Chicago Railway	Pittsburgh, Pa., to Chicago, Ill., and branches	486.83
Pittsburgh, Ohio Valley and Cincinnati Railroad	Bellaire, O., to Powhatan, O.	18.03
Pittsburgh, Youngstown and Ashtabula Railway	Kenwood, Pa., to Ashtabula Harbor, O., and branches	137.56
Rocky Hill Railroad and Transportation Co.	Kingston, N. J., to Rocky Hill, N. J.	2.39
Shamokin Valley and Pottsville Railroad	Sunbury, Pa., to Mt, Carmel, Pa., and branches	40.93
South Chicago and Southern Railroad	Colehour Junction, Ill., to Bernice, Ill., and branches	23.10
Southern Pennsylvania Railway and Mining Company	South Penn Junction, Pa., to Richmond, Pa., and branch	22.00
Terre Haute and Peoria Railroad	Farrington, Ill., to Hervey City, Ill.; Hervey City, Ill., to Decatur Junction, Ill.; and Maroa, Ill., to Farmdale, Ill.	145.07
Tipton Railroad	Tipton, Pa., to terminus	
Union Railroad Company of Baltimore	Baltimore, Md.	7.84
United New Jersey Railroad and Canal Company	New Jersey and Pennsylvania State Line in Delaware River at Trenton, N. J., to Jersey City, N. J.; Camden to South Amboy, N. J., and branches	167.33
Western New York and Pennsylvania Railway	Buffalo, N. Y., to Emporium, Pa., and Oil City, Pa., and branches	563.25
Wheeling Terminal Railway	Martins Ferry, O., to Benwood, W. Va., and branches	9.17
York, Hanover and Frederick Railway	York, Pa., to Frederick, Md., and branch	61.15
Youngstown and Ravenna Railroad	Ravenna Junction to M. V. W. Ry. Junction, Ravenna, O., and Boanna, O., to Niles Junction, O.	2.28
Total Lines Operated Under Contract		6,989.14

ADDENDA "A"—Continued

MILEAGE OPERATED BY THE PENNSYLVANIA RAILROAD COMPANY—Continued

LINES USED UNDER TRACKAGE RIGHTS		Miles Dec. 31st, 1926
Ann Arbor Railroad	Toledo, O.	4.33
Baltimore and Ohio Railroad	Johnstown, Pa.	1.07
	Warwick, O.	.74
	Pleasant City, O., to Mines of Cambridge Coal Company	4.32
	Niles Junction, O., to Ravenna Junction, O.	22.98
	Old River Junction, O., to New River, O.	1.65
	Hempfield Junction to Adamsburg Mine	1.90
	Andrews Run Junction to Edna Mine No. 2	1.32
Baltimore and Ohio Chicago Terminal Railroad	Chicago, Ill.	.38
Belt Railway of Chicago	Chicago, Ill.	10.13
Buffalo Creek Railroad	Buffalo, N. Y.	3.98
Buffalo, Rochester and Pittsburgh Railway	Gates, N. Y.	.33
	Riverside Junction, N. Y., to Bradford, Pa.	9.06
Cambria and Indiana Railway	Manver, Pa., to Yard Limit	1.14
Catonsville Short Line Railroad	Loudon Park, Md., to Catonsville, Md.	3.74
Central Railroad of New Jeresy	Woodbridge, N. J., to north end of Raritan Bay Bridge	1.80
	Newark, N. J.	.31
Cherry Tree and Dixonville Railroad	Cherry Tree, Pa., to Idamar, Pa., and branches	39.07
Chester and Delaware River Railroad	Marcus Hook, Pa.	.33
Chicago and Eastern Illinois Railway	Terre Haute, Ind., to Otter Creek Junction, Ind.	6.00
Chicago Junction Railway	Chicago, Ill.	4.00
Chicago and Western Indiana Railroad	Chicago, Ill.	.03
Chicago, Rock Island & Pacific Railway	Chicago, Ill.	.48

ADDENDA "A"—Continued

MILEAGE OPERATED BY THE PENNSYLVANIA RAILROAD COMPANY—Continued

LINES USED UNDER TRACKAGE RIGHTS		Miles Dec. 31st, 1926
Chicago Union Station Company	Chicago, Ill.	1.42
Cincinnati, Indianapolis & Western Railroad	Indianapolis, Ind.	.01
Cleveland, Cincinnati, Chicago and St. Louis Ry.	Sandusky, O.	1.41
	Columbus, O.	1.02
Cumberland and Pennsylvania Railroad	State Line, Pa.	.46
Delaware, Lackawanna and Western Railroad	Manunka Chunk, N. J., to Stroudsburg, Pa.	17.75
	Buffalo, N. Y.	11.18
Detroit Union Railroad Depot & Station Co.	Detroit, Mich.	3.22
Erie Railroad	Erie Junction, N. Y., to Chemung Junction, N. Y.	5.28
	Oil City, Pa.	.24
Fort Street Union Depot Company	Backus Line, Detroit, Mich., to Fort St. Union Depot Co.	1.23
Grand Trunk Railway	Buffalo, N. Y., to Bridgeburg, Ont.	.90
Huntingdon and Broad Top Mountain Railroad	Mt. Dallas, Pa.	.84
	Huntingdon, Pa.	1.81
Illinois Central Railroad	Decatur Junction, Ill., to Maroa, Ill.	15.44
Indiana Harbor Belt Railroad	State Line to East Chicago, Ind.	7.02
Indianapolis Union Railway	Indianapolis, Ind.	7.55
Johnstown and Stony Creek Railroad	Johnstown, Pa.	.96
Kishacoquillas Valley Railway	Reedsville, Pa.	.23
Lake Erie and Eastern Railroad	Struthers, O., to Girard, O.	8.31
Lehigh Valley Railroad	Gum Run, Pa., and Tomhicken, Pa., to New Boston Jct., Pa.	26.07
	Wilkes-Barre, Pa.	.19
	Buffalo, N. Y.	1.77

ADDENDA "A"—Continued

MILEAGE OPERATED BY THE PENNSYLVANIA RAILROAD COMPANY—Continued

LINES USED UNDER TRACKAGE RIGHTS		Miles Dec. 31st, 1926
Louisville and Nashville Railroad	Louisville, Ky.	.64
Michigan Central Railroad	Bridgeburg, Ont., to End Victoria Yard, Ont.	1.20
	Mackinaw City, Mich.	.81
Monongahela Railway	Brownsville, Pa.	1.00
National Docks Railway	Waldo Avenue, Jersey City, N. J., to Communipaw, N. J.	2.26
New York Central Railroad	Erie, Pa.	.33
	Buffalo, N. Y.	.97
	Girard Junction, Pa., to Erie, Pa.	16.50
	Stoneboro, Pa., to Oil City, Pa.	28.78
New York and Long Branch Railroad	North End Raritan Bay Bridge to Bay Head, N. J.	37.79
Norfolk and Western Railway	Columbus, O.	1.70
Northern Coal and Iron Co.'s Railroad	Buttonwood, Pa., to Wilkes-Barre, Pa.	1.60
Patapsco and Back River Railroad	Pennwood Park, Md.	2.17
Peoria and Pekin Union Railway	Illinois River Bridge to Peoria, Ill.	.17
Pere Marquette Railway	Alexis Junction, Toledo, O., to Carleton, Mich.	25.37
	Grand Rapids, Mich., to Comstock Park, Mich.	....
	Grand Rapids, Mich.	.47
	Muskegon, Mich.	.37
	Delray Jct., Mich., to junction with West Belt Br.—P. O. & D.	4.21
	Junction Ave., Detroit, Mich., to Oak, Mich.	8.47
	Delray, Mich.	.11
Pere Marquette Railway and Wabash Railway	Delray, Mich., to Backus Line, Detroit, Mich.	....
Reading Company	Frackville, Pa., to Wetherill Junction, Pa.	3.00

ADDENDA "A"—Continued

MILEAGE OPERATED BY THE PENNSYLVANIA RAILROAD COMPANY—Continued

LINES USED UNDER TRACKAGE RIGHTS		Miles Dec. 31st, 1926
Stewartstown Railroad	New Freedom, Pa.	.23
St. Charle Air Line	Chicago, Ill.	.96
St. Louis Merchants Bridge Terminal Railway	Willows, Ill., to St. Louis, Mo.	11.00
Terminal Railroad Association of St. Louis	St. Louis, Mo.	3.67
Toledo, Peoria and Western Railway	Farmdale, Ill., to Illinois River Bridge	5.05
Toledo Terminal Railroad	Gould, O., to Walbridge, O.	8.02
Toledo Terminal Railroad and Ann Arbor Railroad	Gould, O., to Hallett, O.	10.71
Tylerdale Connecting Railroad	Tylerdale, Pa.	.26
Union Depot Company (of Columbus, O.)	Columbus, O.	.26
Wabash Railway	Butler, Ind., to Gould, O.	70.83
	Ecorse, Mich., to Delray, Mich.	1.02
	Delray Jct., Mich., to Junction Ave., Detroit, Mich.	2.48
	Delray Jct., Mich., to Carbon Tracks, Detroit, Mich.	.28
	Detroit, Mich.	.88
Washington Terminal	Florida Avenue, Washington, D. C., to South Portal First Street Tunnel	1.60
Western Maryland Railway	State Line, Pa., to Cumberland, Md.	6.35
	Cumberland, Md.	1.57
Wheeling and Lake Erie Railroad	Rayland, O.	2.73
Wilkes-Barre Connecting Railroad	Wilkes-Barre, Pa., to Dorrancetown, Pa.	2.41
	Plains, Pa., to Hudson, Pa.	1.64
Wilkes-Barre and Eastern Railroad	Dorrancetown, Pa., to Plains, Pa.	1.01
Total Lines Used Under Trackage Rights		504.28

ADDENDA "A"—Continued

MILEAGE OPERATED BY THE PENNSYLVANIA RAILROAD COMPANY—Concluded

SUMMARY

MILES OF LINE

	Dec. 31st, 1926
Owned line operated	3,033.59
Line operated under contract	6,989.14
Line used under trackage rights	504.28
Total	10,527.01

MILEAGE OF ALL TRACKS

First track	10,527.01
Second track	4,009.69
Third track	893.07
Fourth track	680.79
Company's sidings	9,849.96
Total	25,960.52

In addition to the foregoing, the Pennsylvania Railroad Company, or Companies controlled by it, own all or a majority interest in the Capital Stock of the railroads indicated below, which are independently operated and have the following mileage:—

	Miles of First Track	*Total Tracks*
Baltimore, Chesapeake & Atlantic Ry. Co.	87.77	106.19
Baltimore & Eastern R. R. Co.	38.17	42.64
Connecting Terminal R. R. Co.	.31	2.91
Long Island R. R. Co.	397.63	979.93
Ohio River & Western Ry. Co.	110.47	122.83
Philadelphia & Beach Haven R. R. Co.	12.11	14.31
Pennsylvania & Atlantic R. R. Co.	59.97	72.07
Rosslyn Connecting R. R. Co.	3.14	5.31
Waynesburg & Washington R. R. Co.	28.19	33.42
West Jersey & Seashore R. R. Co.	375.89	700.36
Total	1,113.65	2,079.97

With the inclusion of this independently operated mileage, the Pennsylvania Railroad System consists of 11,640.66 miles of first main track and 28,040.49 miles of all tracks.

ADDENDA "A"—Continued

The Pennsylvania Railroad Company also controls the following ferry and canal lines:—

	Miles
Ferry—Philadelphia to Camden, N. J.	.53
" —Jersey City to Desbrosses and Cortlandt Streets, New York	2.13
" —Cape Charles to Norfolk, Va.	36.00
Canal—Bordentown to New Brunswick, N. J.	44.00
" —Raven Rock to Trenton, N. J.	22.00
Total	104.66

and also the boat lines of the Baltimore, Chesapeake & Atlantic Railway Company and the Baltimore & Virginia Steamboat Company operating out of Baltimore, Md., on the Chesapeake Bay and its tributaries.

The Pennsylvania Railroad Company, or Companies affiliated in interest with it, are the joint owners of the following railroads and terminal companies:—

		Miles
Akron & Barberton Belt Railroad	(one-fourth interest)	22.86
Akron Union Passenger Depot Company	(one-half ")	.29
Belt Railway of Chicago	(one-thirteenth")	29.96
Calumet Western Railway	(one-fourth ")	3.42
Cherry Tree & Dixonville Railroad	(one-half ")	39.07
Chicago Union Station Company	(one-half ")	1.42
Dayton Union Railway Company	(one-third ")	.54
Fort Wayne Union Railway	(one-fourth ")	1.50
Indianapolis Union Railway	(60% ")	15.95
Lake Erie & Pittsburgh Railway	(one-half ")	27.76
Lorain, Ashland & Southern Railroad	(one-half ")	66.52
Missouri & Illinois Bridge & Belt Railroad	(one-eleventh ")	2.67
Monongahela Railway	(one-third ")	81.21
New York Connecting Railroad	(one-half ")	8.96
Norfolk & Portsmouth Belt Line Railway	(one-eighth ")	14.23
Pittsburgh, Chartiers & Youghiogheny Ry.	(one-half ")	20.41
Sharpsville Railroad	(49% ")	17.85
Terminal Railroad Association of St. Louis	(one-fifteenth ")	59.79
Toledo Terminal Railroad	(9.68% ")	28.59
Tylerdale Connecting Railroad	(one-half ")	1.32
Union Depot Company (Columbus, Ohio)	(one-half ")	.36
Washington Terminal Company	(one-half ")	1.60
Wilkes-Barre Connecting Railroad	(one-half ")	6.66
Zanesville Terminal Railroad	(one-half ")	4.65
Total		457.59

ADDENDA "B"

INCOME STATEMENT OF THE PENNSYLVANIA RAILROAD COMPANY FOR THE YEAR ENDED DECEMBER 31st, 1926

		1926	
Mileage operated (including 67 miles of canals and ferries)		10,594.01	
OPERATING INCOME:			
RAILWAY OPERATING REVENUES	Freight	$497,424,226.40	
	Passenger	147,976,357.37	
	Mail	11,556,809.09	
	Express	17,224,121.04	
	All other transportation	14,091,826.55	
	Incidental	20,974,876.40	
	Joint facility	569,232.82	
Total			$709,817,449.67
RAILWAY OPERATING EXPENSES	Maintenance of way and structures	$92,362,198.32	
	Maintenance of equipment	161,880,738.75	
	Traffic	8,884,633.27	
	Transportation	259,815,201.54	
	Miscellaneous operations	9,228,605.15	
	General	18,642,826.51	
	Transportation for investment—Credit	*453,625.40*	
Total			550,360,578.14
NET REVENUE FROM RAILWAY OPERATIONS			$159,456,871.53
RAILWAY TAX ACCRUALS		$37,110,193.11	
UNCOLLECTIBLE RAILWAY REVENUES		261,610.73	
			37,371,803.84
RAILWAY OPERATING INCOME			$122,085,067.69
HIRE OF EQUIPMENT—DEBIT BALANCE		$14,921,270.97	
JOINT FACILITY RENTS—DEBIT BALANCE		731,039.27	
			15,652,310.24
NET RAILWAY OPERATING INCOME			$106,432,757.45
NON-OPERATING INCOME	Income from Lease of Road	$100,541.75	
	Miscellaneous Rent Income	2,397,274.16	
	Miscellaneous Non-operating Physical Property	52,002.43	
	Separately Operated Properties—Profit	77,125.72	
	Dividend Income	24,038,837.86	
	Income from Funded Securities	6,808,090.89	
	Income from Unfunded Securities and Accounts	3,452,541.02	
	Income from Sinking and Other Reserve Funds	2,958,213.62	
	Release of Premiums on Funded Debt	3,921.25	
	Miscellaneous Income	1,487.32	
Total Non-operating Income			39,890,036.02
GROSS INCOME			$146,322,793.47
DEDUCTIONS FROM GROSS INCOME	Rent for Leased Roads	$45,927,919.03	
	Operating Deficits of Branch Roads borne by The Pennsylvania Railroad Company	206,304.79	
	Miscellaneous Rents	1,226,472.59	
	Miscellaneous Tax Accruals	123,768.68	
	Interest on Funded Debt	30,013,722.75	
	Interest on Unfunded Debt	976,809.59	
	Miscellaneous Income Charges	279,837.53	
Total Deductions from Gross Income			78,754,834.96
NET INCOME (Equal to 13.53% on Capital Stock)			$67,567,958.51
DISPOSITION OF NET INCOME:			
Income applied to Sinking and other Reserve Funds		$4,108,482.75	
Dividend Appropriations of Income (Six and one-half per cent.)		32,451,339.19	
Construction Expenditures during current year on leased and branch roads directly operated, borne by the Pennsylvania Railroad Company		215,810.70	
Advances to leased lines and affiliated companies, borne by the Pennsylvania Railroad Company		521,359.85	
			37,296,992.49
Balance transferred to credit of Profit and Loss			$30,270,966.02

PROFIT AND LOSS STATEMENT

Amount to credit of Profit and Loss, December 31st, 1925		$88,391,547.51
ADD:		
Balance of income for the year	$30,270,966.02	
Sundry net credits	2,296,468.46	
		32,567,434.48
Amount to credit of Profit and Loss, December 31st, 1926		$120,958,981.99

ADDENDA "C"

RETURN ON THE INVESTMENT IN ROAD AND EQUIPMENT

PENNSYLVANIA RAILROAD COMPANY AND LINES DIRECTLY OPERATED

Year Ended December 31st	Investment in Road and Equipment	Net Railway Operating Income	Net Railway Operating Income Per Cent. of Investment in Road and Equipment
1910	$1,432,621,193	$73,094,112	5.10
1911	1,464,339,100	70,114,256	4.79
1912	1,497,922,992	76,742,480	5.12
1913	1,567,750,758	64,469,233	4.11
1914	1,593,380,454	57,990,595	3.64
1915	1,620,990,604	79,532,705	4.91
1916	1,678,654,692	97,025,399	5.78
1917	1,748,098,169	72,869,101	4.17
1918	1,824,962,707	× 23,411,569	× 1.28
1919	1,937,609,317	× 7,862,716	× 0.41
1920	1,955,917,435	Def. × 60,148,959	......
1921	1,965,817,010	37,037,344	1.88
1922	1,975,081,422	73,411,398	3.72
1923	2,052,362,136	83,545,404	4.07
1924	2,108,385,309	78,799,913	3.74
1925	2,147,439,758	100,108,008	4.66
1926	2,217,005,932	106,432,757	4.80

× Based on result of Federal operation and taxes and expenses of the corporations.

Investment in Road and Equipment above stated does not include material and supplies or working capital.

ADDENDA "D"

THE PENNSYLVANIA RAILROAD COMPANY—PERCENTAGE EARNED ON OUTSTANDING CAPITAL STOCK

YEARS 1890 TO 1926

CALENDAR YEAR	NET INCOME	PER CENT. EARNED ON STOCK
1890	$11,716,060	9.52
1891	12,323,160	9.72
1892	10,765,317	8.49
1893	10,546,268	8.16
1894	9,916,072	7.67
1895	10,952,177	8.47
1896	9,823,185	7.60
1897	11,411,914	8.83
1898	10,697,795	8.27
1899	11,036,834	8.54
1900	17,998,390	11.88
1901	23,452,204	11.54
1902	27,458,087	13.44
1903	27,642,907	9.21
1904	28,127,267	9.34
1905	30,238,917	9.99
1906	35,742,701	11.68
1907	33,676,993	10.70
1908	28,287,458	8.99
1909	35,255,188	8.72
1910	37,990,452	9.21
1911	37,531,401	8.27
1912	42,153,964	9.29
1913	41,920,833	8.40
1914	34,090,765	6.83
1915	42,425,322	8.50
1916	52,276,504	10.47
1917	39,281,585	7.87
1918	(A) 44,070,899	8.83
1919	(A) 42,868,098	8.59
1920	(A) 32,801,673	6.57
1921	24,307,669	4.87
1922	(B) 32,382,058	6.49
1923	(D) 51,536,078	10.32
1924	(C) 38,134,677	7.64
1925	62,220,324	12.46
1926	67,567,958	13.53

(A) Includes Government compensation.
(B) Excludes Special Dividend, Pennsylvania Company, amounting to $16,000,000.
(C) Excludes Special Dividend, Pennsylvania Company, amounting to $8,000,000.
(D) Includes $6,681,047 account Federal Control Settlement.

ADDENDA "E"

DIVIDENDS PAID BY
THE PENNSYLVANIA RAILROAD COMPANY

The Pennsylvania Railroad Company has paid a cash return to its Stockholders in every year since 1847. The first installment on subscriptions to the Capital Stock of the Company was paid in April, 1847. In May, 1848, it began to pay interest on these installments at the rate of 6% per annum, and similar payments were made until November 1st, 1855. Beginning with 1856, the payments to the Stockholders were designated as dividends and were at the following rates, those paid in 1856 covering a period of 14 months from November 1st, 1855, to December 31st, 1856:—

CASH DIVIDENDS PAID

Year	Rate	Year	Rate	Year	Rate	
1856	8%	1880	3%	1904	6%	
1857	4	1881	8	1905	6	
1858	6	1882	6½	1906	6½	
1859	6	1883	4½	1907	7	
1860	6	1884	5	1908	6	
1861	6	1885	5	1909	6	
1862	8	1886	5	1910	6	
1863	9	1887	5½	1911	6	
1864	10	1888	5	1912	6	
1865	10	1889	5	1913	6	
1866	9	1890	5½	1914	6	
1867	6	1891	3	1915	6	
1868	8	1892	6	1916	6	
1869	10	1893	5	1917	6	
1870	10	1894	5	1918	6	
1871	10	1895	5	1919	6	
1872	10	1896	5	1920	6	
1873	5	1897	5	1921	4½	
1874	10	1898	5	1922	4½	
1875	8	1899	5	1923	6	
1876	8	1900	6	1924	6	
1877	3½	1901	6	1925	6	
1878	2	1902	6	1926	6¼	
1879	4½	1903	6	Feb., 1927	1¾	Quarterly Dividend.
				May, 1927	1¾	" "

The total cash dividends paid to May, 1927, inclusive, together with interest on Capital Stock subscriptions prior to 1856, amounted to $831,833,733.02.

STOCK AND SCRIP DIVIDENDS

The following Stock and Scrip Dividends, which represent only a part of actual additions to the property and assets made out of income or surplus, were also paid:—

Stock Dividends	
1864	30%
1867	5%
1868	5%

Scrip Dividends Redeemable in Cash or Stock			
1873	5%	1883	4%
1880	4%	1884	2%
1882	2%	1891	3%
1893	2%		

Allotments of Capital Stock were made at various times during the period of 1864 to 1913 at issue prices which resulted in valuable rights on the outstanding stock.

ADDENDA "F"

RECORD OF MARKET PRICES FOR PENNSYLVANIA RAILROAD COMPANY STOCK
(*Dollars Per Share*)

SALES ON PHILADELPHIA STOCK EXCHANGE 1876 TO 1900, INCLUSIVE

Year	*High*	*Low*	*Year*	*High*	*Low*
1876	58⅜	45	1889	56	50¼
1877	49	24¾*	1890	56½	47⅜
1878	35¼	27	1891	57½	49⅝
1879	51⅜	32⅜	1892	57⅜	53
1880	67¼	48	1893	55½	46½
1881	70⅛	59⅝	1894	52⅛	48
1882	65¼	53⅞	1895	57¼	48¾
1883	64¾	56	1896	54¾	49¾
1884	61	48⅞	1897	59½	51⅝
1885	56⅛	45½	1898	61⅜	55⅜
1886	60¼	50⅞	1899	71	61
1887	60	53⅜	1900	74¾	62¼
1888	56⅝	51⅞			

* Pittsburgh riots occurred in 1877.

SALES ON NEW YORK STOCK EXCHANGE† 1901 TO 1926, INCLUSIVE

Year	*High*	*Low*	*Year*	*High*	*Low*
1901	80¾	68½	1914	57¾	51¼
1902	85	73½	1915	61½	51¾
1903	78¾	55⅜	1916	60	55
1904	70	55¾	1917	57⅜	40¼
1905	74	65¾	1918	50⅛	43¼
1906	73¾	61¼	1919	48½	39⅞
1907	70⅝	51¾	1920	44	37⅞
1908	66⅛	54⅜	1921	41¾	32¼
1909	75⅝	63	1922	49¾	33¼
1910	69¼	61¼	1923	47⅞	40⅞
1911	65	59⅛	1924	50	42¼
1912	63⅛	59⅞	1925	55⅜	42½
1913	61⅞	53	1926	57⅛	48⅝

† Listed on New York Stock Exchange in December, 1900.

ADDENDA "G"

GENERAL BALANCE SHEET OF THE PENNSYLVANIA RAILROAD COMPANY

ASSETS — DECEMBER 31st, 1926

INVESTMENTS:			
Investment in Road and Equipment:			
Road		$501,804,350.73	
Equipment		487,544,507.81	
General expenditures		1,222,983.74	
			$990,571,842.28
Improvements on Leased Railway Property:			
Leased lines road		$53,041,622.70	
Leased lines equipment		12,242,751.62	
Leased lines general expenditures		237,501.67	
			65,521,875.99
Sinking Funds	$1,015,721.77		
Less—Pennsylvania R. R. Co. obligations	931,900.00		83,821.77
Deposits in lieu of mortgaged property sold			1,170,051.19
Miscellaneous physical property			964,521.87
Investments in Affiliated Companies:			
Stocks		$273,050,638.84	
Bonds		21,749,028.18	
Notes		67,376,375.26	
Advances		109,973,029.55	
			472,149,071.83
Investment in securities issued, assumed or otherwise carried as a liability			633,528.71
Other Investments:			
Stocks		$77,833,799.37	
Bonds (Including U. S. Liberty Bonds)		32,530,882.61	
Notes (Including U. S. Treasury Notes)		9,194,254.38	
Advances		9,781,374.95	
Miscellaneous		11.00	
			129,340,322.31
CURRENT ASSETS			143,238,812.84
DEFERRED ASSETS			66,636,250.44
UNADJUSTED DEBITS			15,082,263.12
Total			$1,885,392,362.35

ADDENDA "G"—Continued

GENERAL BALANCE SHEET OF THE PENNSYLVANIA RAILROAD COMPANY
DECEMBER 31st, 1926—Continued

LIABILITIES

STOCK:			
apital stock (par value $50. per share)			$499,265,700.00
remium realized on capital stock from January 1st, 1909			7,254,247.63
rants in aid of construction			100.00
MORTGAGE, BONDED AND SECURED DEBT:			
FUNDED DEBT OF THE PENNSYLVANIA RAILROAD COMPANY.			
onsolidated mortgage dollar bonds, 4%, due May 1st, 1943	$2,272,000.00		
onsolidated mortgage sterling and dollar bonds, 3½%, due July 1st, 1945	2,468,260.00		
onsolidated mortgage sterling and dollar bonds, 4%, due May 1st, 1948.	39,837,100.00		
onsolidated mortgage gold bonds, 4½%, due August 1st, 1960	49,000,000.00		
		$93,577,360.00	
eneral mortgage gold bonds, 4½%, Series "A", due June 1st, 1965	$125,000,000.00		
eneral mortgage gold bonds, 5%, Series "B," due December 1st, 1968	50,000,000.00		
eneral mortgage gold bonds, 6%, Series "C," due April 1st, 1970	110,000,000.00		
	$285,000,000.00		
Less—Held by Pennsylvania R. R. Co. (pledged with Trustee)	110,000,000.00		
		175,000,000.00	
en-Year 7% secured gold bonds, due April 1st, 1930		50,000,000.00	
ifteen-year 6½% secured gold bonds, maturing February 1st, 1936		60,000,000.00	
orty-year 5% secured gold bonds, maturing November 1st, 1964		50,000,000.00	
			428,577,360.00
FUNDED DEBT OF ACQUIRED COMPANIES ASSUMED BY THE PENNSYLVANIA RAILROAD COMPANY.			
legheny Valley Ry. Co., general mtg. 4% gold bonds, due March 1st, 1942		$20,000,000.00	
ambria and Clearfield Ry. Co., general mtg. 4% coupon regd. bonds, due February 1st, 1955		2,000,000.00	
ambria and Clearfield R. R. Co., first mtg. 5% coupon regd. bonds, due January 1st, 1941		534,000.00	
learfield and Jefferson Ry. Co., first mtg. 6% bonds, due January 1st, 1927		1,000,000.00	
arrisburg, Portsmouth, Mt. Joy and Lancaster R. R. Co., first mtg. 4% bonds, extended, due July 1st, 1943		700,000.00	
ollidaysburg, Bedford and Cumberland R. R. Co., first mtg. 4% coupon gold bonds, due July 1st, 1951		1,073,000.00	
unction R. R. Co., general mortgage 3½% bonds, due April 1st, 1930		725,000.00	
ennsylvania and North Western R. R. Co., general mtg. 5% bonds, due January 1st, 1930		1,021,000.00	
ittsburgh, Virginia and Charleston Ry. Co., first mtg. 4% bonds, due November 1st, 1943.		6,000,000.00	
unbury and Lewistown Ry. Co., first mortgage 4% bonds, due July 1st, 1936		500,000.00	
unbury, Hazleton and Wilkes-Barre Ry. Co., first mortgage 5% bonds, due May 1st, 1928	$1,000,000.00		
Less—Held in Sinking Fund	931,900.00		
		68,100.00	
unbury, Hazleton and Wilkes-Barre Ry. Co., second mtg. 6% bonds, due May 1st, 1938.		1,349,500.00	
usquehanna, Bloomsburg and Berwick R. R. Co., first mtg. 5% coupon regd. gold bonds, due October 1st, 1952		700,000.00	
estern Pennsylvania R. R. Co., consolidated mortgage 4% bonds, due June 1st, 1928		4,000,000.00	
			39,670,600.00
FUNDED DEBT ASSUMED:			
ennsylvania Company, Guaranteed Trust 3½% Certificates:			
Series "A," due September 1st, 1937	$3,444,000.00		
Series "B," due February 1st, 1941	7,113,000.00		
Series "C," due December 1st, 1942	3,542,000.00		
Series "D," due December 1st, 1944	7,425,000.00		
		$21,524,000.00	
ennsylvania Company, Guaranteed Trust 4% Certificates, Series "E," due May 1st, 1952		8,801,000.00	
			30,325,000.00
GUARANTEED STOCK TRUST CERTIFICATES:			
ew York, Philadelphia and Norfolk R. R., 4% Stock Trust Certificates, due June 1st, 1948			7,478,250.00
quipment trust obligations	$97,321,174.53		
Less—Held by Pennsylvania R. R. Co. (pledged with Trustee)	121,000.00		97,200,174.53
irard Point Storage Company, first mortgage 3½% registered bonds, due April 1st, 1940.			1,695,000.00
ortgages and ground rents payable			3,741,316.85
URRENT LIABILITIES			82,537,534.12
EFERRED LIABILITIES			2,521,479.99
NADJUSTED CREDITS			285,188,201.62
CORPORATE SURPLUS:			
dditions to property through income and surplus		$212,251,146.68	
unded debt retired through income and surplus		4,587,172.18	
inking fund reserves		1,015,721.77	
iscellaneous fund reserves		52,386,997.53	
ppropriated surplus not specifically invested:			
Dividend payable February 28th, 1927		8,737,377.46	
Total appropriated surplus			278,978,415.62
Profit and Loss—balance			120,958,981.99
Total			$1,885,392,362.35

ADDENDA "H"

THE PENNSYLVANIA RAILROAD COMPANY

CLASSIFICATION OF FREIGHT TRAFFIC
ALL LINES DIRECTLY OPERATED

YEAR ENDED DECEMBER 31st, 1926

COMMODITY	1926	
	Tons	Per Cent. of Total
PRODUCTS OF AGRICULTURE		
Wheat	1,183,758	0.48
Corn	972,874	0.40
Oats	465,595	0.19
Other grain	185,253	0.08
Flour and meal	1,179,682	0.48
Other mill products	1,082,568	0.44
Hay, straw, and alfalfa	766,912	0.31
Tobacco	95,665	0.04
Cotton	113,077	0.05
Cotton seed and products, except oil	103,297	0.04
Citrus fruits	358,349	0.15
Other fresh fruits	1,348,954	0.55
Potatoes	1,123,353	0.46
Other fresh vegetables	1,020,004	0.42
Dried fruits and vegetables	135,632	0.06
Other products of agriculture	417,774	0.17
Total	10,552,747	4.32
ANIMALS AND PRODUCTS		
Horses and mules	24,960	0.01
Cattle and calves	575,262	0.24
Sheep and goats	77,891	0.03
Hogs	318,347	0.13
Fresh meats	417,834	0.17
Other packing-house products	132,026	0.06
Poultry	57,284	0.02
Eggs	71,882	0.03
Butter and Cheese	77,383	0.03
Wool	36,478	0.02
Hides and leather	231,139	0.09
Other animals and products	285,343	0.12
Total	2,305,829	0.95
PRODUCTS OF MINES		
Anthracite coal	11,441,526	4.69
Bituminous coal	99,182,673	40.64
Coke	7,878,778	3.23
Iron ore	11,830,963	4.85
Other ores and concentrates	1,070,337	0.44
Base bullion and matte	52,752	0.02
Clay, gravel, sand and stone	20,668,871	8.47
Crude Petroleum	50,907	0.02
Asphaltum	480,624	0.19
Salt	492,704	0.20
Other products of mines	444,154	0.18
Total	153,594,289	62.93
PRODUCTS OF FORESTS		
Logs, posts, poles and cord wood	1,131,615	0.46
Ties	293,447	0.12
Pulp wood	382,927	0.16
Lumber, timber, box shooks, staves and headings	7,131,409	2.92
Other products of forests	457,986	0.19
Total	9,397,384	3.85

ADDENDA "H"—Continued

THE PENNSYLVANIA RAILROAD COMPANY

CLASSIFICATION OF FREIGHT TRAFFIC—Continued
ALL LINES DIRECTLY OPERATED

YEAR ENDED DECEMBER 31st, 1926

COMMODITY	1926	
	Tons	Per Cent. of Total
MANUFACTURES AND MISCELLANEOUS		
Refined petroleum and its products	6,071,847	2.49
Vegetable oils	166,807	0.07
Sugar, syrup, glucose, and molasses	830,669	0.34
Boats, and vessel supplies	4,937	....
Iron, pig and bloom	5,072,358	2.08
Rails and fastenings	492,689	0.20
Bar and sheet iron, structural iron, and iron pipe	8,903,941	3.65
Other metals, pig, bar, and sheet	2,568,505	1.05
Castings, machinery, and boilers	1,693,485	0.69
Cement	2,749,409	1.13
Brick and artificial stone	5,721,404	2.34
Lime and plaster	1,384,901	0.57
Sewer pipe and drain tile	604,330	0.25
Agricultural implements and vehicles other than automobiles	377,276	0.16
Automobiles and autotrucks	808,163	0.33
Household goods and second-hand furniture	35,184	0.02
Furniture (new)	231,315	0.10
Beverages	92,267	0.04
Ice	199,912	0.08
Fertilizers (all kinds)	913,360	0.37
Paper, printed matter, and books	692,868	0.28
Chemicals and explosives	2,221,698	0.91
Textiles	125,113	0.05
Canned goods (all canned food products)	885,873	0.36
Other manufactures and miscellaneous	18,892,289	7.74
Total	61,740,600	25.30
Grand Total, Carload Traffic	237,590,849	97.35
All L. C. L. freight	6,461,578	2.65
Grand Total, Carload and L. C. L. Traffic	244,052,427	100.00

ADDENDA "I"

PENNSYLVANIA RAILROAD SYSTEM

COMBINED OPERATING RESULTS OF ALL TRANSPORTATION COMPANIES FOR THE YEAR ENDED DECEMBER 31st, 1926

		1926	
Mileage operated (including 68 miles canals and ferries)		11,708.66	
OPERATING INCOME:			
RAILWAY OPERATING REVENUES	Freight	$516,846,493	
	Passenger	182,052,959	
	Mail	11,824,102	
	Express	18,065,530	
	All other transportation	15,080,316	
	Incidental	22,535,220	
	Joint facility	584,743	
	Total		$766,989,363
RAILWAY OPERATING EXPENSES	Maintenance of way and structures	$100,429,172	
	Maintenance of equipment	171,106,929	
	Traffic	9,538,457	
	Transportation	284,467,274	
	Miscellaneous operations	9,365,498	
	General	20,107,996	
	Transportation for Investment—*Credit*	*467,618*	
	Total		594,547,708
NET REVENUE FROM RAILWAY OPERATIONS			$172,441,655
RAILWAY TAX ACCRUALS		$40,543,311	
UNCOLLECTIBLE RAILWAY REVENUES		272,755	
			40,816,066
RAILWAY OPERATING INCOME			$131,625,589
HIRE OF EQUIPMENT—DR. BALANCE		$16,494,768	
JOINT FACILITY RENTS—DR. BALANCE		1,979,699	
			18,474,467
NET RAILWAY OPERATING INCOME			$113,151,122

ADDENDA "J"

RETURN ON THE INVESTMENT IN ROAD AND EQUIPMENT
PENNSYLVANIA RAILROAD SYSTEM

Year Ended December 31st	Investment in Road and Equipment	Net Railway Operating Income	Net Railway Operating Income Per Cent. of Investment in Road and Equipment
1910	$1,533,111,360	$77,026,497	5.02
1911	1,568,863,769	73,903,253	4.71
1912	1,606,721,857	80,992,247	5.04
1913	1,681,779,771	67,803,989	4.03
1914	1,710,368,222	61,921,854	3.62
1915	1,739,081,326	83,746,135	4.82
1916	1,799,055,282	102,202,072	5.68
1917	1,872,315,915	77,750,406	4.15
1918	1,952,017,162	× 26,983,353	× 1.38
1919	2,069,968,807	× 9,943,665	× 0.48
1920	2,092,052,738	Def. × 62,852,232	......
1921	2,102,421,811	40,842,192	1.94
1922	2,112,565,888	79,859,730	3.78
1923	2,196,947,406	88,066,460	4.01
1924	2,258,292,092	84,062,516	3.72
1925	2,302,802,826	107,792,415	4.68
1926	2,375,674,983	113,151,122	4.76

× Based on result of Federal operation and taxes and expenses of the corporations.

Investment in Road and Equipment above stated does not include material and supplies or working capital.

ADDENDA "K"

PENNSYLVANIA RAILROAD SYSTEM

(EMBRACING ALL THE TRANSPORTATION COMPANIES)

The following statement gives some interesting information respecting the System on December 31st, 1926, and a comparison with the year 1916:—

The transportation companies in the Pennsylvania Railroad System owned, leased, controlled, or operated under contract, are located in the States of New York, New Jersey, Pennsylvania, Delaware, Maryland, Virginia, West Virginia, Kentucky, Ohio, Illinois, Indiana, Michigan, Missouri and the District of Columbia.

	Years Ended December 31		Per Cent. Increase or Decrease over 1916
	1926	1916	
Miles of First Main Track Operated (including 68 miles of canals and ferries).	11,709	11,645	I. 0.5
Miles of all Tracks Operated	28,040	26,321	I. 6.5
Gross Investment in Road and Equipment	$2,375,674,983	$1,799,055,282	I. 32.1
Other Investments (book value)	192,178,540	167,442,796	I. 14.8
Total Investment	2,567,853,523	1,966,498,078	I. 30.6
Total Capital Stock (par value)	$1,098,900,910	$1,030,690,353	I. 6.6
Total Funded Debt (par value)	1,010,632,981	714,379,065	I. 41.5
Total Capital Obligations	2,109,533,891	1,745,069,418	I. 20.9
Total Capital Stock owned by Companies in System	503,244,715	402,716,029	I. 25.0
Total Funded Debt owned by Companies in System	73,958,880	75,271,898	D. 1.7
Total Capital Obligations owned by Companies in System	577,203,595	477,987,927	I. 20.8
Total Capital Stock held by Public	595,656,195	627,974,324	D. 5.1
Total Funded Debt held by Public	936,674,101	639,107,167	I. 46.6
Total Capital Obligations held by Public	1,532,330,296	1,267,081,491	I. 20.9
Ratio of Capital Stock to Total Capital Obligations held by Public	38.87	49.56	D. 21.6

ADDENDA "K"—Continued

	Years Ended December 31		Per Cent. Increase or Decrease over 1916
	1926	1916	
Number of Locomotives owned	7,200	7,376	D. 2.4
Total Tractive Power (pounds)	343,391,940	269,448,587	I. 27.4
Number of Freight Cars owned	272,168	275,105	D. 1.1
Total Capacity (tons)	14,572,307	13,569,233	I. 7.4
Number of Passenger Train Cars owned	8,268	7,043	I. 17.4
Total Seating Capacity (persons)	352,652	317,140	I. 11.2
Average Number of Employes	217,700	223,768	D. 2.7
Total Compensation	$390,480,093	$211,610,008	I. 84.5
Operating Revenues	$766,989,363	$441,595,604	I. 73.7
Operating Expenses (including taxes, equipment and joint facility rents, etc.)	653,838,241	339,393,532	I. 92.6
Net Railway Operating Income	113,151,122	102,202,072	I. 10.7
Per Cent. Return on Investment in Road and Equipment	4.76	5.68	D. 16.2
Revenue Ton Miles	49,302,755,456	46,717,838,394	I. 5.5
Average Revenue per Ton per Mile (cents)	1.045	0.641	I. 63.0
Average Train Load—Tons (revenue freight)	818.9	699.5	I. 17.1
Average Car Load—Tons (revenue freight)	28.8	27.2	I. 5.9
Passenger Miles	6,561,196,033	4,961,247,631	I. 32.2
Average Revenue per Passenger per Mile (cents)	2.755	1.934	I. 42.5
Number of Stockholders (The Pennsylvania Railroad Company)	141,202	90,388	I. 56.2

ADDENDA "L"

PENNSYLVANIA RAILROAD SYSTEM COMPARED WITH ALL CLASS I RAILROADS IN UNITED STATES

YEAR 1925

Relationship of the Pennsylvania Railroad System (embracing all transportation companies) to all Class I railroads in the United States:

	Per Cent.
Miles of Road	4.90
Miles of Track	7.05
Investment in Road and Equipment	10.38
Revenue Ton Miles	10.92
Passenger Miles	17.91
Total Number of Employes	12.09
Total Operating Revenues	11.76
Total Passenger Equipment Cars	14.86
Total Freight Equipment Cars	11.32
Total Locomotives	11.33
Total Tractive Power of Locomotives	12.93

ADDENDA "M"

EQUIPMENT OF THE PENNSYLVANIA RAILROAD SYSTEM

DECEMBER 31st, 1926

KIND OF EQUIPMENT	Available for Service Dec. 31st, 1926	Capacity of Equipment Available for Service Dec. 31st, 1926
LOCOMOTIVES		(Tractive Power—Pounds)
Passenger—electric	41	2,844,000
Passenger—steam	1,665	60,492,081
Freight—electric	3	300,267
Freight—steam	4,457	243,676,878
Shifting—electric	17	1,221,803
Shifting—steam	1,017	34,856,911
Total	7,200	343,391,940
PASSENGER CAR EQUIPMENT		Seating Capacity—Persons
Passenger—wooden	1,104	70,582
Passenger—wooden—electric	76	4,357
Passenger—steel	2,277	186,556
Passenger—steel—electric	834	56,239
Passenger—steel—cafe	2	120
Parlor—steel	6	252
Dining—steel	173	5,886
Passenger—baggage—wooden	108	4,519
Passenger—baggage—steel	418	19,106
Passenger—baggage—wooden—electric	4	156
Passenger—baggage—steel—electric	60	3,127
Passenger—baggage—mail—steel	20	600
Passenger—baggage—mail—steel—electric	3	96
Baggage—wooden—electric	5	
Baggage—steel—electric	12	
Baggage—mail—wooden	11	
Baggage—mail—steel	229	
Baggage—mail—wooden—electric	3	
Baggage—mail—steel—electric	2	
Baggage—express—wooden	452	
Baggage—express—steel and steel underframe	1,601	
Baggage—express—wooden—electric	8	
Baggage—express—steel—electric	2	
Refrigerator—express—wooden	17	
Refrigerator—express—steel and steel underframe	609	
Postal—steel	117	
Horse—express—wooden	30	
Horse—express—steel	20	
Gasoline motor—steel	20	982
Gasoline motor trailer	1	74
Baggage mail trailer	6	
Crew express	38	
Total	8,268	352,652
FREIGHT CAR EQUIPMENT		Tons
Box—wooden	349	9,872
Box—steel and steel underframe	93,429	4,665,380
Refrigerator—wooden	2	30
Stock—wooden	22	578
Stock—steel underframe	3,352	167,600
Gondola—wooden	218	5,900
Gondola—steel and steel underframe	167,019	9,518,585
Flat—wooden	41	812
Flat—steel	3,991	203,450
Cabin—wooden	607	
Cabin—steel and steel underframe	2,735	
Tank	328	325 — 30,460
		1 — 4,180
		2 — 100
Poling and car droppers and freight transfer	75	
Total	272,168	14,572,307 30,460 4,180

ADDENDA "M"—Continued
EQUIPMENT OF THE PENNSYLVANIA RAILROAD SYSTEM
DECEMBER 31st, 1926—Concluded

KIND OF EQUIPMENT	Available for Service Dec. 31st, 1926
WORK EQUIPMENT	
Cabin	1,016
Tool and block—wooden	543
Tool and block—steel and steel underframe	140
Pile drivers	13
Snow flangers	90
Snow plows	36
Snow sweepers	6
Laboratory test	1
Dynamometer	1
Test weight	26
Clearance	3
Signal instruction	5
Air-brake instruction	6
Valuation	
Inspection	16
Business—wooden	40
Business—steel	7
Supply cars—wooden	99
Supply cars—steel	110
Shop workmen—wooden	154
Emergency cars	51
Calcium distributing cars	9
Miscellaneous service cars	455
Stone and wood—ballast—flat—wooden	257
Stone and wood—ballast—flat—steel and steel underframe	777
Dump box cars	1
Dump cars	180
Dump cars—yard	12
Dump cars—hand cradle	2
Water tank	59
Pick-up cars	28
Grading and spreader cars	37
Derricks	204
Steam shovel	13
Ballast unloader	1
Ditcher	21
Rail loader	67
Ballast cleaning machine	2
Sand digger	1
Experimental sweeper	1
FLOATING WORK EQUIPMENT	
Flat scows	22
Floats	5
Row boats	9
Dredges	2
Pile drivers	3
Motor boats	1
Tug boats	1
Derrick scows	1
Total	4,534
FLOATING EQUIPMENT	
Ferry boats	18
Passenger and freight steamboats	20
Tug boats	50
Steam and harbor lighters	10
Grain and other barges	178
Canal barges	10
Car floats	111
Motor and gasoline boats	2
Grain elevators	2
Coal scows	2
Mooring scows	1
Total	404
Total valuation of equipment as per General Ledger	$712,097,505

ADDENDA "N"

ALL COMPANIES IN THE SYSTEM

DECEMBER 31st, 1926

The Pennsylvania Railroad System consists of over 600 constituent corporations, gradually reduced through acquisition, merger, or otherwise to the number indicated below.

Active companies:	
Railroad operating companies	11
Lines operated under lease or contract	51
Ferry operating companies	1
Total transportation companies in the Pennsylvania Railroad System	63
Electric railway companies	1
Warehouse companies	3
Water supply companies	14
Real estate companies	7
Miscellaneous companies	13
Total active companies	101
Inactive companies:	
Railroad companies	14
Ferry companies	2
Warehouse companies	1
Water supply companies	3
Miscellaneous companies	2
Total inactive companies	22
Total companies	123

In addition to the above, there are Companies Jointly Owned and used with other railroad systems:—

Active:	
Individual operating companies	14
Roads under lease or contract	2
Bridge companies	1
Terminal companies	9
Miscellaneous companies	5
Total	31
Inactive:	
Railroad companies	4
Total companies embraced in System including those jointly owned with other railroad systems	158

INDEX

A

D

J

N

PAGE

W